The Spanish Atlantic World, 1492–1825

The Spanish Atlantic World, 1492–1825

From Kingdoms to Colonies to Independence

KENNETH J. ANDRIEN
Southern Methodist University

OXFORD
UNIVERSITY PRESS

Oxford University Press is a department of the University of Oxford.
It furthers the University's objective of excellence in research, scholarship,
and education by publishing worldwide. Oxford is a registered trade mark of
Oxford University Press in the UK and in certain other countries.

Published in the United States of America by Oxford University Press
198 Madison Avenue, New York, NY 10016, United States of America.

© Kenneth J. Andrien 2025

All rights reserved. No part of this publication may be reproduced, stored in a retrieval system, transmitted, used for text and data mining, or used for training artificial intelligence, in any form or by any means, without the prior permission in writing of Oxford University Press, or as expressly permitted by law, by license or under terms agreed with the appropriate reprographics rights organization. Inquiries concerning reproduction outside the scope of the above should be sent to the Rights Department, Oxford University Press, at the address above.

You must not circulate this work in any other form
and you must impose this same condition on any acquirer.

CIP data is on file at the Library of Congress.

ISBN 9780190238834 (pbk)
ISBN 9780190238827 (hbk)

Printed by Integrated Books International, United States of America

The manufacturer's authorized representative in the EU for product safety is
Oxford University Press España S.A., Parque Empresarial San Fernando de Henares,
Avenida de Castilla, 2 – 28830 Madrid (www.oup.es/en).

To Anne and Madelyn

Acknowledgments

The foundations of this study rest on my own many years of archival research in Spain, Italy, and Latin America and on the work of scholars too numerous to mention from several different disciplines. The specific origins of this book go back to 2007, when Jack P. Greene and Philip D. Morgan unexpectedly asked me to write a chapter on the Spanish Atlantic world for their forthcoming anthology, *Atlantic History: A Critical Appraisal* (Oxford University Press, 2009). Given the short deadline they offered me, I declined at first. Nonetheless, I had been thinking and teaching about Atlantic history at the Ohio State University for some time, and my colleague Allan J. Kuethe (Paul Whitfield Horn Professor Emeritus, Texas Tech University) and I were writing a book on the Spanish Bourbon dynasty's reform program in the eighteenth century using an Atlantic focus. As a result, I eventually accepted the challenge of writing a chapter for the Greene–Morgan collection. Afterward, I continued working with Allan Kuethe to complete our study entitled *The Spanish Atlantic World in the Eighteenth Century: War and the Bourbon Reforms, 1713–1796* (Cambridge University Press, 2014). In a very real sense, this current book is an outgrowth of the inquiries that resulted in the chapter for the Greene–Morgan anthology and the book completed with Allan Kuethe. I am thankful for the conversations I shared with all three men about the Atlantic world, particularly Allan, and they have influenced the shape of this current study. In fact, much of the substance of Chapter 4 is drawn from the book that Allan and I coauthored, and the research on the early Bourbon period was done almost exclusively by Allan in Paris at the French Archives des affaires étrangères and Archives nationales de France. I am also grateful to my colleagues at Southern Methodist University, who provided a supportive and collegial intellectual environment, particularly Kenneth M. Hamilton, Daniel Orlovsky, Kathleen Wellman, Edward Countryman, Neil Foley, and John Chavez, as well as nonhistorians Robert Gregory, Luigi Manzetti, and Adam Herring. I received generous research funds from the Edmund J. and Louise W. Kahn Chair fund to do research in Spain, Italy, and Peru. Moreover, I participated in conferences held at Louisiana State University; the Universidad de Medellín in Colombia; the Escuela de Estudios Hispano-Americanos in Seville, Spain; and the (AHILA) Association of European Latin Americanists conference in Berlin and at meetings of the TePaske seminar, where I shared some early ideas that shaped this current work. I also thank those who attended those meetings, who gave me generous and useful feedback.

Scholars in history, anthropology, archaeology, art history, and geography, as well as specialists in literary and cultural studies, have all made substantial contributions to Atlantic studies, and I have drawn on their work in producing this book. In this study, some scholars may find that my interpretation of the data included in their work differs from their own views. When dealing with the findings of other scholars, I do not attempt merely to summarize and reconcile conflicting interpretations. Instead, I used the data presented in studies by other scholars (even those I deeply respect) to come to my own, occasionally different conclusions, based on my years of research and writing. I apologize in advance for taking this license, but I felt compelled to offer my own interpretation of past events. The book also represents the uneven evolution of the field of Atlantic and Spanish American studies. Some topics are given perhaps more cursory treatment than they might deserve because current scholarship, including my own, has given less attention to these topics. Others may receive what appears to be more, or even disproportionate, attention, but this too reflects the state of the field. Moreover, for some periods, particularly for the seventeenth century, documentation for this study is less abundant, which limits what can be covered. Throughout the book, the chapters follow a chronological presentation, rather than a topical series, because I believe my readers will find this approach easier to follow and more informative, given the broad scope of the topic. The history of the Spanish Atlantic world from its inception, following the voyage of Christopher Columbus in 1492, until its slow-motion collapse between 1808 and 1825 is a compelling story, but I make no claim to speak the final word on the subject. Others will undoubtedly follow, add greater depth, and offer different interpretations of the evolution of the Spanish Atlantic world during this period, but these are my own current views on the subject.

The intellectual journey that produced this book began many years ago, when I entered the graduate program at Duke University, under the scholarly direction of John J. TePaske. John directed all of his graduate students to prepare a major field that encompassed both Spain and Latin America. In all my work since graduate school, I have maintained that broad perspective, focusing principally on the Andean region and its links to Europe over the sixteenth, seventeenth, and eighteenth centuries. For much of that time, scholars of colonial Latin America had emphasized local or regional studies of urban and rural groups (such as merchants, *encomenderos*, artisans, women, and enslaved people), Indigenous communities and their resistance to Spanish oppression, and agricultural holdings (particularly landed estates, called haciendas and plantations). These studies preferred to examine both elites and common people from a local or regional perspective. This scholarship seldom connected local or regional events to the wider Atlantic world. Likewise, scholars studying marginalized groups in colonial society—such as petty traders, innkeepers, small farmers, Amerindian villagers and miners, enslaved individuals, and poor

Spaniards or *castas* (people of mixed racial ancestry) living in colonial cities have found it difficult to link their everyday experiences to the broader Atlantic world. Given the transatlantic focus of my own work, however, when the subfield of Atlantic studies began to emerge, moving to that category of analysis seemed a natural expansion of my own scholarly focus as my career matured. As a result, this study is an outgrowth of my own scholarly past and a sign of how Latin American history has evolved to take its place in this growing field of Atlantic studies.

I have been fortunate to know an extremely intelligent and accomplished group of colleagues who have helped me along this intellectual odyssey. I have already mentioned Jack Greene, Philip Morgan, and, of course, my collaborator, Allan Kuethe, but there are many others whose work helped to shape this study. The published works and conversations over the years with Rolena Adorno, Mark A. Burkholder, Peter J. Bakewell, Geoffrey Parker, Jeremy Baskes, Kris Lane, Christiana Borchart de Moreno, Kendall Brown, John Fisher, Luis Miguel Glave, Carlos Contreras, José Hernández Palomo, Douglas Inglis, Brian Hamnett, Donna Guy, Margarita Suárez, William Taylor, the late John TePaske, Kenneth Hamilton, Jane Mangan, Barbara Mundy, Gabriel Paquette, Adrian Pearce, Allan Gallay, John Brooke, Stephanie Shaw, Stephanie Smith, Ana María Presta, Sherwin Bryant, Alcira Dueñas, Cameron Jones, and Spencer Tyce (among others) have taught me a great deal, and I sincerely thank them. I also thank a former graduate student, Luis García, whose dissertation at Southern Methodist University, later published as an award-winning book (*Frontera Armada: Prácticas Militares en el Noreste Histórico, Siglos XVII al XIX*) on the impact of the Reconquista on the evolution of the northern frontier of New Spain, led me to rethink the influence of Spain's medieval past on Spanish colonialism in the Americas. More recently, Karen B. Graubart has developed these ideas in a fine book on the topic, *Republics of Difference: Religious and Racial Self-Governance in the Spanish Atlantic World*. I would also like to give special thanks to my friend and colleague Lyman L. Johnson, who read the entire manuscript and offered numerous constructive and helpful comments. Lyman's generosity and long experience as the founding editor of the Diálogos series at the University of New Mexico Press have shown him to be a paragon of responsible leadership in the profession, and I hope the final draft of this book justifies his efforts on my behalf. I also owe Mark A. Burkholder a debt because an important article that he wrote in 2016 in *Colonial Latin American Review*, "Spain's America: From Kingdoms to Colonies," helped clarify my ideas at a crucial stage of the writing process and gave me the inspiration for the subtitle of the book. I would also like to thank Susan Ferber, who did her customary careful copy-editing of the draft of the manuscript and Niko Pfund both at Oxford University Press, who expedited the publication process at a crucial stage. Finally, I would like to thank two excellent production editors, Cathryn Steele at Oxford and Vasuki Ravichandran at Straive, a partner production company of Oxford University Press.

Three particularly kind and generous colleagues, Allan J. Kuethe, Rolena Adorno, and Barbara E. Mundy, also helped enormously at the later stages of the project. Allan took the time during a trip to Spain to secure permissions to publish three pictures used in Chapter 4 from the Museo del Prado and the Museo Naval in Madrid, while Rolena gave me guidance on how to secure permissions and images for the pictures from Guaman Poma's masterpiece, which the Royal Danish Library provided, along with high-resolution images and the permission to publish them in Chapter 3. Barbara also provided camera-ready images for additional pictures used in that same chapter, and the Museo Pedro de Osma in Lima and the Benson Collection at the University of Texas Library gave high-resolution images and permission to publish them.

I thank my wife, Anne, who has endured and supported yet another of my scholarly projects. During the course of our long marriage, Anne had to learn Spanish and take trips to exotic (and not so exotic) locales in Europe and Latin America. She has been a true partner in everything that I have done for the past forty-four years. I dedicate this book to her and to our granddaughter, Madelyn Nicole Andrien.

I completed the final stages of this book after leaving Southern Methodist University and moving back to Columbus, Ohio, where our family lives. A few months after relocating from Dallas, Texas, to Columbus, the COVID-19 pandemic broke out, which to date has taken the lives of over one million people in the United States. During these trying times, my wife, Anne, and I took care of our granddaughter, Madelyn, two or three days each week so that her parents could work from home in peace and quiet after their work offices shut down. Even after the day care centers in Ohio reopened, we continued to care for her periodically because we just enjoyed her company. We found it impossible to fret about the different stages of the pandemic while watching Madelyn grow and develop from a baby into a charming, lively, and sometimes willful five-year-old child. Now she is in school each day, but we have the memories of how she brightened up our days. I dedicate this book to Madelyn so that she may know, and someday understand, what Grandpa was doing in his office during her afternoon naps on the days that we looked after her.

Dallas, Texas, and Columbus, Ohio

Table of Contents

List of Figures — xiii

Introduction: A History of the Spanish Atlantic World: Prospects and Possibilities — 1

1. The Reconquista and the Institutional Origins of Spanish Overseas Expansion — 20

2. New World Beginnings to the Institutional Consolidation of the Spanish Atlantic World, 1492–1610 — 52

3. The Mature Colonial Order and the Drift toward Greater Autonomy, 1610–1700 — 95

4. War and Reform in the Spanish Atlantic World, 1700–1796 — 140

5. The Collapse of the Spanish Atlantic World, 1796–1825 — 185

6. Conclusion: From Kingdoms to Colonies to Independence, 1492–1825 — 225

Glossary of Terms — 235
Bibliography — 243
Index — 257

List of Figures

1.1 Map of the chronology of the Reconquista — 47
Adapted from Joseph F. O'Callaghan, *A History of Medieval Spain* (Ithaca, NY: Cornell University Press, 1975), Map 3, p. 108; Map 4, p. 199; Map 5, p. 252; and Map 6, p. 355.

2.1 Inca checkerboard tunic like those worn by the warriors at Cajamarca — 53
Dallas Museum of Art: 5122425.

2.2 Marriages of Martín García de Loyola to Beatriz Ñusta and Juan de Borja to Lorenza Ñusta, seventeenth century — 59
Museo Pedro de Osma, Lima.

2.3 Map of viceregal political units: New Spain and Central America — 74
Adapted from Cathryn L. Lombardi, John V. Lombardi, with K. Lynn Stoner, *Latin American History: A Teaching Atlas* (Madison: University of Wisconsin Press, 1983), p. 28.

2.4 Map of viceregal political units: South America and Panama — 75
Adapted from Cathryn L. Lombardi, John V. Lombardi, with K. Lynn Stoner, *Latin American History: A Teaching Atlas* (Madison: University of Wisconsin Press, 1983), p. 29.

2.5 Relaciones Geográficas Map of Teozacoalco, 1580 — 85
Benson Latin American Collection, The General Libraries, University of Texas at Austin (JGI xxv-3).

2.6 New World gold and silver output in millions of pesos of 272 maravedís, 1492–1610 — 86
John J. TePaske and edited by Kendall W. Brown, *A New World of Gold and Silver* (Leiden and Boston, Brill, 2010), Tables 1–2, p. 20.

3.1 The author, Felipe Guaman Poma de Ayala, on the road to Lima — 97
El primer nueva corónica y buen gobierno, p. 1093, 1095, GkS 2232 4. Courtesy of the Royal Library of Denmark, Copenhagen.

3.2 A dinner involving a priest, a mestizo, a mulatto, and an Andean — 125
El primer nueva corónica y buen gobierno, p. 603, 617, GkS 2232 4. Courtesy of the Royal Library of Denmark, Copenhagen.

3.3 A *corregidor* and his lieutenant uncovering a naked, sleeping Andean woman — 126
El primer nueva corónica y Buen gobierno, p. 503, 507, GkS 2232 4. Courtesy of the Royal Library of Denmark, Copenhagen.

3.4 Lust and licentiousness among Spanish men and women — 127
El primer nueva corónica y Buen gobierno, p. 534, 538, GkS 2232 4. Courtesy of the Royal Library of Denmark, Copenhagen.

3.5 Virgin of Bethlehem, eighteenth century — 129
Museo Pedro de Osma, Lima.

xiv   LIST OF FIGURES

3.6 New World gold and silver output in millions of pesos of 272 maravedís, 1492–1810 — 131
John J. TePaske and edited by Kendall W. Brown, *A New World of Gold and Silver* (Leiden and Boston, Brill, 2010), Table 1–2, p. 20.

3.7 New World gold and silver output in millions of pesos of 272 maravedís, 1581–1710 — 131
John J. TePaske and edited by Kendall W. Brown, *A New World of Gold and Silver* (Leiden and Boston, Brill, 2010), Table 1–2, p. 20; Table 7.2, p. 314, Table 7.3, p. 315.

4.1 Julio Alberoni by Rafael Tegeo — 147
Museo Naval, Madrid: 00816.

4.2 José Patiño by Rafael Tegeo — 151
Museo Naval, Madrid: 00818.

4.3 Zenón de Somodevilla, Marqués de la Ensenada, by Jacopo Amigoni — 155
Museo del Prado, Madrid: P02939.

4.4 Map of eighteenth-century viceroyalties and intendencies in South America — 166
Adapted from Cathryn L. Lombardi, John V. Lombardi, with K. Lynn Stoner, *Latin American History: A Teaching Atlas* (Madison: University of Wisconsin Press, 1983), p. 32.

4.5 New World gold and silver output in millions of pesos of 272 maravedis, 1492–1810 — 177
John J. TePaske and edited by Kendall W. Brown, *A New World of Gold and Silver* (Leiden and Boston, Brill, 2010), Table 1–2, p. 20.

4.6 Remittances of public revenue to Spain, three-year moving average — 178
Jacques A. Barbier, "Towards a New Chronology for Bourbon Colonialism: The 'Depositaría de Indias' of Cádiz, 1722–1789," *Ibero-Amerikanisches Archiv* 6, no. 4 (1980): 335–53; Jacques A. Barbier and Herbert S. Klein, "Revolutionary Wars and Public Finances: The Madrid Treasury, 1784–1807," *Journal of Economic History* 41, no. 2 (June 1981): 315–37; Carlos Marichal, "Beneficios y costes fiscales del colonialismo: Las remesas Americanas a España, 1760–1814," *Revista de Historia Económica* XV, no. 3 (Otoño–Invierno, 1997): 475–505.

5.1 Map of wars in Peru/Río de la Plata front — 197
Based on a map from John Fletcher, *The Wars of Spanish American Independence, 1809–29* (Oxford: Osprey, 2013), 50, 54.

5.2 Map of the wars in New Spain — 199
Based on maps from Anthony McFarlane, *War and Independence in Spanish America* (New York: Routledge, 2014), 250; and John Fletcher, *The Wars of Spanish American Independence, 1809–29* (Oxford: Osprey, 2013), 36.

5.3 Map of campaigns of Bolívar and San Martín in South America — 210
Based on maps from Cathryn L. Lombardi and John V. Lombardi, with K. Lynn Stoner, *Latin America: A Teaching Atlas* (Madison: Conference on Latin American History and the University of Wisconsin Press, 1983), 48; and John Fletcher, *The Wars of Spanish American Independence, 1809–29* (Oxford: Osprey, 2013), 40, 54.

Introduction
A History of the Spanish Atlantic World: Prospects and Possibilities

The overseas enterprises of Spain expanded dramatically following the first voyage of Christopher Columbus in 1492.[1] Even before this historic Atlantic crossing, Spaniards had explored and then launched an invasion of the Canary Islands, conquering the archipelago between 1478 and 1493. The Canaries then served as both a base and a proving ground for the invasion and conquest of Spanish America, known as the Indies. After 1492, Spain's possessions expanded from a few isolated Caribbean outposts, such as Española, Cuba, and Puerto Rico, to include the most densely populated regions of Mexico as the army of Fernando Cortés and his Amerindian allies overthrew the Aztec (Mexica) Empire between 1519 and 1521. From central Mexico, the Spanish invaders moved southward to annex the Maya domains in southern Mexico and Central America. Within a decade, the equally stunning victories of Francisco Pizarro, Diego de Almagro, and their Indigenous allies initiated the process that eventually brought down the Inca Empire (*Tawantinsuyu*), giving the Spaniards control over extensive human and mineral resources in the Andean region of South America.[2] A less famous Spanish expedition under Gonzalo Jiménez de Quesada raided, explored, and established settlements in present-day Colombia between 1536 and 1537.[3] Over the course of the

---

[1] The expansion into the Indies was sponsored and largely funded by Queen Isabel of Castile, so these domains were annexed as an accessory union with that kingdom. When Ferdinand and Isabel married in 1469 and consolidated their rule ten years later, the union was dynastic, and in most respects Castile and Aragon remained separate political entities until the accession of the Bourbon king, Philip V, in 1700. As a result, most of the first conquistadors were from Castile, not Aragon. Nonetheless, for the sake of simplicity, I will use the term *Spaniard* to describe them. J. H. Elliott, *Imperial Spain, 1469–1716* (1963; London: Penguin, 2002), 15–76; Henry Kamen, *Spain, 1469–1714: A Society of Conflict* (New York: Pearson Longman, 2006), 1–59.

[2] The Spanish narrative of how they conquered the Andes is presented in John Hemming, *The Conquest of the Incas* (New York: Harcourt Brace Jovanovich, 1970). For a very different view from the Inca perspective, see Titu Cusi Yupanqui, *History of How the Spaniards Arrived in Peru*, trans. with intro. Catherine Julien (Indianapolis, IN: Hackett, 2006).

[3] The Native American groups that Jiménez de Quesada encountered were the Muísca, Tunja, and Panches, who had a long history of fighting with each other. At the end of his expedition, Jiménez de Quesada met an expedition led by Sebastián de Benalcázar coming from Peru and another from Venezuela, led by Nicolás Federmán, representing the Welser Company. This

sixteenth century, the conquistadors, followed by Crown bureaucrats and Catholic clergymen, slowly but firmly consolidated control over the central regions of Mexico and the most populous regions of South America. These possessions collectively served as the foundation of the Spanish Atlantic world. By 1600, the Spaniards claimed control over a vast region extending from the current southwest of the United States to the southern tip of South America.[4] It was a massive domain that brought unimaginable wealth to the Kingdoms of Spain for over three hundred years.[5] This wealth, however, came at the expense of the conquered Indigenous peoples, and later people of mixed racial ancestry, and enslaved Africans brought to the Indies. For three hundred years, the Spanish Atlantic world inspired wonder, envy, and later the predatory attention of other European powers.

Political and Institutional Culture of the Spanish Atlantic World

The Spanish Atlantic world was bound together by a common loyalty to the Spanish monarch, the Roman Catholic Church, and a series of interlocking ties of clientage, family connections, and political alliances on both the imperial and the local levels. The Crown established the New World's largest professional bureaucracy to govern, tax, and control the dense Indigenous populations and wealth of the Indies, which gave institutional stability. These Crown officials also established strict mercantile regulations over the flow of commerce across the Atlantic. The Church provided the moral and ethical foundations of the Spanish Atlantic world and a crusading spirit to convert the Indigenous population, while the Crown founded the Holy Office of the Inquisition to impose rigid Roman Catholic orthodoxy. The ties forged between the Crown and elites in the Indies offered political stability, but they were potentially brittle if policy disagreements, Crown demands, or local conflicts undermined networks of loyalty. Spain's European wars put tremendous fiscal pressure throughout the Spanish Atlantic world as the Crown tried to take larger shares

---

German commercial and banking house financed many of the wars of King Charles I in Europe and was given the right to settle Venezuela for the Spanish Crown. Of the nearly 800 men who started the expedition to the Colombian highlands, only 179 survived. For the story of the Jiménez de Quesada expedition, see J. Michael Francis, *Invading Colombia: Spanish Accounts of the Gonzalo Jiménez de Quesada Expedition of Conquest* (University Park: Pennsylvania State University Press, 2007).

[4] This did not include Brazil, which by papal donation was a Portuguese possession, only tied to the Spanish monarchy dynastically from 1580 to 1640. Elliott, *Imperial Spain*, 63.

[5] In using *Spain*, I refer to the union of Castile and Aragon and their territories in Europe from the accession to their respective thrones of Ferdinand of Aragon and Isabel of Castile in 1479.

INTRODUCTION: A HISTORY OF THE ATLANTIC WORLD   3

of revenue, particularly from Castile and the Indies, to fight increasingly expensive foreign conflicts. These wars nearly led to the collapse of the Spanish system in the second half of the seventeenth century and throughout the eighteenth century. Such intense fiscal pressure only escalated early in the next century and undermined the whole Spanish Atlantic world, leading to its ultimate collapse by 1825.

The political and institutional culture of the Spanish Atlantic world evolved in five distinct stages over three hundred years. Each stage led to changes in the shared set of political values, beliefs, knowledge, and the faith in secular and religious institutions, particularly among elites, which undergirded political/religious processes and supported them.[6] Social, economic, and cultural changes more broadly were most often affected directly or indirectly by changes in political and institutional culture. Shifts in the on-the-ground implementation of policies or political practices often inflected or altered politics at the local or regional level.

The first stage of this evolving political and institutional culture emerged during the conquest of the Indies, and it drew inspiration from the violence, military traditions, and evangelical Christian zeal that characterized the seven hundred-year struggle in Iberia against the Muslims known as the Reconquista.[7] The final moment of this long conflict came with the fall of the last Muslim Kingdom of Granada in 1492, the year that Columbus made his momentous voyage. The struggles with the Muslims shaped the Spanish monarchy, as well as numerous other institutional, religious, and military practices that Spanish settlers brought with them to the Indies.[8] The original Spanish conquistadors

---

[6] This definition of political culture describes the long-term and salient process of historical change in the Spanish Atlantic world, and it does not attempt, as some political scientists have, to test and measure hypotheses about political culture. For a fine survey of the ways that the concept of political culture has evolved in history and political science, see Ronald P. Formisano, "The Concept of Political Culture," *The Journal of Interdisciplinary History* 31, no. 3 (Winter 2001): 393–426. For a more cultural history definition of the concept in the Latin American context, see Nils Jacobsen and Christóbal Aljovín de Losada, who argue, "By political culture we mean a perspective on the processes of change and continuity in any human polity or its component parts which privileges, symbols, discourses, rituals, customs, norms, values, and attitudes of individuals or groups for understanding the construction, consolidation, and dismantling of power constellations and institutions." See "How Interests and Values Seldom Come Alone or: The Utility of a Pragmatic Perspective on Political Culture," in *Political Culture in the Andes*, ed. Nils Jacobsen and Cristóbal Aljovín de Losada (Durham, NC: Duke University Press, 2005), 58.

[7] Such individual actors could be powerful elites or even ordinary people who had the courage and charisma to influence events. A prime example of an ordinary man who shaped local events was the illiterate Aymara peasant, Tomás Katari, who uncovered local corruption and whose actions prompted a major Indigenous rebellion in Chayanta, north of the mining town of Potosí. See Sergio Serulnikov, *Subverting Colonial Authority: Challenges to Spanish Rule in the Eighteenth-Century Southern Andes* (Durham, NC: Duke University Press, 2003), 4–5, 126–31, 148–58, 186–94, 218–27.

[8] The influence of the Reconquista on the direction and form of Spanish overseas expansion has been recognized by historians for many years. See, for example, Silvio Zavala, *Las instituciones*

effectively ruled in the Indies by dividing Indigenous towns in the Indies into grants of encomienda, drawing taxes and labor service from their Indigenous charges, in return for military protection and converting the native peoples to Roman Catholicism. The Crown had awarded similar types of encomienda grants in the Reconquista to individual nobles and military orders, usually as a temporary measure to control new lands taken in battle from the Muslims.[9] In addition, a militant evangelical brand of Christianity emerged from the Reconquista in Iberia, as many Christian Spanish laymen and clerics saw themselves on a divine mission to bring the Roman Catholic faith to the Indigenous peoples of the Americas.[10] The conquistadors also brought other religious traditions of medieval Spain, such as Catholic mysticism, the tradition of establishing Roman Catholic sodalities, selling indulgences (to forgive past sins), the reverence for relics, and the belief in miraculous images and shrines.

In the second stage, the government in Madrid eventually replaced the political and fiscal duties of holders of encomienda grants, called *encomenderos*, with royally appointed officials. The Church took over the responsibility for the religious conversion of the Indigenous peoples. As a result, many aspects of the Reconquista's influence over the Spanish Atlantic world diminished over time, particularly in the more populated, central regions of the Indies. The Crown was able to take control in the Indies because the most important political and institutional arrangement to emerge from this long struggle with the Muslims was the formation of a strong Spanish monarchy. This process began with the dynastic marriage in 1469 between the heirs of the two largest Christian kingdoms in Iberia, Isabel of Castile and Ferdinand of Aragon (known as the Catholic kings). The marriage of Ferdinand and Isabel produced not a unified nation-state, but what historian J. H. Elliott has labeled a "composite monarchy," composed of different provinces or kingdoms united only by a common

---

jurídicas en la conquista de América (Madrid: Imprenta Helénica, 1935); Charles Verlinden, *Précédents médiévaux de la Colonie en Amérique* (Mexico City: I.P.G.H., 1954); and more recently Luis Weckmann, *The Medieval Heritage of Mexico*, trans. Frances M. López-Morillas (New York: Fordham University Press, 1992). For a collection of "classic" essays dealing with this issue, see James Muldoon and Felipe Fernández Armesto, *The Medieval Frontiers of Latin Christendom: Expansion, Contraction, Continuity* (2008; repr., London: Routledge, 2016). The links between medieval Spain and the foundation of the Spanish Indies have not been a central issue of concern for most historians of the Spanish Atlantic world; one notable exception is the recent work by Karen Graubart. See Karen B. Graubart, "Learning from the *Qadi*: The Jurisdiction of Local Rule in the Early Colonial Andes," *Hispanic American Historical Review* 95, no. 2 (May 2015): 195–228; and Karen B. Graubart, *Republics of Difference: Religious and Racial Self-Governance in the Spanish Atlantic World* (New York: Oxford University Press, 2022).

[9] The encomienda in Spain usually involved a grant of land, but in the Indies, this was not the case; the *encomendero* only received the right to collect taxes and labor service.

[10] An early book that covers this millennial mission of the mendicantas is: John Leddy Phelan, *The Millennial Kingdom of the Franciscans in the New World* (Berkeley: University of California Press, 1970).

monarch. This was the prevailing form of monarchy in most of early modern Europe. The union of Castile and Aragon consisted of several political units, each jealously guarding its own laws, privileges, and semi-independent status.[11] Composite monarchy was a negotiated political order: good government in the Spanish kingdoms involved a contract, with the monarch providing protection and respect for local laws and privileges, in return for the loyalty and support of the people in each separate kingdom or province.

According to the seventeenth-century Spanish-born jurist who served in the Viceroyalty of Peru, Juan de Solórzano y Pereira, there were two basic forms of composite monarchy. One involved a province or kingdom that acquired a new territory and subjected it to the laws and privileges of the dominant power, called an *accessory union*. An example of such an accessory union was the Spanish Indies in the sixteenth century, which was originally considered a legal appendage of Castile, subject to the laws of that kingdom. Another form of composite monarchy was a looser confederation, or *aeque principaliter* (equally important), in which each province or kingdom demanded to be treated as a distinct entity, subject to its own laws and privileges, with its unique relationship to the monarch. An example of an *aeque principaliter* was the union between Castile and the other kingdoms and provinces of the monarchy, such as Aragon, Catalonia, Valencia, Sicily, Naples, and later Portugal, where each maintained their own laws, languages, and political traditions, united only by a common monarch. This more decentralized form of composite monarchy had access to great resources, yet it preserved the traditional position of influential local groups—aristocrats, urban oligarchs, state bureaucrats, influential members of the Church, mercantile groups, and the military—at both the center and the peripheral provinces of the monarchy. The king frequently tried to cement the relationship by dispensing patronage to members of the nobility and university-trained lawyers (*letrados*) in each region, allowing them to serve on royal advisory councils. The Crown also respected the representative institutions that gave voice to these wide-ranging elite groups, such as the representative assembly or parliament (*cortes*) of each province or kingdom and important city councils.[12] The composite monarchy of Castile and Aragon (later known as

---

[11] An important marker of this composite monarchy was that Ferdinand was considered only the consort of Isabel in Castile, not the king, and Isabel enjoyed this more limited status in Aragon. Even when their grandson, Charles of Ghent, inherited both thrones in 1516, he was not crowned king of Spain, but had to swear to observe the laws and privileges of each separate kingdom in front of its representative assembly, or *cortes*, before he could claim its allegiance and recognition as monarch. J. H. Elliott, "A Europe of Composite Monarchies," *Past and Present* 42 (February 1969): 50–52.

[12] Elliott, "Europe of Composite Monarchies," 53–55; and Antonio Feros, "Governance," in *Lexicon of the Hispanic Baroque: Transatlantic Exchange and Transformation*, ed. Evonne Levy and Kenneth Mills (Austin: University of Texas Press, 2013), 140–44.

Spain) also had the flexibility and political strength to sponsor the voyages of Columbus, undermine the power of the original conquistadors, and later annex the Indies as an accessory union by the mid-sixteenth century to create a Spanish Atlantic world.[13]

In the third stage of this evolution, political and legal relationships between the Indies and Spain evolved into a looser, more autonomous union over the course of the seventeenth century. The corpus of written laws produced by Crown-appointed bureaucrats in the Indies, combined with local customs and practices, defined a sense of the common good and shaped a distinct legal system, or *derecho indiano*, in the Spanish Indies. The power of local officials in the Indies only grew as the fiscally strapped Spanish Crown began public auctions to sell appointments even for important judicial offices in the seventeenth century (treasury offices in 1633, local magistracies or *corregimientos* in 1678, and high court or *audiencia* judgeships in 1687).[14] Often, these purchasers used their position to enrich themselves and their friends and families, viewing their positions as a personal sinecure, not just as loyal service to the monarchy. As Spain's power in Europe and over the Indies waned, the American provinces effectively operated as a more autonomous union or an *aeque principaliter*, which altered the political and institutional culture of the Spanish Atlantic world.

The fourth stage began after 1700 when the French Bourbon monarch, Philip V, inherited the throne of Spain; the king and his ministers sought to end this drift toward greater autonomy in the Indies by strengthening royal power throughout the Spanish Atlantic world. Over the course of the century, they sought to use the wealth of the Indies to rebuild the Spanish economy and to centralize power in a more absolutist state. Philip and his successors during the eighteenth century responded with a thoroughgoing reform of the political relationships in Spain and the empire to curb smuggling, curtail the power of interest groups (such as commercial guilds and even the Church), modernize

---

[13] One more recent way of examining the structure of Iberian monarchies argues that they were polycentric, with "many different interlinked centers that interacted not only with the king but also among themselves, thus actively participating in forging the polity." See Pedro Cardim, Tamar Herzog, José Javier Ruiz Ibánez, and Gaetano Sabatini, eds., *Polycentric Monarchies: How Did Early Modern Spain and Portugal Achieve and Maintain a Global Hegemony?* (2012; repr., Eastbourne, UK: Sussex Academic Press, 2014), 4. I would argue that this is more a slight change in emphasis from the argument Elliott made about an *aeque principaliter*, rather than a new theory of the structure of early modern Iberian monarchies.

[14] Kenneth J. Andrien, *Crisis and Decline: The Viceroyalty of Peru in the Seventeenth Century* (Albuquerque: University of New Mexico Press, 1985), 103–29; Mark A. Burkholder and D. S. Chandler, *From Impotence to Authority: The Spanish Crown and the American Audiencias* (Columbia: University of Missouri Press, 1977), 13–15, 81–83, 139–44; and Alberto Yalí Román, "Sobre alcaldías mayors y corregimientos en Indias," *Jahrbuch für Geschichte von Staat, Wirtschaft, und Gesellschaft Lateinamerikas* 9 (1974): 1–39.

state finances, establish firmer control over the empire, replenish depleted royal coffers, and rebuild Spanish military might. In short, successive Bourbon monarchs attempted to turn the composite monarchy of the Habsburgs into a stronger, more centralized state apparatus to enhance royal authority, potentially transforming the political and institutional culture of Spain and its Atlantic world. Spain also had to fight in Europe and the Americas to keep rival colonial powers from gaining direct commercial access to the Spanish Indies.[15] War and reform thus enjoyed a symbiotic relationship, as conflicts sometimes interfered with Crown attempts at renovation and at other times encouraged reform as Spain's ministers attempted to prepare for impending conflicts with rivals. Paying for these wars led the Crown to exert intense fiscal pressure to raise taxes needed to support these ongoing and increasingly expensive conflicts.

In the fifth and final stage, the outbreak of European wars associated with the French Revolution in 1789 disrupted transatlantic trade and local economies throughout the Spanish Atlantic world. Wars with revolutionary France in 1793 and 1795 led to a series of disastrous defeats, forcing the Spanish Crown to sue for peace and revive the traditional alliance with France. This precipitated wars with Great Britain, France's principal foe, in 1796 and 1804 that led to the loss of most of the Spanish navy and effectively disrupted commercial ties between Spain and the Indies. Although the monarchy survived colonial rebellions and these defeats at the hands of increasingly belligerent European rivals, Crown power was undermined. As a result, when the French emperor, Napoleon Bonaparte, sent an army to invade Iberia in 1807, he forced the abdication of the Bourbon monarch, Charles IV, and compelled his son and heir, Ferdinand, to renounce his claim to the throne. This led to a constitutional crisis in the Spanish Atlantic world over where sovereignty resided in the absence of a monarch. The crisis of legitimacy, in turn, set in motion a series of conflicts in the Indies that led to the slow collapse of the Spanish Atlantic world between 1808 and 1825.

---

[15] When the Crown tried to impose an empire-wide set of taxes to support a standing army for Spain (called the Union of Arms) in 1625, for example, it produced a series of imbroglios that ultimately contributed to revolts in Catalonia and Portugal and even led to serious political unrest in New Spain. For the origins of the Catalan Revolt, see J. H. Elliott, *The Revolt of the Catalans: A Study in the Decline of Spain, 1598–1640* (Cambridge: Cambridge University Press, 1963); for unrest during this time period in New Spain, see, J. I. Israel, *Race, Class, and Politics in Colonial Mexico, 1610–1670* (Oxford: Oxford University Press, 1975), 135–60; and, more recently, Angela Ballone, *The 1624 Tumult of Mexico in Perspective (c. 1620–1650): Authority and Conflict Resolution in the Iberian Atlantic* (Leiden: Brill, 2018). In the Viceroyalty of Peru, venal officeholders simply failed to implement any new levies capable of meeting the quota set for the Union of Arms, despite the Crown sending a special commissioner, Hernando de Valencia, to secure the implementation of a plan to meet royal expectations. See Andrien, *Crisis and Decline*, 143–54.

Change, Diversity, and Everyday Life in the Spanish Atlantic World

The impact of long-term, largely impersonal historical changes in political and institutional culture varied, sometimes substantially, across the vast agglomeration of landscapes, climates, disease environments, and cultures that comprised the Spanish Atlantic world. The Spanish Atlantic encompassed small Caribbean settlements, remote frontier outposts, densely populated central regions of North and South America, and the Iberian kingdoms; each region also had stark climatic and geographical differences. Charting the impact of such long-term historical changes across time and space is complicated further by the fact that Indigenous, European, and African lifeways, while distinct, also became intertwined over time in the Atlantic basin, producing a hybrid colonial order that differed in each region of the Spanish Atlantic world. Although violence and coercion were an integral part of the subjugation of the Indigenous and African populations, these subordinated peoples managed to incorporate these changes into their own political, social, economic, and religious customs, producing a constantly evolving mosaic that varied over time and in each locale of the massive Spanish Atlantic world. Furthermore, Spanish efforts at evangelization prompted profound religious changes, as Roman Catholic clergymen attempted to convert millions of Indigenous people to their faith. Nevertheless, some Indigenous and African religious practices persisted, particularly in frontier regions. Intermarriage and casual sexual unions among Europeans, Indigenous peoples, and enslaved Africans led to a racial, ethnic, and cultural mixture. With this incredible diversity, it is no small wonder that the impact of long-term historical changes in political and institutional culture varied across the Spanish Atlantic world.

The precise chronology for such long-term changes also differed, with politics, social change, economic life, culture, and even religious narratives moving at different paces across the regions of Spain and the Indies. Throughout the Spanish Indies, the Crown began to consolidate its control over the original conquistadors by sending Crown-appointed officials to govern beginning in the 1550s and 1560s. During this period, the Crown also organized trade between Spain and the Indies into a system of convoys, proceeding from Seville (and, after 1717, Cádiz) to a few licensed ports in the Americas, which lasted until the second half of the eighteenth century. Socioeconomic changes, however, proceeded more incrementally, as the mining economy spread and spurred the development of other sectors, such as agriculture, grazing, artisan crafts, and textile production. Likewise, after the optimistic efforts by the religious orders to convert the Indigenous peoples, periodic signs that Amerindians stubbornly clung to pre-Columbian religious practices continued to bedevil Roman Catholic clergymen intent on preserving the religious purity of the

Spanish Atlantic world. In addition, although cultural changes became embedded in the Indies, artistic traditions, the adoption of the Castilian language, and even alphabetic writing, particularly in the Andes, moved unevenly and more slowly. In short, the Indies remained a new world that was not entirely European, Indigenous, or African.

The pace of such longer- and shorter-term changes over time profoundly influenced many residing in the Spanish Atlantic world, although this differed because of unique local conditions. According to anthropologist George Marcus, an approach that takes into account such diversity can create the "crucible for integrating the micro and the macro, combining the accounts of impersonal systems into representations of local life as cultural forms both autonomous and constituted by the larger order."[16] This study attempts to recreate the lives of real people within their broad historical context, without reducing their experiences merely as reflections of deep, long-term forces of change. Some of these individual actors played prominent roles in the events of their day, while others were swept up in the larger forces that shaped their lives. To illustrate how individuals dealt with these long- and shorter-term historical processes, each chapter ends with a biographical portrait.

The Spanish Atlantic world had evolved from connections, interactions, and exchanges that began with the voyages of Christopher Columbus and extended into the early nineteenth century. The Spanish expansion into the Atlantic islands started even before 1492, but these efforts did not have the lasting significance of the Columbian voyages. Despite its ethnic, cultural, and geographic diversity, the Spanish Atlantic world constituted a defined political, economic, and religious space that held together from the sixteenth to the early nineteenth century.[17]

European Expansion, Competition, and Conflict in the Atlantic Basin

The Spanish Atlantic world represented the first great wave of European overseas expansion across the Atlantic Ocean.[18] From the time of Columbus,

---

[16] George E. Marcus, "Contemporary Problems of Ethnography in the World System," in *Writing Culture: The Poetics and Politics of Ethnography*, ed. James Clifford and George E. Marcus (Berkeley: University of California Press, 1986), 170.

[17] Control of the Indies also had a profound influence over the metropolis; the massive influx of American silver that fueled the imperial aspirations of the Crown in Europe provides only the most obvious example of this impact. Earl J. Hamilton, *American Treasure, and the Price Revolution in Spain, 1501–1650* (Cambridge, MA: Harvard University Press, 1934); and, more recently, John J. TePaske, *A New World of Gold and Silver*, ed. Kendall W. Brown (Leiden: Brill, 2010).

[18] The Portuguese, who had pioneered European expansion into Africa and the Far East, did not firmly establish their Atlantic colony in Brazil until the mid-sixteenth century. See A. J. R. Russell-Wood, "The Portuguese Atlantic, 1415–1808," in *Atlantic History: A Critical*

prospective Spanish conquistadors signed and notarized agreements (called *capitulaciones*) with the Crown, specifying the responsibilities of all parties to the contract, including spreading the Roman Catholic faith among any native groups encountered.[19] These contracts with the monarchy sometimes provided for additional investors in the enterprise or served as leverage to gain private funding from wealthy merchants, nobles, or even churchmen. The intent of these overseas expeditions of trade, conquest, and colonization was to improve the lives and well-being of the largely middle-class Spanish conquistadors and settlers, well beyond what they could hope to attain in Spain. By maintaining ties with the metropolis, overseas settlements also promised benefits for Spain and the monarchy. In some cases, particularly for clergymen, these enterprises included a utopian element, converting and saving the souls of Native peoples and creating an ethical and moral society.[20] These *capitulaciones* authorizing overseas ventures resembled the agreements that the Christian kings made with various noble and civic groups to fight against the Muslims during the Reconquista to create a Christian Spain.

French, Dutch, and English efforts at colonization followed over a century later, and their overseas colonies were shaped by a set of European political and economic customs and values that had changed markedly since the voyages of Columbus. In the sixteenth century, Spain's competitors in the Atlantic world often began with privateering ventures to raid Spanish and Portuguese shipping. As they founded colonies, early Dutch, English, French, and Portuguese explorers and colonists received contracts from their respective Crowns, which resembled the Spanish *capitulaciones*. The early English overseas ventures of Walter Raleigh, for example, received Crown patents that authorized the establishment of colonies in Ireland or the Americas in the name of the Crown, not Parliament.[21] Later colonial efforts in the seventeenth century relied on more advanced economic tools, such as joint-stock companies, to fund the founding of colonies in the Atlantic world. The Dutch colonial enterprises in the Atlantic world, for example, were launched by a state-licensed joint-stock company, the Dutch West India Company (Geoctroyeerde Westindische Compagnie), in 1621. The Dutch colonists were either employees of the West India Company or free settlers. The company devoted large resources to gaining footholds in Africa to participate in the trade of enslaved individuals, and it also launched a fleet of twenty-six ships and thirty-three hundred soldiers to capture the

---

Appraisal, ed. Jack P. Greene and Philip D. Morgan (New York: Oxford University Press, 2009), 81–109.

[19] For an excellent example of how this process worked, see Francis, *Invading Colombia*, 19–33.

[20] For a comparison with the aims and aspirations of early English colonial enterprises, see Alan Gallay, *Walter Raleigh: Architect of Empire* (New York: Basic Books, 2019), 339–43.

[21] For a comparison with early English colonial enterprises, see Gallay, *Walter Raleigh*, 81–84.

Brazilian capital of Salvador de Bahia in 1626 in an effort to gain control over this lucrative Portuguese sugar-producing province and the global commerce in sugar. When a Spanish–Portuguese joint expedition recaptured the city a year later, the Dutch West India Company returned to Brazil in 1630 and captured the city of Recife in Pernambuco, which they held until 1654, when a large Portuguese force retook the province. Meanwhile, the English used joint-stock companies to establish a colony in Virginia in 1607, while religious separatists, the Pilgrims in 1621 and later the Puritans, used such companies to found colonies in New England. The French also used a joint-stock company to establish small colonial enterprises in Canada and the Caribbean.

The earlier Spanish invaders of the late fifteenth and early sixteenth centuries came to the Americas in search of wealth valued in their home country, and they found it in large deposits of precious metals (particularly silver) and rich agricultural lands. Later European settlers of the Americas found fewer deposits of such valued resources as they set up their own overseas settlements, but initially they tried to imitate the earlier successful patterns of expansion pioneered by the Spaniards. They penetrated the Spanish Atlantic world through contraband commerce, and in some instances military incursions, which led to periodic wars as the French settled in Haiti (on the island of Española in 1625); the Dutch colonized Curacao in 1634, off the coast of Venezuela; and the English took Jamaica in 1655. The settlements of these later European colonists also interacted with those of the Spanish, particularly along frontier zones in North and South America. Indeed, the histories of the Spanish, English, French, and Dutch Atlantic worlds became "mutually entangled" over time.[22]

Apart from losing some of its Caribbean possessions, from the sixteenth century onward, Spain also had to fight in Europe and the Americas to keep rival colonial powers from gaining direct commercial access to Spanish possessions in the Indies. In 1493, the papacy had divided the non-European world, awarding control over evangelization of Native peoples in Asia, Africa, and Brazil to Portugal and the bulk of the Americas to Spain. This papal bull was verified in 1494 by the Treaty of Tordesillas between the two Iberian monarchies. As a result of these agreements, the Spanish and Portuguese claimed complete sovereignty over the lands and sea lanes outside their Atlantic domains. The Spanish monarchy set up the New World's largest professional bureaucracy to govern, tax, and control the people and wealth of the Indies. Crown officials established strict mercantile regulations over the flow of commerce across the

---

[22] See the American Historical Review forum: Eliga H. Gould, "Entangled Histories, Entangled World: The English-Speaking Atlantic as a Spanish Periphery," *American Historical Review* 112, no. 3 (June 2007): 786; Jorge Cañizares-Esguerra, "Entangled Histories: Borderland Historiographies in New Clothes," *American Historical Review* 112, no. 3 (June 2007): 787–99.

Atlantic. Finally, Spaniards imposed a tight Roman Catholic orthodoxy, establishing the Holy Office of the Inquisition in their capitals of Lima, Mexico City, and later Cartagena de Indias (in current-day Colombia). The political, economic, and religious policies of the Spaniards were collectively intended to establish an Atlantic world that was "closed" to outside influence, particularly non-Catholics.

The other European powers challenged these claims by supporting voyages of exploration, licensing privateers to prey on Iberian shipping, engaging in contraband commerce with the Indies, and dispatching their own competing colonial enterprises. Spanish and Portuguese diplomats in Amsterdam, London, and Paris repeatedly protested against such infringements on these waters and lands, but to no avail. The Dutch, French, and English all had seafaring histories, shipbuilding industries, seaports on the Atlantic, and vibrant merchant communities to finance overseas expansion.[23] The result was ongoing conflict in the Atlantic world, which only intensified in the eighteenth and early nineteenth centuries as Spain, Portugal, and European rivals all successfully implanted competing colonial enterprises in the New World. Indeed, Spanish efforts to centralize power and replace the composite monarchy that emerged from the Reconquista with a more centralized, absolutist form of government during the eighteenth-century, and Bourbon reforms were partly a response to these imperial threats.

What Is Atlantic History?

Studying the Spanish Atlantic allows for a comparative examination of how events in Europe, Africa, and the Americas influenced each other, as well as an examination of the interconnections of global, regional, and local processes.[24] It is a departure from much previous scholarship on early Latin American history, which emphasized local or regional studies of urban and rural groups (such as merchants, *encomenderos*, artisans, women, and even enslaved individuals), Indigenous communities, and their resistance to Spanish oppression. The Atlantic perspective, however, provides a broad framework

---

[23] Kenneth J. Andrien, "The Age of Exploration, c. 1500–1650," in *The Ashgate Research Companion to Modern Imperial Histories*, ed. Philippa Levine and John Marriott (Surrey, UK: Ashgate, 2012), 27–32.

[24] According to Jack P. Greene and Phillip D. Morgan, Atlantic history is "a framework, an angle of vision, an arena of analysis...that historians have devised to help them organize the study of some of the most important developments of the early modern era: the emergence in the fifteenth century and the subsequent growth of the Atlantic basin as a site for demographic, economic, social, cultural, and other forms of exchange surrounding the Atlantic Ocean." Greene and Morgan, *Atlantic History*, 3, 10.

to study important historical changes without regard to local political borders and even encourages comparisons with the Portuguese, Dutch, French, and English empires. It also highlights the differences within the Spanish Atlantic world, between the densely populated central regions and the more sparsely settled frontier zones—where Spanish rule was more insecure and various Indigenous groups challenged their control, along with competing European powers. Frontier regions such as Florida, northern New Spain, Chile, and Paraguay saw different Indigenous and later European groups interact, trade, and often compete for hegemony. Moreover, an Atlantic perspective emphasizes the world of merchants and maritime commercial exchanges. Such a broad perspective also places renewed emphasis on movement, particularly migration back and forth across the Atlantic Ocean. Wars also connected the Spanish Atlantic world; conflicts in Europe often spread to America and beyond, while the commerce in enslaved people sometimes led to wars among African polities. Moreover, it brings scholarly attention to the role of Africa, the trade of enslaved peoples, and the lives of enslaved and free Africans living in the Indies. It short, an Atlantic perspective encourages students of Spain and early Latin America to explore a wide range of topics and relationships and to see old problems from a different viewpoint.

Atlantic history has emerged as a full-blown, recognized subfield in a number of disciplines since the 1990s, leading to an impressive list of scholarly books, articles, and even journals dedicated to the subject. These works broaden and deepen an understanding of the Atlantic world, dealing with the interconnections among global, regional, and local processes linking the four continents surrounding the Atlantic basin—Europe, North and South America, and Africa. Studies using the Atlantic as an analytic framework have tended to fall into three basic typologies identified in a pioneering study by historian David Armitage.[25] Circum-Atlantic histories provide a transnational view of the region, viewing the Atlantic basin as a unified zone of exchange, circulation, and the transmission of people, ideas, goods, and even warfare. The emphasis here is on the whole Atlantic region, rather than specific imperial, national, regional, or local histories. An excellent example of circum-Atlantic history is Joseph C. Miller's *Way of Death: Merchant Capitalism and the Angolan Slave Trade, 1730–1830*.[26] The second approach to doing Atlantic history, which Armitage calls transatlantic history, involves international comparisons across the ocean and the continents that face onto it. A recent example of transatlantic

---

[25] David Armitage, "Three Concepts of Atlantic History," in *The British Atlantic World, 1500–1800*, ed. Armitage and Michael J. Braddick (Basingstoke, UK: Palgrave Macmillan, 2008), 15–27.

[26] Joseph C. Miller, *Way of Death: Merchant Capitalism and the Angolan Slave Trade, 1730–1830* (Madison: University of Wisconsin Press, 1988).

history is J. H. Elliott's *Empires of the Atlantic World: Britain and Spain in the Americas, 1492–1830*.[27] The third approach identified by Armitage is cis-Atlantic history, which examines particular places, regions, empires, and even institutions within a wider Atlantic context, focusing on the interplay between local events and a wider web of connections or comparisons. It is this third framework of analysis that will serve as the basis for this study of the changing political and institutional culture of the Spanish Atlantic world from the voyage of Christopher Columbus in 1492 to the culmination of the independence movements in Spanish America by 1825. This book presents the Spanish Atlantic world as a cohesive unit, whereby events in the metropolis and the colonies had a constant and enduring impact on each other. The Indies and Spain were linked not just by a common legal system, ideology of empire, bureaucratic ties, and Roman Catholicism but also by facing the same challenges of dynastic ambitions, warfare, commerce, and the migrations of people and ideas across the vast Atlantic basin.

Organization of the Book

The book is a broad survey of the chronological evolution of political and institutional culture in the Spanish Atlantic world from its inception in 1492 to its dissolution by 1825; it is divided into an introduction, five chapters, and a conclusion. Each of these chapters demonstrates the long-term changes in Spanish colonialism that shaped the Spanish Atlantic world over time: the early influence of the Reconquista, the evolution of the Spanish composite monarchy in the Spanish Atlantic world to a more centralized state, and how the precise chronology of changes in political, social, economic, religious, and cultural life varied over time. These broad changes also shaped the parameters of individual lives throughout this diverse landscape over three hundred years. As a result, every chapter ends with an individual life story, which illustrates the influence of the larger historical changes over the lives of people living in that historical period.

Chapter 1, "The Reconquista and the Institutional Origins of Spanish Overseas Expansion," examines the ways that the seven hundred–year Reconquista of the Iberian Peninsula shaped the institutions and mental attitudes of the first freewheeling Spanish invaders and churchmen sent to evangelize the Indigenous peoples of the Indies. Institutions such as the encomienda, the reliance on

---

[27] The broadly gauged analysis by J. H. Elliott's *Empires of the Atlantic World: Britain and Spain in the Americas, 1492–1830* (New Haven, CT: Yale University Press, 2006) compares the evolution of the British and Spanish Atlantic empires over the entire colonial period.

Indigenous allies, using Amerindian leaders as intermediaries to control and tax their communities for the Spaniards, and forms of military organization all derived from Reconquista traditions. It will also show how a composite monarchy emerged under the Catholic kings and how it both ended the Reconquista and sponsored the voyage of Christopher Columbus. The whole overseas enterprise depended on belief in one monarchy and one religion in the Spanish Atlantic world. While the Indigenous peoples and their customs, beliefs, and actions also helped influence the evolution of the Spanish colonies, they were essentially excluded from most positions of power in the conquest era. The chapter ends with the story of how a single individual, a Jewish convert, Luis de Santángel, played a key role in convincing Queen Isabel to sponsor and partially fund the momentous voyage of Christopher Columbus.

Chapter 2, "New World Beginnings to the Institutional Consolidation of the Spanish Atlantic World, 1492–1610," traces the dramatic expansion of Spanish power in the Indies over the course of the sixteenth century, from a few small Caribbean outposts to the mainland of North and South America. It examines the early reliance on the independent-minded Spanish invaders, who established a pillaging conquest socioeconomic system based on grants of encomienda, to a more established colonial order supervised by Crown-appointed bureaucrats, churchmen, and settlers who came to rule, convert, and populate the new lands of the Indies. This led to the consolidation of a political and institutional culture, which incorporated the Indies into the Spanish composite monarchy as an accessory union, subject to the laws and institutions of its Iberian metropole. It also explores the emergence of a market economy, first based on the extraction of precious metals and then diversifying into a series of commercial, agropastoral, and artisanal activities. This process involved the exchange of plants and animals, as well as the introduction of deadly European diseases that decimated the Indigenous population of the Indies. The chapter ends with the story of the mysterious origins of a servant woman, Catalina, who became a pawn in a power struggle between predatory, corrupt colonial officials in Cuba and a wealthy Spanish official and his family returning to Spain. The case of Catalina demonstrates the fluid nature of new colonial societies in relation to more stable European social hierarchies.

Chapter 3, "The Mature Colonial Order and the Drift toward Greater Autonomy, 1610–1700," covers the consolidation and evolution of the political and institutional culture of the Spanish Atlantic world as local elites began to exert greater influence over the affairs of the Indies. After the most virulent epidemics had passed and the Native American population began to recover, a more stratified Spanish patriarchal society emerged, and the cultural and religious traditions of Europeans, Amerindians, and Africans merged to create a rich social mixture. Enslaved Africans supplemented the labor force, particularly in those areas that had suffered the worst population losses from disease, and Spanish settlers began populating the borderlands in northern Mexico, Texas, and New Mexico in North America and into frontier regions of South America, such as Chile and the Río de la Plata. The Crown bureaucracy, created in the previous century, progressively fell under the control of local colonial elites, particularly after the Crown auctioned even high-ranking fiscal and judicial appointments, giving these local groups greater political power and autonomy. This gradually changed the political relationship between Spain and the Indies from an accessory union to the more independent provinces of an *aeque principaliter*. The chapter ends with the case of an Afro-Peruvian mystic, Ursula de Jesús, an enslaved woman who was able to secure her freedom but who continued to work in the Lima convent of Santa Clara. Ursula gained fame for her ability to communicate with the dead in purgatory, a liminal space between heaven and hell. Despite her reputation for these divinely inspired visions, Ursula could not escape the hierarchical society that developed over the century, with its prejudices against people of African descent.

Chapter 4, "War and Reform in the Spanish Atlantic World, 1700–1796," examines the Bourbon dynasty's efforts to replace the composite monarchy of the Habsburgs with a more centralized, absolutist state apparatus over the course of the eighteenth century, which reshaped the political and institutional relationship between Spain and the Indies. In large part, these reforms attempted to strengthen Spain in the face of threats from European rivals. They were influenced by intellectual currents in Europe associated with the Enlightenment, and their impact varied in each region of the empire, as political interests contested to oppose or force the implementation of the changes. In some cases, they even provoked violent colonial responses from 1765 to 1783. War with Spain's rivals also added drama that shaped the reform process. These conflicts could periodically disrupt the reforming impulse, while on other occasions, war and past defeats could be used as justifications to advance new innovations in the Spanish Atlantic. In the end, the reform impulse stalled after 1796, and Crown efforts to drain wealth from the clergy and the laity weakened the Church and diminished public support for the monarchy. Finally, the chapter explains how the wars associated with the French Revolution in the 1790s led to fears about the spread of revolutionary ideas from France and suspicions about a suspected revolt of enslaved peoples in Buenos Aires in 1795. Crown officials in the city arrested a prosperous merchant and a French citizen, Juan Barbarín, as a leader of the plot, leading to his financial ruin and exile. Barbarín was a casualty of the hysteria in Buenos Aires, shaped by fears of the spread of revolution and of the large, recently imported enslaved African population in the viceregal capital.

The fifth chapter, "The Collapse of the Spanish Atlantic World, 1796–1825," presents the consequences of the major wars that accompanied the French

Revolution in Europe, culminating in the French invasion of Iberia, the abdication of the Bourbon monarchs, and the ensuing Peninsular War. The tumult in Spain promoted a serious constitutional crisis, which had ramifications in the Indies, where many Creoles believed that without a legitimate monarch, sovereignty reverted to the people. As a result, some Creole elites felt emboldened to create councils (juntas) to rule, at least until a legitimate monarch returned to the throne. Others remained steadfastly loyal to the Crown. The conflicts that emerged became increasingly violent and bloody, as both sides recruited the popular sectors, Indigenous communities, and enslaved Africans. In the metropolis, liberals favoring a constitutional monarchy wrote and promulgated the Constitution of 1812, but when the Bourbon king, Ferdinand, returned in late 1813, he soon abrogated the liberal constitution and sent armies to the Indies in an ultimately futile attempt to finish off any colonial resistance. In the end, the bitter wars in the Indies led to the independence of Mexico and Central America in 1822 and in South America by 1825. This chapter ends with the case of a controversial mestizo royalist leader, Agustín Agualongo, who believed that loyalist groups were more willing to protect the rights of enslaved and Indigenous people than the rebel leader, Simón Bolívar. Agualongo's career demonstrates the enduring appeal of loyalty to the Crown, despite the rise and ultimate victory of the rebel groups.

The conclusion, "From Kingdoms to Colonies to Independence, 1492–1825" examines the changing political and institutional culture of the Spanish Atlantic world from its inception after 1492 to its political dissolution in 1825, showing how it evolved from an accessory union to a more autonomous union and then to a more centralized, absolutist state during the eighteenth century. This reversal of the autonomous union in the seventeenth century led to unrest and even rebellions that paved the way for the move for independence after the French invasion of Iberia in 1807. Over the course of more than three hundred years, the Spanish Indies had evolved from kingdoms to colonies to independent nations, resulting in the fracturing of the Spanish Atlantic world. Independence led to political instability, economic decline, and social disorder in both Iberia and the former Spanish Indies. With deep divisions among elites over the future path of the independent states, much effective power passed to regional warlords, called *caudillos*. Regionalism, not strong nation-states, characterized much of the early nineteenth century in Spain and the newly independent Latin American nations, leading to strife, instability, and economic decline.

The Spanish Atlantic World, 1492–1825

The Spanish conquistadors initiated the first major wave of European expansion into the Americas, and by the end of the sixteenth century, Spain claimed sovereignty over a massive land mass stretching from New Mexico to the southern tip of South America, populated by millions of non-European peoples. The Spanish Crown also gained control over vast resources, particularly precious metals, along with fertile lands that produced a wide range of animals, foodstuffs, and tropical products. These valued commodities allowed the Spanish Indies to maintain commercial ties first across the Atlantic and later across the Pacific Ocean to China. The Crown tried to exert strict controls over commerce in the Spanish Atlantic world, but a thriving network of intercolonial and contraband trade links expanded beyond legally approved commercial markets in Spain.

Loyalty to the Spanish monarchy provided the political control while the Roman Catholic Church gave the moral and ethical principles that held the Spanish Atlantic world together for over three hundred years. After some initial debates over how to deal with the Indigenous peoples, the Crown adopted a policy of evangelizing them into the Catholic fold, bringing millions of new members into the Church. In so doing, the Spanish attempted to impose their faith, language, culture, and moral and ethical practices on the new subjects. The Indigenous and African peoples adopted the Roman Catholic religion, but in most cases they interpreted it to meet their own needs and expectations. As the seven hundred years of the Reconquista demonstrated, competing religions and their different moral and ethical traditions had produced nothing in Iberia but warfare and disorder. As a result, the monarchy and the Church determined that only Roman Catholicism would prevail in the Spanish Indies. The Spanish monarchs, Ferdinand and Isabel, began the process of imposing religious uniformity in Spain by expelling any Jews who would not convert to Catholicism and later forced the conversion of the Muslim population. This imposition of Catholic orthodoxy in Spain presaged the crusading evangelization efforts in the Indies. The large-scale introduction of enslaved Africans introduced new racial, cultural, and religious traditions into this world, but Spanish authorities demanded that they, too, convert to Catholicism. Nonetheless, the large presence of non-European peoples made the Spanish Atlantic world a multiracial, multiethnic entity, with the descendants of the Spanish settlers at the apex of a hierarchical society. Moreover, this social and ethnic mixture varied in different geographical regions of the Spanish Indies. In the Viceroyalty of Peru, for example, the Indigenous peoples remained the majority in the Andean highlands, while on the coast Spanish and African groups became more numerous as the Amerindians succumbed to epidemic diseases.

The Crown established no real institutions of representative government in the Indies, but upper-crust Creoles and peninsular-born Spaniards gained power and influence through informal channels based on clientage, family ties, corruption, and influence peddling. By the early eighteenth century, these informal mechanisms weakened the Crown's political, fiscal, and economic control over the Indies, and a series of reforms in the eighteenth century attempted to reverse this trend toward greater autonomy by tightening administrative, fiscal, and social controls. These reforms undermined the political and religious balance in the Spanish Atlantic world, which alienated local elites and popular groups, weakened the power of the Church, and ultimately undermined loyalty to the monarchy by the early nineteenth century. In essence, by the late eighteenth century, the Madrid government treated the Indies not as separate kingdoms united by a common monarch, but as dependent colonies, subordinated to the metropole, Spain. Although this vast agglomeration of lands and peoples had made Spain a great power, it also produced endless conflict with European rivals as these powers founded competing colonies and tried to penetrate the markets and gain access to the wealth of the Spanish Indies. In the end, the enormous fiscal pressures of war finally undermined the political, religious, and cultural ties that had bound this vast Spanish Atlantic world together, leading to its collapse by 1825.

ID
The Reconquista and the Institutional Origins of Spanish Overseas Expansion

A certain Pelayo, who was the sword-bearer of kings Wittiza and Roderick, oppressed by the authority of the Ishmaelites, had come to Asturias with his sister. On account of his sister, the aforementioned Munnuza dispatched Pelayo to Córdoba as his envoy; but before he returned, Munnuza married his sister through some ruse. When Pelayo returned, he by no means approved of it, and since he had already been thinking about the salvation of the Church, he hastened to bring this about with all of his courage. Then the evil Tārik sent soldiers to Munnuza, who were to arrest Pelayo and lead him back to Córdoba in chains.[1]

When Spain began its overseas expansion to the Indies, following the first voyage of Christopher Columbus in 1492, it had a political and institutional culture shaped by the military and crusading traditions established during the long struggle between Christians and Muslims in Iberia, known as the Reconquista. As they gained more territory from the Muslims over time, the Christian kings had to develop various methods for living side by side with Muslim and Jewish minorities under their jurisdiction. This interaction with non-Christians shaped administrative practices, institutions, religious values, and legal traditions, which had a profound influence on how the first conquistadors would deal with the Indigenous peoples of the Americas. These institutional, legal, and cultural arrangements derived from Roman law, but also from Islamic law and governance, leading to indirect rule and a degree of local autonomy in return for loyalty and paying taxes. Moreover, conflict along the Muslim–Christian frontier zones was omnipresent, so Christian monarchs relied on armies drawn from noble retainers, civic militias, and the military orders of Santiago, Calatrava, and Alcántara. Christian Spain became a "society organized for war,"

---

[1] Simon Barton, *Conquerors, Brides, and Concubines: Interfaith Relations and Social Power in Medieval Iberia* (Philadelphia: University of Pennsylvania Press, 2015), 20.

which developed a strong militant crusading impulse.[2] The relative geographic isolation of Iberia from western Europe allowed the Christian kingdoms to build a political and institutional culture shaped largely by this unique heritage. Castile and Aragon also had an ongoing tradition of trade in both the Atlantic and the Mediterranean. When Columbus and his flotilla of three small ships set sail from Palos de la Frontera, it represented not only the advance of European overseas expansion, but also the military, legal, commercial, and religious crusading traditions of medieval Iberia.

The struggles between Christians and Muslims in Iberia began in 711 CE when Muslim invaders from North Africa swept across the Iberian Peninsula and defeated the weak, decentralized Visigothic Kingdom of Spain, leaving only a small Christian enclave in parts of modern-day Asturias and Galicia. The first leader of this early Christian-controlled territory in northeastern Spain was the celebrated Visigothic nobleman, Pelayo. As the opening quotation of this chapter indicates, the conflict between a Muslim invader, Munnuza, and Pelayo over the Berber's marriage to his sister provided a motivation for Pelayo to lead the Christian revolt in Asturias and Galicia. The Muslim leadership ordered the arrest of Pelayo, but according to legend, Pelayo escaped from his captivity, became the leader of the Kingdom of Asturias, and led an attack on the Muslim invaders. This Christian revolt produced the decisive victory at Covadonga around 722 CE, which halted the Muslim advance, secured the independence of the Kingdom of Asturias, and began the over seven hundred-year Reconquista. The final victory in this long series of struggles did not occur until 1492 when the Christian forces captured the last Muslim stronghold in Granada.

The union of the two largest Christian monarchies in Iberia, with the marriage of Ferdinand of Aragon and Isabel of Castile in 1469, produced a powerful dynastic monarchy capable of securing this final Christian victory. The monarchs could muster their combined resources with the assistance of noblemen, members of the civic militias, and the military orders to launch a religious crusade against Muslim Granada. The capitulation of the last Muslim stronghold signaled the triumph of Christianity in Iberia and the final goal of the 770-year struggle begun by the legendary Pelayo at Covadonga. It was against the backdrop of this historic triumph that Isabel of Castile decided to sponsor the expedition of Christopher Columbus. When the first Spanish invaders and subsequent settlers arrived in the New World, they brought with them crusading religious fervor, military traditions, and a political and institutional culture

---

[2] This idea is taken from the title and the book on the civic militias during the Reconquista: James F. Powers, *A Society Organized for War: The Iberian Municipal Militias in the Central Middle Ages, 1000–1284* (Berkeley: University of California Press, 1988).

shaped by these medieval traditions, which they adapted to their New World surroundings.

The Muslim Invasion and the Christian Kingdoms' Reconquista

In 711 CE, the Muslim governor of Tangier, Tārik Ibn Ziyād, invaded from North Africa with seven thousand mostly Berber soldiers and defeated Roderick, the ruler of the Visigoths, at the Battle of Guadalete. The king was killed in the fighting, along with much of his aristocratic entourage, which made it difficult to muster effective resistance to the invaders. Tārik and his army then captured the city of Córdoba after a prolonged siege. In 712, another Muslim army of eighteen thousand men, commanded by the governor of North Africa, Musa ibn Nāsayr, entered Iberia, and these two armies jointly captured the Visigothic capital of Toledo.[3] The remnants of the Visigothic nobles were able to retain only a small enclave in parts of today's Asturias and Galicia. This remote, mountainous region, which had resisted both the Romans and the Visigoths, ironically became the nucleus of the Christian resistance against the Muslim invaders. Others among the Visigothic elite fled across the Pyrenees Mountains as the Muslims advanced. Those who remained behind either reached an accommodation with their Muslim overlords or were captured, enslaved, or executed. Within two years, the Muslims began establishing their authority in Iberia, setting up rule south of the Duero River, a region they called al-Andalus.

Although a Muslim army pushed into France, its advance was halted by a Frankish force under the command of Charles Martel in a decisive battle near Tours and Poitiers in 732 CE. The Muslims apparently sought plunder, but cold weather and an overly long supply line contributed to halting their advance. After the defeat in 732 CE, the Muslim invaders retreated across the Pyrenees and, together with those who remained behind in Iberia, they concentrated their efforts on ruling al-Andalus, squabbling with each other over power, and raiding the small Christian outposts in the north of the peninsula.

Factional strife plagued the Muslim world in the eighth century, with ramifications that spread even to al-Andalus. In 750 CE, the Abbasid family wrested control of the Muslim capital of the caliphate in Damascus from the ruling Umayyad dynasty. A key member of the defeated dynasty, Abd al-Rahmān, fled the city to North Africa, where he raised an army and crossed into the Iberian Peninsula in 756 CE, defeating the Muslim Qaysite ruling dynasty in Córdoba.

---

[3] Derek W. Lomax, *The Reconquest of Spain* (London: Longman, 1978), 14–16.

He then set up his own emirate with its capital at Córdoba and began taking control over al-Andalus and calling himself Abd al-Rahmān I. During his lifetime, Abd al-Rahmān I made Córdoba the capital of al-Andalus, expanding the city and beginning construction of a great mosque (*mesquita*) in 780 CE. His emirate was theoretically a vassal of the caliph in Damascus (and later in Baghdad, where the Abbasids made their capital), but in reality he operated virtually independently. Although factionalism plagued al-Andalus after the death of Abd al-Rahmān I in 788 CE, Córdoba remained a major political, economic, and cultural center of the Islamic world with a population estimated at one hundred thousand inhabitants at its apogee.[4] When Abd al-Rahmān III became emir in 912 CE, he attempted to control the various political factions in al-Andalus and proclaimed himself caliph, making al-Andalus an independent authority, theoretically equal in status to the caliph in Baghdad. After his death in 961, however, factionalism erupted anew as provincial leaders broke free of the central authority in Córdoba. By 1031, these various provincial leaders abolished the caliphate, as approximately thirty separate city states, called *taifas*, emerged in the politically divided al-Andalus.[5]

While the bulk of al-Andalus remained under Muslim control, the rugged country to the northwest, encompassing parts of current-day Asturias and Galicia, remained under Christian jurisdiction. The Visigothic nobleman, Pelayo, became king of this Christian Kingdom of Asturias and halted the Muslim effort to conquer the region.[6] The region was poor, but over time, more and more Christians migrated there. The Christians slowly moved southward into the Duero River valley, a region largely ignored by the Muslims, who concentrated their efforts in the more populous and fertile regions of central and southern Iberia. The Christians continued to expand southward, and raids for plunder and land characterized the frontier zones separating Christian and Muslim Iberia. Over the next several centuries, the Kingdom of Asturias evolved into four separate Christian polities: Portugal, Castile-León, Navarre, and Aragon. There was no plan for reconquest among the Christian kingdoms, which often fought with each other and sometimes allied with Muslim fighters, as much as they sought to defeat the Muslims of al-Andalus. As divisions and civil war eventually led to the breakup of the caliphate in Córdoba by 1031 CE, the Christian kingdoms began to gain the military advantage, and Portugal, Castile-León, and Aragon annexed new lands.

---

[4] William D. Phillips Jr. and Carla Rahn Phillips, *A Concise History of Spain* (New York: Cambridge University Press, 2010), 62.

[5] Lomax, *Reconquest of Spain*, 49.

[6] Ibid., 25; the precise date of the Battle of Covadonga and even the authenticity of Pelayo and the historic battle are disputed.

When Alfonso VI of Castile-León captured Toledo in 1086 CE, the Muslim ruler of the *taifa* kingdom of Seville requested aid from an expansionary Berber kingdom in the western Sahara, the Almoravids. The Berber leader, Yūsuf ibn-Tāshfīn, crossed the straits with an army that eventually controlled much of al-Andalus, uniting most of the area under their rule. The Almoravids demanded strict adherence to the tenets of Islam and were much less tolerant of non-Muslims, forcing many Christians and Jews living in al-Andalus to flee to Christian-controlled territories.[7] When the Almoravid Empire in North Africa and Iberia began to fracture by 1145, a new fundamentalist Islamic group, the Almohads, extended their control from Marrakesh to Tripoli.[8] In 1172, the Almohads crossed into al-Andalus, first capturing Seville and later conquering a large portion of Muslim Spain, supplanting the Almoravids. When King Alfonso VIII of Castile tried to halt their northern advance in 1195, an Almohad army inflicted a crushing defeat on his large Christian force at the Battle of Alarcos, near Ciudad Real. King Alfonso barely escaped with his life.[9]

By the time of Alfonso VIII, the Christian armies that fought at Alarcos and similar battles were not professional soldiers who owed allegiance to any particular monarch, but a hodgepodge of troops drawn from the king's royal guard, retainers of loyal nobles, and urban civic militias. Along the frontiers of the Muslim and Christian polities, civilians lived in fear of physical attack, as bands of soldiers from one side or the other crossed the borders in search of plunder. Often these forays were supported directly by the monarchs, who occasionally led them, while other times they were commanded by noblemen (called *adelantados*, usually operating under contract with a monarch) who mustered soldiers to attack and take plunder from their enemies. The Crown drew on this tradition of naming *adelantados* among the leaders of the early Spanish conquistadors in the New World battles with the Indigenous peoples. Armed groups formed on noble estates to defend against such frontier attacks in medieval Iberia, and the Christian nobles established fortresses to help guard the land. Local cities and towns of all sizes also armed and trained civic militias to defend their locality and even to fight in the monarch's wars. All urban citizens (*vecinos*) had an obligation to obtain arms and fight when called on; political rights and citizenship were tied to military service. In return, the cities received special privileges (*fueros*) from the Crown, such as immunity from certain taxes and control over local political institutions.[10]

Another force available to the Christian monarchs was the military orders, a group of ecclesiastical knights formed to fight the Almohad threat in the twelfth century. The first of these orders was a branch of the Cistercians, Calatrava,

---

[7] Ibid., 68–71.   [8] Ibid., 112–15.   [9] Ibid., 118–20.
[10] Powers, *Society Organized for War*, 93–112.

organized in 1164 CE, whose knights had the same status as monks of the order and were subject to its rules, including celibacy. The next of the military orders was Santiago, formed in 1175 when Pope Alexander III issued a command subjecting the knights directly to the Holy See and laid down its rules, including the right of members to marry. The final order was Alcántara, licensed by Pope Alexander III in 1176, and it was organized under the same rules as Calatrava, but it largely confined its activities to León.[11] The military orders staffed fortifications and could be summoned to fight on behalf of the Crown, but the number of brethren probably rarely exceeded two hundred at any one time in the thirteenth century.[12]

When Pope Innocent III called for the fractious Christian kingdoms to unite in a crusade against the Almohads, military forces from Castile, Aragon, and Navarre, along with some French knights heeding the pope's call, assembled at Toledo. The army may have reached 100,000 men, making it the largest Christian army ever brought together in the Iberian Peninsula. The Almohads marched north with an even larger army of 120,000 soldiers and met the Christian force at Las Navas de Tolosa in July 1212 CE. At first, the battle went badly for the combined Christian army, after the Almohad caliph, Muhammad al-Nāsir, committed a portion of his reserves to the fight. As the Christian line came under attack, some soldiers began to flee, causing King Alfonso VIII of Castile to consider suicide rather than face another crushing defeat like Alarcos. Instead, however, the Christian commander recovered his composure, committed his reserves, and persuaded the fleeing soldiers to return to the fray. When a detachment of Christian soldiers broke through a line of chained enslaved people protecting the caliph, Muhammad al-Nāsir fled the battlefield. With the flight of their caliph, the Almohad army began a retreat, which soon degenerated into a rout. It was an overwhelming Christian victory, which turned the tide in the conflict.[13] The defeat marked the end for the Almohads in al-Andalus.

In the aftermath of Las Navas de Tolosa, Alfonso VIII concentrated on opening a passageway into Andalusia and capturing Baeza and Úbeda, selling the Muslim population of the latter town into slavery. However, illness in the Christian army forced the Castilian king to return to Toledo and the victory celebrations that awaited him. The death of Alfonso VIII in 1214 CE and the unexpected passing of his son and heir, Henry I, meant that any plans to follow up the victory over the Almohads would have to wait, as the Crown passed to Alfonso's young grandson, Ferdinand III, a teenager at the time of his accession

---

[11] Sam Zeno Conedera, S.J., *Ecclesiastical Knights: The Military Orders in Castile* (New York: Fordham University Press, 2015), 36–46.
[12] Ibid., 85.   [13] Lomax, *Reconquest of Spain*, 124–28.

to the throne. The young king had to consolidate his power over the fractious nobility of Castile, anxious to take advantage of a potentially weak young king.[14]

Many Muslims in al-Andalus had grown restive under the puritanical rule of the Almohads, particularly after the caliph, Muhammad al-Nāsir, retired to Marrakesh after his defeat at Las Navas de Tolosa. When the caliph died in 1213 CE, he was succeeded by Yusuf II, then a young boy. The young ruler unexpectedly died after being gored by a cow in 1224, causing a succession crisis as three claimants vied for the throne.[15] In this time of uncertainty, a number of city rulers in Muslim al-Andalus rebelled against the Almohads, often with the aid of Christian kings. Once again, the king of Castile, Ferdinand III, took the lead in forging alliances with disenchanted Muslim rulers to push the Almohads from Iberia. Ferdinand III turned his attention to conquering Córdoba, which fell in 1236, followed by Murcia in 1243 and Jaén in 1246. Ferdinand then captured the most important city in southern Spain, Seville, in 1248 with the aid of the Muslim king of Granada. After Seville fell, Granada became a tributary of Castile, paying an annual sum in gold.[16]

Ferdinand's contemporary, Jaume (James) I of Aragon (also known as the Conqueror), launched a campaign against Mallorca, which fell to his armies in 1230 CE. He then turned his attention southward to the *taifa* kingdom of Valencia. In 1238, his armies captured the city of Valencia, and by 1248 he had conquered the whole kingdom, with its large Muslim population. As a result of James's conquests, the Muslim population within the borders of the Kingdom of Aragon had tripled.[17] By 1250, the only independent Muslim polity on the Iberian Peninsula was the Kingdom of Granada, surrounded by Aragon to the north and Castile to the west and south. The religious crusading spirit that motivated these successes of the Christian kingdoms against the Muslims continued until the final Christian victory in 1492. This religious zeal also drove the first Spanish conquests in the Americas in the late fifteenth and sixteenth centuries.

Christian–Muslim Frontiers (*Fronteras*)

The military successes of James I and Ferdinand III left their kingdoms with large territorial gains, and to consolidate them, the monarchs colonized the

---

[14] Ibid., 129–31.
[15] The three claimants to the caliphate after the death of Yusuf II were his great-uncle, Abu Muhammad Abd al-Wahid in Marrakesh, Abu Muhammad al-Bayyasi in Córdoba, and al-Adil in Seville. Ibid., 136–37.
[16] Ibid., 142–54.
[17] David Nirenberg, *Communities of Violence: Persecution of Minorities in the Middle Ages* (1996; repr., Princeton, NJ: Princeton University Press, 2015), 22–23.

frontier zones with Christian settlers.[18] Crown officials oversaw the settlement of Andalusia, Murcia, Valencia, and Mallorca, with lands going to nobles, clergy, and ordinary people, particularly soldiers who had participated in military engagements.[19] The military orders also received lands, usually in grants of encomienda, giving them sovereignty over the land and the ability to collect tribute from those Muslims (called Mudéjars) who remained in each region. Many upper- and middle-class Muslims left the newly acquired Christian zones for Granada or North Africa, preferring to heed the views of Muslim scholars, who argued that no Muslim could live a virtuous life among nonbelievers. As one former Muslim resident of Seville wrote, "Seville, through our fault you are in slavery, and we have become foreigners in Spain."[20] Most Muslims who remained behind were either peasants who were unwilling or unable to abandon their smallholdings or urban residents, such as artisans, merchants, or tradesmen. In Valencia, King James I followed the long-standing tradition of allowing Muslims to retain their property and worship their faith freely, as long as they recognized the sovereignty of the Aragonese Crown and paid special taxes.

When Ferdinand III captured Seville in 1248 CE, he ordered the Muslim population to leave the city. He made his own entry into Seville on December 22 and heard mass in the city mosque, which had been rededicated as a Roman Catholic cathedral. Many Muslims undoubtedly remained in the city, and some of those who left later returned, but Seville did not establish a separate district (*morería*) for the Muslim population until 1483.[21] Nonetheless, the property and personal effects left behind by the Muslims who fled were redistributed to soldiers who participated in the siege. The king charged Bishop Raimundo of Segovia in 1252 with making a definitive distribution of property in the city and its hinterland, and royal commissioners in 1255 and 1263 finished the task. Forty-three noblemen, magnates, and bishops and the military orders received large estates in the region. Some two hundred knights and foot soldiers received smaller holdings, and additional property went to support the city council, the newly established archdiocese, and a few modest plots of land for the king. The monarch's principal gain was the tax revenues from the region. In general, the

---

[18] To historians of the United States, the term *frontier* conjures up the work of Frederick Jackson Turner, which most scholars no longer accept, and they prefer to use the term *borderlands*. This is not true of historians of medieval Spain, who view the frontier as a zone of interaction, either peaceful or hostile. The Spanish word for such a zone, *frontera*, most easily translates into "frontier." For an explanation of this idea, see Thomas Devaney, *Enemies in the Plaza: Urban Spectacle and the End of Spanish Frontier Culture, 1460–1492* (Philadelphia: University of Pennsylvania Press, 2015), 10–11.

[19] Joseph F. O'Callahan, *A History of Medieval Spain* (Ithaca, NY: Cornell University Press, 1975), 473.

[20] Lomax, *Reconquest of Spain*, 154.   [21] Graubart, *Republics of Difference*, 44–46.

grants were modest; the Crown did not want to create new sources of noble wealth and power in the conquered lands.[22]

Christian colonization of newly captured lands in the Kingdom of Aragon was also a royal priority, particularly after the Crown suppressed a Muslim revolt in Murcia in 1266 CE. Ten thousand Catalan and Aragonese Christians settled in the province, but Muslims remained the majority. A similar situation prevailed in Valencia, where Muslims and Jews were often moved from the cities and strategic locations and replaced by Christian settlers, but Muslims still formed the majority of the overall population.[23] The Crown usually provided the Christian settlers with a house, a few acres of agricultural fields, and orchards or vineyards. The setters could prosper by using cheap Muslim laborers to help work their properties. Larger tracts of land went to the nobility, although Muslim resident laborers still cultivated it as they had before the reconquest, but they worked for Christian, not Muslim, overlords. The same basic pattern also held for Mallorca.[24]

To attract Christian settlers to the newly acquired lands, the kings of Portugal, Castile, and Aragon offered a variety of privileges and exemptions from royal taxes (called *fueros*) for a stipulated time period. In 1310, Ferdinand IV of Castile, for example, even offered amnesty to criminals to settle Gibraltar.[25] Most commonly, the king offered cities such *fueros* to attract Christian settlers; Seville, for example, received the same privileges and immunities granted to Toledo in 1251.[26] Such royal incentives and the prospect of economic opportunity provided by owning land drew settlers to the cities and to rural zones in these frontier regions, leading to a period of immigration and social mobility. The Crown even offered incentives to Jewish settlers, extending the right to travel and move about freely to relocate in the frontier zones. Such royal incentives, assurances of safe conduct, and the prospect of new lands and markets led to the steady growth of the Jewish population throughout Andalusia during the thirteenth century.[27]

Although the newly conquered frontiers offered economic opportunity, they were also fluid, diverse, and even unstable zones of transition, often punctuated by violent clashes across the borderlands. Raiding parties periodically crossed the border between Castile and Granada as Christian and Muslim soldiers created periods of anxiety and calls for revenge. The economic repercussions of these frontier raids were considerable—lost trade, burned crops and property, ransoms for captives, and the cost of arming local troops and manning

---

[22] Ibid., 154–55.
[23] O'Callahan, *History of Medieval Spain*, 474.   [24] Ibid.
[25] Jonathan Ray, *The Sephardic Frontier: The Reconquista and the Jewish Community in Medieval Iberia* (Ithaca, NY: Cornell University Press, 2006), 28.
[26] Lomax, *Reconquest of Spain*, 155.   [27] Ray, *Sephardic Frontier*, 13.

fortresses to defend against the incursions of raiding parties. Elites and local peasants alike suffered depredations and losses in frontier combat.[28]

Frontiers were also zones of social interaction among the Abrahamic faiths of Iberia, which posed challenges that long predated the Christian victories of the thirteenth century. The Catholic Church opposed the laity having sexual relations with people of other faiths, but in the disorderly years after the initial Muslim invasion in 711 CE, Muslim men often took Christian wives. Such kinship alliances allowed the Muslims to consolidate power in the immediate aftermath of the conquest and legitimated their position as overlords. It also provided a legal means for transferring the landed wealth of the Visigothic elite to Muslims. Even the Visigothic landed aristocracy could benefit from such alliances, which helped them defend their economic interests and keep their landed wealth.[29] The Muslim rulers of al-Andalus also took Christian brides and concubines into their harem, and interfaith marriages at the lower levels of society were apparently not uncommon. Muslim women, however, seldom took Christian husbands.[30] At the same time, such alliances caused friction. In either case, interfaith marriages between Muslim men and Christian women appear to have been a strategic tool in pacifying the regions and consolidating Muslim power in the immediate aftermath of the conquest; such sexual unions also symbolized the ultimate act of submission to the Muslim conquerors.[31] This was probably one of the causes of Pelayo's anger over the apparent forced marriage of his sister to the Berber Munnuza. Moreover, Berbers were considered inferior by Arabs in the new Muslim order, which also made the marriage seem unequal and difficult to accept for a Christian nobleman. Over time, these formal interfaith marriages probably became less useful and common, although there is considerable evidence that Muslim men still valued Christian concubines.[32]

By the twelfth century, Christians sought to erect barriers to social and sexual interaction and assimilation. Eminent Church theologian Thomas Aquinas, in his *Suma Theologica* (composed between 1265 and 1274), inveighed against interfaith marriages, which he argued would lead to discord over which faith any offspring of the marriage should be brought up in. The son of Ferdinand III, Alfonso X (known as *el Sabio*, or the Wise) created a legal code, the Siete Partidas (completed by 1265 CE), which drew inspiration from canon law and strongly condemned interfaith marriages. As the seventh part of the legal code stated, "A difference of religion is the sixth thing that operates as an impediment to marriage. For no Christian should marry a Jewess, Moorish woman, a heretic, or any woman who does not profess the Christian religion, and if he

---

[28] Devaney, *Enemies in the Plaza*, 20–21.
[29] Barton, *Conquerors, Brides, and Concubines*, 15–17.
[30] Ibid., 19, 32.   [31] Ibid., 41.   [32] Ibid., 31.

does so the marriage will not be valid."[33] Pope Innocent III also issued decrees against interfaith marriages, and at the Fourth Lateran Council of 1215, he supported having Muslims and Jews wear distinctive dress to draw visible boundaries between Christians and nonbelievers to avoid the dangers of interfaith sexual relations and marriages.[34] The shift in the political balance of power in favor of the Christian kingdoms, along with the incorporation of larger Muslim and Jewish populations in the frontier zones, probably explains this hardening of attitudes by church and state regarding interfaith unions. The papacy's efforts to characterize the conflict against the Muslims as a holy crusade also reflected this harder-line stance. At the same time, regulating interfaith sex and marriage was consistent with the efforts of Jewish and Muslim leaders' prohibitions on intimate relations between their people and nonbelievers.[35] Despite the religious prohibitions against interfaith sexual unions, the Spanish conquistadors in the sixteenth century used such unions with Indigenous women of noble blood to forge kinship alliances that helped them consolidate power in the years after the Spanish invasion of the Americas.

The Reconquista was a southward movement of the Christian kingdoms into regions held by Muslim polities. The impulse behind this movement was a militant Christian crusading zeal to extend the faith throughout the Iberian Peninsula, much as early generations of Christians had tried to recapture the Holy Lands. Conquest also involved settlement, however, and the Christian kings used institutions, such as the encomienda, to govern and profit from lands taken from the Muslims.[36] The Christian kings encouraged settlers from other parts of the peninsula to migrate and settle newly conquered lands taken from Muslim enemies. Moreover, they forged kinship and military alliances with Muslims when it suited their purposes, often to fight against fellow Christian enemies. The Reconquista often involved messy diplomatic maneuvers to advance the overall goals of the crusade against Islam. The Christian movement reached temporary political and territorial limits and halted periodically before again renewing hostilities with the Muslims. The last Muslim Kingdom of Granada held out until 1492, but the tide had turned decisively in favor of the Christian kingdoms by the end of the thirteenth century. As the Reconquista reached its territorial limits in Iberia, expansion of the Iberian Christian kingdoms continued in the Mediterranean and then to Africa, to the Madeira and Canary Islands, and finally across the Atlantic Ocean to the Indies. The religious crusading zeal displayed in Iberia during the reconquest also motivated the Spanish conquistadors to invade, settle, and evangelize the Indigenous peoples of the New World in the late fifteenth and sixteenth centuries.

[33] Ibid., 63.   [34] Ibid., 64.   [35] Ibid., 75.
[36] J. H. Elliott, "The Spanish Conquest and Settlement of America," in *The Cambridge History of Latin America*, ed. Leslie Bethell, Vol. 1 (Cambridge: Cambridge University Press, 1984), 149–50.

Muslims, Christians, and *Convivencia*

The Christian conquests of the thirteenth century brought large numbers of Muslims under the jurisdiction of the Kingdoms of Castile and Aragon. In the Kingdom of Aragon, for example, there were six thousand Mudéjars in Catalonia, mostly concentrated around the Ebro River valley, and in Aragon itself there were two hundred thousand Muslims, comprising as much as 35 percent of the total population. In Valencia, Mudéjars remained the overwhelming majority, comprising up to 80 percent of the population, which was concentrated largely in the countryside.[37] By the fourteenth century, however, as a result of Christian and Jewish migration, Mudéjars made up only 50 percent of Valencia's population.[38] In Castile, the Muslim population remained a scattered minority, except in Andalusia. Consequently, in much of the Iberian Peninsula, Christians and Muslims lived and worked in close proximity. This coexistence, or *convivencia*, was not without competition, periodic outbreaks of violence, suspicion, and even hatred. Nonetheless, Muslims and Christians were united by a web of social and economic relationships. The monarchs depended on taxes levied on the Muslim community or *aljama*, and many nobles, particularly in Valencia, depended on Mudéjar peasants to work their lands. Urban bankers extended credit to those same nobles, dependent on Muslim peasants, and merchants, artisans, and farmers of all faiths did business with each other. Religious toleration was not a political policy, but the result of the necessities of material life, which is why it could break down so easily, especially when these economic relationships were under stress.

Muslims in Iberia were legally vassals of the Crown, and the kings of Castile and Aragon drew on the *dhimmi* system of Islamic tradition and law in structuring the relationship between the monarch and his Muslim subjects. When Muslim states dominated the Iberian Peninsula, unconverted religious minorities under Islamic law were accorded *ahd al-dhimma*, or a special pact of protection accorded to "people of the book." Christians and Jews living under their control could retain their religious freedom and some level of political and economic power if they paid a special poll tax (*jizya*).[39] Christians were then allowed rights to liberty and property and to live by their own laws and religious practices—if they did not contradict Muslim laws. As a result, when the Christian kings conquered a region, they negotiated the surrender of the Muslim residents by extending terms reflecting the *dhimma* tradition, which

---

[37] Nirenberg, *Communities of Violence*, 23.
[38] Mark D. Meyerson, *The Muslims of Valencia in the Age of Fernando and Isabel: Between Coexistence and Crusade* (Berkeley: University of California Press, 1991), 14.
[39] Janina M. Safran, *Defining Boundaries in al-Andalus: Muslims, Christians, and Jews in Islamic Iberia* (Ithaca, NY: Cornell University Press, 2013), 9–10.

both sides understood to give the Muslims certain political, religious, and legal rights as vassals of the king of Castile, Portugal, or Aragon. The Muslim *aljama* was a corporate structure that afforded rights and privileges, but also obligations, such as paying special taxes to the king. This form of *convivencia* was not always permanent or stable because the Muslim *aljama* and the Christian monarchs attempted to redefine the relationships over time, leading to acts of violent resistance by Muslims. Moreover, many Mudéjar communities saw such rights and privileges as royal vassals as little more than terms of surrender, viewing restrictions imposed on their community by the Christian king as an affront. The numerous Muslim rebellions, particularly in Valencia, attest to such discontent in the reign of James I and his successors.

Muslim scholars were skeptical that the Mudéjars could live a virtuous life under the sovereignty of nonbelievers because of the primacy of Islamic law, or Shariah. The Shariah derived from the Qur'ān, the direct revelation of God (Allah) and the Sunnah, which related the statements and deeds of the prophet, Muhammad, preserved by legal scholars in written form in the Hadith (reports or accounts of the Prophet Muhammad).[40] Although it encompassed both secular and religious practices, the Shariah served as a moral and ethical guide to all private and public behavior, and Muslims had to obey its precepts. The Christian monarchs recognized Islamic law, and they established a separate corporate legal identity for Muslims within their kingdoms as long as these vassals did not violate the legal code of the Christian overlords. As a result, the Crown permitted a whole network of experts in Shariah and separate courts, staffed by trained Muslim judges, to adjudicate in matters relating to the Muslim *aljama*. This was particularly important in the Kingdom of Aragon, where Muslims were the majority population in provinces such as Valencia.

Although judicial practices varied across the Kingdoms of Castile and Aragon, the chief Muslim official in both kingdoms was the *qādī mayor de aljamas* (Hispanicized as *alcalde mayor de aljamas*), appointed by the king.[41] The *qādī mayor* position was a lifetime appointment, and its functions were primarily judicial, serving as an appeals court to all lower Muslim courts. The *qādī mayor* also served as a royal scribe, informing the various Muslim communities of royal laws and decisions, mediating disputes among Mudéjar families on appeal from lower Muslim courts. Moreover, he supervised the collection of the king's taxes in the Muslim *aljamas*. From 1458 CE, the position in Aragon was held by Mohamat Bellvis, and the Crown granted him the right to pass on the position to his son. This family dominated the office until the

---

[40] Meyerson, *Muslims of Valencia*, 185.
[41] Ibid., 101–2; Karen B. Graubart, "Learning from the *Qadi*," 205.

forced mass conversions to Christianity began in Aragon in 1525.[42] In effect, this royal appointee was the intermediary between the king and his Muslim vassals, including those Muslims residing on noble estates or in the cities, which made the office an extension of Crown authority into Muslim communities throughout Aragon and Castile.

Although the kings of Castile and Aragon had to rely on the contributions (*servicios*) from the *cortes* of their respective realms for revenue, there were few institutional restraints on the demands for taxes from the Mudéjars. Indeed, any legal and institutional protections afforded Mudéjars in both Christian kingdoms was based in part on important fiscal contributions of the *aljama* to the monarchy. Long-term policy considerations argued for royal moderation, not rapacity, on the king's demands for revenue. After all, too much fiscal pressure could prove devastating to the Muslim community and provoke a revolt. Over the long term, taxes from the Mudéjars provided a consistent, reliable source of royal income, apart from contributions voted by the different *cortes* of the kingdoms. Nonetheless, during frequent times of war the monarchs tended to escalate their demands on the Mudéjars, sometimes forcing them to borrow money to meet the royal exactions and maintain community solvency. As the Crown of Aragon expanded into the Mediterranean and the kings of Castile sought to centralize their control and curtail powers of the nobility and the cities, fiscal pressure on the Mudéjars tended to rise.[43]

Even legal privileges afforded Muslim communities depended on royal benevolence. Over time, royal officials, the Christian nobles, and urban authorities tended to erode the power of Muslim officials in the *aljama*. Mudéjars did not have to resolve all disputes in Islamic courts, and Christian courts had the power to overrule Muslim officials. Although *aljama* officials held some administrative, legal, and religious authority in their communities, they were not governors or legislators vested with real executive and legislative authority. Indeed, Mudéjar communities and their Islamic legal authorities were vulnerable in Christian Iberia. Mudéjars in Castile and Aragon tended to speak romance languages, and Arabic was not commonly spoken in Valencia by the fourteenth century.[44] Over time, Mudéjar communities became more assimilated and less reliant on Islamic institutions.

Since much of Muslim law was based on religious principles, the Christian kings of Iberia tended to allow the Mudéjar communities control over many local legal disputes in the *aljama* if their decisions did not violate Crown laws. Muslim legal experts could serve as notaries, enforce Islamic law, and judge cases within Muslim communities. Muslim tax collectors worked as fiscal

---

[42] Meyerson, *Muslims of Valencia*, 102.   [43] Ibid., 169.
[44] Meyerson, *Muslims of Valencia*, 227–28.

intermediaries between the *aljama* and the Christian monarchs. Muslim city councils also directed local civic affairs in the *morería*. In short, a parallel set of governmental institutions, based on Islamic law and custom, existed within the Christian kingdoms to regulate civic life. Nonetheless, tensions and instability resulted from this power-sharing arrangement because the monarchs could sometimes exploit the Muslim communities to provide financial assistance, particularly in wartime. Toleration of Islamic law and legal institutions was a practical way for the Christian kings to coexist with their Muslim vassals, but this *convivencia* could break down in times of economic stress, such as war, leading to tensions and even periodic outbreaks of violence between a king and his Muslim subjects and also between Christians and Muslims. Such outbreaks of violence and the gradual erosion of Muslim legal institutions paved the way for the forced conversion of these Muslim communities in the late fifteenth and early sixteenth centuries. Nonetheless, this tradition of tolerating a certain amount of self-rule was later extended to settled Indigenous communities in the Indies, with Spanish authorities allowing local Amerindian elites some latitude in controlling their own community affairs, particularly in the early years after the conquest. The principal difference was that from the outset, the Spaniards demanded that the Indigenous peoples convert to Roman Catholicism.

Jews, Christians, and *Convivencia*

Jews of the Iberian Peninsula were a tolerated minority population, largely grouped in urban neighborhoods known as *juderías* in Castile and *juerias* in the Kingdom of Aragon. Roman law and Catholic Church law both sanctioned the toleration of Jews living under Christian rule, and monarchs in medieval Spain restricted but tolerated the presence of Jews in their kingdoms.[45] By the thirteenth century, estimates for the Kingdom of Aragon placed the Jewish population at approximately twenty thousand in Aragon, twenty-five thousand in Catalonia, and ten thousand in Valencia.[46] They occupied an important role in the Iberian kingdoms as moneylenders, artisans, agriculturalists, winemakers, merchants, and public officials, often acting as key advisors to the monarchs of Castile and Aragon. In the Kingdom of Aragon, however, in 1283 CE Jews were forbidden from holding high offices in a move to placate members of the nobility, who had grown jealous of Jewish power and wealth.[47] Jews were much more

---

[45] Mark R. Cohen, *Under the Crescent and Cross: The Jews in the Middle Ages* (Princeton, NJ: Princeton University Press, 1994), 17–51.

[46] Nirenberg, *Communities of Violence*, 26–27.

[47] Mark D. Meyerson, *Jews in an Iberian Frontier Kingdom: Society, Economy, and Politics in Morvedre, 1248–1391* (Leiden: Brill, 2004), 64–65.

prosperous than the Mudéjars, and they paid large sums in taxes to the monarchies of Castile and Aragon. They were also much more assimilated than Muslims; although many retained a knowledge of Hebrew, virtually all Jews spoke one of the peninsula's Romance languages.[48] Given their clustering in urban areas, Jews depended directly on the king and royal officials, and few lived within the seigneurial jurisdiction of the nobility. The threat of Christian violence and an overall sense of insecurity characterized the *convivencia* of Jews living alongside the Christians and Mudéjars of the Iberian kingdoms.

The thirteenth-century conquests of Ferdinand III of Castile and James I of Aragon gave Jews an unprecedented opportunity to gain greater freedom and economic opportunity by colonizing new frontier zones, along with those Christians moving there. Jews also served the Christian monarchs in prominent positions, such as royal scribes, tax collectors, and other public capacities. For wealthier Jews, the frontier zones represented new social and economic opportunities. The Crown facilitated this movement by giving Jews the right to move freely to the frontier zones, where they could establish new Jewish communities in urban areas and own land in rural zones. The Jewish communities of Iberia were more stratified than those of the Mudéjars, but the majority of the Jewish frontier settlers were men and women of modest means and social status. Some of these Jewish settlers left their home communities to escape punishment for crimes, while others simply sought new economic opportunities in the frontier.[49] For example, in 1248 CE, Jews established a community in Morvedre, outside Valencia, which became a thriving center. Jews in Morvedre became involved in growing grapes for kosher wine; they also served as merchants and artisans, and some were Crown officials, such as tax collectors. Others even operated as Crown bailiffs in the region. To encourage Jewish settlement in Morvedre, the Crown gave the growing community tax abatements until 1274, when the Jewish community had grown sufficiently to pay greater sums.[50] The newly conquered frontier zones promised a more dynamic and open society than the long-established urban communities of Christian Castile and Aragon.

Like the Mudéjars, the Jews of Iberia were vassals of the king in the Iberian Peninsula, and monarchs also gave Jewish communities (called *kahal* or *kehilla*) some local judicial and religious autonomy. Unlike the large and recently conquered Muslim communities, Jewish *kahals* were small and generally older communities, and each evolved with slightly different legal and institutional structures. Some communities governed themselves according to Jewish law (*halakha*), while others relied on local precedents and a mixture of Jewish and

---

[48] Nirenberg, *Communities of Violence*, 27.
[49] Meyerson, *Jews in an Iberian Frontier Kingdom*, 24.   [50] Ibid., 17, 24–30.

Christian legal traditions. Nevertheless, most Jews lived in defined urban, often walled, *juderías* ruled by a town council made up of either appointed or elected officials with defined terms of office. These officials also consulted with notable Jewish families, communal elders, rabbis, and Crown officials.[51] Jewish officials in frontier provinces probably only had a rudimentary knowledge of *halakha*, and they governed largely by applying local customary law.[52]

Given the social and economic stratification in most *kahals*, an oligarchy of wealthy families dominated community politics. Iberian Jewry produced numerous Jewish scholars (*hakhamim*) whose mastery of Jewish law gave them an influential role in communal government, and their reputations as religious scholars often extended beyond their own *kahal*.[53] When disputes arose between Christians and Jews or in cases that might lead to capital punishment, Christian courts had jurisdiction. Jews could bypass Jewish courts and take disputes directly to Christian magistrates. Such practices of giving a certain amount of local control to Jews and Muslims were extended to the settled Indigenous communities in the Indies, particularly in the early period of Spanish rule.

By the thirteenth century, the Christian kings of the Iberian Peninsula began to extend royal authority and regularize institutions of royal governance, including in the Jewish communities. Crown authorities began appointing Crown rabbis to Jewish communities, who played an important role in either collecting or supervising the collection of royal taxes. These rabbis also served as primary judges and courts of appeal in cases within *kahals*. Members of the community also had to consult with the royal rabbi when choosing their local leaders in the Crown of Aragon during the reign of James I. These royally appointed rabbis could have jurisdiction over a single community or a particular region. Sometimes royal interference in communal justice and politics provoked opposition, and communities even opposed the choice of individual rabbis. When James I of Aragon decided to appoint a Jewish notable, Salamon Alconstantini, as rabbi of Zaragoza, rival Jewish clans successfully blocked the appointment, which went to an opponent of Alconstantini, Salamon Avenbruch. In 1304 CE, King James II of Aragon appointed a chief rabbi over Aragon, but he had no authority over Catalonia and Valencia's Jewish communities. There was never a chief rabbi with jurisdiction over all of the Kingdom of Aragon, and no such appointment in Castile existed until the late fourteenth century, when the king established the office of Rab de la Corte.[54] An appointment of a chief rabbi for all of Portuguese Jewry came only in 1373, when King Ferdinand I confirmed Judah Aben Menir as *arrabi mor*.[55]

---

[51] Ray, *Sephardic Frontier*, 106.   [52] Ibid., 108.   [53] Ibid., 113.
[54] Ibid., 114–18.   [55] Ibid., 124–30.

In both Castile and Aragon, monarchs put increasing fiscal pressure on Jewish communities, particularly as they became embroiled in wars. As vassals of the Crown, Jews had to pay as much in taxes as their monarchs could wring from the *kahals*. At the same time, the monarchs shielded the Jews from the meddling of municipal, seigneurial, and even local royal officials. To meet the increasing fiscal demands of the monarchs, many wealthier Jews engaged in moneylending at high rates of interest. Christians were bound by Church law, which forbade them from engaging in usury, but the law did not bind Jews from moneylending at interest. The Crown in Aragon tried to set the official maximum interest rate at 20 percent in loans to Christians, but in practice, many Jewish lenders charged rates well above the legal limit. Forty percent of the Jewish community in Morvedre lent money to urban and rural residents of the region in 1348 CE. After a series of poor harvests in the region, one noble complained that his tenants owed the astounding sum of thirty thousand sous to Jewish moneylenders.[56] Tensions surrounding Jewish moneylending escalated in times of increasing royal fiscal pressure, as Jews pushed to collect debts to meet royal demands. Since the debtors, mostly Christians, also faced increased fiscal pressure from the Crown, they naturally resented Jewish efforts to collect the money owed, which highlighted the economic power that Jews exercised over the Christian population. Jews later served as moneylenders and merchants in Spain's overseas possessions in the Indies. Apart from moneylending, Jews also took positions in the royal government, often as tax collectors, another position that put them in conflict with local Christians. In short, the Jewish community was caught between the exactions of the Crown and the hostility of the Christian community, much like the more numerous Mudéjar population.

The *convivencia* of Christians and Jews was always marred by rising episodes of violence directed against the Jewish minority, which peaked in 1391 CE with a series of pogroms (massacres) beginning in Seville. Even before events in Seville, however, anti-Semitism was on the rise. When the bubonic plague struck Iberia around 1343, many blamed the toleration of the Jews for God's wrath. Members of the nobility stoked the unrest in the intervening years between the onset of the plague and the pogroms of 1391, partly as a means of opposing the centralizing efforts and fiscal pressure of the Castilian monarchy. Christians (particularly the nobility) resented the status of the Jews (as special vassals of the Crown) and directed their resentment at the Jews partly to get back at the king, seen as the Jews' protector. Violence erupted in Seville in 1391, provoked by the vitriolic anti-Jewish preaching of Ferrand Martínez, archdeacon of Ecija.

---

[56] Meyerson, *Jews in an Iberian Frontier Kingdom*, 177, 201. In the fifteenth-century Kingdom of Valencia, one sou was worth twelve diners and twenty sous comprised one pound. Ibid., xi.

Violence and forced conversions spread first throughout Andalusia and then to Old and New Castile. On July 9, 1391, the violence reached Valencia as mobs marched on the city's *judería*, killing over two hundred residents and forcing the rest to receive baptism as Christians. Of the twenty-five hundred members of Valencia's Jewish community, perhaps only two hundred escaped death or baptism, many by fleeing to Morvedre, where the bailiff, Bonafonat de Sant Feliu, and the nobles evacuated the city's Jewish population to the local castle.[57] Violence then spread to Catalonia and Mallorca. The presence of the king and his retainers in Zaragoza probably spared Aragon from the Christian mobs that terrorized most of the Kingdom of Castile and parts of Valencia. This escalation of violence against Jews and later Muslims proved a turning point in the relations between interfaith groups living in Iberia, culminating in forced conversions for Jews in 1492.

The violence of 1391 CE devastated Iberian Jewry and led to the forced conversion of thousands of Jews, who became known as *conversos*, or New Christians. Church officials and laymen of all sorts voiced suspicions about whether the New Christians clandestinely practiced Judaism. Given that most *converso* families had been baptized forcibly in 1391 and during the months and years immediately afterward, it is not unlikely that some regretted accepting baptism and still tried to practice Jewish rites in secrecy. The close ties that many *conversos* maintained with Jewish families also encouraged the fears of Christians. In Valencia, for example, the Jewish population had abandoned the city, but many New Christians kept up friendships with the Jews of Morvedre, sometimes celebrating holiday dinners and attending festivals together.[58] Fear and animosity against the New Christians remained barely beneath the surface of everyday life, sometimes leading to outbreaks of violence.

While Jews shared the same legal and social status as Muslims as special vassals of the Christian monarchs, they were more closely tied to the Crown than the Mudéjars. The Jewish *kahals* were older, more Hispanicized, and wealthier than their Muslim counterparts. Moreover, while they maintained some parallel legal and governmental institutions, they were not as extensive and powerful as in the Muslim *aljamas*. Some Jewish communities even relied on a mixture of Jewish and Christian legal principles. Nonetheless, Jews were always a vulnerable minority; *convivencia* between Christians and Jews was fragile and the threat of violence against Jews was omnipresent. Apart from traditional anti-Semitism, anger directed against Jewish tax collectors, moneylenders who charged high interest rates, and even local resentment against the centralizing

---

[57] Ibid., 272.
[58] Mark D. Meyerson, *A Jewish Renaissance in Fifteenth-Century Spain* (Princeton, NJ: Princeton University Press, 2004), 35–45.

efforts of the Christian monarchs all contributed in various ways to undermine the fragile *convivencia* in medieval Iberia. Vulnerable Jewish communities were caught between often-hostile regional and local interest groups and the growing power of the kings in the Christian monarchies of the Iberian Peninsula, which culminated in the Crown-ordered forced conversions of 1492.

The Union of the Crowns: Formation of a Composite Monarchy

The violence, social instability, and periodic anti-Semitic riots resulted in part from divisions and economic difficulties that plagued the Crown of Aragon in the fifteenth century as the plagues subsided. After the Muslim conquests of James I in the thirteenth century, the Kingdom of Aragon began expanding into the Mediterranean, acquiring the Balearic Islands and Sicily. By the fifteenth century, it had added Sardinia and Naples to the Aragonese patrimony. The basis of this Mediterranean empire was the export of textiles, and the economic center of the kingdom was Barcelona. Merchants from Barcelona and later Valencia plied commercial routes to France, Italy, Corsica, Sardinia, Sicily, and the Islamic Mediterranean. They also established trade links in northwestern Europe, in Bruges and later in Antwerp, both in Belgium.[59] By the fifteenth century, however, a series of internal problems disrupted the economic life of the kingdom, particularly in Catalonia. Plague had devastated Barcelona and its hinterland in 1347 and 1397 CE, which reduced the population of Catalonia from 430,000 in 1365 to 350,000 in 1378 CE.[60] In this time of disease and famine, peasants and lords clashed in the countryside, banks in Barcelona failed, and urban unrest divided the populace of the city. In addition, a civil war from 1462 to 1472 pitted the nobles against the Crown, which they believed was attempting to centralize power and usurp the traditional laws and privileges of Catalonia. Although King John II emerged victorious, the formerly prosperous Mediterranean empire of the Kingdom of Aragon faced a period of crippling political and economic crisis.

When Ferdinand succeeded King John in 1479 CE, he faced an imposing array of problems in the city of Barcelona and the countryside, which he resolved by reinforcing Aragonese constitutional principles. In Catalonia, for example, the city of Barcelona was divided into two opposing factions, the

---

[59] William D. Phillips Jr. and Carla Rahn Phillips, "Spain in the Fifteenth Century," in *Transatlantic Encounters: Europeans and Andeans in the Sixteenth Century*, ed. Kenneth J. Andrien and Rolena Adorno (Berkeley: University of California Press, 1991), 25.

[60] Elliott, *Imperial Spain*, 37.

Biga, composed of urban rentiers and large-scale merchants, and the *Busca*, clothiers, smaller-scale merchants, members of the urban professions, and artisans. Several wealthy families of the *Biga* had traditionally controlled city political affairs, and members of the *Busca* challenged their virtual monopoly on the city council and the Generalitat, a standing committee of the Catalan *cortes*. To resolve the imbroglio that divided the city, Ferdinand had members of these governing institutions chosen by lot, effectively breaking the monopoly of the narrow oligarchy.[61] In addition, the peasantry of the Catalan countryside, known as *Remença*, rebelled against noble landowners who used laws binding laborers to their lands, known as the six evil customs. According to these laws, Catalan peasants had to pay a large payment (*remença*) to their lord to be relieved of their feudal obligations and leave the estate.[62] After the bubonic plague, some rural workers wanted to use the labor shortage to gain better terms on other noble estates and, in some cases, leave their traditional estates. Ferdinand intervened in the struggle with the Sentencia de Guadalupe in 1486, which abolished the six evil customs and freed the peasantry from serfdom, but it ensured that the nobles received monetary compensation and retained legal ownership of their lands. In short, Ferdinand ended the most pressing urban and rural conflicts in Catalonia not by centralizing power, but by enacting reforms that brought old constitutional institutions into working order once again.

Although Castile had a much more prosperous economy in the fifteenth century than Aragon, political divisions between the Crown and the nobility threatened the kingdom's future. The core of Castile's economy was the wool trade to northern Europe, particularly the Netherlands. The sheep growers' guild (*mesta*) regulated the grazing of merino sheep across Castile, with some of the largest and most important herds owned by high nobility (*grandees*) in the kingdom. Resident Castilian merchants in places such as Antwerp sold the wool to Flemish cloth manufacturers, and a growing cloth industry also began to flourish in north-central Castilian cities such as Burgos. Moreover, the trade fair at Medina del Campo was the most important in Europe, with merchants coming from Seville, Burgos, Valencia, and Barcelona, joining Flemings, Italians, Irish, and Portuguese. Medina del Campo became the one of the commercial and financial hubs of Europe.[63] Nevertheless, during the reign of Henry IV (1454–1474 CE), restive members of the Castilian nobility rose up against the weak monarch between 1465 and 1474, despite his attempt to placate them with

---

[61] John Edwards, *The Spain of the Catholic Monarchs, 1474–1520* (Oxford: Blackwell, 2000), 64–66; Elliott, *Imperial Spain*, 40, 80–81.
[62] Edwards, *Spain of the Catholic Monarchs*, 157; Elliott, *Imperial Spain*, 37–38, 81.
[63] Phillips and Phillips, "Spain in the Fifteenth Century," 26–28.

honors and grants of lands and towns.[64] The opposition to the king coalesced around his half-brother, Alfonso, whom many nobles recognized as the true king. When Alfonso died unexpectedly in 1468, opposition nobles shifted their loyalty to his sister, Isabel. As a part of the treaty to end the civil war, King Henry was forced to make Isabel his successor to the throne, dispossessing his only child, a daughter, Juana, whom his enemies disparagingly called Juana la Beltraneja. The rumor at court held that her real father was the king's favorite, Beltrán de la Cueva.[65]

The recognition of Isabel as heir to the Castilian throne made her marriage a matter of international interest. King Henry IV favored a marriage for his half-sister with Alfonso V of Portugal, a rising, expansionary power in Europe. As part of his designation of Isabel as his heir, Henry claimed veto power over her choice of a husband. Many nobles outside the king's inner circle favored a union with the heir to the Kingdom of Aragon, Ferdinand, uniting Castile and Aragon. In the end, Isabel chose a union with Ferdinand and Aragon, and they married secretly in Valladolid in 1469 CE, fearing that Henry would try to stop the wedding. Isabel's half-brother, the king, denounced the union and tried to acknowledge the rights of Juana as his successor. Nevertheless, Ferdinand managed to gain the support of members of the Castilian nobility and the towns, so when Henry died in December 1474, Isabel proclaimed herself queen.

It was not until 1479 CE that Ferdinand and Isabel brought Castile under her control. Early that same year, John II of Aragon died, making Ferdinand king and uniting Castile and Aragon under the couple's leadership. The union was purely a dynastic, composite monarchy, and the laws and institutions of both kingdoms remained separate and largely unchanged. In fact, there was no guarantee that the two kingdoms might not separate after the death of Ferdinand and Isabel. The Catholic kings, as they came to be called, first turned their energies to ending the strife and civil war that plagued Castile. Unlike in Aragon, where Ferdinand eschewed asserting royal power and respected and reaffirmed traditional local constitutional privileges, in Castile the Catholic kings more forcefully centralized the power of the monarchy. Their very different solutions to the disorder in both Castile and Aragon were consistent with the laws and traditions of both kingdoms.

---

[64] William D. Phillips Jr., *Enrique IV and the Crisis of Fifteenth-Century Castile* (Cambridge, MA: Medieval Academy of America, 1978), 42–52.

[65] According to some contemporary accounts, particularly those opponents of the king who tried to put his half-brother, Alfonso, on the throne, Henry IV engaged in same-sex relationships. Henry had apparently not consummated his first marriage with Blanca of Navarre and allegedly gave his second wife, Juana, to his favorite, Beltrán de la Cueva, who was the supposed father of his daughter, called Juana la Beltraneja. The queen later had a child when Henry was away on an extended military mission, allegedly by her keeper. Peggy K. Liss, *Isabel the Queen: Life and Times* (New York: Oxford University Press, 1992), 60, 61, 68.

When Ferdinand and Isabel turned to the problem of re-establishing peace and order in Castile, they called a *cortes* held at Madrigal in 1476, where the monarchs received support from the municipalities. The most effective measure taken at Madrigal was the creation of the Santa Hermandad, a rural police force and judicial tribunal to establish order in the countryside. Later that same year, the grand mastership of the military order of Santiago fell vacant, and Isabel secured the appointment of Ferdinand. When similar positions opened at Calatrava and Alcántara in 1487 and 1494, they too went to Ferdinand, giving the Crown control over 194 encomiendas and annual rents exceeding 145,000 ducats.[66] Ferdinand and Isabel then turned to the power of the restive nobility, and by the Act of Resumption of 1480, they deprived the nobles of half the revenues and lands they had alienated or taken since 1464. In that same year, they reformed the Council of Castile, which advised the monarchs on appointments, acted as a court of justice, and supervised the local governments in the kingdom. In making appointments to this powerful body, the monarchs favored members of the lesser nobility, gentry, townsmen, and lawyers, rather than just influential aristocrats. Finally, the monarchs dramatically expanded the number of Crown-appointed magistrates (*corregidores*) to the principal towns and cities of Castile, naming forty-four magistrates by 1475.[67] Although these *corregidores* had no power over justice and administration in lands controlled by the nobility, they expanded royal control and sharply curtailed attempts by the restive nobles to expand their jurisdiction over the towns of Castile.

In 1480, Ferdinand and Isabel established the Holy Office of the Inquisition to reform the corrupt Castilian Catholic Church and bring it under closer Crown control. As the monarchs wrote to their ambassador in Rome in 1488, "The Church has never been in such ruin and governed as it is now; all the income that it should be spending on the poor and on charitable works is being wasted on material matters, while the service of God and the good of the Church are totally neglected."[68] This desire to revitalize the Church and its wayward clergy and bishops emerged from the same crusading zeal that motivated the Reconquista. The Inquisition was also a powerful tool for dealing with the widely mistrusted *conversos*, whom many Catholics suspected of secretly practicing Judaism. After the forced conversions of the Muslims between 1500 and 1525, the Holy Office extended its jurisdiction over these

---

[66] The ducado, or ducat, was originally a coin (originally in gold but later silver) whose value probably changed over time, but its standard worth was 375 maravedís in the fifteenth century. John Lynch, *Bourbon Spain, 1700–1808* (Oxford: Blackwell, 1989), xi.

[67] Edwards, *Spain of the Catholic Monarchs*, 56; Elliott, *Imperial Spain*, 86–99.

[68] Quoted in John Lynch, *New Worlds: A Religious History of Latin America* (New Haven, CT: Yale University Press, 2012), 1.

converts, called Moriscos. The Inquisition's jurisdiction only prevailed in Castile until 1487, when it was extended to the Kingdom of Aragon, making it the only Crown council with equal jurisdiction in both kingdoms.

In 1482, Ferdinand and Isabel turned to mustering the resources of Castile and Aragon to end the long Reconquista by attacking the last independent Muslim Kingdom of Granada. The Catholic kings mobilized the fractious nobles of Castile and Aragon, along with civic militias, and the military orders to fight in this crusade to rid the peninsula of the last Muslim stronghold. Granada fell to the Catholic kings on January 6, 1492, ending the long Reconquista with a decisive Christian victory. For Ferdinand and Isabel, the triumph appeared to be the culmination of their reign; the monarchs even wanted to move their capital to Granada, and to this day they remain buried together in the city cathedral.

On March 31, 1492, the Catholic kings made the first of two momentous decisions, both an outgrowth of the crusading zeal that led to the fall of Granada. The first was to force all the Jews in their kingdoms either to convert to Catholicism or to leave Spain before July 31. Ferdinand and Isabel already had issued laws limiting the rights of Jews, an ironic twist since Ferdinand had Jewish ancestors. In 1480, the monarchs had already forced Jews to live in segregated communities, ended the jurisdiction of Jewish courts, and authorized expelling Jews from Seville, Córdoba, and Cádiz.[69] Although the statistics are unreliable, it is likely that 120,000 to 150,000 Jews fled the country in 1492 rather than convert, going to North Africa, Italy, France, Germany, and Portugal.[70] They had to sell their property and goods and face an uncertain and dangerous diaspora. Although their motives are unclear, the Catholic monarchs undoubtedly responded to the tide of anti-Semitism in their kingdoms and pressure from the Church, particularly the Inquisition, to gain control over the *converso* population by ending the temptations of having the presence of a practicing Jewish community living nearby. Subsequently, all converts fell under the jurisdiction of the Holy Office.[71]

The second major decision came on April 17, 1492, to support the voyage of Christopher Columbus to sail west to Asia. Under the terms of the agreement between Isabel and Columbus (called the Capitulaciones of Santa Fé), Columbus was made an admiral, viceroy, and governor general over any lands he discovered, along with the right to a tenth of any treasure he uncovered. He was also given the right to trade duty free with any inhabitants of the lands he encountered. Columbus received financial support to outfit three ships for the

---

[69] Ibid., 267–68.   [70] Elliott, *Imperial Spain*, 109.   [71] Ibid., 110.

voyage from private investors and from Isabel of Castile, whose kingdom had a long history of Atlantic expansion. The savvy queen secured funding for Columbus in an imaginative way. She apparently used some of the wealth at hand with the fall of Granada to buy at the cost of 16,400,000 maravedís half of the town of Palos de la Frontera, a prominent Atlantic port of Castile with twenty-seven hundred inhabitants. Isabel then commanded the town's citizens to outfit two ships (the *Niña* and the *Santa María*) in payment for taxes owed to the Crown as a royal city and further commanded the citizenry to provide mariners for the voyage.[72] The merchant family of Martín Alonso Pinzón in Palos, sensing that the voyage might pay dividends, also invested in the enterprise by outfitting a third ship, the *Pinta*.[73] Some sources also indicate that the queen may have used 1,140,000 maravedís from the treasury of the Santa Hermandad to provide additional funding for the voyage. As a result, without taking money directly from the normal operating funds of the royal treasury, Isabel financed at least an important portion of the first voyage of Columbus.[74] The pious queen also entrusted the Genoese seaman with any "business that touches the service of God and the expansion of the Catholic Faith."[75] Columbus departed from Palos de la Frontera on August 3, 1492, on the first of four voyages that ultimately led to the creation of the Spanish Atlantic world.

---

[72] Escritura de venta que otorgó D. Pedro de Silva, a favor de los Reyes Católicos, de la mitad de la villa de Palos, Archivo General de Simancas, Patrimonio real, 35, 5; and Mandamiento de don Juan de Silva, conde de Cifuentes, asistente de Sevilla, y del Consejo, y a sus hermanos, don Pedro, y don Lope de Silva, para que entreguen a Juan de Cepeda, trinchante de doña Isabel, princesa de Portugal, la mitad de la villa de Palos con su Fortaleza y demás vendido por ellos a SS.AA. Archivo General de Simancas, Registro de Sello de Corte, 350, 1492-06-23.

[73] Felipe Fernández-Armesto, *Columbus* (New York: Oxford University Press), 62.

[74] There is considerable controversy among Columbus scholars about how much Isabel did or did not contribute to the first voyage of Columbus and how she raised the funding. In their biography of Columbus, William D. Phillips Jr. and Carla Rahn Phillips argue that Luis Santángel shifted 1,140,000 maravedís from the Santa Hermandad to fund the voyage; see William D. Phillips Jr. and Carla Rahn Phillips, *The Worlds of Christopher Columbus* (Cambridge: Cambridge University Press, 1992), 134. That figure was cited by Felipe Fernández-Armesto in his biography, *Columbus*, 62; that same author, in a later work, wrote, "Columbus' project could be financed at no direct cost to the king and queen (the old nonsense about Isabella pawning her jewels to meet Columbus' cost is another myth), there seemed no reason not to let Columbus sail"; see Felipe Fernández-Armesto, *Pathfinders: A Global History of Exploration* (New York: W. W. Norton, 2006), 163–64. In still another slightly different version, Santángel provided 1.4 million maravedís from the treasury of the Santa Hermandad and Columbus provided 500,000 maravedís advanced by Genoese and Florentine friends of Columbus, while the seaport town of Palos donated two caravels and Columbus leased a third vessel, the *Santa María*. See William S. Maltby, *The Rise and Fall of the Spanish Empire* (New York: Palgrave Macmillan, 2009), 22. These cited documents give credence to the version that I have used in the text, but they hardly provide definitive evidence on the subject. Indeed, it is unlikely that the question will ever be fully resolved unless personal financial documents of Columbus, Isabel of Castile, or contemporary merchants are unearthed in a Spanish archive.

[75] Liss, *Isabel the Queen*, 290.

Luis de Santángel: *Converso* Courtier and the Voyage of Columbus

The life of Luis de Santángel demonstrates the continuities between Iberia of the Reconquista and Spanish overseas expansion. Santángel was a wealthy and influential *converso* from Valencia, who excelled in business and in various financial and state projects for the Aragonese court. The grandfather of Luis Santángel, Noah Chinillo, was a Jewish cloth merchant from Daroca (in Aragon) who converted to Christianity in 1414 CE during the time when the Dominican Vincent Ferrer was preaching throughout Castile to force the conversion of Jews to Christianity. Chinillo later moved to Valencia, where he added to his wealth by running the Malta salt works and serving as a tax farmer in the Kingdom of Aragon.[76] By the 1470s, his grandson, Luis Santángel, had emerged as an influential courtier, performing a number of important tasks for Ferdinand, who described him as "the good Aragonese, excellent, well beloved councilor."[77] By the 1480s, Luis Santángel had served as secretary, manager of the king's household accounts (*escribano de ración y contador mayor*), and secretary of the Santa Hermandad. Despite his prominence, as a *converso*, Santángel was always under suspicion by the Inquisition. His mother, Brianda Bessant, herself from a *converso* family, was imprisoned by the Holy Office in 1487 for practicing Judaism. She was ultimately declared innocent and freed in 1488, possibly with the intervention of the king, but only after spending over one year in the Inquisitorial prison.[78] The Inquisition punished several other family members, indicating the dangers facing even prominent, well-connected *conversos* in fifteenth-century Spain.

Despite his many accomplishments at court, Luis Santángel's most significant service to the Catholic kings was his role in securing the support of Isabel of Castile for the first voyage of Columbus. Columbus came to the Spanish court in 1486 after failing to get Portuguese support for his idea of reaching Asia by sailing west. After he failed to gain Queen Isabel's financial backing, he decided to seek funding at the French court. When Luis Santángel heard about Columbus's departure for France, he requested an audience with the queen to gain her support for the project. Santángel emphasized that Spain would benefit even if the mariner did not land in Asia, since much could be learned about sailing across the Atlantic. He also argued that Columbus was an experienced navigator, and if another country sponsored the voyage, Spain would lose any rewards and respect to whoever backed Columbus. Queen Isabel was

---

[76] Dolores Sloan, *The Sephardic Jews of Spain and Portugal: Survival of an Imperiled Culture in the Fifteenth and Sixteenth Centuries* (London: McFarland, 2009), 78–79.
[77] Ibid., 82.   [78] Ibid., 89–92.

apparently convinced by Santángel's arguments. According to some accounts, Santángel allegedly found 1,140,000 maravedís in the treasury of the Santa Hermandad to support the venture. He also offered to advance a personal loan to help fund the enterprise.[79] In this way, a *converso* businessman and courtier played a key role in establishing the Spanish Atlantic world.

Conclusion

The Reconquista was both a series of military engagements and a great movement of the Christian kingdoms and their subjects southward dating from 711 CE to its culmination with the fall of Granada in 1492. As Fig. 1.1 indicates, the remote Christian enclave of Asturias in northwestern Iberia slowly expanded south to populate the lands north of the Duero River. This Christian migration proceeded more quickly after the Muslim caliphate, centered in Córdoba, fragmented into a series of thirty smaller *taifa* kingdoms. The Reconquista was not just a series of military engagements but also a frontier war, with hit-and-run raids, plunder, and a steady migration of people and livestock in search of land for settlements and pastures. In this second phase of the Reconquista after 1061, the Christian kingdoms of Portugal in the west, Aragon in the east, and Castile in the center became separate polities, sometimes at war with each other, not just the Muslims.

It was also the period of *convivencia*, when Christians, Muslims, and Jews lived together in these Christian monarchies. Jews and Muslims had their own parallel legal and governmental institutions (although subordinate to Christian laws) to resolve local community disputes. The treatment of these religious minorities varied in each region of the Christian kingdoms, with their rights and privileges protected by the monarch, particularly in areas where their numbers, economic importance, and political clout were most pronounced. After the great Christian victory at Las Navas de Tolosa in 1212, the Christian kingdoms expanded more rapidly southward until the Muslims held only their last stronghold of Granada. The growth of the Christian kingdoms quickened in the thirteenth and fourteenth centuries, leading to the breakdown of this more peaceful era of toleration or *convivencia*, particularly after the bubonic plague spread across Iberia after 1343. With the rising power of the Christians, pogroms directed against the Jews and forced conversions took place across much of the peninsula in the 1390s. Pressure on Muslim communities also heightened. The stability of *convivencia* was always precarious, and violence and intolerance on

---

[79] Ibid., 87. The exact amounts invested are in dispute; see Phillips and Phillips, *Worlds of Christopher Columbus*, 132–34; Liss, *Isabel the Queen*, 289.

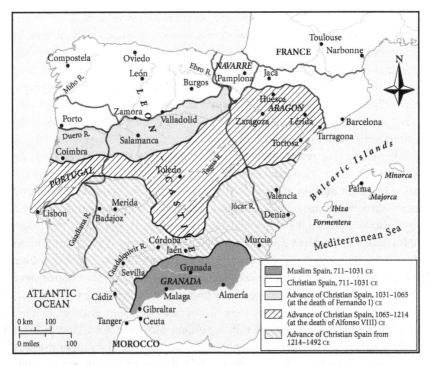

Fig. 1.1 Map of the chronology of the Reconquista.
Source: Adapted from Joseph F. O'Callaghan, *A History of Medieval Spain* (Ithaca, NY: Cornell University Press, 1975), Map 3, p. 108; Map 4, p. 199; Map 5, p. 252; and Map 6, p. 355.

the part of the Christian population were omnipresent, particularly as the Christian kingdoms expanded their authority over the peninsula.

The marriage of Ferdinand of Aragon and Isabel of Castile in 1469 united the two largest kingdoms in Iberia, forming a dynastic or composite monarchy, with each separate kingdom keeping its own laws, institutions, and political traditions. Nonetheless, this powerful union allowed the monarchs to pool resources and bring the Reconquista to a close with the fall of the last Muslim stronghold, Granada, in 1492. This victory only accentuated the era of intolerance that began in the aftermath of the plagues in the 1390s. After the fall of Granada, the Catholic kings expelled the Jews in 1492 or forced them to convert to Catholicism. The Muslims suffered the same fate of forced conversion to Christianity beginning in 1499 in Castile and Navarre in 1515, but in areas with large Muslim populations, the forced conversions came later, in the early 1520s in Valencia and in 1525 in Aragon.[80] The year 1492 also

---

[80] James S. Amelang, *Parallel Histories: Muslims and Jews in Inquisitorial Spain* (Baton Rouge: Louisiana State University Press, 2013), 8.

saw the Catholic kings support the momentous voyage of Christopher Columbus, which began the creation of a Spanish Atlantic world, shaped by the political, religious, and institutional culture developed during the seven hundred-year Reconquista. In essence, the Spaniards took the lessons from their holy war to the Americas. Although ethnically, culturally, and geographically diverse, this Spanish Atlantic world constituted a defined political, cultural, economic, and religious space, united by adherence to one monarchy and one orthodox Roman Catholic faith.

After Columbus returned from his first voyage in the spring of 1493, the Spanish composite monarchy embarked on its overseas expansion across the Atlantic, a continuation of the crusading spirit of the Reconquista. The Crown established the terms of each conquest expedition with a contract, called a *capitulación*, between the king and the leader (frequently given the title *adelantado*), much as they had done with nobles raiding across the Muslim borders during the Reconquista. The original Spanish conquistadors were drawn from the middle class and most were not professional soldiers, but they came from a society where martial skills were widely known. The polyglot Christian armies that fought against the Muslims were drawn from the king's guardsmen, civic militias, noble retainers, and the military orders. Moreover, the Christian kings had a long tradition of forging alliances with dissident Muslim groups to attack a common enemy, just as King Ferdinand III relied on an alliance with Granada to conquer Seville. The new lands were incorporated into the composite monarchy as an accessory union, tied to the laws and institutional practices of Castile, which had supported and funded the original voyages of Columbus.

The first Spanish conquistadors, and the settlers from Iberia who followed, brought the political values, beliefs, knowledge, and institutions (secular and religious) that would shape the basic political, religious, social, and economic order in the New World. This Iberian political and institutional culture was forged during the Reconquista and later applied in stages to Spanish possessions in the New World, particularly after the Crown began to send bureaucrats and churchmen to govern and evangelize in the Indies. Although the subjected Indigenous peoples had their own customs, religious beliefs, and socioeconomic practices, they were forced into a subordinate social position over time. Likewise, when Africans (brought largely as enslaved people) came to the Indies, they occupied an even more inferior social position in the Spanish Indies. Both groups were largely excluded from taking part in the Spanish political order and from most religious positions in the Roman Catholic Church in the conquest era. Despite their subservient position in the emerging political, religious, and socioeconomic order, Indigenous peoples and Africans and their traditions, over time, played an important role in the evolution of the Spanish Atlantic world.

When they arrived in the Indies, Spanish conquistadors used diplomatic skills honed during the Reconquista to make alliances with Indigenous groups to overthrow the Aztec and Inca states. They initially strengthened these alliances with Indigenous allies by taking Amerindian wives or concubines, just as Muslim and Visigothic families intermarried early in the Reconquista. The conquistadors also largely abandoned this practice when they had consolidated power, just as Christians, Muslims, and Jews erected barriers to interfaith sexual contact over time. Moreover, the initial conquistadors drew on the Muslim *dhimmi* tradition of working through Indigenous clan leaders to collect taxes and make labor assignments. They also would allow Indigenous clan leaders to settle many of the disputes that periodically arose among the citizens of Indigenous communities, according to their own customary laws, as Muslim judges and Jewish rabbis had administered justice in their communities under Christian rule. This process was simplified in the Indies by the early decision to convert all the Indigenous people to Christianity, so there was only one accepted religion and legal tradition, not three as in medieval Spain, at least until the forced conversions. This decision to evangelize the inhabitants of the Indies also served as a justification for the Spanish invasion and settlement in the New World, turning the conquest into a moral crusade to save the souls of the New World natives, just as the Reconquista had been a moral crusade against Muslims. Both the Reconquista and the Spanish New World conquests received the blessings of the papacy in 1496 CE, which divided the responsibility for converting the Indigenous peoples of the New World between Spain and Portugal, the leaders in European overseas expansion at the time. The Indigenous people of the New World also became vassals of the Crown, paying special taxes in return for privileges granted by the Crown and duties or obligations, such as forced labor in the mines and textile workshops of the Indies, resembling the way the Christian kings had treated their Muslim and Jewish subjects in medieval Spain. The conquistadors also relied on a Reconquista institution, the encomienda, which they used in modified form to distribute the spoils of conquest, much as the Christian kings of Castile had done in the thirteenth century. Along the frontiers of the emerging empire in the New World, the Crown relied on a mix of regular troops and civic militias, tying military service to citizenship. In short, the Spanish who settled the Indies could not escape their long Reconquista traditions, which shaped their early efforts to conquer and settle the lands that would comprise the emerging Spanish Atlantic world.

Timeline: The Reconquista and the Institutional Origins of Spanish Overseas Expansion

711 CE	Muslims invade Iberia and defeat the Visigothic King Roderick at the Battle of Guadalete
722	Legendary Christian victory at Covadonga, establishing the independence of the Kingdom of Asturias
732	Muslim advance into Europe halted by Frankish forces under Charles Martel at the Battle of Tours and Poitiers
756	Abd al-Rahmān I sets up the Muslim capital at Córdoba and establishes an emirate ruling over al-Andalus, beginning the construction of the great mosque in 780
912	Abd al-Rahmān III becomes emir and proclaims himself caliph, making al-Andalus independent of Baghdad
1031	Provincial leaders abolish the caliphate, establishing thirty independent Muslim *taifa* city states
1086	Asturias evolves into four separate kingdoms: Castile-León, Navarre, Aragon, and Portugal, and Alfonso VI of Castile captures Toledo, leading Muslim states to appeal to fundamentalist Almoravids to enter Iberia and establish control over Muslim al-Andalus
1164	Military order of Calatrava founded as a branch of the Cistercian order
1172	A new fundamentalist group, the Almohads, crosses from North Africa and supplants the Almoravids
1175	Military order of Santiago founded subjected to the pope
1176	Military order of Alcántara founded as a branch of the Cistercian order
1195	Almohads defeat King Alfonso VIII of Castile at Alarcos
1212	Christian victory at Las Navas de Tolosa turns tide in favor of Christian kingdoms in the Reconquista
1214	Ferdinand III accedes to the throne and conquers Córdoba in 1236, Murcia in 1242, Jaén in 1246, and Seville in 1248
1230	James I of Aragon (the Conqueror) conquers Mallorca, as well as all of Valencia in 1248, leaving Granada as the only independent Muslim polity in Iberia
1265	Alfonso X of Castile (*el Sabio*) completes the legal code, Siete Partidas
1343	Bubonic plague hits the Iberian Peninsula
1391	Pogroms directed against the Jewish communities of Iberia, beginning in Seville, leading to the death or forced conversion of the Jews
1462–73	Civil war in the Kingdom of Aragon, pitting nobles against the Crown
1469	Secret marriage of Isabel of Castile and Ferdinand of Aragon

1473	Violence against Jews in Córdoba spreads across Andalusia
1474–79	Death of Henry IV leads to civil war over Isabel's succession to the throne of Castile, but she prevails and accedes to the throne in 1479
1479	Ferdinand accedes to the throne of the Kingdom of Aragon
1480	Act of Resumption in Castile deprives nobles of half of the lands alienated or taken since 1464
1480	Ferdinand and Isabel establish the Inquisition
1486	Sentencia de Guadalupe ends six evil customs and serfdom in Catalonia with compensation to the nobility
1492	Granada falls to Ferdinand and Isabel on January 6
1492	On March 31, Jews are forced to convert or leave Castile/Aragon
1492	On April 17, Isabel supports and provides funding for the voyage of Christopher Columbus
1499	Forced conversions of the Muslims of Castile
1515	Forced conversions of the Muslims of Navarre
1525	Forced conversions of the Muslims of Aragon (forced conversions in Valencia took place a few years earlier)

2

New World Beginnings to the Institutional Consolidation of the Spanish Atlantic World, 1492–1610

On November 16, 1532, a group of only 168 Spaniards, positioned in the northern city of Cajamarca, confronted an Inca force of tens of thousands of seasoned combat veterans, who had just achieved victory in a bloody civil war between their commander, Atahualpa, the Sapa Inca (unique Inca or emperor), and his half-brother Huascar. Both emerged as rival claimants for the imperial throne after the unexpected death of their father, the Sapa Inca Huayna Capac. Experienced commanders led both the small Spanish force and the large Inca host. Atahualpa divided his army into three separate formations. The bulk of the army remained close to the Inca camp, overlooking the city of Cajamarca, ready to attack when ordered. A second force of around 20,000 men deployed in a flanking movement to block any attempt by the Spanish troops to flee the city. A third column of perhaps 6,000 men was composed of soldiers, servants, and household staff of Atahualpa, who commanded this group himself while seated on an elaborate palanquin (litter). The soldiers formed the front of the Inca's formation, dressed in tunics of alternating white and black squares in a checkerboard pattern (called *tocapu*) with red on the upper part, around the soldiers' shoulders (see Fig. 2.1). This last group advanced slowly toward the gates of Cajamarca, a distance of two to four miles.[1]

The Inca force halted several hundred yards from the city gates and waited, perhaps to heighten the fear and anxiety of the Spaniards positioned in buildings around the city's main square. Atahualpa probably anticipated a panicky attack or even an attempted flight by the Spaniards, who surely would have been overwhelmed by the superior Inca army in any open field battle. Instead, the Spaniards waited fearfully and impatiently until the Inca force advanced into the city. According to young Pedro Pizarro, a cousin of the principal

---

[1] The most detailed account of the incident at Cajamarca is found in Adam Herring, *Art and Vision in the Inca Empire: Andeans and Europeans at Cajamarca* (Cambridge: Cambridge University Press, 2015), particularly 79–117. Another important study of the incident is Gonzalo Lamana, *Domination without Dominance: Inca–Spanish Encounters in Early Colonial Peru* (Durham, NC: Duke University Press, 2008), 53–64.

Fig. 2.1 Inca checkerboard tunic like those worn by the warriors at Cajamarca.
Source: Dallas Museum of Art: 5122425.

Spanish commander, "I saw many Spaniards urinate without noticing it out of pure terror."[2] The Inca soldiers and retainers moved to the central square, which resounded with the chants, music, and singing of the Inca troops. Atahualpa remained seated on his palanquin, probably awaiting the surrender of his vastly outnumbered Spanish foe. After the expected capitulation, he no doubt anticipated a traditional meal with the Spaniards, complete with ritual drinking of fermented maize beer (*chicha*). It was a pattern based on a long-tested Inca policy of intimidation, followed by diplomacy and the inevitable acceptance of vassalage by former enemies.[3]

The Spanish commanders concealed their small but well-armed force in the buildings that surrounded the city's main square. According to most chronicles of the event, a Spanish Dominican friar, Vicente de Valverde, went to meet the

---

[2] Hemming, *Conquest of the Incas*, 38.
[3] See Herring, *Art and Vision*, 116–17; for Inca ritual drinking patterns, see Thomas B. F. Cummins, *Toasts with the Inca: Andean Abstraction and Colonial Images on Quero Vessels* (Ann Arbor: University of Michigan Press, 2002).

Sapa Inca, and after a brief exchange, Atahualpa rose to address his followers.[4] The Spanish commander, Francisco Pizarro, then gave the signal for his subordinate, Pedro de Candía, to fire the army's cannon into the tightly packed Inca soldiers and retainers. Heavily armed foot soldiers and cavalrymen then sprang from their concealment shouting their war cry, "Santiago!" and attacked the Inca's followers, offering no quarter. Amid what must have been a terrifying din of horse hooves, weapons firing, the clanking of armor, and deadly slashing of Spanish steel blades, the Andean troops panicked, trampling each other to escape from their entrapment in the enclosed square. Those at the rear flung themselves against a fifteen-foot wall on one side of the plaza, which finally gave way, as the desperate and probably terrified retainers tried to flee through the opening. During the slaughter and mayhem, Pizarro and a small party of Spaniards captured Atahualpa, pulling him from his palanquin, while the remainder of the Spanish force used their horses, lances, swords, and firearms to slaughter the Andeans who remained in the square, even pursuing those who fled through the wall to the surrounding plain. The few who managed to reach the larger Inca force merely spread fear and disorder among the troops, who fled the field. By nightfall, thousands of Inca soldiers lay dead, and the Spaniards held Atahualpa captive. After extracting a ransom of gold and silver from the captive Atahualpa, the Spaniards tried and executed him.[5]

One year after the slaughter at Cajamarca, Francisco Pizarro and his small army entered Cusco, the Inca capital. Within weeks of arriving in the city, Pizarro oversaw the coronation of a kinsman of the defeated Huascar, Manco Inca, as the new Sapa Inca. The forces of Manco Inca, in alliance with the Spaniards, then defeated the remaining armies who had followed Atahualpa in the civil war, bringing an unstable peace to the Inca realm. In the ensuing two and a half years, tensions had risen steadily between the allies, particularly as the Spaniards became increasingly greedy and arrogant. The conquistadors even beat and imprisoned the Sapa Inca when he displeased them, and Gonzalo Pizarro took the ruler's principal wife (*coya*) as his mistress. In 1536, an angry and thoroughly disillusioned Manco Inca managed to slip unnoticed from Cusco. He somehow raised an army of nearly 100,000 men, who besieged the

---

[4] According to some accounts of the event, Valverde offered Atahualpa a breviary, which the Sapa Inca threw to the ground. See Patricia Seed, "Failing to Marvel: Atahualpa's Encounter with the Word," *Latin American Research Review* 26, no. 1 (Winter 1991): 7–32; and Sabine MacCormack, "Atahualpa and the Book," *Dispositio* 14, no. 36–38 (1989): 141–68.

[5] According to Gonzalo Lamana, Atahualpa sent the Spaniards to fetch the ransom by stripping the gold and silver from the Temple of the Sun in Cusco and the coastal shrine of Pachacamac; both had been centers of support for his rival and half-brother, Huascar. In effect, Atahualpa was using the Spaniards to punish his enemies. He also had the captive Huascar killed to remove him as a threat while Atahualpa remained a captive of the Spaniards. See Lamana, *Domination without Dominance*, 66–92; Heming, *Conquest of the Incas*, 54.

capital city. The large Inca force hurled flaming stones to burn the thatched roofs of Cusco's houses to force the 190 Spaniards and their numerous Indigenous allies (opposed to Manco as Sapa Inca) defending the city to fight them in the open field. In August 1536, Manco's forces attacked the Spanish coastal capital of Lima and defeated two Spanish forces sent to relieve the Spaniards who were tenuously holding on to Cusco.[6] Conflict also erupted between two rival leaders of the Spanish expedition, Francisco Pizarro and Diego de Almagro, further complicating the political scene, leading to civil wars among the conquistadors that continued off and on for over a decade. With a mixture of grit and determination, however, the desperate Spanish defenders and their allies survived numerous attacks, burning rooftops, and shortages of food and water to break out of their encirclement and take the Inca fortress of Sacsayhuamán, just outside Cusco. Finally, in February 1539, the Inca force abandoned the siege, and Manco Inca retreated to a remote fortress in Vilcabamba, where he and his successors remained until a Spanish army eventually conquered the city and executed the last Sapa Inca, Tupac Amaru, in 1572. It was not until the fall of Vilcabamba that the Spaniards finally subdued the last vestiges of the Inca state.[7] Armed with the optimism, confidence, and religious zeal of the Reconquista, the Spaniards and their Indigenous allies had toppled the massive Inca Empire, the largest and most well-organized Indigenous polity in the Americas.

The dynastic monarchy of Castile and Aragon had the political flexibility to incorporate the new domains in the Americas, much as the Crown had done with European kingdoms, such as Naples or Sicily. These new possessions in the Indies remained volatile and unstable in the early years as the conquistadors attempted to consolidate their rule, particularly over the large, densely populated regions in the Andes and Mexico. In these early years, periodic wars erupted among the fractious conquistadors, and Indigenous uprisings, particularly in the Andes, made Spanish rule tenuous. At first, the Spanish relied on institutions and traditions utilized during the Reconquista, such as the encomienda to draw surplus resources from the Indigenous communities to reward the conquistadors and consolidate power in the Indies. By 1610, the rule of the freelancing conquistadors had been replaced by more permanent political and institutional arrangements as the Indies became incorporated into the

---

[6] Inca kinship groups formed factions, particularly those who had supported Atahualpa in the civil war, which opposed the accession of Manco Inca and fought in the city and its environs against his forces besieging the Inca capital. For a detailed discussion of these factional alignments and how they influenced the political situation from 1532 to 1570, see Danielle Tina Anthony, "Intimate Invasion: Andeans and Europeans in 16th Century Peru" (Ph.D. diss., The Ohio State University, 2018).

[7] Ibid., 189–220.

Spanish monarchy as an accessory union, subject to the laws, taxes, and institutions of Castile. As the Crown established permanent institutions to govern the Indies, Roman Catholic priests and friars worked to convert the Indigenous inhabitants to Catholicism and a stable, prosperous economy evolved, particularly after the Spanish settlers discovered rich deposits of gold and silver.

The Turbulent Conquest Era

The dramatic events at Cajamarca in 1532 were just an important step in Spanish overseas expansion, which began with the first voyage of Christopher Columbus in 1492. Columbus established the first small settlement on the island of Española in 1492, when he left some men behind after losing his flagship, the *Santa María*.[8] This failed initial attempt at settlement was followed by other more thriving efforts, particularly after the discovery of gold deposits on Española and other Caribbean islands. Columbus and his family could not manage these early communities effectively, and dissatisfaction among the colonists and the continued decline of the Indigenous population led the Crown to assume governance of the islands by 1502. The Crown established the basic structures of government with a royally appointed governor (from 1502), a high court (*audiencia*) to administer justice in 1511, and treasury offices to collect taxes. Spanish authorities also encouraged the Church to send missionaries, followed by the creation of three bishoprics for the islands. These early Caribbean outposts served as a proving ground for Spanish rule in the Americas, where the Crown and settlers from Iberia firmly established a political and material culture that extended to mainland settlements in subsequent years.[9]

When the Caribbean gold deposits were exhausted and the Indigenous population had largely died off from enslavement, the introduction of European diseases, and overwork, Portuguese slave vessels supplied African bondsmen as Spanish colonists turned to planting sugar cane, introduced from the Canary and Madeira Islands. The production of foodstuffs, however, came to overtake the modest sugar industry in the Caribbean later in the sixteenth century, with enslaved Africans often substituting for Indigenous labor on Spanish farms, *trapiches* (sugar mills), and *ingenios* (sugar plantations).[10] As they had done in

---

[8] Phillips and Phillips, *Worlds of Christopher Columbus*, 191.
[9] Stuart B. Schwartz, "The Iberian Atlantic to 1650," in *The Oxford Handbook of Atlantic History*, ed. Nicholas Canny and Philip Morgan (Oxford: Oxford University Press, 2011), 149–52.
[10] David Wheat, *Atlantic Africa and the Spanish Caribbean, 1570–1640* (Chapel Hill: University of North Carolina Press, 2016), 8–9, 182–92, 194–97, 255–56; Genaro Rodríguez Morel, "The Sugar Economy of Española in the Sixteenth Century," in *Tropical Babylons: Sugar and the Making of the*

settling Christian frontiers of Iberia during the Reconquista, Spanish authorities encouraged married couples or Spanish women to populate these early settlements to promote morality and social stability and to discourage racial mixture. Over time, the Spanish invasion of the New World proceeded from these Caribbean Islands to Mexico and then to Peru, as new expeditions fanned out across North and South America to incorporate rich new lands into the Crown's domain. Spanish leaders of these expeditions (usually called *adelantados*), such as Fernando Cortés, led efforts at trade and conquest from Cuba to the mainland of North America, gaining control of the land and peoples in central Mexico and Central America. Francisco Pizarro later undertook three separate expeditions to South America from Panama, and on the third, he achieved his military successes beginning at Cajamarca in 1532.

When the Spanish conquistadors encountered dense, wealthy Indigenous populations, their initial military successes had to be consolidated by carefully cultivating diplomatic alliances with Indigenous allies. After Fernando Cortés launched an expedition to the mainland of North America in 1519 CE, he immediately began forging political and military alliances with the enemies of the large Aztec (Mexica) empire, such as the warlike Tlaxcalans. In the Spanish siege of the Aztec capital of Tenochtitlan in 1521, as many as twenty-four thousand Indigenous allies participated—as soldiers, porters, cooks, translators, guides, and spies. Indeed, it is possible to view the Spanish invasion of central Mexico as initiating a full-scale Indigenous rebellion against Aztec rule, with the Spaniards playing an important role, most often directing these larger armies of Indigenous allies. Amerindian allies also participated in later conquests in Central America; a letter in 1567 estimated that Tlaxcala alone provided twenty thousand soldiers for conquests throughout Mesoamerica.[11] Indigenous allies also played a major role in the Spanish invasion of the Andes. The initial accounts from the forces of Francisco Pizarro included bitter complaints regarding the hostile landscape, hunger, and plagues of insects, disease, and the omnipresent humidity that rotted the clothes on their backs as they made their way through the Inca realm. Fears of failure plagued the small Spanish force, at least until they began attracting Indigenous allies, first along the coast and later in the highlands, such as the Huanca communities of Jauja.

Atlantic World, 1450–1680, ed. Stuart B. Schwartz (Chapel Hill: University of North Carolina Press, 2004), 85–114; and Alejandro de la Fuente, "Sugar and Slavery in Early Colonial Cuba," in Schwartz, *Tropical Babylons*, 115–57. See also Alejandro de la Fuente, with the collaboration of César García del Pino and Bernardo Iglesias Delgado, *Havana and the Atlantic in the Sixteenth Century* (Chapel Hill: University of North Carolina Press, 2008), 46, 47, 136–46.

[11] Laura E. Matthew and Michael R. Oudijk, eds., *Indian Conquistadors: Indigenous Allies in the Conquest of Mesoamerica* (Norman: University of Oklahoma Press, 2007), 35. The essays in this volume provide convincing evidence of the broad range of actions that Indigenous allies made possible.

The Spanish accounts of peril and the hostile environment then faded as Indigenous allies gave the Spanish force confidence to overcome the obstacles that had seemed so daunting just a few months earlier.[12]

After the overthrow of the powerful Aztec Empire in 1521, the Spanish leader Fernando Cortés recognized that the Spaniards were just one among many ethnic groups in the valley of Mexico vying to control the lands of the fallen Aztec Empire, so such alliances with Indigenous groups continued.[13] In Peru, the Spaniards even supported the efforts of Manco Inca against the generals who had remained loyal to Atahualpa before his death, at least until frayed relations led the Sapa Inca to besiege Cusco and attempt unsuccessfully to expel the Spaniards from the Inca domains in 1536. For their part, the Indigenous ethnic groups had a tradition of forging alliances to maintain or extend their power, so the Spaniards and the Indigenous ethnic groups both well understood the value of such alliances, particularly in times of political instability in central Mexico and the Andes during the conquest era.

Since the power of the early conquistadors was often so insecure, the Spanish invaders forged kinship ties with powerful Indigenous ethnic groups to consolidate their wealth, power, and status, often marrying or taking as concubines the daughters of Indigenous elites. Fernando Cortés and several of his officers, for example, took Indigenous concubines, who bore them several children. These women represented the spoils of war, but they also served to tie the Europeans to important Indigenous families.[14] Inca nobles also often married their daughters to provincial rulers or newly incorporated ethnic leaders. A mural in the entrance of the Jesuit church in Cusco (see Fig. 2.2) depicts on the left the marriage of Beatriz Ñuesta, the daughter of Sayre Tupac, the brother of Manco Inca in Vilcabamba, to Martín García de Loyola, the nephew of the founder of the Jesuit order, Ignatius Loyola. To the right of this couple is Juan de Borja, who is marrying doña Lorenza Ñuesta, the daughter of Beatriz and García de Loyola, uniting the Inca royal family with one of the most prominent grandee families of Spain. The Spaniards had promised Sayre Tupac lands and tribute monies from communities in the Cusco region to establish him as an alternative leader to supplant the hostile Vilcabamba ruler.[15] Between the two

[12] Heidi V. Scott, *Contested Territory: Mapping Peru in the Sixteenth and Seventeenth Centuries* (Notre Dame, IN: University of Notre Dame Press, 2009), 20–33.

[13] Michel R. Oudijk and Matthew Restall, "Mesoamerican Conquistadors in the Sixteenth Century," in Matthew and Oudijk, *Indian Conquistadors*, 38.

[14] See Matthew Restall, *When Cortés Met Montezuma: The True Story of the Meeting That Changed History* (New York: Ecco, Harper Collins, 2018), 286–87, 305–7. Restall emphasizes the forced nature of these relationships and portrays Cortés and his officers as sexual exploiters, which they undoubtedly were, but there was also likely a political calculation behind establishing these kinship ties.

[15] Titu Cusi Yupanqui, *History of How the Spaniards Arrived*, x, xi, 147.

Fig. 2.2 Marriages of Martín García de Loyola to Beatriz Ñusta and Juan de Borja to Lorenza Ñusta, seventeenth century.
Source: Museo Pedro de Osma, Lima.

couples is the founder of the Jesuit order, Ignatius Loyola, depicted as a saint. The upper left of the painting shows members of the Inca elite, while on the right are prominent Spaniards. The painting not only demonstrates the kinship ties across two generations between Spanish and Inca elites, but also represents the transfer of power from the Inca nobility to Spanish and clerical elites. Just as kinship alliances between the Muslims and Visigoth families allowed for the consolidation of power in the early years of the Reconquista, so too did strategic marriages allow Spaniards to consolidate their gains in Peru, even after the unsuccessful rebellion of Manco Inca. As time passed and the Spaniards established their power in various regions of the Indies, however, such marriages became less common, particularly as more Spanish women migrated to the New World.

Strategic marriages or informal unions between Spanish conquistadors and Indigenous women also produced children of mixed blood (*mestizos*), complicating the colonial social structure. Spanish fathers sometimes supported and acknowledged their mestizo offspring, even sending them to Spain to live with close relatives, so that they would be raised as Christians with Iberian cultural values, rather than living in the New World with their Indigenous kinsmen. This was the case with Lorenza Ñuesta, the child of Martín García Loyola and Beatriz Ñuesta. Another famous example was el Inca Garcilaso de la Vega, whose Spanish father sent him to Spain, where he spent the rest of his life, later writing his famous history, *Royal Commentaries of the Incas* (1609) and *General History of Peru* (1617). Such blended families emerged in Iberian cities, particularly Seville. According to Spanish law, paternal rights (*patria potestad*) allowed fathers to take children from the care of their Indigenous mothers as long as they provided for the child's material and spiritual well-being. Some fathers even gave dowries for young mestizas so that they could arrange a suitable marriage either in Spain or in the Indies. These blended families did not disappear after the first generation of conquistadors; middle- and lower-class Spaniards in the New World married or cohabited with Indigenous women, particularly in urban areas where Indigenous and Spanish citizens interacted on a daily basis. It was quite uncommon in this early period for an elite Spanish woman to marry an Indigenous man, however, even a member of the Amerindian nobility. A few Spanish fathers also provided legacies for their mestizo children in their wills. During the sixteenth century, Spanish mixed-race families residing in Iberia or the Indies were often composed of mestizo half-siblings, cousins, mothers, and fathers.[16]

To divide the spoils and ensure their wealth and status, expedition leaders parceled out grants of encomienda to loyal followers, which allowed them rights to collect taxes and labor services from a designated group of Indigenous towns in return for military protection and religious instruction. The encomienda allowed the conquistadors to drain excess resources from the existing Amerindian economies, and they avoided the struggles and privation later experienced by English colonists at Jamestown and Plymouth. The encomienda was an institution used by the Crown during the Reconquista to give the right to the lands and taxes, but the New World encomienda never included a title to Indigenous lands as part of the grant. These New World grants gave the holder (called an *encomendero*) social status and economic

---

[16] This information is taken from Jane E. Mangan, *Transatlantic Obligations: Creating the Bonds of Family in Conquest-Era Peru and Spain* (New York: Oxford University Press, 2016).

wealth—a source of capital and labor to buy property, engage in mining, or pursue commercial opportunities. Indeed, the disposable income and labor service provided by an encomienda could serve as the centerpiece of a diverse investment portfolio in the early years of the Spanish conquest. The Pizarro family, for example, grew rich from the investments they made from capital and labor services provided by their encomiendas, and Fernando Cortés established a series of landed estates with the labor provided by the thirty thousand Indigenous charges granted to him with his populous encomiendas in Oaxaca and Morelos.[17] Encomienda grants could usually only be passed down for two to three generations before they reverted to the Crown, and *encomenderos* continuously lobbied the Crown to have the grants held by their families in perpetuity. In 1555 CE, for example, the Peruvian *encomenderos* offered the normally cash-poor Spanish Crown seven to nine million ducats for granting perpetual encomiendas. Church officials and Indigenous ethnic lords in the Andes vigorously opposed the proposal. At a meeting in 1561 at Mama in the Andean highlands above Lima, Dominican friar Domingo de Santo Tomás and the ethnic lord of Jauja, Cusichaq, argued that encomiendas should be granted to the natural Indigenous lords of the region, not to Spanish conquistadors. Cusichaq, seconded by Santo Tomás, argued that his people had been poorly rewarded for past services to the Crown, and he and the other Indigenous leaders would offer one hundred thousand gold castellanos, a sum greater than the Spanish *encomenderos* had pledged, to receive lordship over their own peoples.[18] Such offers must have sorely tempted the perpetually indebted King Philip II, who had been forced recently to declare bankruptcy, but in the end, he and his advisors did not accept either offer. Instead, the king listened to churchmen opposed to the encomienda, which the king feared would create a new Spanish or Indigenous aristocracy in the Indies capable of challenging the power of the Crown.[19]

Spanish expansion across the Atlantic created social tensions, tangled loyalties, and emotional distress. The Crown sent a royal edict to Peru in 1544 ordering all that married Spanish men bring their wives to the New World or return to Spain. While some men complied, others did not. One of the conquistadors

---

[17] See Rafael Varón Gabai, *Francisco Pizarro and His Brothers: The Illusion of Power in Sixteenth-Century Peru* (Norman: University of Oklahoma Press, 1997); G. Micheal Riley, *Fernando Cortés and Marquesado in Morelos: A Case Study in the Socioeconomic Development of Sixteenth-Century Mexico* (Albuquerque: University of New Mexico Press, 1973). For an excellent series of case studies on how *encomenderos* won and often lost great fortunes, see Ana María Presta, *Los encomenderos de La Plata, 1550–1600* (Lima: Instituto de Estudios Peruanos, 2000), especially 139–248.

[18] John V. Murra, "Nos hazen mucha ventaja: The Early European Perception of Andean Achievement," in Andrien and Adorno, *Transatlantic Encounters*, 81–83; 1 gold castellano equaled 450 maravedís.

[19] Lawrence A. Clayton, *Bartolomé de las Casas: A Biography* (Cambridge: Cambridge University Press, 2012), 432.

of Peru, for example, Francisco Noguerol de Ulloa, left Spain not only to make his fortune in the New World, but also apparently to get away from his wife, Beatriz de Villasur. While in Peru, Noguerol participated in the conquest and the struggles among rival factions of the conquistadors. During this time, his sisters, doña Inés and doña Francisca, nuns in the Benedictine convent of San Pedro de las Dueñas (in León, Spain), wrote to tell Noguerol that Beatriz had died and urged him to return to Spain. Noguerol had no desire to return because he had amassed a small fortune, gained an encomienda, and later successfully courted and married a rich widow, Catalina de Vergara. His new wife made returning to Spain a condition of accepting Noguerol's proposal, however, so they left Peru in 1554. Upon arriving, the couple found out that Beatriz de Villasur was alive and demanding that Noguerol come to live with her as her husband. Noguerol was an unwitting bigamist, who was subject to prosecution in both clerical and civil courts. In the end, the civil courts remanded the case to clerical authorities, and Noguerol and Catalina de Vergara petitioned the pope to intervene in 1558. Pope Paul IV finally declared the couple legally married, and they lived together until Noguerol's death in 1581. The matter was not completely resolved until 1583, when Catalina de Vergara paid 1,387,500 maravedís as a settlement to Beatriz de Villasur, by then a sick elderly woman.[20]

Although the encomienda was central to the acquisition of wealth and power in the conquest era, over the generations many conquistadors and their families lost this wealth, power, and influence. Some conquistadors longed for the adventure and wealth that new expeditions could bring, but the risks were daunting. Juan Ortiz de Zárate, for example, was a wealthy *encomendero* and entrepreneur in Charcas (now Bolivia), most often in partnership with his brother, Lope de Mendieta. From Orduña in the Basque region, in the 1540s the two men sought their fortunes in Peru with considerable success, amassing rich encomiendas and landholdings and engaging in successful commercial ventures. In 1565, the lure of potentially lucrative new conquests prompted the restless Ortiz de Zárate to petition the Crown for permission to outfit an expedition for resettling Buenos Aires in the Río de la Plata. The original Spanish settlers had abandoned the region in 1536 because of hostile Indigenous attacks and a lack of readily exploitable resources. By the 1560s, however, the discovery of silver in Paraguay and the prospect of having an Atlantic port to transport silver from Charcas to Spain led the Crown to approve Ortiz de Zárate's plan of mounting of a new expedition. Ortiz de Zárate borrowed heavily to fund the expensive enterprise and, when the expedition faltered, he went even more

---

[20] The story of Francisco Noguerol de Ulloa and his two wives is found in Alexandra Parma Cook and Noble David Cook, *Good Faith and Truthful Ignorance: A Case of Transatlantic Bigamy* (Durham, NC: Duke University Press, 1991).

deeply into debt. When he died in Paraguay in 1576, the family's wealth and power collapsed under the weight of these accumulated debts.[21]

Another prominent Spanish official and entrepreneur, Juan Polo de Ondegardo y Zárate, flourished in Charcas after migrating to Peru from Valladolid in Spain.[22] After coming to Peru, Polo de Ondegardo became an authority on the Incas, an influential loyalist fighting on behalf of the Crown in the disputes with the *encomenderos*, and later a prominent *encomendero*, miner, and landowner. Despite his legendary wealth and power, when Polo de Ondegardo died in 1575, his strong-willed wife, Jerónima de Peñalosa, spent lavishly to arrange favorable marriages for her children. She also supported several relatives who were receiving their education in Spain. Over time, the declining Indigenous population on the family encomiendas and some poor business decisions squandered the rest of Polo de Ondegardo's formerly large estate. In the end, the family lacked the money to finish building a chapel in the Church of San Francisco in La Plata, where Polo de Ondegardo's body was buried. The angry friars compelled his wife to remove his remains from their resting place in 1592, and the family suffered the indignity of having to send his bones to Spain for burial.

The Encomienda and the "Struggle for Justice"

After the conquistadors encountered diverse, populous Amerindian societies in the Indies, word spread to Europe about abuses of the encomienda system and the nature of the Indigenous peoples. Intellectuals in Spain began to debate about both the humanity and the proper social role of Indigenous peoples in the emerging Spanish Atlantic world. These intellectuals struggled with basic questions such as, Were the Amerindians "beasts" (mere brutes incapable of living in civilized society), "barbarians" (rude outsiders best kept apart from civilized

---

[21] For the life of Juan Ortiz de Zárate, see Presta, *Los encomenderos de La Plata*, 139–94.

[22] Juan Polo de Ondegardo y Zárate is sometimes referred to as Polo Ondegardo or Polo de Ondegardo. The confusion apparently stems in part from the name Polo, which is an uncommon but not unknown Spanish or Italian first name. For a reference to Polo Ondegardo, see Presta, *Los encomenderos de La Plata*, chap. 6. According to Ana María Presta and Catherine Julien, the official's first name was Polo, and he was named after his paternal grandfather, a Milanese businessman who moved to Valladolid. They do admit, however, that he was referred to in documents and signed his name as Licenciado Polo, when the more common linking of the title to his surname would be Licenciado Ondegardo. See Ana María Presta and Catherine Julien, "Polo Ondegardo (ca. 1520–1575)," in *Guide to Documentary Sources for Andean Studies*, ed. Joanne Pillsbury et al. (Norman: University of Oklahoma Press, 2008), 3:529. Other sources, such as Franklin Pease G. Y., refer to this sixteenth-century figure as Juan Polo de Ondegardo. See Franklin Pease G. Y., *Las crónicas y los Andes* (Mexico City: Fondo de Cultura Económica, 1995), 34, 40, 126, 286, 353, 382, 432, 558, 569. So too do Gary Urton and Adriana Von Hagen in *Encyclopedia of the Incas* (New York: Rowman & Littlefield, 2015), 223.

people), or "brothers" (men and women capable of accepting Christianity and being "restored" to civility)?[23] In 1512, King Ferdinand convened a group of learned theologians and officials to debate the issue, and the resulting Laws of Burgos decisively declared Amerindians brothers—free and entitled to own property and receive wages for their labors and suited for instruction in the Catholic faith.[24]

One of the provisions of the Laws of Burgos was the Requirement, which called for an official proclamation to be read before any battle between Spaniards and Amerindians in the New World.[25] The document, usually spoken aloud in Latin or Castilian, demanded that the Indigenous people accept Christianity and the political authority of the king or face subjugation, enslavement, or death. According to the Requirement, failure to heed the summons to Christianity would lead the Spaniards to "take you and your wives and your children, and shall make slaves of them, and such shall sell and dispose of them as their Highnesses may command; and we shall take away your goods, and shall do all the harm and damage that we can, as to vassals who do not obey, and refuse to receive their lord, and resist and contradict him; and we protest that the deaths and losses which shall accrue from this are your fault, and not that of their Highnesses."[26] The absurdity of reading a document in a language that opponents did not understand provoked criticism then and now, and the Dominican Bartolomé de las Casas wrote that he did not know whether to laugh or to cry when he learned about the Requirement. Nonetheless, the Requirement actually drew on the Islamic ritual of demanding submission before engaging in a holy war, or *jihad*. According to this tradition, the prophet Muhammed would write to enemies before beginning a jihad: "Now I invite you to Islam (surrender to Allah)."[27] The Requirement was a Christian summons to convert to the "superior Christian faith" or face the consequences of war, which mimicked the Islamic warning given before beginning a holy war. It also served to justify the Spanish conquests and institutions such as the encomienda. No one knows how often the Requirement was read, but it remained unaltered for twenty years before the Crown and the conquistadors abandoned what they apparently viewed as a farcical practice.

---

[23] Elliott, *Empires of the Atlantic World*, 66; the characterization of the debate over the nature of the Amerindian about whether to consider them beasts, barbarians, or brothers was made by J. H. Elliott in a public lecture at the Ohio State University conference on "Early European Encounters with the Americas," held October 9–11, 1986.

[24] Elliott, *Empires of the Atlantic World*, 68. The pioneering work on this topic is Lewis Hanke, *The Spanish Struggle for Justice in the Conquest of the Americas* (Philadelphia: University of Pennsylvania Press, 1949).

[25] Clayton, *Bartolomé de las Casas*, 67.   [26] Hanke, *Spanish Struggle for Justice*, 33.

[27] Patricia Seed, *Ceremonies of Possession in Europe's Conquest of the New World, 1492–1640* (Cambridge: Cambridge University Press, 1995), 69–77.

Over the ensuing decades, reports of abuses perpetrated by the *encomenderos* against the Native American peoples cast doubt on the Crown's claims to secure the protection and evangelization of these Indigenous brothers. Quarrels among the *encomenderos* and the jealousy of those who did not receive a grant also threatened to impede order and stability in the Indies and even disrupt the evangelization process. Advocates of Amerindian rights, such as the Dominicans Bartolomé de las Casas and Domingo de Santo Tomás, urged the Crown to end the encomienda and grant the right to supervise the evangelization of Amerindians directly to the Church. Las Casas and his allies at court even persuaded King Charles I to issue the New Laws in 1542, which demanded an end to Amerindian slavery; that no Amerindian be sent without cause to labor in the mines; a just system of taxation for the Indigenous people; that encomiendas held by public officials revert to the Crown; and, most controversially, that all encomienda grants end with the life of the current holder. The New Laws stirred so much contentiousness that the viceroy of New Spain, Antonio de Mendoza, suspended enforcing them. In Peru, the New Laws prompted a rebellion of the *encomenderos*, led by Gonzalo Pizarro, who defeated and killed the first viceroy sent from Spain, Blasco Nuñez Vela. The king felt compelled to revoke the New Laws, but the debate over the encomienda and the evangelization of the Native peoples continued in Spain and the Indies.

Spanish intellectuals opposing the views of Las Casas, such as the king's chaplain Juan Ginés de Sepúlveda, argued (citing Aristotle) that "inferior" beings, such as the Indigenous peoples, were by nature slaves, not worthy or capable of becoming full citizens. This dispute reached a climax in 1550 when King Charles I convened a meeting in Valladolid, with both Las Casas and Sepúlveda on hand to debate the issue of Amerindian rights. After hearing both sides, the Crown eventually sided with Las Casas and suppressed Sepúlveda's views.[28] Two years later, Las Casas published his polemical denunciation of the conquest, *The Briefest Relation of the Destruction of the Indies*, which alleged all manner of abuses perpetrated by the conquistadors/*encomenderos* on the Indigenous population. After its landmark decision in favor of Las Casas and his position, the Crown reiterated its view that the Amerindians were free men, capable of conversion to Christianity. At the same time, the Indigenous people had the legal status of children (neophytes)—free people who could be made into good citizens, evangelized, and governed, but who also owed the Crown taxes and labor service. In this way, the Native American peoples occupied a subordinate position in an organic, hierarchically organized multiracial society,

---

[28] Elliott, *Empires of the Atlantic World*, 76–77.

governed first by *encomenderos* and later by Crown-appointed bureaucrats and instructed by the Church in the Roman Catholic faith.

Despite this Crown decision, some conquistadors, such as Bernal Díaz del Castillo, wrote detailed accounts of the conquest, defending the actions of the conquistadors and refuting the contentions of churchmen such as Bartolomé de las Casas.[29] Bernal Díaz was known at court, where he defended the encomienda and met his foe, Las Casas, around the time of the Valladolid debate.[30] The ostensible reason for writing his account at the age of eighty-four was "to extol our heroic feats and exploits in conquering New Spain," to present an eyewitness account of the common soldiers, and to correct the errors and exaggerations of earlier accounts by learned men, such as Francisco López de Gómara.[31] He shaped his account as an extended *probanza de méritos*, a legal document sent to the Crown to attain a reward for services to the king, normally complete with eyewitness testimony verifying the truthfulness of the assertions and certified by a notary. This narrative structure was meant to give readers greater confidence about the truth of the account. At the same time, Bernal Díaz wrote this document to refute the charges of clerics, particularly Las Casas, saying, "Those evil slanderers do not even want us to be given the preference and recompense His Majesty has ordered the viceroys, presidents, and governor to give."[32] To counter the charges of his critics, Bernal Díaz constantly explained that the conquistadors won only with the favor of God and that they continually strove to convert the Indigenous peoples, only fighting when first attacked. In short, the account of Bernal Díaz defended the conquest, extolled the bravery and religiosity of the conquistadors, and invoked divine favor, all to counter his enemies and win the favor of the king. In doing so, he minimized the violence and the greed displayed by the conquistadors in this early period of Spanish colonialism.

In keeping with the Crown's position after the Valladolid debate, royal officials in the New World separated the Indigenous peoples into a subordinate, legal corporate category, the República de Indios, giving them access to their traditional landholdings in return for paying a head tax, or tribute, and serving

---

[29] The account of Bernal Díaz del Castillo was a much more sophisticated account of the conquest of New Spain, which has been translated into numerous English-language editions, such as the recent work by Bernal Díaz del Castillo, *The True History of the Conquest of New Spain*, trans. and intro. Jane Burke and Tod Humphrey (London: Hackett, 2012). The much less polished work of Bernardo de Vargas Machuca has been translated recently; see Bernardo de Vargas Machuca, *Defending the Conquest: Bernardo de Vargas Machuca's Defense and Discourse of the Western Conquests*, ed. Kris Lane, trans. Timothy Johnson (State College: Pennsylvania State University Press, 2010). The link between such accounts and the denunciations of Las Casas are made most clearly and eloquently by Rolena Adorno in *The Polemics of Possession in Spanish American Narrative* (New Haven, CT: Yale University Press, 2007).

[30] Clayton, *Bartolomé de Las Casas*, 347.

[31] Díaz del Castillo, *True History*, 1.   [32] Ibid., 2.

periodic labor service. The payment of tribute indicated that the Indigenous people of the Indies were subjugated vassals of the Crown. The Crown limited the freedom of movement of the Indigenous peoples, but granted them access to Spanish courts, the right to military protection, and the privilege of instruction in Roman Catholicism. Much like the Jews and Muslims under Christian rule during the Reconquista, Indigenous people in the New World were allowed to adhere to their own community laws (as long as they did not conflict with Spanish law or Roman Catholic orthodoxy). They were also ruled by traditional ethnic leaders (called *caciques* by Spaniards), who served as intermediaries between the Indigenous communities and Spanish officials, much as Muslim and Jewish officials had during the Reconquista. The Spanish *encomenderos*, and later Crown-appointed bureaucrats, supervised the collection of taxes and the assignment of labor service. These Spanish officials also oversaw the interaction between Indigenous communities and the República de Españoles, formed by Spaniards from Iberia, people of Spanish descent born in the Indies (called Creoles), people of mixed ancestry (*castas*), and free and enslaved Africans. The República de Españoles was subject to the laws of Castile, with its own privileges but also obligations, such as paying taxes and serving the Crown. These were fundamentally legal categories, however, and interaction between Spaniards and Indigenous peoples was commonplace, leading to a growing number of people of mixed blood, particularly in urban areas.

Although Roman Catholic clergymen such as Bartolomé de las Casas tried to defend the rights of Amerindians, Spaniards in the New World frequently enslaved the Indigenous peoples of the Indies. The Crown allowed the enslavement of captives taken in a "just war"; it did not even outlaw Amerindian slavery permanently until the New Laws of 1542. Nonetheless, Spaniards used legal loopholes to enslave many thousands of Indigenous people over the course of the sixteenth century, sometimes even taking them to Spain. Enslaved Indigenous people, captured in the Indies, were visible on the streets of Spanish cities, particularly Seville, identified by the royal *R* or *G* brand on their faces. After the passage of the New Laws, the Crown empowered Gregorio López Tovar, a lawyer on the Council of the Indies, to conduct an inspection to verify the legal status of Amerindians residing in the archbishopric of Seville. López investigated numerous cases in the region of Seville and freed over one hundred formerly enslaved individuals.[33] Nonetheless, the enslavement of Indigenous peoples continued, particularly along the northern frontier of Mexico, where Spaniards used the excuse of fighting a just war to take captives, which they then sold throughout the Caribbean and in the frontier regions. Spaniards also

---

[33] Nancy E. van Deusen, *Global Indios: The Indigenous Struggle for Justice in Sixteenth-Century Spain* (Durham, NC: Duke University Press, 2015), 98–124.

bought enslaved Indigenous people captured by hostile Amerindian ethnic groups, who actively participated in enslaving enemies and selling them to other tribes or to Spanish colonists. Such practices continued along the frontiers with little official interference into the nineteenth century.

The Emerging Colonial Socioeconomic Order

To ensure Spanish control in the populous central regions of Mexico and the Andes, the conquistadors either founded cities or transformed existing Indigenous cities as centers of control, much like in Iberia when they captured cities previously ruled by Muslim polities during the Reconquista. They even founded some of these colonial urban centers on the site of Indigenous capitals, such as Tenochtitlan and Cusco, and modeled them on famous European urban spaces, like Seville or Naples. On August 13, 1521, for example, the Spanish ruling elite founded Mexico City on what they claimed were the ruins of the depopulated former Mexica capital. The new capital city would have a central plaza, with the governor's palace, a Roman Catholic cathedral, and the building of the city governing council, or *cabildo*. Nonetheless, after the fall of Tenochtitlan, a city of perhaps 100,000 to 150,000 residents before the Spanish invasion, the city's Indigenous residents did return; despite the epidemics that plagued the capital city in the 1560s, it had an Indigenous population of around 75,000.[34] Even the pre-Columbian division of Tenochtitlan/Mexico City into four Indigenous sectors of Moyotlan, Teopan, Atzacoalco, and Cuepopan endured, with Indigenous portions of the city governed by a local Indigenous cabildo and a governor, drawn from the Mexica elite. Traditional Mexica religious festivals, adapted to Roman Catholic rituals, also continued. In fact, on June 28, 1575, the Indigenous governor of the city, Antonio de Valeriano, flanked by the Mexica mayors (*alcaldes*), appeared before the Spanish cabildo of Mexico City. They petitioned the city to allocate a large sum of money for the construction of an aqueduct to supply water from Chapultepec to the city's southwestern quadrant, particularly the large Indigenous marketplace (*tianguis*). The viceroy supported the plan, and despite the amounts involved in the construction, the Spanish cabildo reluctantly approved the costly project.[35] In Tenochtitlan/Mexico City, the conquistadors did not destroy the Indigenous city. Instead, a hybrid urban space evolved that was both European and Mexican.

---

[34] This paragraph is drawn from Barbara E. Mundy, *The Death of Aztec Tenochtitlan and the Life of Mexico City* (Austin: University of Texas Press, 2015), 79–80.
[35] Ibid., 190–93.

While the Spanish conquistadors built the capital of New Spain on the preexisting Aztec capital, Francisco Pizarro founded a new capital city, the City of the Kings, or Lima, on the coast of the Viceroyalty of Peru. Indigenous men and women came to the city in search of work and opportunity. Males usually migrated as young adults to work as laborers or in a variety of lower-skilled positions. Initially, Spanish authorities tried to confine the city's Indigenous residents to the parish of San Lázaro, but over time the Amerindians spread throughout the city. Urban society in Lima offered opportunities for social mobility, and Indigenous men became fishermen, shoemakers, artisans, silversmiths, scribes, and tailors. Many Indigenous women originally came to Lima as domestic servants, but like their male counterparts, they could learn Castilian, join religious sodalities, and engage in petty industry or commerce, such as selling *chicha* and foodstuffs and weaving or sewing. The more prosperous Indigenous citizens of Lima also advanced credit, employed poorer residents, and even owned enslaved individuals.[36] A new and growing city offered opportunities to participate in and prosper from the emerging markets of the Peruvian coast. In this environment, large numbers of Indigenous people became more Hispanicized and Christian, interacting with the Spanish and African populations of the bustling viceregal capital.

By the middle of the sixteenth century, the encomienda system began to decline in the wealthy, densely populated central areas of Mexico and Peru, although it persisted for longer periods along the frontiers of the empire. Squabbles among the fractious conquistadors led to disorder, particularly in Peru, and the onset of European epidemic diseases dramatically reduced the Amerindian population in the central zones of the Spanish Indies. In Mexico, for example, the Indigenous population declined from 20 to 25 million before the European invasion in 1519 to under 1.5 million a century later.[37] This demographic disaster depleted what had been extremely lucrative encomiendas. Moreover, Crown authorities wanted to limit the political and economic power of the often-unruly *encomenderos*, while many Church officials wanted to gain control over evangelizing the Indigenous peoples. The rise of new colonial cities, such as Lima, and the discovery of fabulously rich gold and especially silver mines—such as Zacatecas (1546), Guanajuato (1550), and Sombrete (1558) in New Spain and at Carabaya (pre-Columbian), Potosí (1549), and Oruro (1608) in the Viceroyalty of Peru—also attracted a new influx of migrants from Castile. Many of these newer settlers resented the political, social, and economic

---

[36] Karen M. Graubart, *With Our Labor and Sweat: Indigenous Women and the Formation of Colonial Society in Peru, 1550–1700* (Stanford, CA: Stanford University Press, 2007), 63–92.

[37] Woodrow Borah and Sherburne Cook, *The Aboriginal Population of Mexico on the Eve of the Spanish Conquest* (Berkeley: University of California Press, 1963), pp. 4, 88.

dominance of those first conquistadors, who monopolized the encomiendas and access to wealth and labor.

The Spanish conquistadors of the sixteenth century sought sources of wealth esteemed in their homeland, and they found it in large deposits of precious metals (particularly silver), rich lands, and dense Amerindian populations, whose labor would help exploit these resources. To the Spanish conquistadors and later settlers, precious metals promised wealth, social advancement, and security, which would allow Spain to assert its military power to stop the splintering of Christendom and fight the dual threats of Protestantism and Islam.[38] On a practical level, Europeans viewed precious metals as a valuable commercial commodity (in great demand in the Far East). Gold and silver were also important for metallic currency that facilitated economic exchanges and were valued as a form of elite adornment, particularly in jewelry. By controlling the source of precious metals in the Indies, Spain thus added to its own wealth and power, while depriving its European enemies of control over these valuable resources. To extract this wealth, Spanish settlers needed to harness the labor of the Indigenous populations of central Mexico and the Andes to mine these reservoirs of silver and gold, while the rich lands of these regions provided the food, transport animals, and other supplies needed to sustain the mines and their Indigenous laborers. In short, gold and silver equaled wealth and power to enrich the Spanish settlers and metropolitan Spain, enhance trade, and advance Roman Catholic orthodoxy.

The mining cities of the Indies grew rapidly as Spaniards mustered the necessary resources to extract the rich supplies of gold and silver. The new mining city of Potosí in Upper Peru (Bolivia) grew to 160,000 inhabitants by 1611. The productivity of Potosí's silver mines benefited greatly from the amalgamation process, using mercury in refining ore to increase the volume of silver extracted from base rock. This burgeoning mining city was supplied by llama trains (*trajines*) carrying a range of locally produced goods, foodstuffs, and European wares.[39] Since the region had been largely uninhabited before the town's founding in 1549, Spanish officials created an elaborate forced labor system based on the Inca system of cyclical state corvée labor or *m'ita* (Hispanicized as *mita*). Viceroy Francisco de Toledo (1569–81) organized the mita, which originally intended to send over thirteen thousand laborers from as far away as Cusco each year to labor in the mines of Potosí. Mita laborers often performed the

---

[38] For an excellent comparison of how the English viewed gold and silver in this period, see Gallay, *Walter Raleigh*, 364–66.

[39] Luis Miguel Glave, *Trajinantes: Caminos indígenas en la sociedad colonial, siglos XVI/XVII* (Lima: Instituto de Apoyo Agrario, 1989).

more dangerous low-skill jobs such as ore cutters or carriers, who ascended long rope ladders out of the mine shaft with heavy sacks of ore on their backs. A smaller mita provided a steady stream of laborers at the Peruvian mercury mine at Huancavelica. Potosí also attracted large numbers of wage laborers (called *mingas*), who were often mita labors who chose to take higher-skilled jobs that paid better wages after learning how to work in the mines. Often accompanying the forced (mita) and wage (*minga*) laborers to the city, Indigenous women dominated the city's marketplace, selling everything from foodstuffs to *chicha* and offering credit to workers and their families.[40]

Working conditions at the Potosí mines were punishing, with workers frequently laboring underground for much of the week. Cave-ins and other accidents at the mines happened, leading to the maiming or death of Indigenous workers. Bad ventilation at the mines and working underground for several days led many mine workers to contract silicosis, a lung disease caused by inhaling tiny pieces of glass-like rocks. According to one critic, Potosí was a "fierce beast" that swallowed workers alive.[41] Working at the mills processing silver ore was equally dangerous and potentially deadly because exposure to clouds of silica dust, mercury, lead, and zinc sickened many. Working the hydraulic and horse-powered ore-crushing machines could also lead to broken bones or even death for Indigenous workers. Toxic mercury fumes at the Huancavelica mercury mines produced serious long-term health risks for workers. It is no small wonder that contemporaries referred to Potosí's rich hill as "Blood Mountain."[42]

In the north Andes, the Crown also allocated forced laborers to work in the woolen textile mills (called *obrajes*) of the region, where the worst working conditions paralleled those at Potosí. In the mill at San Ildefonso in Ambato, the local *encomendero*, Antonio López de Galarza, forced Indigenous workers from the town of Pelileo to work in what locals called a "torture chamber." Indigenous men, women, children, and even elderly people were commonly beaten, whipped, starved, shackled to their workstations, deprived of sleep, and even locked in a dungeon at night. When workers escaped, Galarza and his henchmen forced family members to substitute for them. To replace those who died or escaped, enslaved people working at the mill kidnapped Indigenous adults and even children. Each worker had to meet a quota, and those who

---

[40] Much of this material on Potosí is drawn from an excellent book by Jane E. Mangan, *Trading Rolls: Gender, Ethnicity, and the Urban Economy in Colonial Potosí* (Durham, NC: Duke University Press, 2005), especially 48–75.
[41] Kris Lane, *Potosí: The Silver City That Changed the World* (Berkeley: University of California Press, 2019), 74.
[42] Ibid., 78.

failed to do so suffered a variety of severe punishments, most commonly whippings. The workers frequently contracted debts, which bound them to the mill until they or their family members repaid the deficit. Mill owners often failed to provide food and clothing, so workers had to rely on family members for necessities. Indigenous kinsmen, particularly women, worked alongside their children to help meet the quotas. Workers without family support too often died of starvation, overwork, illness, or excessive beatings.[43]

Mines in New Spain were located in more remote northern provinces, but early on, Indigenous workers sold their labor for wages and forced labor became rare, since working conditions were apparently better than in many Andean mines or obrajes. Slave labor endured at some sites, however, such as the remote northern mining city of Parral.[44] The most pressing problem in exploiting these silver deposits was defending the long supply lines from central Mexico to the northern mines from hostile Amerindian raiders, whom the Spaniards called Chichimecas. These fierce warriors resisted Spanish settlement on their lands, prompting a prolonged, intermittent conflict in the present-day Bajío region, from 1550 to the 1590s. As a result, Crown officials from 1560 began to establish missions, military bases (called *presidios*), and new towns, often populated by peaceful, Christian Indigenous groups from central Mexico. The staunchest allies of Fernando Cortés, the Tlaxcalans, sent settlers to northern Mexico, Texas, and even New Mexico, where they established towns along with Catholic missionaries. From the 1520s, the Crown encouraged peaceful Otomí Indigenous groups to settle the region around Querétaro. These towns served as a military bastion protecting the trade routes from the silver mines to Mexico City, but the prosperity of Tlaxcalan settlements also attracted Chichimeca groups who wanted to settle, farm, and gain protection from other enemy groups. The Crown's plan was to use the Tlaxcalans and the Otomí as a civilizing force in the region, who could teach the migratory hunters of the north how to be sedentary, Christian members of society in New Spain.[45] Despite Crown efforts to secure the frontiers of the Indies, these regions had few mineral or other natural resources, and they remained barely under Crown control.

---

[43] Rachel Corr, *Interwoven: Andean Lives in Colonial Ecuador's Textile Economy* (Tucson: University of Arizona Press, 2018), 40–51.

[44] Andrés Reséndez, *The Other Slavery: The Uncovered Story of Indian Enslavement in America* (Boston: Houghton Mifflin Harcourt, 2016), 115.

[45] The most important works dealing with settling the frontiers of New Spain with Indigenous allies are Sean F. McEnroe, *From Colony to Nationhood in Mexico: Laying the Foundations, 1560–1840* (Cambridge: Cambridge University Press, 2012); and John Tutino, *Making a New World: Founding Capitalism in the Bajío and Spanish North America* (Durham, NC: Duke University Press, 2011), especially 63–120.

The Crown and the Imposition of a Castilian Political and Institutional Order

In contrast to frontier zones, the populous central regions of Mexico and the Andes exploited and profited from resources such as silver mining, which shaped the political and institutional culture of the sixteenth-century Spanish Indies. Silver was a valuable asset but it could be easily stolen, smuggled, or sold illicitly. The Spaniards also had to govern large, wealthy, sedentary Amerindian populations living in central regions who could not be ignored, pushed aside, or simply isolated on reservations. Besides, they served as a needed labor force to exploit the resources valued by the Spanish settlers. As the power of the *encomenderos* waned, the Crown sent bureaucrats, churchmen, and other settlers to rule, convert, and populate the newly acquired lands, supplanting the conquistadors. These bureaucrats and clergymen attempted to impose the governmental and religious system of Iberia implanted by Ferdinand and Isabel at the end of the Reconquista. In Spain, the Crown established the Casa de la Contratación, or Board of Trade (1503), to control colonial commerce, gather navigational information, license travelers crossing the Atlantic, and inspect cargos entering Seville to see that foreigners did not participate clandestinely in commerce with the Indies and that everyone paid the proper duties. The Crown established the Council of the Indies in 1524, just three years after the fall of the Aztec Empire brought millions of Indigenous people and vast resources under royal control. The council served as a court of appeals in civil cases, a legislative body, and an executive authority to enforce laws for the Indies. The Council of the Indies also recommended legislation for the king's approval, dispatched royal inspectors to the Indies to ensure good governance, and served as a court of appeals in civil cases heard before colonial courts.

In America, the Crown set up an extensive bureaucracy to rule the newly conquered lands, headed by a viceroy in each of the two major political units, the Viceroyalties of New Spain and Peru (see Figs. 2.3 and 2.4). New Spain encompassed all the lands in southern portions of what are now the United States, the Caribbean, Mexico, and Central America to the borders of current-day Panama. The Viceroyalty of Peru included all the territory from Panama to the southern tip of South America, except for Brazil, which fell under Portuguese control. The viceroy was the king's personal representative in the New World—the supreme military commander, the chief executive authority—and as a member of the high court of the capital cities of Lima and Mexico City, he could issue laws, subject to Crown approval (called *bandos*). The viceroy exercised significant control over patronage to Crown offices in the Indies, whether he appointed some local bureaucrats directly, made interim appointments (pending Crown approval), or influenced the selection of officials named

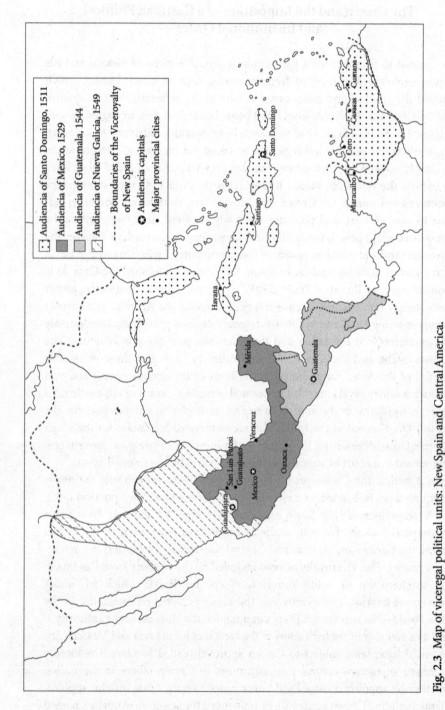

Fig. 2.3 Map of viceregal political units: New Spain and Central America.

Source: Adapted from Cathryn L. Lombardi, John V. Lombardi, with K. Lynn Stoner, *Latin American History: A Teaching Atlas* (Madison: University of Wisconsin Press, 1983), p. 28.

Fig. 2.4 Map of viceregal political units: South America and Panama.
Source: Adapted from Cathryn L. Lombardi, John V. Lombardi, with K. Lynn Stoner, *Latin American History: A Teaching Atlas* (Madison: University of Wisconsin Press, 1983), p. 29.

in Madrid. Governing in the Indies relied on the viceroy and those loyal retainers (*criados*), who accompanied him in his entourage to the New World. Once installed in office, a successful viceroy would place retainers in key bureaucratic positions, where they would establish ties of clientage and corruption and even marry into local elite families to govern successfully. This also gave the viceroy a vehicle for gauging the concerns and attitudes of local elites, so that he could make more informed decisions that were more sensitive to local concerns. All sides profited handsomely from such political arrangements.

Within these two massive territorial units, the metropolitan government founded a series of high courts, called *audiencias* (six in Peru and four in New Spain), to hear civil and criminal cases (for the jurisdiction of the *audiencias*). The Council of the Indies could hear appeals of decisions in civil matters; *audiencia* rulings in criminal cases were final. These key justices also forged ties to local elites and often the viceroy to gain power, exert influence over local affairs, and enrich themselves. The courts in the capitals of Lima and Mexico City were the most prestigious of the *audiencias*, and the justices there were the best paid, but in practice each *audiencia* operated as an independent court of law. These justices worked with the viceroys to enforce legislation sent from Spain and to issue any necessary laws dealing with local matters. The Crown effectively used this bureaucracy to annex the Indies and subordinate it to the laws of Castile. In the sixteenth century, judicial authority was deemed superior to administrative and legislative responsibilities, so members of the *audiencia* usually had advanced degrees in the law.

To limit the regional power of the *encomenderos*, authorities in Spain created a network of Crown-appointed rural magistrates (*corregidores de indios*) to regulate contact between Spaniards and Amerindians, to collect the head tax or tribute, and to oversee the assignment of forced (corvée) labor service for state projects. The *corregidores de indios* were the link regulating all political and economic ties between the Spanish and caste populations and the Indigenous communities. The Crown also established a network of treasury offices in all major ports, mining centers, and agricultural zones to collect royal taxes levied on colonial subjects. Magistrates (*corregidores de españoles*) also served in municipalities to hear court cases and to regulate local affairs in conjunction with the city council (cabildo). During the previous century, Isabel had used these officials to limit the power of the nobility in Spain at the end of the Reconquista. Only Spaniards and Creoles could hold offices in the Crown bureaucracy, and candidates for such offices had to prove that they were old Christians, untainted by Jewish, Muslim, or later Indigenous and African blood. These officials served at the regional and local levels to implement policies of the Crown, the viceroys, and the *audiencias*, but they became notorious for corruption, influence peddling, and embezzling tax money at the local level to enrich themselves.

As colonial trade grew during the sixteenth century, the Crown promulgated strict regulations on the flow of goods to and from the Indies. Commerce was funneled through Spain's Atlantic port of Seville (and after 1717 through Cádiz) and policed by the Casa de la Contratación, which inspected ship cargos from the Indies to ensure that everyone had paid Crown-levied taxes on imported goods and to search for contraband. The Crown also established a series of licensed ports in the Indies, under the watchful eye of Crown-appointed treasury officials at these port cities.[46] From 1564, all trade went in legally sanctioned annual convoys (*flotas y galeones*) dispatched from Seville to designated locations, where trade fairs held at Veracruz, Cartagena, and Portobelo exchanged European wares for colonial products, particularly silver.[47] Merchant guilds (*consulados*) in Seville, Mexico City, and Lima regulated commercial transactions in the transatlantic trade between Spain and the Indies. The system was designed by mercantilist officials, who aimed to protect colonial markets from outside penetration and to direct resources from the Indies to metropolitan Spain. In short, by the first decade of the seventeenth century, the turbulent early years of the Spanish invasion and conquest of the New World gave way to a more stable colonial political, economic, and religious order that reflected the political and institutional culture envisaged by the Spanish Crown.

The Crown and its bureaucrats in the New World designed this government to plan and manage the emerging colonial societies and economies. This ambitious plan involved more than merely governing. Through the Crown's labor, tax, and commercial policies, the colonial regimes attempted to redirect the flow of labor and goods from the Indies to Europe, thereby siphoning the wealth of the Indies to meet the military and economic needs of Spain. This effectively created a new colonial society that relied on the labor and taxes of the densely populated Indigenous societies of the Andes and central Mexico. The colonial regime also deprived Indigenous ethnic communities of access to political power and forced their conversion to Christianity. The basic institutional structure of the colonial system took form under the viceregency of Martín Enríquez in New Spain (1568–80) and Francisco de Toledo in Peru (1569–81). Both men built a strong, effective colonial state (on the foundations established by their predecessors) meant to siphon the wealth of the Indies to bolster the monarchy in its struggles for hegemony in Europe.

All subordinate treasuries in the Viceroyalties of New Spain and Peru sent surplus income to treasury offices in the capitals of Mexico City and Lima, called the *cajas matriz*. Treasury income in Lima fluctuated between 1580 and 1610 from under 2,250,000 pesos de ocho (or 272 maravedís) and nearly 4,250,000 pesos. Mexico City's treasury collected lesser amounts, fluctuating between nearly 1,225,000 pesos de ocho and 2,750,000 pesos during this same

---

[46] By 1717, the merchant guild moved from Seville to Cádiz. Clarence Haring, *The Spanish Empire in America* (New York: Harcourt, Brace & World, 1952), 302.

[47] The fleets seldom sailed annually, and by the early eighteenth century the intervals between fleets could be more than a decade. See Geoffrey Walker, *Spanish Politics and Imperial Trade, 1700–1789* (Bloomington: Indiana University Press, 1979).

period.[48] The royal bureaucracy established by the Crown was clearly functioning well, collecting large amounts of revenue mostly from taxes on mining production, but other lucrative tax levies included Amerindian tribute, taxes on commerce, and royal monopolies. Beginning in the 1580s, these two central treasuries remitted large amounts of revenue to Castile, normally accounting for approximately 36 percent of expenditures (Mexico City), and remittances reached 51 percent from Lima (1607–1610).[49] In short, the royal government apparatus made large profits by the late sixteenth and early seventeenth centuries and treasury officials in the viceregal capitals sent a significant percentage of this income to Madrid. Spanish colonialism paid rich financial dividends to the Crown.

The Roman Catholic Church and Evangelization

While the Crown profited from the wealth of the Indies, it entrusted Roman Catholic clergymen with evangelizing and ministering to the Amerindians in the two viceroyalties. At first, the religious orders—primarily the Franciscans, Dominicans, Augustinians, and Mercedarians, and later the Jesuits—played a leading role in evangelizing the Indigenous peoples.[50] The first official mission to New Spain began on May 13, 1524, when twelve Franciscan friars (corresponding to the first twelve apostles) arrived to begin evangelizing the Native peoples. Over time, members of the secular clergy established parishes under the overall supervision of prelates (seven in New Spain and eight in Peru).[51] The regular orders maintained a number of rural parishes, and they kept missions in the frontier zones of the empire. Over the years, however, the Crown tended to favor the secular clergy. The pope had given the Spanish king control over a share (two-ninths) of the tithes paid to the Church in 1501, as well as the right to submit a rank-ordered list of candidates, from which the pope would

---

[48] John J. TePaske and Herbert S. Klein, "The Seventeenth Century Crisis in New Spain: Myth or Reality," *Past and Present* 90 (February 1981): 121.

[49] Ibid., 133; John J. TePaske and Herbert S. Klein, *The Royal Treasuries of the Spanish Empire in America*, vol. 1, Peru (Durham, NC: Duke University Press, 1982), 290–303; and Andrien, *Crisis and Decline*, 67.

[50] The orders were called *regular clergy* because they lived according to the rules, or *regula*, established by the founder of the order. In Europe, the religious orders most commonly lived communally in religious houses or monasteries. Charles Gibson, *Spain in America* (New York: Harper & Row, 1966), 77.

[51] In contrast to the religious orders, the secular clergy ministered directly to the laity, or *saeculum*, and they were subject to the authority of the local bishop. The secular clergy were composed of the hierarchy of bishops, the cathedral chapters, and the parish clergy. The archbishoprics of Lima in Peru and Mexico City in New Spain were the central seat of clerical power in the New World. Ibid.

choose bishops in the Indies in 1508. These privileges were a reward to the Spanish Crown for the huge potential influx of new Indigenous converts brought into the Catholic Church, making the Spanish conquest of the Indies like extending the crusading aspects of the Reconquista to new lands outside Iberia.[52] In New Spain, for example, the Crown expanded the number of secular dioceses beyond Mexico City (1527) to include Guatemala (1534), Oaxaca (1535), Michoacan, (1536), Chiapas (1538), and Guadalajara (1548). With each new diocese, the Church created a distinct ecclesiastical governing structure, subject to canon law, and the bishop was responsible for supervising all the secular clergy in his jurisdiction. These parish priests administered the sacraments and oversaw the imposition of Roman Catholic orthodoxy in their parishes (*doctrinas*).[53] In 1574, the president of the Council of the Indies oversaw the passage of the Ordenanza del Patronazgo, which established public examinations for any secular clergymen to ensure that they were fluent in the Indigenous language of the laity and demanded that all priests live full-time in their parish.[54] The orders, who reported primarily to the heads of their order and the pope, always remained more independent of royal authority. Throughout the sixteenth century, Spaniards and Creoles dominated positions in both the regular and the secular clergy, and after some early experiments with admitting Amerindians as priests and friars, the orders generally excluded Indigenous peoples from taking holy orders.

The evangelization process sometimes ran into resistance from Indigenous communities unwilling to abandon their old deities, particularly in times of defeat, plague, and crisis. In New Spain, members of the Franciscan order recorded an exchange of speeches (called *coloquios*) with lords and spiritual leaders of Tenochtitlan, which demonstrated the sometimes-ambivalent response of the Mexica elite to Roman Catholicism. According to these men, "You also say that those we worship are not gods. This way of speaking is entirely new to us, and very scandalous.... There has never been a time remembered when they were not worshiped, honored, and esteemed.... It would be a fickle, foolish thing for us to destroy the most ancient laws and customs left by the first inhabitants of the land.... And we are accustomed to them and we have

---

[52] Haring, *Spanish Empire in America*, 167–70.
[53] John Frederick Schwaller, *The History of the Catholic Church in Latin America: From Conquest to Revolution and Beyond* (New York: New York University Press, 2011), 76–77.
[54] Stafford Poole, *Juan de Ovando: Governing the Spanish Empire in the Reign of Philip II* (Norman: University of Oklahoma Press, 2004), 150–52. Although it concerns New Spain, the key article on this law is John Frederick Schwaller, "The Ordenanza del Patronazgo in New Spain," *The Americas* 42, no. 3 (January 1986): 253–74. The law also called for replacing the regular orders with secular clergy in Indigenous parishes, but the orders convinced King Philip II to rescind the sections dealing with this matter, and the orders continued to administer their parishes.

them impressed on our hearts."[55] The Mexica lords ended with a warning to the Franciscans: "You should take care not to do anything to stir up or incite your vassals to some evil deed."[56]

While the Mexica lords were reluctant to abandon fully their old gods, the Maya of the Yucatan Peninsula apparently experimented with drawing spiritual power from traditional gods and the Christian God, a practice that many in the Roman Catholic hierarchy viewed as *idolatry*. The Yucatan Peninsula was densely populated with Maya, but there were no deposits of gold, silver, or other commodities that the Spaniards valued, so the region remained a frontier in New Spain. Local Franciscans, who arrived to convert the Maya, wielded greater power there than the few Crown officials and *encomenderos* in the region. Since the friars lacked the manpower to instruct all the Maya, after baptizing them, they taught the children of elite Mayans Catholic theology, to assist the friars in teaching Maya families Christian precepts. In 1562, however, the Franciscans discovered shocking evidence of human sacrifices, even on the altars of Catholic churches; in some cases, children had been tied to crosses and had their hearts extracted. Moreover, the friars found idols in caves and buried in churches, even under the altars.

The Franciscan leader Diego de Landa, who was a student of Maya history and culture, felt betrayed, particularly when he discovered that these idolatrous practices were often committed by the very elite Maya youths that the friars had trained and entrusted to assist them in evangelizing their people. Without any clear legal right to do so, Landa began an ad hoc inquisition, arresting and trying 4,500 Maya and subjecting many to judicial torture, which led to the deaths of 158 people. When the new bishop of the Yucatan, Francisco de Toral, arrived, he stopped the proceedings and eventually sent Diego de Landa to Spain for discipline for employing such extralegal punishments. Church authorities ultimately cleared Landa and later sent him back to the Yucatan as a bishop, but no further idolatry trials ensued. In all likelihood, this "idolatry" of the Maya represented their efforts to incorporate Catholic ritual and dogma into their own "superior" religious framework and culture.[57] Indigenous civilizations, such as the Yucatec Maya, had a long history of accepting the religious power from alien gods while retaining their own local deities. Christian priests, monks, and friars, however, demanded the complete abandonment of these so-called false deities once the Indigenous peoples had converted.

---

[55] Kenneth Mills, William B. Taylor, and Sandra Lauderdale Graham, *Colonial Latin America: A Documentary History* (Wilmington, DE: Scholarly Resources, 2002), 21–22.
[56] Ibid., 22.
[57] The idolatry trials and their aftermath are covered in detail by Inga Clendinnen, *Ambivalent Conquests: Maya and Spaniard in the Yucatan, 1517–1570* (Cambridge: Cambridge University Press, 1987), 57–92.

In Peru, Indigenous resistance to Catholicism even threatened to turn violent. A nativist millenarian movement called Taqui Onqoy (meaning "dancing sickness" in Quechua) came to the attention of Church authorities in 1564. According to adherents (*taquiongos*), the Andean gods were angry at the inattention of the Indigenous people, who had not made the necessary sacrifices to them, and they ordered that everyone purge the Andes of Spanish–Catholic impurities. According to followers of Taqui Onqoy, the traditional deities, called *huacas*, would enter the bodies of humans, making them talk, tremble, and dance. The *taquiongos* predicted a convulsive struggle to vanquish the Spaniards, their God, and any Andeans who would not renounce Christianity. Spanish authorities responded quickly and decisively to this threat, dispatching a dedicated and morally upright priest, Cristóbal de Albornoz, to capture and punish the *taquiongos*. In an anti-idolatry campaign that lasted two years, Albornoz arrested eight thousand participants and meted out punishments ranging from permanent exile for leaders to requiring that lesser participants serve local priests or receive mandatory religious instruction. The movement crumbled under the pressure, effectively ending this particular threat to evangelization.

In sixteenth-century Spain, images of Christ and the Virgin Mary reputed to be associated with miracles proliferated, but in the Indies, miraculous image shrines were not common until the 1570s. Statues and paintings of Jesus, Mary, and some saints were found in many places reputed to be sacred, but the link between such images and miracles was not yet strong. Church synods said little about images with miraculous reputations among the laity, and writings by monks, friars, and priests seldom dealt with image shrines. In New Spain, for example, churchmen documented only twenty-two such image shrines until the 1580s. In the first decades of the seventeenth century, however, the numbers of shrines associated with miraculous events increased dramatically.[58] The famous miracle of our Lady of Guadalupe and her imprint on the cloak of the Indian seer, Juan Diego, occurred in 1531, but the image and cult of Guadalupe really grew by the middle of the next century.[59]

The Church sought to impose religious orthodoxy in the Republica de Españoles in the Indies, much as it did between 1492 and 1525 in the Kingdoms of Spain. The Crown established the Holy Office of the Inquisition in Lima and Mexico City by 1570, followed by a third office in Cartagena in 1605.[60]

---

[58] William B. Taylor, *Theater of a Thousand Wonders: A History of Miraculous Images and Shrines in New Spain* (Cambridge: Cambridge University Press, 2016), 40–52.

[59] Ibid., 44.

[60] Historians rightly stress the monarchy's use of the Inquisition to police the behavior of *conversos* and Moriscos, but another major responsibility of the tribunal was to reform the Spanish Church, which had grown lax and materialistic. See Lynch, *New Worlds*, 1.

Clergymen had accompanied the original conquistadors, and the Church launched a moral crusade to evangelize all the Indigenous inhabitants of the central regions. The Church also sent missionaries to convert Amerindians in the frontier areas, such as Nueva Galicia (in northern New Spain) and Chile. Indeed, the Papal Donation of 1493 gave Spain the task of converting the Indigenous peoples of the New World, and the Spanish monarchy justified its continued occupation of the Indies because of the potential to reap a huge harvest of Amerindian souls. The Crown and the Church collectively attempted to create a Spanish Atlantic world that was Catholic, orthodox, and closed to what they perceived as pernicious outside religious and cultural influences, particularly Protestantism, Judaism, and Islam.

Overseas Expansion and the Advance of Science

The discovery of the Indies led to a series of breakthroughs in Iberian science, as the Crown championed advances in knowledge not viewed as a threat to Roman Catholic orthodoxy. Although Columbus believed to his death that he had discovered a sea route to Asia, it was soon apparent to most observers that the Indies was a new world, not predicted by European cosmographers. European Renaissance cosmography was the science that integrated classical intellectual traditions—Aristotelian natural philosophy, Euclidean geometry, and Ptolemaic geography—with the aim of providing a complete description and understanding of the universe.[61] The Spanish king could use the emerging political and religious institutions implanted in the Indies to gain the knowledge to understand the Indies, govern it more effectively, and profit from its bountiful resources. The Casa de la Contratación, for example, was a court that not only licensed travelers to the New World and adjudicated commercial disputes, but also hired cosmographers to compile navigational information and create maps to train pilots and sea captains traveling to the Indies. The Council of the Indies also collected navigational information. The potential discovery of new plants, animals, medicines, and other valuable resources also spurred scientific inquiry. The Spanish authorities not only cared about the availability of precious metals in the Indies, but also sought to profit from its other natural resources.

The president of the Council of the Indies, Juan de Ovando, began a more systematic compilation of information about the New World, and in 1572, he created the position of chief cosmographer-chronicler of the Council of the

---

[61] María M. Portuondo, *Secret Science: Spanish Cosmography and the New World* (Chicago: University of Chicago Press, 2009), 20-21.

Indies, appointing Juan López de Velasco to the position.[62] López de Velasco's duties included writing a history of the Indies, collecting information about the local geography and national resources, and censoring books about the New World. The Crown viewed this information as state secrets to be kept from Spain's rivals until the seventeenth century, when King Philip III allowed much of it to be published.

The Crown charged officials in the Indies—such as archbishops, bishops, clerics, viceroys, *audiencia* judges, governors, mayors, city council members, Indigenous clan leaders, captains, pilots, admirals, and even some ordinary citizens—with writing reports about the natural resources, flora, fauna, climate, and natural history of their particular region. These reports went directly to the Casa de la Contratación and the Council of the Indies, where Crown officials filed and analyzed them for their practical commercial and scientific information. The Casa de la Contratación and the Council of the Indies became a clearinghouse for useful scientific information about the Indies, which these officials could use to train pilots, captains, and others traveling to the Indies. Crown officials also wanted to find out which natural resources of the Indies had commercial value in Europe. *Cascarilla*, the bark of a small tree, for example, found in the Caribbean, the North Andes, and some other tropical locations, was rich in quinine and was used as a tonic, a stimulant, and a treatment for various types of fevers. Geographical knowledge of latitude and longitude allowed the Spaniards to make more accurate maps to travel more safely across the Atlantic and to settle territorial claims, such as where the line established by the Treaty of Tordesillas was located, dividing the areas of influence of Spain and Portugal. Moreover, the more Spanish officials learned about the New World, the more effectively they could govern and profit from the wealth of their new provinces.[63]

When the Spanish Crown appointed Juan López de Velasco, the king charged him with writing a definitive chronicle-atlas of the New World. King Philip had already commissioned not only maps of Spain's cities, but also a geographical map picturing Spain as single entity, under the control of the monarchy. The king wanted a similar geographical map of the Indies. To achieve this goal, López de Velasco created a survey (with fifty questions) concerning local history, natural history, economic data, trade, and navigational and geographical information, including maps of each locale. This questionnaire, known as the Relaciones Geográficas, was sent to officials in the New World, who had to answer the questions and produce the maps. In many cases, however, Crown

---

[62] Antonio Barrera-Osorio, *Experiencing Nature: The Spanish American Scientific Revolution* (Austin: University of Texas Press, 2006), 92; Portuondo, *Secret Science*, 172–83.

[63] Barrera-Osorio, *Experiencing Nature*, 91–94; Jorge Cañizares-Esguerra, *Nature, Empire, and Nation: Explorations of the History of Science in the Iberian World* (Stanford, CA: Stanford University Press, 2006), 14–45.

bureaucrats in the Indies delegated local priests and Indigenous clan leaders to answer the questions and draw the maps.[64]

By 1584, the Viceroyalty of New Spain had produced ninety-eight maps, most drawn by Native artists, but they were all utterly unsuitable for making a definitive chronicle-atlas for King Philip II. A map from the Relaciones Geográficas of Teozacoalco, for example, a remote Mixtec-speaking region in New Spain, features a circular map of the community with its boundaries defined by pictographic toponyms (see Fig. 2.5). The interior of the map has toponyms, stylized symbols for buildings, written notations in Castilian (probably inserted by a priest or local Spanish official), and the community's logographic place name as it was depicted in the Mixtec language. The figures on the left show Mixtec royal genealogies—ruling families composed of four separate dynasties. In short, the map represents an Indigenous vision of space and history, with the community at the center, with its hierarchical and ordered internal structure and the history of its ruling families. The map was not intended as the sort of territorial unit fenced in by geographical borders that López de Velasco had envisaged.[65] According to art historian Barbara Mundy, these maps showed "New Spain to be an archipelago of individual and separate communities, each with a unique sense of identity."[66] For López de Velasco, these Indigenous maps proved useless for fulfilling King Philip's charge to create a single master map of New Spain as a unified geographical entity under the control of the Spanish composite monarchy. Despite conveying important information about the people and places of his possessions across the Atlantic, the maps did not employ the sort of European geographical representations the king would have expected and wanted as a sign of his power throughout a united Spanish Atlantic world.

Scientific breakthroughs were a necessary component of Spanish overseas expansion, but the exchange of plants, animals, and microorganisms truly transformed life in both Spain and the Indies. In this so-called Columbian Exchange, products from the Americas circulated in Europe, Africa, and Asia and European, African, and Asian products traveled to the Americas, changing the diet, culture, commercial exchanges, and lifestyles of people throughout the Atlantic world and beyond. Products such as American pumpkins, peanuts, potatoes, corn, and tomatoes became mainstays of European diets, along with peppers, cacao, beans, and vanilla. European livestock—cattle, sheep, pigs, and horses—thrived in the Americas, along with grains such as wheat, rice, barley,

---

[64] Barbara E. Mundy, *The Mapping of New Spain: Indigenous Cartography and the Maps of the Relaciones Geográficas* (Chicago: University of Chicago Press, 1996), 17–44; Barrera-Osorio, *Experiencing Nature*, 94–98; Portuondo, *Secret Science*, 211–21, 292–94.
[65] Mundy, *Mapping of New Spain*, 112–17, 159–61, 165–66.   [66] Ibid., 214.

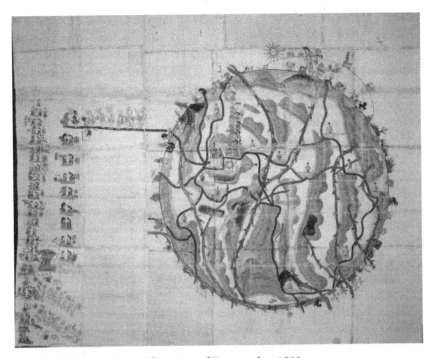

Fig. 2.5 Relaciones Geográficas Map of Teozacoalco, 1580.
Source: Benson Latin American Collection, The General Libraries, University of Texas at Austin (JGI xxv-3).

and oats, as well as new crops, such as sugar, bananas, grapes, and a variety of citrus fruits. Not all foreign imports had salutary consequences, however. European diseases such as smallpox, influenza, typhus, measles, malaria, and diphtheria led to a demographic catastrophe among the Indigenous people of the New World, who had no immunities to them. Many scholars postulate that syphilis may have originated in the Indies and spread through sexual contact to other parts of the world.[67]

Silver, Gold, and the Colonial Economic Order

The Crown bureaucracy in the Indies annually oversaw the mining and taxation of large quantities of gold and silver production. The decade-by-decade total of officially registered bullion output in gold outstripped that of silver

---

[67] The seminal work on the Columbian Exchange is Alfred W. Crosby, *The Columbian Exchange: Biological and Cultural Consequences of 1492* (Westport, CT: Greenwood Press, 1972).

until the 1540s, when silver mining began to dominate (see Fig. 2.6). The gold came first from the Caribbean and later from Chile, Ecuador, and Colombia. Silver lodes discovered in both the Viceroyalties of New Spain and Peru by the mid-sixteenth century led to this dramatic rise in output. Crown accounts of silver production rose from a low of 340,000 pesos of silver mined in the 1520s to over 100 million silver pesos in the 1580s, reaching a peak of 121,810,000 pesos in the period 1600–1610. Gold production during that period rose steadily until the 1530s to over 11 million pesos, then declined for two decades to the 1550s; it fluctuated between 10,180,000 and 12,750,000 pesos over the next eighty years. Thereafter, gold output began to fall. In the period when silver dominated the production of precious metals, the output of Spain's New World silver mines accounted for between 76 and 96 percent of all New World mining production. Gold remained the far scarcer metal, totaling 107,210,000 pesos during the entire period 1492 to 1610, while silver output reached 517,670,000 pesos, nearly five times as much, over the same span. These official figures do not account for contraband, which contemporaries estimated at 17 to 20 percent of the total mined annually.[68] Nonetheless, this influx of precious metals flowing into Europe, and also to bullion-starved markets in Asia, allowed Spanish and Portuguese merchants to secure luxury goods from China and India to sell in the Indies and Europe.

Years	Silver	Gold	Total
1492–1500	0	0.7	0.7
1501–1510	0	8.2	8.2
1511–1520	0	7.21	7.21
1521–1530	0.34	3.92	4.26
1531–1540	7.55	11.12	18.67
1541–1550	28.12	8.73	36.85
1551–1560	42.71	10.64	53.35
1561–1570	56.05	8.85	64.9
1571–1580	71.47	13	84.47
1581–1590	100.19	10.18	110.37
1591–1600	113.4	11.91	125.31
1601–1610	121.81	12.75	134.56

Fig. 2.6 New World Gold and Silver Output in millions of pesos of 272 Maravedis, 1492–1610.

Source: John J. TePaske and edited by Kendall W. Brown, *A New World of Gold and Silver* (Leiden and Boston, Brill, 2010), Tables 1–2, p. 20.

[68] These numbers are taken from J. TePaske, *New World of Gold and Silver*, Tables 1 and 2, 20. The numbers in their current form were published by Kenneth J. Andrien, "Economies, American: Spanish Territories," in *The Princeton Companion to Atlantic History*, ed. Joseph C. Miller et al. (Princeton, NJ: Princeton University Press, 2015), 170–74.

Despite the best efforts of Spain to monopolize commerce with the Indies, Genoese, French, English, and especially Portuguese traders penetrated colonial markets. Portuguese merchants, many of them Sephardic Jews who arrived after the expulsion of 1492, were particularly effective in trading enslaved Africans to the Spanish Indies. They opened a factory (*feitoria*) in Seville by 1500 to secure access to Andalusian wheat and wine for their African garrisons, which they exchanged for enslaved Africans, gold, and Asian spices. In the Indies, Portuguese merchant communities supplied enslaved individuals throughout the Spanish possessions, especially as the Amerindian population declined in the second half of the sixteenth century.[69] These commercial activities only expanded when Philip II inherited the Portuguese crown in 1580, after the childless king, Sebastian, was killed in battle on an ill-fated crusade to Morocco. When influential Portuguese nobles opposed the union with Spain, King Philip reinforced his claim by dispatching the Duke of Alba and 15,500 troops, who crossed the border on June 19, 1580. This sealed his case for uniting the thrones of Iberia under his rule.[70] The Spanish Crown tried to keep the imperial possessions of Spain and Portugal separate, just as King Philip attempted to govern Castile, Aragon, and Portugal according to their own laws and institutions, but this proved largely impossible in commercial matters. The diaspora of Portuguese merchants throughout the Spanish Atlantic world only accelerated its commercial ties in the Indies after the union of both Crowns. In Lima, for example, the Portuguese merchants were the largest foreign population in the city, and in Puerto Rico, they outnumbered the Castilian settlers. The settlement of Brazil only accelerated these commercial ties by mid-century and continued into the seventeenth century.[71]

Despite the incursions of Spain's rivals into commerce with the Indies, legal and contraband gold and silver by 1610 permitted the Spanish monarchy to pursue an aggressive foreign policy in Europe, leading to a series of expensive and ultimately unsuccessful wars with European rivals. The Castilian treasury's normal tax revenues barely met the normal operating expenses of the royal household and the government. Taxes returned from Aragon were even more meager and had to be approved by the *cortes* of each of the Aragonese realms. Extraordinary expenses such as war had to be financed by borrowing from bankers throughout Europe. The influx of gold and especially silver from the Indies allowed King Charles I (1516–56) and his son Philip II (1556–98) to use this unpledged income as collateral for loans. The largest legal imports of

---

[69] Wheat, *Atlantic Africa*, 181–216.
[70] Geoffrey Parker, *Imprudent King: A New Life of Philip II* (New Haven, CT: Yale University Press, 2014), 270.
[71] Daviken Studnicki-Gizbert, *A Nation upon the Ocean Sea: Portugal's Atlantic Diaspora and the Crisis of the Spanish Empire, 1492–1640* (Oxford: Oxford University Press, 2007), 17–39.

precious metals came in the latter half of Philip II's reign, which allowed him to finance his wars in Italy, Flanders, and Germany, including his outfitting of the disastrous voyage of the Great Armada in 1588, which aimed to invade England. During the reign of Philip II, the financial burdens of these wars forced the Crown to declare bankruptcy three times. These expensive wars drained capital from Spain to foreign bankers, particularly in northern Europe. As a result, precious metals did not develop or diversify the economic base of Spain by 1610, contributing to the political and economic decline of the metropolis later in the century. Ironically, this influx of precious metals from the Indies both produced the rise of northern European capitalism and encouraged disastrous military entanglements, which contributed to the overall decline of Spain in the seventeenth century.

From the early seventeenth century, commerce in legal and contraband goods in the Indies was organized around a series of internal regional markets connected to the emerging economy of the Atlantic world.[72] The introduction of European-style market exchanges began slowly at first, but the discovery of gold and particularly silver led to an accelerated expansion and integration of regional market economies by the late sixteenth century. Historian James Lockhart used a railroad metaphor to describe this expanding network of colonial markets and their links to the wider world.[73] The central transportation route for railroads is the trunk line, with smaller, subsidiary feeder lines connected to it. In New Spain, the principal avenue for market exchanges, or trunk line, extended through the port city of Veracruz to Puebla and Mexico City. It then moved northward to the major mining districts, particularly Zacatecas. Feeder lines proceeded southward to Oaxaca and Guatemala, east to Yucatan, and west to Acapulco. In the Viceroyalty of Peru, the trunk line was more abstract. It went from the viceregal capital of Lima, first by sea to Arica and then inland through Arequipa and the populous Indigenous zones of Bolivia, to its terminus at the silver mines at the famous "red mountain" of Potosí. Feeder lines extended north to Quito, south to Chile, and east to Cusco. The products of economic exchanges along the Peruvian trunk and feeder lines were then shipped by sea to Panama and transported by river and overland across the isthmus to Portobelo on the Caribbean coast. In this way, the goods produced in the Pacific trading zone became a vital component in the Spanish Atlantic

---

[72] The emphasis on the relationship between internal markets and international trade was the subject of a pioneering study by Carlos Sempat Assadourian, *El sistema de la economía colonial: El mercado interior, regiones, y espacio económico* (Mexico City: Editorial Nueva Imagen, 1983).
[73] James Lockhart, "Trunk Lines and Feeder Lines: The Spanish Reaction to American Resources," in Andrien and Adorno, *Transatlantic Encounters*, 90–120.

world.[74] These awkward series of trade routes paid little attention to geographical realities or economic rationality, particularly the Peruvian trading system. Nonetheless, it made sense to mercantilists in Spain seeking to control markets, maximize wealth (particularly bullion), and keep out their European rivals. Any Spanish or Indigenous communities located along the trunk line became progressively drawn into market exchanges, while those on the smaller, subsidiary feeder lines took longer to feel the influence of the new economic order.

The Mysterious Catalina: Indian or Spaniard?

By the early seventeenth century, the Caribbean was far from the centers of political power, dense Amerindian populations, and mineral wealth in the Spanish Indies, yet it was a strategic area protecting the sea lanes to Mexico and northern South America. The commercial hub of the region was Havana, Cuba, where the *flotas* and *galeones* reunited to get provisions for the return voyage to Seville. It was in Havana that a series of imbroglios began involving Crown officials; a well-heeled notary, Francisco de Ludeña; his family; and an enigmatic servant girl, who were waiting for the fleet to take on water and provisions for the trip back to Spain. While in the city, local Crown authorities detained Ludeña for taking an Amerindian servant named Catalina to Spain, a practice strictly forbidden by Crown law. Bureaucrats in Havana frequently tried to extract bribes or confiscate goods from travelers returning to Spain to supplement their meager salaries, but the case of this young servant girl proved particularly complicated. For his part, Ludeña claimed that Catalina was a Spanish woman entrusted to his care, while his accusers contended that her lowly status as a servant, her appearance (dark skinned and short), and her lack of an education or refinement proved that she was an Amerindian from Cartagena, where Ludeña had worked for several years.

The city constable, Francisco Báez, denounced the royal notary and filed charges, complaining that Ludeña had planned to transport a seventeen-year-old Amerindian servant girl to Spain. The accusation was so serious that authorities jailed Ludeña and sequestered his property before he could leave. Báez found a series of witnesses willing to testify against the wealthy notary from Cartagena. When questioned about her identity, Catalina at first said that

---

[74] The trade with the Far East through Manila was only tangentially related to the Atlantic trade, but one recent study of the volume of American silver passing to Asia indicates that it became increasingly important over time. See William Schell Jr., "Silver Symbiosis: ReOrienting Mexican Economic History," *Hispanic American Historical Review* 81, no. 1 (February 2001): 89–133.

she was from Guadaira in Castile, the daughter of Anton de Mairena, a short, dark-complected Spanish laborer with straight black hair, and a peasant woman, Catalina Rodríguez. Later, she contradicted her this testimony, admitting that she was an *india* (Amerindian) from Cartagena. While Báez compiled evidence about Catalina's identity, Ludeña argued that Catalina's testimony was unreliable and coerced and that she was ignorant and uneducated, with no real will of her own. Ludeña then argued that he had taken Catalina into his service while living in Spain as a favor to a friend, Rodrigo Caro, and his wife Isabel. The couple had begged him to take and raise her, a poverty-stricken orphan. As the trial progressed, it became clear that Catalina was merely a pawn in the power struggle between Ludeña and his accusers.

It became obvious that Ludeña treated the servant girl more like a slave than a member of his household. He frequently beat her, provided her with little more than food and clothing, and assigned her demeaning tasks in Cartagena. The judge, Melchior Suárez de Poago, finally absolved Francisco de Ludeña of all charges, but Báez filed an appeal with the Audiencia of Santo Domingo. After a delay of several months, Ludeña, his family, and his servants, including Catalina, returned to Spain. When the family disembarked in Seville, however, officials from the Casa de la Contratación pressed charges against Ludeña for failing to show the proper documentation authorizing their return to Spain. The paperwork had been confiscated and retained by officials in Havana. Ludeña eventually was released from custody, but throughout the proceedings, the identity of Catalina remained a mystery.[75]

The controversy surrounding the case of Catalina's identity demonstrates the difficulty of trying to maintain unambiguous categories of race, caste, and ethnicity in the ever-changing Spanish Atlantic world. Much as religious authorities in Spain had difficulty rooting out crypto-Jews or Muslims from the *converso* and Morisco communities, authorities in the Americas could not easily resolve the racial or ethnic origins of this poor servant girl. Once removed from the more orderly European world of rigid social hierarchies, records could be falsified and a person could "pass" for someone of a higher or, in the case of Catalina, lower social position. The case demonstrates how biases, self-interest, and outright lies enter into the historical record, making it difficult to determine the real identity of historical actors, even those leaving a lengthy paper trail in modern archives.

---

[75] The case of Catalina is presented in more detail in Noble David Cook, "The Mysterious Catalina: Indian or Spaniard," in *The Human Tradition in Colonial Latin America*, ed. Kenneth J. Andrien (New York: Rowman & Littlefield, 2013), 77–95.

Conclusion

By 1610, the Spanish Crown had implanted a large bureaucracy in the Indies and enacted a great number of laws meant to assert royal authority over the Spanish and Indigenous populations. Given the preeminence of judicial authority in the Castilian political and institutional structure, most of the colonial councils and tribunals, such as the *audiencias*, were courts that also exercised administrative and legislative powers. High offices in the Indies interpreted the law, and the men appointed to fill these offices had advanced university degrees in Castilian jurisprudence. In this way, the power of the early conquistadors had been subordinated fully by royally appointed Crown bureaucrats in the populous central regions of the Indies. This process of political consolidation took place during the 1560s in New Spain and about a decade later in the Viceroyalty of Peru. The steady flow of commerce and private and public remittances of income from the Indies testify to the overall fiscal success of this bureaucratic order. Spanish colonialism paid dividends to the Crown as the governmental apparatus in the central areas collected taxes efficiently and remitted significant amounts of public revenue to Madrid. Private revenues derived from commerce also flowed steadily to the metropole by the late sixteenth century.

Political control over frontier zones took much longer, however, and followed a different chronology. The last Inca fortress of Vilcabamba did not fall until 1572, and the Chichimec Wars in northern New Spain (fought largely to protect the northern silver mining zones around Zacatecas) extended from the 1550s to approximately 1590. The Crown dispatched soldiers and colonists to found towns and military bases (presidios), even dispatching Indigenous allies, such as the Tlaxcalans, to the region to settle and to attract the Chichimecas to the sites and become sedentary farmers. Nonetheless, governmental institutions remained much weaker in these peripheral zones, and illegal activities, such as taking enslaved Indigenous individuals, continued unabated, unlike in the more populous central regions. Lands even farther north in New Spain remained largely in the hands of Indigenous groups, and the jungle regions on the eastern slopes of the Andes also remained largely outside Spanish control.

Socioeconomic change in the Spanish Atlantic world preceded adjustments in key political and institutional arrangements in the central regions of New Spain and Peru. The consolidation of Crown political power and the regularization of transatlantic commerce in the convoy system, directed through only a few licensed ports by 1564, promoted relatively safe commerce across the Atlantic Ocean. This also stimulated the exchange of European wares for precious metals from mining centers such as Zacatecas and San Luis Potosí in New

Spain and the legendary red mountain of Potosí in the Andes to Spain. Silver was easily smuggled, however, so the Crown created and paid for its bureaucracy in New Spain and Peru to control and tax the resources of the Indies. The mining of silver in New Spain also led to the use of coerced Indigenous labor, which gave way by the 1540s to wage labor. In the Andes, the colonial state organized corveé or mita labor, sending over thirteen thousand Indigenous laborers to Potosí, and these workers played a crucial role in stimulating mining production. With the growth of mining in these regions more remote from traditional population centers, the nexus of trunk and feeder lines became increasingly complex as market exchanges expanded in geographical scale and prominence. All of these economic changes also promoted migration, as Indigenous communities moved to take advantage of new market opportunities as laborers and consumers in the emerging colonial economic order.

The chronology of religious conversion diverged in certain ways from political and socioeconomic change. The Roman Catholic Church worked in partnership with Crown officials in the Indies to convert the Indigenous peoples and inculcate them with Iberian cultural values. The bulk of the Indigenous conversions took place in the first half of the sixteenth century, largely before the full consolidation of the Crown bureaucracy. The evangelization of Indigenous communities in the central zones proceeded apace as large numbers of Amerindians embraced baptism and Church rituals and practices and as Indigenous cults gave way to the official rituals and dogmas of Spanish Catholicism. Evidence of persistent pre-Columbian religious practices emerged, however, among the Maya of the Yucatan and with the Taqui Onqoy movement in the Andes. Evangelization along peripheral frontier zones also proceeded much more slowly than in populous central regions because clergymen found it difficult to convert migratory groups in northern New Spain and in remote jungle regions of the Andes. The growth of miraculous image shrines, such as the cult of the Virgin of Guadalupe in New Spain, evolved only haltingly in this formative era.

By the end of the sixteenth century, the Crown had implanted a political and institutional culture, based on Castilian traditions, to control the fractious conquistadors, gain access to the rich resources of the Indies, and enforce an orderly society with rigid social hierarchies. Crown bureaucrats and churchmen tried, for example, to separate the Native peoples into their own legal, corporate República de Indios. The purpose of such a legal entity was to facilitate conversion, collect taxes more effectively, and force the Indigenous peoples to provide labor service for the colonial economy. For their part, regular and secular clergymen attempted to police the purity of the faith among members of the República de Españoles with the Holy Office of the Inquisition by 1570. Nonetheless, a hybrid social order emerged in the Indies with a growing number of people of mixed racial ancestry, demonstrating the flaws in Crown policies of racial separation. The complexity of this developing colonial society and the inability to maintain rigid social and racial categories is manifest in the case of the mysterious Catalina, a servant of the notary Francisco de Ludeña. Catalina was a mere pawn in the struggles over race and ethnicity in the Indies because her identity as either a Spaniard or an Amerindian was apparently impossible to prove. The discovery of the Indies prompted a revolution in scientific knowledge, natural history, and navigational techniques, which also brought the Spanish Atlantic world closer together. In short, by 1600, the Spaniards exercised a claim to control the region extending from the southwest of North America to the southern tip of South America, incorporating this vast region as an accessory union with Castile. This domain brought great wealth and power to the Kingdoms of Spain and forged the creation of the Spanish Atlantic world.

Timeline: New World Beginnings to the Consolidation of the Spanish Atlantic World, 1492–1610

1492	During his first voyage, Columbus establishes the first settlement on Española
1502	The Spanish Crown appoints a royal governor on Española
1503	The Crown establishes the Board of Trade (Casa de la Contratación) to control commerce, gain valuable geographic and navigational information, and serve as a court to hear commercial cases
1511	The Crown appoints a high court, *audiencia*, on Española
1519–21	Fernando Cortés leads a joint Spanish–Amerindian expedition that overthrows the Aztec/Mexica Empire and in 1521 founds Mexico City on the site of the Aztec capital of Tenochtitlan
1524	The Crown establishes the Council of the Indies as an appellate court in civil cases, a legislative body, and to recommend executive actions to the king
1532	On November 16, 168 Spaniards ambush the Inca at Cajamarca and capture the Sapa Inca, Atahualpa
1536–39	Manco Inca's Rebellion
1542	The Crown issues the New Laws, which, among other provisions, outlaw Amerindian slavery and order that all encomienda grants revert to the Crown with the death of the current holder
1550	Debate in Valladolid between Bartolomé de las Casas and Juan Ginés de Sepúlveda over the treatment of the Indigenous people of the Indies
1552	Las Casas publishes *The Briefest Relation of the Destruction of the Indies*

1562	Diego de Landa and the Franciscans discover signs of idolatry and begin extralegal trials and punishments against the Maya in the Yucatan Peninsula
1564	The Crown establishes the convoy system of *flotas* and *galeones* to protect trade routes from Spain to the Indies
1564–66	Taqui Onqoy millenarian movement is discovered in the Andes and suppressed by Roman Catholic clergy
1570	Holy Office of the Inquisition is established in Lima and Mexico City
1568–80	Viceroy Martín Enríquez establishes the institutional structure of colonial governance in New Spain
1569–80	Viceroy Francisco de Toledo establishes the institutional structure of colonial governance in Peru
1571	King Philip II appoints Juan López de Velasco cosmographer-chronicler of the Council of the Indies and charges him with writing a chronicle-atlas of the Indies
1572	Fall of the last Inca outpost at Vilcabamba and the execution of the last Sapa Inca, Tupac Amaru
1580	King Philip II inherits the throne of Portugal and sends the Duke of Alba with fifteen thousand troops to secure his claim, uniting Portugal with Castile, Aragon, and Navarre

3

The Mature Colonial Order and the Drift toward Greater Autonomy, 1610–1700

> His holy Catholic Royal Majesty inquires of Ayala, the author, in order to know about everything that exists in the kingdom of the Peruvian Indies, for the sake of good government and justice and to relieve the Indians from their travails and misfortunes so that the poor Indians of the aforementioned kingdom will respond and speak to his Majesty.
>
> Felipe Guaman Poma de Ayala, ca. 1615
> *El primer nueva corónica y buen gobierno*

After the turbulent conquest era, the Spanish Atlantic world underwent a long period of expansion and consolidation. By 1610, Spaniards had subjugated the major Indigenous civilizations in central Mexico and the Andes; ended the disruptive civil wars among the fractious conquistadors, particularly in South America; and imposed an extensive imperial bureaucracy to consolidate their dominance. The great epidemics that had devastated the Indigenous peoples slowly passed, and by the 1650s most Amerindian populations began to recover.[1] Immigration from Castile continued, and a stratified colonial Spanish-controlled society emerged in the Indies. Ever larger numbers of enslaved Africans and Indigenous people were imported to work in the cities, in mining, and in burgeoning plantation economies. The expansion of market economies continued apace as the nexus of trunk and feeder lines grew steadily and became more complex, extending well beyond the original transatlantic markets and the centers of pre-Columbian Indigenous populations. Spanish landed estates emerged to meet the demand for hides, meat, wool, grains, and draft animals. Over time, settlers moved to frontier zones in northern Mexico, the northern coast of South America, and the southern tip of the continent. Silver mining still predominated in the central regions of the Indies, but colonial economies became

---

[1] The one notable exception to this pattern of demographic recovery is the Audiencia of Quito, where the Indigenous population grew from in-migration until the 1690s, when a demographic decline took place. See Karen Vieira Powers, *Andean Journeys: Migration, Ethnogenesis, and the State in Colonial Quito* (Albuquerque: University of New Mexico Press, 1995), 45–80.

more diverse and self-sufficient. Intercolonial trade links in legal and contraband goods expanded throughout the Indies, extending even to Spanish Pacific holdings in the Philippines and from there to China. The primitive conquest economy, drawn from Reconquista traditions and based on the encomienda and mining, gave way to a more stable, self-sufficient, and mature socioeconomic order in the overseas possessions. It was a time of profound, yet largely evolutionary, political, economic, social, and cultural change.

Gradual but significant changes in the political and institutional culture of the Spanish Atlantic world also took place during the seventeenth century, as political ties between the bureaucracy in the Indies and the metropole progressively loosened. Spanish authorities became increasingly preoccupied with fighting wars against rivals in Europe, which slowly depleted the resources of the Crown and led to defeats on land and sea. As Spain's power in Europe diminished, the ability to control the actions of bureaucrats in the Indies declined. The cash-strapped Spanish monarchy increasingly relied heavily on tax farming and the sale of key bureaucratic appointments in the Indies, which allowed power to pass into the hands of local interest groups often more concerned with advancing their own fortunes than with meeting the needs of the increasingly desperate metropolis. The Madrid government tried to apply greater fiscal pressure on the treasuries of the Indies, but to no avail. The lethargic Spanish governments in Peru and, to a lesser extent in New Spain, failed to stem declines in treasury income flowing into the central treasuries in Mexico City and Lima, resulting in lesser remittances of revenue to beleaguered Spain.[2] The political and institutional relationship between Castile and the Indies evolved from being a more tightly controlled set of institutions of an accessory union to the greater autonomy of an *aeque principaliter*.

The transformations that incorporated the Indigenous populations of the Indies into the Atlantic world led to cultural changes, such as the formation of a new group of Indigenous intellectuals (called *indios ladinos*) literate in both Castilian (and sometimes Latin) and their Indigenous language. One example is the Native Andean writer, Felipe Guaman Poma de Ayala, the author of *El primer nueva corónica y buen gobierno*, completed around 1615. By his own account, Guaman Poma began a long overland trek from his home in Lucanas in the Andean central highlands to Lima, accompanied by his son, a horse, and two dogs. Guaman Poma carried a massive manuscript (1,189 pages with 398 illustrations) that he had written, in a mixture of Castilian and Quechua, over a period of thirty years (see Fig. 3.1). This impressive book detailed life before and after the foundation of the Inca realm, along with the abuses visited on the

---

[2] TePaske and Klein, "Seventeenth Century Crisis," Graph 1.

THE MATURE COLONIAL ORDER 97

Fig. 3.1 The author, Felipe Guaman Poma de Ayala, on the road to Lima.
Source: El primer nueva corónica y buen gobierno, p. 1093, 1095, GkS 2232 4. Courtesy of the Royal Library of Denmark, Copenhagen.

Native Andean peoples by their Spanish overlords since 1532. Guaman Poma's achievement in writing his book is all the more impressive because before 1532, the Andean peoples apparently lacked both a system of alphabetic writing and an artistic tradition of figurative art. The intended audience for this monumental work was none other than King Philip III of Spain. Beset by robbers, vagabonds, low-born Indigenous ne'er-do-wells, and a host of rapacious Spanish officials on the road to Lima, Guaman Poma still managed to reach the capital city and send his precious manuscript to Madrid. Although it is unlikely that Philip III ever read *El primer nueva corónica y buen gobierno*, the work remains an outstanding example of the social and cultural changes that demonstrated the delusion that the Indigenous and Spanish societies could remain separate in two "republicas," each with their own rights and privileges. Instead, Guaman Poma represents the hybrid colonial culture and society that emerged over the course of the seventeenth century in the Spanish Atlantic world.[3]

Greater Political Autonomy for the Indies in the Mature Colonial Order

While the mature period produced fundamental changes in the Indies, it was a time of war, defeat, and decline in Europe for the metropolis. Following the assertive imperialism of Philip II (1556–98), his son and successor, King Philip III (1598–1621), made few modifications in the Spanish Atlantic world. During his reign, there was peace and retrenchment in Europe, while tax remittances and commerce with the Indies remained substantial. Peace did not bring fiscal moderation, since the king spent lavishly on the arts, pomp and ceremony at court, and expressions of baroque piety. With the accession of Philip IV (1621–65), however, Spain pursued a more active, militant policy in Europe, leading to a series of expensive foreign wars. Given that official silver remittances from the Indies had begun to decline, the Crown was forced to finance its European wars through a ruinous set of policies—borrowing from foreign and domestic bankers, debasing royal currencies, and selling appointments to public offices throughout the empire. Faced with these spiraling fiscal pressures, the king's chief minister (*válido*), the Count Duke of Olivares, attempted to assess each constituent part of the Spanish monarchy (including the Indies) with a special levy, called the Union of Arms, which was designed to support a permanent, standing military force to defend the monarchy. This unprecedented

---

[3] The manuscript is currently located in the National Library of Denmark and Copenhagen University, and a full online version of the manuscript and the pictures drawn by Guaman Poma may be found at http://www.kb.dk/en/nb/tema/poma.

attempt at royal centralization by the Spanish monarchy provoked bitter dissent throughout the Spanish Atlantic world. By 1640, Spain was on the verge of bankruptcy and collapse, particularly after Catalonia and Portugal revolted against Castilian domination in 1640. Although the Portuguese ultimately prevailed and won their independence, the Catalans were subdued and forced to remain under Habsburg control. Nevertheless, Spain suffered defeat on sea and on land to the Dutch and French. During the reign of the sickly and inept Charles II (1665–1700), the metropolis continued its overall political, economic, and social decline.[4]

By the early seventeenth century, the Spanish Crown had established an extensive royal bureaucracy in the Indies, headed by viceroys in New Spain and Peru, but over time this governmental system became more responsive to local concerns than to royal ones. The fiscal structure of this government was based on the mineral wealth of the Indies and on the labor and taxes of the Indigenous population. The viceregal courts in Lima and Mexico City were attempts to replicate the royal court in Madrid, filled with pomp and ceremony that embodied the ritual production and negotiation of power relations in the Spanish Atlantic world. In 1607, the Crown established a panel, the Tribunal of Accounts, in Lima and Mexico City to audit the annual accounts of every treasury office in the two viceroyalties. The viceroys made patronage appointments to numerous colonial offices as they attempted to manage relations with the various *audiencias, corregidores*, and city councils and the Church hierarchy of their vast realms.[5] They also struggled to balance the needs of the Crown and the increasingly powerful viceregal political, social, and economic interest groups.[6]

The Crown bureaucracy in the Indies underwent significant modifications amid the turmoil in the metropolis during the seventeenth century. The viceroys and key bureaucrats had always exercised power and influence in the government

---

[4] After Charles II died childless in 1700, the situation only worsened during the War of the Spanish Succession, when armies of the Austrian Habsburg and French Bourbon claimants to the throne fought with their Spanish partisans to determine who would replace the last of the Spanish Habsburg dynasty. Although the Bourbon candidate prevailed by 1713 and was crowned as Philip V (1700–1746), Spain remained politically divided and economically prostrate. See Henry Kamen, *Spain in the Later Seventeenth Century* (London: Longman, 1980); and Henry Kamen, *The War of the Succession in Spain, 1700–1715* (Bloomington: Indiana University Press, 1969).

[5] Alejandro Cañeque, *The King's Living Image: The Culture and Politics of Viceregal Power in Colonial Mexico* (London: Routledge, 2004), 120.

[6] Despite the institutional similarities of the colonial regimes in New Spain and Peru, political power tended to be more centralized in the South American viceroyalty. The Aztec Empire had been a loosely organized tribute-collecting confederation, with numerous, largely independent urban centers. By contrast, Peru had few large pre-Columbian urban centers and a governmental structure built on the legacy of the highly centralized Inca realm. This insight has been most clearly articulated by Gabriela Ramos, "Indigenous Intellectuals in Andean Colonial Cities," in *Indigenous Intellectuals: Knowledge, Power, and Colonial Culture in Mexico and the Andes*, ed. Gabriela Ramos and Yanna Yannakakis (Durham, NC: Duke University Press, 2014), 22.

through informal channels based on clientage, family connections, corruption, and influence peddling, but over the course of the century, local interest groups gained great power. Spain traditionally sold only low-level government offices, but the fiscally strapped Spanish Crown began the unprecedented policy of selling appointments to key bureaucratic posts (treasury offices in 1633, *corregimientos* by 1678, *audiencia* judgeships in 1687, and even the viceregal thrones by 1700). Such positions carried important judicial and policy roles, which weakened Crown authority throughout the New World. Before the sales, the viceroys exercised significant control over patronage in the Indies, whether they had appointed some local bureaucrats directly, made interim appointments (pending confirmation by the Crown), or influenced the selection of officials named in Madrid. The sale of key bureaucratic appointments allowed local elites direct access to power, which undermined the patronage power of the viceroys. The new policy also allowed Creoles (people of European descent born in the Indies) to purchase key posts directly, even in their own cities and towns, allowing locals to gain unprecedented political clout.[7] While this policy may have helped the Crown to co-opt local elites in New Spain and Peru, the purchasers were often less qualified people with strong local connections who viewed their position as a personal possession, rather than a public trust. The practice in the Viceroyalty of Peru became so widespread during the period that sometimes several purchasers had to wait their turn to assume an office.

Corruption, graft, influence peddling, and slipshod government practices abounded, as venal officeholders used their positions to advance business interests and enrich themselves and their allies at the expense of the embattled metropolis, particularly in Peru. Among the first purchasers of treasury offices in Lima were Baltásar de Becerra and Juan de Quesada y Sotomayor, both wealthy, prominent merchants whose families had been long-time residents in the city.[8] Quesada had even been caught trafficking in contraband goods before he purchased his appointment as treasurer of the Lima *caja real* in 1634. In the South Sea armada of 1624, for example, royal inspectors found that the total value of registered merchandise was 9,340,000 pesos, but this included 7,955,124 pesos of contraband, or 85 percent of the total value of the goods in the Portobelo fair. In this same armada of 1624, Quesada had 215,900 pesos of merchandise, but 209,198 pesos of these goods were unregistered contraband.[9]

---

[7] Andrien, *Crisis and Decline*, 103–29; and Burkholder and Chandler, *From Impotence to Authority*, passim.

[8] Quesada purchased his treasury appointment while on business in Spain in 1634, without the knowledge of the viceroy, the Count of Chinchón, who denounced Quesada as a merchant with little talent for the job and many outstanding debts in the city. Quesada's offer of 18,750 pesos for the position overruled the viceroy's concerns. Andrien, *Crisis and Decline*, 115–16.

[9] Enriqueta Vila Vilar, "Las Ferias de Portobelo: Apariencia y realidad del comercio con Indias," *Anuario de Estudios Americanos* XXXIX (1982): 65.

While the armada of 1624 may have been an exceptionally corrupt affair, it indicates that such illegal shenanigans were an embedded part of the fleet system, even before the sale of treasury offices nearly a decade later.

Despite his reputation as a prominent merchant and contrabandist, when he went to Spain on business, Quesada purchased the treasurer's post in his native Lima, without anyone in Madrid consulting the viceroy, the Conde de Chinchón. When word of the purchase reached Lima in 1637, Chinchón wrote an indignant letter to Madrid denouncing Quesada. The viceroy strongly objected to merchants serving in such important appointments, especially Quesada, who had outstanding debts in the city and little training or background for the job. Quesada's generous offer of nearly 19,000 pesos for the post sufficiently impressed officials in Madrid, and they ignored the viceroy's misgivings. The financial distress of the Crown led authorities in Madrid to sell appointments to the highest bidder, allowing members of the Lima elite to put their own candidates directly into strategic offices. Years after taking office, Quesada notoriously used his political influence and connections in the merchant community to gain command of the treasury fleet to Panama in 1648, giving him and his Peruvian merchant colleagues the opportunity to smuggle contraband merchandise virtually without supervision.[10]

Treasury officers often failed to produce accurate accounts of income and expenditures in their jurisdiction, making it impossible for the Crown to monitor their actions. In 1651, for example, an inspection of the treasury office at the mining center of Potosí found that no official accounts of income and expenditures had been kept for twenty years.[11] *Corregidores de indios* were notoriously corrupt, and contemporaries estimated that tribute debts in the Viceroyalty of Peru had reached 1,654,057 pesos by 1630. The Tribunal of Accounts was also behind in its audits, which made oversight of these problems difficult. By mid-century, the tribunal in Lima failed to either audit or receive thirty-two accounts from the treasury at Oruro, twenty-nine from Arequipa, forty from La Paz, fourteen from Huancavelica, and forty-five from the Huánuco office. Royal inspection tours of the Lima treasury (*visita generals*) in 1664, 1669, and 1677 failed to make any improvements in the fiscal administration of the viceroyalty.[12]

In 1650, members of the perpetually backlogged Tribunal of Accounts nevertheless uncovered a debt of 45,409 pesos in the central treasury office of Lima. The treasury officials responsible for the debt, Bartolomé Astete de Ulloa and Juan de Quesada, blamed their deceased colleague, Baltásar de Becerra, a wealthy

---

[10] Members of his family had accumulated fortunes exceeding 200,000 pesos. Ibid., 120–21.
[11] Kenneth J. Andrien, "Corruption, Inefficiency, and Imperial Decline in the Seventeenth-Century Viceroyalty of Peru," *The Americas* XLI (July 1984): 7.
[12] Ibid., 6.

merchant who had advanced the treasury money to cover shortfalls in legal income to meet pressing treasury expenses. They claimed that when the elderly Astete was ill and Quesada was dealing with treasury matters in Callao, Becerra must have taken out funds in excess of the original loans. Although Becerra and Quesada had purchased their appointments, the embarrassed officials blamed the Crown policy of selling future appointments to the treasury office. According to Astete and Quesada, by 1650, three men were in line to take up positions in the treasury office—Sebastián de Navarrete, Francisco de Guerra, and Bartolomé Torres Cavallón—and they had conspired with Becerra to create the shortfall as an excuse to replace them. The confusing case was made even more complicated when the inspector dispatched by the Tribunal of Accounts to investigate the scandal found 58,361 pesos missing for the period 1648-50 and an additional 46,600 pesos in a chest carelessly pushed to a corner in the treasury office itself. Since Becerra had died early in 1649, he could not answer for the shortfall, and neither Astete nor Quesada had an explanation for these hidden or mislaid funds. In the end, the Council of the Indies found Becerra, Astete, and Quesada responsible for all the missing money, fined both living men 2,500 pesos, and suspended them from office for four years.[13] This level of corruption, inefficiency, and graft among these venal officeholders in Peru occurred as Spain was fighting a series of disastrous and costly foreign wars in Europe.[14]

The collusion between government officials and local mining interests in Potosí produced a notorious and scandalous corruption case in 1648. Widespread rumors that the mint produced debased coins prompted King Philip IV to dispatch a special prosecutor, Francisco Nestares Marín, then president of the Audiencia of Charcas, with broad powers to investigate the allegations. The royal inspector soon found out that silver merchants (*mercaderes de plata*), headed by Potosí's richest man, Francisco Gómez de la Rocha, were behind the

---

[13] Andrien, *Crisis and Decline*, 127-28.

[14] Two scholars of colonial New Spain take a much different view of office sales in that viceroyalty. According to Alejandro Cañeque, "In the case of the sale of offices...it is quite clear that they cannot be considered a corrupt practice whatsoever." See Cañeque, *King's Living Image*, 177; in a recent article, Christoph Rosenmüller argues, "The sale of appointments, if anything, strengthened the crown because it help to co-opt mercantile or bourgeois sectors while weakening the influence on patronage by the aristocratic and jurist (*letrado*) circles at court, whose aims were often at odds with those of the crown." Christoph Rosenmüller, "'Corrupted by Ambition': Justice and Patronage in Imperial New Spain and Spain, 1650–1755," *Hispanic America Historical Review* 96, no. 1 (February 2016): 13; Christoph Rosenmüller, *Corruption and Justice in Colonial Mexico, 1650–1755* (Cambridge: Cambridge University Press, 2019), 123-95. Neither historian examined who actually purchased these offices, what their socioeconomic connections were in New Spain, or the fiscal consequences of the sales on the viceregal treasury. The practice in the Viceroyalty of Peru clearly had pernicious effects on royal authority, measured by who bought the offices and the fiscal impact of their actions. Among those involved in the scandals in Lima in 1650, only Bartolomé Astete de Ulloa had not purchased his appointment. See Kenneth J. Andrien, "The Sale of Fiscal Offices and the Decline of Royal Authority in the Viceroyalty of Peru, 1633–1700," *Hispanic American Historical Review* 62, no. 1 (February 1982): 49-71.

debasement of currency at the mint. According to the testimony of staff members at the mint, Rocha and his associates forced out anyone who did not take their bribes, and they loaned money or paid off the local *corregidor* and even some *audiencia* judges at Charcas to ensure their silence. When he failed to take such bribes, Nestares Marín received numerous death threats, hired assassins shot out the windows of his apartment above the mint, and he was burned in effigy in the main square outside his office. Rocha allegedly paid a female cook to poison the prosecutor's food with mercury, but other servants informed authorities of the plan. In late January 1650, Nestares Marín sentenced Rocha to death and had his body hanged from a scaffold on the city's main plaza as a grisly reminder of the price of betraying the Crown. Other executions followed, breaking or at least weakening the ring of corrupt silver merchants. In return for eliminating a 1.5 percent tax on silver production, Nestares Marín cut a deal with the miners and silver merchants to keep the mint's coinage just under the royal standards, but much less debased than in years past.[15]

Almost as scandalous and dangerous as the crisis at the Potosí mint was the declining productivity of the region's famous silver mines. The decline was tied to lower-quality ore at the mine heads, but also to ongoing abuses of the mita system. By the seventeenth century, many Andeans had fled their towns to avoid the draft, while others utilized a legal loophole that allowed them to buy their way out of serving by paying the wage of a wage laborer (*minga*). These so-called *indios de faltriquera* (literally pocket or purse Indians) exacerbated production declines at the silver mines, as many miners (*azogueros*) left their increasingly unproductive mines unworked and lived off the cash payments from the *indios de faltriquera*.[16] The crisis of the forced labor system led the viceroy to appoint a special prosecutor, Francisco de la Cruz, in 1659 with the task of reorganizing the mita and eliminating payments to miners from *indios de faltriquera*.[17] Cruz soon determined that these cash payments to the miners totaled 587,000 pesos annually, while the royal fifth each year amounted to barely 300,000 pesos.[18] When Cruz ordered all mita deliveries in silver stopped and tried to reorganize the whole forced labor draft, he alienated the region's miners, the silver merchants, and their corrupt allies in the government. Apparently, these entrenched local elites arranged to poison the prosecutor's chocolate, and Cruz died mysteriously in his sleep on April 23, 1660.[19] When a new viceroy, the Count of Lemos, took office in 1667, he ordered a fresh

---

[15] Kris Lane, *Potosí: The Silver City*, 127–33.
[16] Jeffrey A. Cole, *The Potosí Mita, 1573–1700: Compulsory Indian Labor in the Andes* (Stanford, CA: Stanford University Press, 1985), 56–58, 79–80.
[17] Cruz was the bishop-elect of Santa Marta and he was appointed by the viceroy, the Conde de Alba de Liste, to investigate the mita. Ibid., 91.
[18] Ibid., 92.   [19] Ibid., 93.

investigation of the Potosí mines and the mita, which revealed that widespread abuses had continued unabated since the death of Cruz. In 1670, the frustrated viceroy took the bold step of recommending that the whole corrupt and abusive mita system be abolished.[20] Nonetheless, the Crown feared that such a dramatic policy change would lead to the total collapse of the silver mines at Potosí, so the mita remained. As a result, the mita, supported by the local miners, the silver merchants, and their cronies in the local government, continued to operate as before.

Colonial law also reflected the rising influence of local power brokers in the Spanish Indies. After the conquest of the Americas, Castilian law formed the foundation of the colonial legal system, but by 1614 the Crown decreed that legislation formulated specifically for the New World would have the force of law. Both Crown officials and local settlers played a role in the creation of this discrete body of law, or *derecho indiano*. According to *derecho indiano*, public officials throughout the Indies had the prerogative (*arbitrio judicial*) to resist or delay the imposition of any controversial laws whenever they felt that new legislation violated local customs or notions of justice and the common good. Colonial officials never administered justice by adhering mechanically to written laws, but often exercised their *arbitrio judicial* to forge compromises between royal objectives and local ideas about proper custom and what they perceived to be communal fairness. As Crown power declined and venal officeholders took power, they could manipulate these provisions in the law to advance local or regional interests over the needs of Madrid. By the mid-seventeenth century, this tension between peninsular and colonial conceptions of justice had produced a colonial legal system that was in some respects distinct from that of Castile.[21] In fact, in 1680 the Crown finally completed a compilation of colonial law known as the *Recopilación de leyes de los reynos de las Indias*.[22] These political and legal changes slowly began to transform the relationship of the Indies to the Spanish monarchy, making it more autonomous from the political, legal, and institutional traditions of Castile.

The sale of high public offices and the corruption of local officials was most pronounced in the Viceroyalty of Peru. In the central treasury office in Lima, venal officeholders failed to implement new tax policies that might have alleviated the fiscal penury of the Crown by increasing treasury revenues and remittances to Spain.[23] Instead, remittances of public revenue from the Peruvian

---

[20] Ibid., 100.

[21] Charles Cutter, *The Legal Culture of Northern New Spain, 1700–1810* (Albuquerque: University of New Mexico Press, 1995), 30–36.

[22] Kenneth J. Andrien, "Legal and Administrative Documents," in Pillsbury et al., *Guide to Documentary Sources*, 108, 114.

[23] Andrien, *Crisis and Decline*, 60–61; Margarita Suárez, *Desafíos transatlánticos: Mercaderes, banqueros, y el estado en el Perú virreinal, 1600–1700* (Lima: Pontificia Universidad Católica del Perú/Instituto Riva Agüero, 2001), 141–86.

treasuries to Spain fell dramatically over the course of the century, from 51 percent of total income in the period 1607–10 to only 5 percent in the last decade of the century, as treasury officials in Lima retained these funds to meet local needs.[24] The decline in treasury remittances from New Spain was also significant but far less dramatic—from over 9 million pesos (88 percent of total revenues) to just over 2.7 million pesos (62 percent of total revenues).[25] Treasury officials, particularly in Peru, failed to meet the pressing fiscal demands of the beleaguered government in Madrid. Nonetheless, the empowerment of these Creole elites in the government did little to better the lot of the great mass of Amerindian, African, and mixed-blooded peoples in the Indies, who occupied the lowest positions in the colonial socioeconomic order.

One of the most obvious examples of colonial bureaucrats retaining Crown revenues to meet local (rather than metropolitan) needs occurred in New Spain with the seventeenth-century effort to drain the lakes surrounding Mexico City—the Real Desagüe de Huehuetoca. The Mexica capital of Tenochtitlan had been built around an island in Lake Texcoco, and when the Spanish founded Mexico City on the site, they tried to drain the lake, but flooding in the capital was an ongoing problem. Crown officials decided to enact an expensive, large-scale drainage project, which began on November 28, 1607. Floods had seriously damaged the capital city in 1604 and 1607, threatening property and the lives of the citizenry.[26] The principal architect of the project, Enrico Martínez, devised a plan that involved perforating the hills running along the basin's northwestern margin to create a tunnel that was 4 miles long and ran as deep as 184 feet underground. The work engaged 60,000 Indigenous male laborers (most of them forced into service by the viceregal government) and 1,664 women to cook their rations, along with hundreds of paid artisans and supervisors.[27] The effort was miraculously completed in less than a year, although the dangerous work took a heavy toll on the laborers.[28] The entire project had involved confiscating Amerindian land, and it was financed by forced donations and taxes on property, paid for largely by the middle and lower classes. In the end, the entire Desagüe was over 40,000 feet long. Over time, the tunnel section deteriorated, and in 1629 the city again flooded because the tunnel of Martínez was too constricted to allow the free flow of water.[29] As a result, Amerindian laborers were utilized once again to turn the tunnel of Martínez into a large, open trench. The Carmelite designer of the new plan, Fray Andrés de San Miguel, estimated that a trench from Mexico City to the outlet of the

---

[24] Andrien, *Crisis and Decline*, 67.
[25] TePaske and Klein, "Seventeenth Century Crisis," Table 4.
[26] Vera S. Candiani, *Dreaming of Dry Land: Environmental Transformation in Colonial Mexico City* (Stanford, CA: Stanford University Press, 2014), 1.
[27] Ibid., 50.   [28] Ibid., 61.   [29] Ibid., 51.

Desagüe involved moving fifteen million cubic feet of earth.[30] Oversight of the project went to the Franciscan order, but when they left the project in 1691, the Desagüe largely failed to protect the city from serious, periodic flooding. The open trench eroded over time and the flow of water remained inconsistent, which led to the accumulation of debris in the trench. The project continued for the next two centuries. Despite the ongoing threat of flooding, neither the redirection of large sums of Crown revenues nor seventeenth-century advances in science and technology could solve the complex problem of successfully draining the lakes around Mexico City to prevent flooding.

The Church and Evangelization in the Indies

Although the Roman Catholic Church remained a powerful partner with the Crown, the religious orders and the hierarchy of the secular clergy retained considerable independence from royal control. The religious orders in both Spain and the Indies were subject to the head of their order and ultimately to the pope in Rome, but even the secular clergy enjoyed a degree of independence from Crown authority. The *patronato real* in 1504 gave the Crown the right to nominate all bishops in the Indies (and after 1523 in Spain), but in practice, many of these prelates defended episcopal authority vigorously, particularly against any incursions on clerical privileges by Crown officials, such as the viceroy. Indeed, the viceroy of New Spain, the Marqués de Mancera, complained to the Crown in 1665: "The discord between viceroys and archbishops in this kingdom is so old and continuous that it seems to be congenital to both posts, with irreparable damage to the cause of God, Your Majesty, and our people and vassals, following from this lack of conformity between the heads."[31] The archbishops of Mexico and Lima were surrounded by the same pomp and ceremony as the viceregal court, and they guarded their prerogatives and rituals zealously. Disputes all too often erupted between archbishops and viceroys, for example, over whether the prelate had the right to sit under a canopy (*quitasol*), an honor that the viceroys claimed as their exclusive privilege. Clergymen were also subject to canon law, not temporal laws, and they possessed the right to be tried in clerical courts for any offense. This relative autonomy of the Church and its prelates produced ongoing friction.

Although relations between civil and ecclesiastical authorities sometimes became strained in the Viceroyalty of Peru, they broke down completely on two

---

[30] Ibid., 85.   [31] Cañeque, *King's Living Image*, 94.

notable occasions in the Viceroyalty of New Spain during the seventeenth century.[32] In his efforts to harness the fiscal potential of the Indies to support the monarchy's ambitions in Europe, King Philip IV's chief minister, the Count Duke of Olivares, dispatched a determined reformer, the Marqués de Gelves, to New Spain with specific instructions to curtail corruption and inefficiency in government and increase remittances of public revenue to Spain in 1621.[33] The marqués soon ran afoul of the *audiencia* and the Creole oligarchy, led by the archbishop of Mexico, Juan Pérez de la Serna. By 1624, relations between the two men had deteriorated so badly that the archbishop excommunicated the viceroy, but Gelves disputed the prelate's authority to do so. The viceroy then ordered the *audiencia* to exile the recalcitrant archbishop. He withdrew as far as Teotihuacan and refused to leave, declaring the viceroy a tyrant and ordering a clerical strike.[34] The next day, the churches of the capital closed. In response, violent riots erupted in Mexico City that overthrew the viceroy, who barely escaped with his life to sanctuary in the city's Franciscan priory.[35]

Even after the riots that deposed Gelves, political unrest simmered and then intensified when the Count Duke ordered the extension of the Union of Arms to the New World in 1627, which threatened even higher taxes for New Spain. To restore order and tranquility in New Spain, Olivares sent a special visitor general to Mexico City in 1639, naming one of his protégés to the post, clergyman Juan de Palafox y Mendoza. The count duke also convinced the king to name Palafox the bishop of Puebla de los Angeles.[36] Palafox quickly made enemies after taking up his duties in 1640 by ordering the mendicant friars, particularly the Franciscans, to vacate their lucrative Indigenous parishes in Puebla in favor of secular clergy.[37] He then quarreled with the Jesuits, demanding that they pay the tithe, a 10 percent tax on all the produce of rural properties. The arrival of the visitor general in Mexico City and his quarrels with the religious orders concerned the viceroy, the Duke of Escalona, whose cousin, the Duke of Braganza, had led the rebellion of Portugal against the Spanish Crown in 1640. When the viceroy attempted to block the visitor general's plans to crack down on political corruption and inefficiency, Palafox utilized the duke's family ties to the Portuguese rebels as an excuse to remove him from office. The visitor general

---

[32] The most notable conflict between the viceroy of Peru and the archbishop of Lima occurred during the tenure of Baltásar de la Cueva Enríquez, the Conde de Castellar (1672–78), and Archbishop Melchor de Liñan y Cisneros, leading to the recall of the viceroy, a move unprecedented in the century. Andrien, *Crisis and Decline*, 184–89.

[33] Cayetana Alvarez de Toledo, *Politics and Reform in Spain and Viceregal Mexico: The Life and Thought of Juan de Palafox, 1600–1659* (Oxford: Oxford University Press, 2004), 46–47.

[34] Cañeque, *King's Living Image*, 76.

[35] Israel, *Race, Class, and Politics*, 135–60. The most complete, recent study of this period is Ballone, *1624 Tumult of Mexico*.

[36] Alvarez de Toledo, *Politics and Reform*, 51.   [37] Ibid., 65–74.

then used his influence with Olivares to have the viceroy confined and later recalled to Spain in June 1642. Meanwhile, Palafox served as interim viceroy until the arrival of the new viceroy, the Count of Salvatierra, in November.[38] The political conflicts continued, this time between the prelate and the new viceroy, ultimately leading the Count of Salvatierra and his allies to secure the removal and recall of Palafox in 1649.[39] New Spain had suffered twenty-eight years of political discord, fueled in large part by the friction between civil and ecclesiastical leaders.

The Crown also applied great fiscal pressure on the Viceroyalty of Peru, but by this time, treasury offices were sold, and these venal officeholders devised strategies to resist imposing new levies. Instead, they used other, less controversial fiscal expedients to raise money, largely from clerical organizations and later from prominent merchants. In 1629, the Count Duke of Olivares imposed a yearly levy of 650,000 ducats on the viceroyalty, and the Count of Chinchón, the viceroy during this period, postponed action of the issue for a decade, when he finally agreed to double the sales tax (*alcabala*) and the tax on the armada (*avería*); he also levied a port tax of two reales on domestic wine. Elite interest groups opposed the new taxes, and treasury officers with strong local ties in the viceregal capital failed to collect the levies effectively. Instead, they relied on the sale of government annuities (*juros*) in 1639, 1640, and 1641, which produced nearly two million ducats in revenue.[40] A *juro* was a contract whereby a person, corporate group, or institution agreed to advance capital to the Crown in return for an annual pension of 5 percent of the annuities value. Although some miners and merchants purchased the annuities in the sales from 1639 to 1641, most of the purchasers were clerical institutions seeking a secure outlet for their surplus income that paid modest annual interest payments that did not qualify as usury. In addition to the sale of *juros*, treasury officers in Lima contracted loans and interest-free donations (*donativos*) from private citizens, particularly wealthy members of the Lima merchant guild, to bolster income at the office. The sale of *juros*, loans, and donations allowed treasury officers to draw money from local elites and the previously tax-exempt holdings of the Roman Catholic Church, all without exacerbating the tensions between the government,

---

[38] While Palafox was a protégé of Olivares, he sponsored reformist policies that paid greater heed to local interests and customs rather than simply favoring greater centralization; in this case, he was sensitive to the needs of the Creole population. Alvarez de Toledo, *Politics and Reform*, passim.

[39] Ibid., 102–3. It is significant that the patron of Palafox, the Count Duke of Oliveres, had fallen from power in 1643, and Crown officials were fearful of disruptions of the political order in the aftermath of popular upheavals in Naples and Sicily in 1647 and 1648, respectively. Ibid., 244.

[40] A sale of annuities in 1608 had produced over one million ducats, which set the precedent for later sales. During this period, a ducat was 11 reales or 350 maravedís. AGI, Lima, 1171, Cédula, September 6, 1608.

local elites, and the Church that plagued New Spain during this period. At the same time, it left the treasury deeply in debt; by the 1660s, total income at the central treasury at Lima began a precipitous decline, and remittances of money to Spain fell off dramatically.[41]

Although founded by Ferdinand and Isabel to reform the Church and monitor orthodoxy, the Holy Office of the Inquisition was also drawn into the political conflicts of the seventeenth century. The Inquisition had broad judicial powers to investigate heresy and other crimes against the Church, such as bigamy, blasphemy, witchcraft, divination, idolatry, and sexual malfeasance by clergymen.[42] When Juan de Palafox was interim viceroy of New Spain, for example, he strongly urged the Holy Office to begin an investigation of Portuguese merchants in the capital (after the Portuguese rebellion against Philip IV) for allegedly being crypto-Jews, which ultimately led to large-scale arrests and public punishments (*autos-da-fé*) in the period from 1646 to 1649. In that era, such heresies were termed "a homicide of the souls," which not only jeopardized the salvation of those who practiced Judaism or Protestantism, but also by extension threatened the salvation of everyone in society, including the monarch.[43] The Catholic hierarchy saw religious purity as a clear social goal, viewing religious toleration as promoting social disorder, which jeopardized the moral foundations of the whole Spanish Atlantic world.

Despite the efforts of the Crown and the Inquisition to impose Roman Catholic orthodoxy, evidence drawn from Inquisitorial court records indicates that common folk expressed doubts and dissenting views about salvation, sex, and other religious issues that challenged Church doctrine. Atheists, relativists (who found truth in other religions), and skeptics apparently abounded. Jewish and Muslim converts in Iberia, for example, were reluctant to believe that their ancestors suffered eternal damnation for their beliefs, and some took the position that each person could be saved by adhering to his or her own law. Heterodox religious thinking thrived in the Indies, where bureaucratic and social controls remained weaker than in Iberia. These dissenting thinkers, favoring freedom of conscience and religious relativism, proved difficult for the Inquisitors to eradicate. Nevertheless, the cases of unorthodox behavior brought before the Holy Office were denounced, often from the same popular sector, which indicates that most citizens likely viewed religious toleration and the presence of

---

[41] For the short- and long-term effects of the sale of *juros*, see Kenneth J. Andrien, "The Sale of Juros and the Politics of Reform in the Viceroyalty of Peru, 1608–1695," *Journal of Latin American Studies* 13 (May 1981): 1–19.
[42] Schwaller, *History of the Catholic Church*, 86.
[43] Kimberly Lynne, *Between the Court and Confessional: The Politics of Spanish Inquisitors* (Cambridge: Cambridge University Press, 2013), 307.

relativists and atheists as transgressions and perhaps even serious crimes worthy of prosecution by the Inquisition.[44]

Spanish clergymen considered the Indigenous peoples of the New World neophytes and not subject to the Inquisition's discipline, but the bishops still exerted authority to root out any forms of pre-Columbian religious practices. After all, a crucial component of incorporating the Indies into the Spanish Atlantic world involved the conversion of millions of Amerindians to Roman Catholicism. The Spanish invaders, later colonists, and clerics even justified their overthrow of the Amerindian polities and their continued presence in the Indies by vowing to convert and secure eternal salvation for the Indigenous peoples within the Roman Catholic Church. At first, it seemed as though the Indigenous converts eagerly embraced baptism and the outward displays of Catholic piety—the veneration of the cross, colorful devotional objects, ornate churches, cults of the saints, and the ritual use of music, dances, and prayer. Over time, churchmen uncovered disturbing evidence of enduring pre-Christian religious practices. Whereas clergymen demanded that converts to Catholicism abandon their "pagan" beliefs for Christianity, some Indigenous people just attempted to incorporate Catholic dogma into their own preexisting religious framework to produce a hybrid faith.

Churchmen divided over what this evidence of hybrid religious practices represented, with some hard-liners terming them idolatry and the work of the devil, which had to be extirpated by force, if necessary. As the Jesuit Pablo José de Arriaga stated in 1621, "A common error (among Andeans) is their tendency to carry water on both shoulders, to have recourse to both religions at once.... Most of the Indians have not yet had their *huacas* and *conopas* taken away from them, their festivals disturbed nor their abuses and superstitions punished, and so they think their lies compatible with our truth and their idolatry with our faith."[45] Indeed, Arriaga even wrote a manual for priests in the Andes to help them identify and root out any such forms of idolatry. Others, such as the archbishop of Lima, Gonzalo de Campo, saw these deviant religious customs as "religious error," which could be countered by gentle persuasion and education in the faith. According to the archbishop, "I found a variety of opinions about this when I arrived in Lima; and among the serious and most important men there were those who told me that it (idolatry) was the invention and (a product of the) greed of the *visitadores* who used their titles to enrich

---

[44] The most important book on this intriguing subject is Stuart B. Schwartz, *All Can Be Saved: Religious Tolerance and Salvation in the Iberian Atlantic World* (New Haven, CT: Yale University Press, 2008), passim.

[45] Pablo José de Arriaga, *The Extirpation of Idolatry in Peru*, trans. L. Clark Keating (1621; repr., Lexington: University of Kentucky Press, 1968), 72–73. Also quoted in Kenneth Mills and William B. Taylor, eds., *Colonial Spanish America: A Documentary History* (Wilmington, DE: Scholarly Resources, 1998), 241.

themselves, and that this did serious injustice to the Indians.... Others said that there was some idolatry, but not as much as was claimed."[46] This religious debate within the Roman Catholic hierarchy divided clergymen for much of the century.

The most serious attempts to stamp out pre-Columbian religious practices began in 1609 in the archbishopric of Lima, when a priest in the highland parish of San Damián de Checa (southeast of Lima in the province of Huarochirí), Francisco de Avila, produced disturbing evidence of persisting "pagan religious rituals" in the region. Before Avila's revelations, however, his parishioners alleged that he had committed numerous abuses of his priestly authority, including engaging in scandalous sexual relationships with local women. In his defense, Avila rallied his own supporters and produced evidence of widespread idolatry in the region, possibly to divert attention from the allegations of abuse against him. Avila's revelations made an immediate impression on Archbishop Lobo Guerrero, along with the viceroy, the Marqués de Montesclaros, and the Jesuit provincial. All were hard-liners, sympathetic to advocates of forceful evangelization and the extirpation of idolatry, and they viewed any non-Christian practices as the work of the devil. These authorities cleared Avila of all charges against him and named him judge inspector of idolatry, with authority to begin a formal campaign to root out and punish idolatry throughout the archbishopric.

Over time, these visitations acquired a more definite set of legal and religious policies governing their conduct, which culminated in the publication of Arriaga's manual for extirpators in 1621.[47] Teams of extirpators, usually consisting of a clergyman (*visitador*), accompanied by an attorney (*fiscal*), a notary, a scribe, and two or three Jesuit priests, roamed the highland Indigenous villages to uncover and punish idolatry. Upon entering a parish, the visitor called on locals to denounce any idolatrous practices, and then the team collected evidence and rendered verdicts. Punishments could vary, depending on the severity of the crime and the degree of repentance shown by the guilty parties, from severe public lashings, exile, or mandatory religious instruction to the death penalty. The inspection team usually left one or more Jesuits behind to provide additional religious education to the community.

Despite mounting evidence of hybrid religious practices, many clergymen adamantly opposed the idolatry trials, carried out in the archdiocese of Lima.[48] Bishops in Arequipa, Huamanga, Cusco, and Trujillo, for example, refused to

---

[46] Quoted in Kenneth Mills, *Idolatry and Its Enemies: Colonial Andean Religion and Extirpation, 1640–1750* (Princeton, NJ: Princeton University Press, 1998), 37.

[47] Pierre Duviols, *La destrucción de las religiones andinas (conquista y la colonia)*, trans. Albor Maruenda (1971; repr., Mexico City: Universidad Autónoma de México, 1977), 185–89, 405–13; Mills, *Idolatry and Its Enemies*, 26–38; Nicholas Griffiths, *The Cross and the Serpent: Religious Resurgence in Colonial Peru* (Norman: University of Oklahoma Press, 1996), 28–32.

[48] Mills, *Idolatry and Its Enemies*, 33–38; Griffiths, *Cross and the Serpent*, 55–64.

admit idolatry teams to their dioceses, contending that the Indigenous people were guilty only of religious error and superstition, which could be handled effectively with education, rather than forceful methods involving punishment. In the archdiocese of Lima, however, the extirpation campaigns continued between 1609 and 1627 and then again from 1641 to 1671, when another hard-line archbishop, Pedro de Villagómez, vigorously supported them. In one form or another, cycles of idolatry trials ebbed and flowed in the archbishopric of Lima throughout the seventeenth century, until they finally ended around 1750.

Idolatry trials conducted by the regular clergy also took place in New Spain under the supervision of the local bishop and his appointed prosecutor, or *provisor*. In practice, church officials in Mexico City and Oaxaca delegated the task of prosecuting idolatry and sorcery cases to a select group of secular clergy called *jueces de comisión* or *jueces de idolatrías*.[49] In the archdiocese of Mexico and in Oaxaca, idolatry trials escalated from 1571 to the 1660s.[50] During this phase of the extirpation trials, most communal pre-Columbian religious practices had been suppressed, but individual Native religious specialists still met with small groups to carry out rituals that many clergymen defined as idolatrous. These trials involved dedicated secular clergymen such as Hernando Ruiz Alarcón and Jacinto de la Serna in the archdiocese of Mexico and Gonzalo Balsalobre in the diocese of Oaxaca, who knew Indigenous languages and identified activities centered on calendrical, life cycle, and healing activities that they considered tied to Native religious practices.[51] As time went on, the extirpators attempted to standardize, institutionalize, and centralize their procedures and punishments for uncovering, confronting, and punishing native ritual practices. They even established a special prison in the center of Oaxaca City to confine those guilty of idolatry, much as the Jesuits did in Lima during this period.[52]

Apart from their evangelization and extirpation responsibilities, the regular and secular clergy supported schools, hospitals, orphanages, and houses for pious or wayward women (*recogimientos*), which required substantial financial resources.[53] Such activities complemented the governing efforts of secular authorities, demonstrating the interdependency of Crown and clerical agencies, despite periodic differences, such as those in New Spain from the 1620s to the 1640s. Church bodies, particularly the secular clergy, depended on their tithe income and also the bequests of wealthy believers and pious works (*obras pias*)

---

[49] David Tavárez, *The Invisible War: Indigenous Devotions, Discipline, and Dissent in Colonial Mexico* (Stanford, CA: Stanford University Press, 2011), 16–17.
[50] Ibid., 18–21.   [51] Ibid., 74–76, 97–99, 112–23.   [52] Ibid., 187–91.
[53] For an excellent study of the *recogimiento* in seventeenth-century Lima, see Nancy E. van Deusen, *Between the Sacred and the Worldly: The Institutional and Cultural Practice of Recogimiento in Colonial Lima* (Stanford, CA: Stanford University Press, 2001).

foundations created to support their spiritual activities. The most common form of these pious works was the chantry (*capellanía*), a financial bequest to support a certain number of masses for the soul of the donor, family members, or close friends. If the donor gave cash, Church officials invested the funds, and the interest earned on the principle provided income for clergy to say the required masses. Donors could also give the proceeds from rents on urban property or rural land or a percentage of the produce from an estate to pay for a chantry. Other donors placed liens on properties that paid annual interest to the Church to support the chantry. Dioceses managed these pious works and endowments according to canon law through a clerical agency known as the Chantry and Pious Works Court (Juzgado de Capellaías y Obras Pias). When cash became available to this agency, it often lent the money to secular authorities or the laity at modest interest rates of 3 to 5 percent to avoid the sin of usury. In some dioceses the amounts managed by the agency could be considerable, and the money lent to local creditors formed a large portion of the loans extended to fuel the local economy.[54]

Male and female religious orders also relied on bequests from the laity, pious works, and property to support their various pastoral and social welfare activities. Although the mendicant orders were forbidden to acquire material goods, they supported themselves with charitable bequests. Over time, however, bequests allowed them to purchase or gain control over urban and rural property. The Jesuits, who were not a mendicant order, established a lucrative network of rural estates to support their colleges, founded in principal cities in the Indies. Many of these estates produced cloth, foodstuffs, and export crops for commercial markets, and by the early eighteenth century the order had accumulated substantial assets. Even female religious houses controlled considerable amounts of wealth, which they also invested in local economies. When a woman entered a convent, for example, her family customarily presented a dowry; the highest amounts supported the prestigious nuns of the black veil, who ran large households in the convent and monopolized leadership positions. More modest dowries came from women of less wealthy or prestigious families, who became nuns of the white veil, who occupied lower-level positions in the religious house. In the large convent of Santa Catalina in Cusco, for example, the nuns established lucrative chantries and invested the dowries of nuns in local enterprises, forging business alliances with regional elites, extending credit, securing and managing urban and rural properties, running textile mills, and buying and selling local produce. The whole symbiotic network of economic ties both

---

[54] Schwaller, *History of the Catholic Church*, 82–83; for more detail on these issues, see John Frederick Schwaller, *Origins of Church Wealth in Mexico: Ecclesiastical Revenues and Church Finances, 1523–1600* (Albuquerque: University of New Mexico Press, 1985).

ensured the prosperity of the convent and provided substantial credit and investment assets that fueled the local economy of the seventeenth-century Cusco region.[55] Such relationships made the institutions of the Church key actors in local economies throughout the Indies.

The militant religious zeal that emerged from the Reconquista gave way to baroque piety in the seventeenth century, leading to the founding of image shrines and the religious practices associated with them in the Indies. These shrines embodied the sense of wonder and astonishment that accompanied feeling the presence of the divine, where miracles could happen in the daily lives of believers.[56] A large number of these sacred images or shrines were associated with the Virgin Mary and Jesus. In New Spain, Mexico City and the Valley of Mexico served as the centers of the sacred. In the capital, the Virgin of Guadalupe and the Virgin of los Remedios were the most famous shrines/cults in the viceroyalty, but secondary shrines in other cities gained fame as painted copies of these images were placed in provincial cities.[57] The cathedral chapter of Mexico City oversaw the construction of the shrine to our Lady of Guadalupe in Tepeyac, one of the most popular devotional places in New Spain. In the period from 1680 to 1720, these image/shrines grew more popular and developed a large following of devoted Catholics and institutional support deepened, with a lively ceremonial life, full-time chaplains, and construction projects to honor the sacred images.[58] Despite concerns by some members of the Church hierarchy that such popular devotions could turn into idolatry, their popularity continued to grow throughout the century.[59]

Social Change in the Seventeenth Century

As racial and ethnic diversity spread, Crown authorities and Spanish settlers tried to enforce rigid social hierarchies, with European and Creole males at the apex. One of the mechanisms to police this social order was purity of the blood (*limpieza de sangre*) that emerged from the medieval Reconquista. In Spain, this meant proving that a person came from an Old Christian lineage, free of any taint of Jewish or Muslim blood. To enter a university, join a religious order, obtain a government position, or even travel to the Indies, Spaniards had to appear before the Holy Office of the Inquisition, along with witnesses and the requisite Church records, to prove that they came from Old Christian families.

---

[55] Katherine Burns, *Colonial Habits: Convents and the Spiritual Economy of Cuzco, Peru* (Durham, NC: Duke University Press, 1999), passim.
[56] Taylor, *Theater of a Thousand Wonders*, 55.
[57] Ibid., 60–61, 64.   [58] Ibid., 72.   [59] Ibid., 76.

If successful, the Inquisition would issue a certification of purity of the blood (*probanza de limpieza de sangre*). In the Indies, the Inquisition also had to certify that all petitioners were free from any taint of Indigenous or African blood. Because Black people were associated with slavery and Amerindians with idolatry, such ancestry usually excluded people from claiming *limpieza de sangre* and kept them from attaining elite status. The exceptions were members of the Indigenous nobility, but only if they proved descent from a family of committed Roman Catholics, who had converted early in the conquest era.[60] Purity of the blood often proved difficult to ascertain in the mobile, unpredictable colonial societies.

Membership in religious confraternities (*cofradias*) provided people throughout the Indies with community activities and social networks, but also reinforced social and racial hierarchies. Confraternities were usually organized around the veneration of a saint, religious image, or religious practice and provided opportunities for ritual piety and charitable activities. Membership in most confraternities was restricted to certain ethnic or racial groups. Some only extended membership to people of pure European descent. Others existed for enslaved persons, people of mixed racial ancestry, or Indigenous groups. Still others were founded by occupational groups, such as silversmiths or shoemakers. Members usually paid dues to support activities and even to allow some confraternities to hire the services of a priest to serve as a chaplain, who led processions or provided for the spiritual needs of members. Confraternities played an active role in organizing religious celebrations of Church holidays or a saint's feast day. Despite reinforcing social hierarchies, confraternities facilitated the spread of Roman Catholic beliefs and religious practices.[61]

Craft guilds also attempted to strengthen social hierarchies while serving their primary purpose of regulating artisan production, prices, and wages. Nearly all major cities in the Indies had some version of guild-based manufacturing, which controlled essential craft technologies, found necessary raw materials, recruited laborers, and regulated prices and the quality of goods and services. Guilds also founded religious confraternities that united craft production with Roman Catholic religious practices. They policed their membership by recruiting apprentices and journeyman only from certain social groups. Silversmiths generally only admitted apprentices of European blood to their ranks, but less prestigious artisan crafts were more open to people of mixed racial ancestry. While artisans in some cities employed enslaved African laborers or mixed-race workers

---

[60] The most important book on *limpieza de sangre* is María Elena Martínez, *Geneological Fictions: Limpieza de Sangre, Religion, and Gender in Colonial Mexico* (Stanford, CA: Stanford University Press, 2008).

[61] Schwaller, *History of the Catholic Church*, 84–85.

to assist them, such employees seldom reached the lofty goal of becoming master craftsmen. Women were commonly excluded from guild membership. In this way, the guild structure attempted to mirror the social hierarchies of the larger society.[62] Guilds only operated effectively in more established colonial cities, such as the viceregal capitals, and were either weak or nonexistent in many provincial urban areas.

By the seventeenth century, most settlers believed that social status, honor, and wealth were divinely assigned at birth, and human efforts at social mobility threatened God's natural order. Crown officials, for example, issued sumptuary laws that attempted to limit the consumption of certain luxury goods. This legislation forbade commoners from carrying swords or from dressing above their social station in silks or other expensive materials. They also tried to restrict the use of honorific titles, such as *don* or *doña*, which conveyed honor, status, and even real privileges, such as freedom from judicial torture, some tax exemptions, and the right to wear a sword. Towns in the Indies were usually constructed on a grid pattern, with the central plaza surrounded by a major church or cathedral, the houses of prominent citizens, and perhaps religious houses of the regular clergy. Where citizens resided reflected their social status and standing. In the minds of people in the Spanish Atlantic world, widespread social mobility signaled disorder, not a valuable way to reward merit.

Attempts to impose immutable social hierarchies were always imperfect, and the rising amount of racial mixing made for a diverse colonial social and cultural landscape. Europeans continued to immigrate to the Indies. To supplement Indigenous laborers, enslaved Africans were imported in larger numbers, from almost one thousand annually in the sixteenth century to two thousand each year in the seventeenth century.[63] Adding to this ethnic mix was the Amerindian population. European rule had not destroyed Indigenous and African culture in the Indies; instead, it produced a constantly evolving society that varied over time and across geographical space. It also differed in many respects from Iberian culture. In the Caribbean and coastal regions of New Spain and Peru, African and European cultures intermingled, while in the central regions of both viceroyalties European, Indigenous, and mestizo (mixed European and Amerindian blood) influences remained strong.

Cities in the Indies served as centers of racial and cultural interaction among the Indigenous, African, and European residents, which contributed to the erosion of rigid social hierarchies. After founding new cities or setting up residence

---

[62] Lyman L. Johnson, *Workshop of Revolution: Plebeian Buenos Aires and the Atlantic World, 1776–1810* (Durham, NC: Duke University Press, 2011), 11.

[63] Gabriel Paquette, *The European Seaborne Empires: From the Thirty Years War to the Age of Revolutions* (New Haven, CT: Yale University Press, 2019), 135.

in pre-Columbian urban areas, such as Mexico City–Tenochtitlan, Spanish officials tried to segregate the Indigenous population into special neighborhoods, allegedly to protect them from exploitation by Spaniards. Over time, Indigenous people, Africans, and mixed-race urban residents circulated throughout most colonial cities. When Lima became the capital of the Viceroyalty of Peru in 1535, for example, the Indigenous residents of the city were located in the parish of San Lázaro; they were later relocated in 1570 to Santiago del Cercado, a neighborhood set aside for Amerindians serving their mita rotation in the city. By the census of 1613, however, it was clear that 1,173 Indigenous residents of Lima (excluding the nearly 350 residents of the Cercado) were scattered throughout the city. Most of them practiced a trade, as tailors, shoemakers, silk weavers, hatters, slaughterhouse workers, carders, button makers, farmers, fisherman, and domestic servants.[64] In short, the Spanish, Creole, Indigenous, African, and mixed-race residents of Lima interacted with each other across the city's vibrant but culturally mixed urban landscape.

Social interaction among the races occurred in urban centers, particularly as Indigenous residents participated in market exchanges. In the former Inca Empire, for example, textiles were an art form, and cloth made from the finest camelid wool (*cumbi*) was a sign of wealth and prestige, restricted to Indigenous elites. The founding of Spanish cities attracted Indigenous migrants from all social classes, who had the potential to acquire wealth from market exchanges. Textiles became a commodity in urban market economies throughout Peru, and even fine *cumbi* could be bought, owned, and exchanged by all Indigenous customers, regardless of social status. In late-sixteenth- and seventeenth-century La Plata (in Bolivia), Indigenous women of modest birth who had attained wealth as grocery store owners (*pulperías*), moneylenders, or market vendors could buy previously unobtainable items, even textiles made of fine *cumbi*. Doña Ana Paico, for example, married a local *kuraka* (Indigenous clan leader), but she came from a humble family. Nonetheless, in her will doña Ana boasted owning houses, estates, animals, rich clothing (made from *cumbi*), and jewelry produced locally and imported from Spain. Women such as doña Ana could mix these traditional elite textiles with Spanish dresses, fabrics, and jewelry, creating a new hybrid social presence that often hid their humble origins.[65]

---

[64] Paul Charney, "Much Too Worthy..." Indians in Seventeenth-Century Lima," in *City Indians in Spain's American Empire*, ed. Dana Velasco Murillo, Mark Lentz, and Margarita R. Ochoa (Brighton, UK: Sussex Academic Press, 2012), 89; see also Paul Charney, *Indian Society in the Valley of Lima, Peru, 1532–1824* (Lanham, MD: University Press of America, 2001).

[65] This use of material culture to demonstrate social mobility in urban centers is drawn from an important article by Ana María Presta, "Undressing the *Coya* and Dressing Indian Women: Market Economy, Clothing, and Identities in the Colonial Andes, La Plata (Charcas), Late Sixteenth and Early Seventeenth Centuries," *Hispanic American Historical Review* 90, no. 1 (February 2010): 68–70.

Spaniards and the Native peoples also interacted in rural zones, but no single pattern of land tenure predominated in the seventeenth century. Indigenous farmers maintained their communal landholdings, where they engaged in farming and livestock raising. As the Indigenous population declined from the sixteenth century, however, Europeans alienated vacant lands, usually forming private estates (most commonly called *haciendas*). In each region, the type of European landholding depended on the crops or animals raised; demands of consumers; distance and strength of market demand; availability of investment capital, labor, and good arable land; and the local climate. Spaniards also developed plantations, utilizing enslaved Africans or Indigenous laborers to grow tropical crops, such as sugar cane, for both local and international markets. Some Indigenous workers increasingly abandoned their traditional villages to work on different types of Spanish estates, often to avoid state labor service or to earn cash to pay their tribute obligations.

As the network of market economies of the Spanish Atlantic world became more diverse and interconnected, the Indigenous peoples of New Spain and Peru participated more actively in commercial exchanges as buyers, sellers, and laborers. European modes of production expanded, and the Indigenous peoples adapted traditional kinship institutions to the rapidly changing economic landscape. State demands for tribute paid in specie encouraged Amerindians to work in mines, in textile mills (*obrajes*), on Spanish estates, or as merchants supplying needed goods to mining zones and urban centers. In the Andes, such movements led to the formation of communities of migrants (called *forasteros*), who had no rights to communal lands but could claim lower tribute rates and exemption from mita drafts. By 1646, over 36 percent of the Indigenous population (subject to the forced labor draft or mita of Potosí) was officially listed as *forasteros*; by 1683, that number had risen to 54 percent.

Despite pervasive migration, significant numbers of *forasteros* maintained links with their home communities. Much of the migration in the Cusco region, for example, was relatively short range, as Amerindians sought jobs in the city or took over unoccupied agricultural lands, but they still contributed tribute and labor services to their home communities. In other cases, migrants left their communities permanently, leading to a reformulation of traditional lifestyles, social practices, and cultural identities. Sometimes they took on Spanish cultural values and in other cases they adopted Indigenous lifeways. On the North Andean estate of Guachalá (in Cayambe, Ecuador), for example, migrants from several ethnic groups throughout the northern portions of the Audiencia of Quito came to seek work, with each retaining their ethnic surname. Apparently, members of the ethnic groups intermarried, abandoning old surnames, and forged a new eclectic mix of ideas about community and ethnicity on the estate that were Andean rather than Spanish.[66] The Indigenous peoples of central Mexico, with their long tradition of market exchanges before the arrival of the Spaniards, were even more likely than the counterparts in the Andes to sell their labor, exchange goods and services, and migrate to areas of economic opportunity.

As the Indigenous peoples interacted with the Spanish colonizers and the colonial economy, they increasingly defended their interests by utilizing the court system. Although they had the legal status of neophytes, they took advantage of any rights provided by the colonial government to defend their land, water rights, and labor practices. In Peru, they flooded the *audiencias* with petitions and suits, often giving power of attorney to Spanish lawyers to represent their legal interests in cases involving tribute and labor assessments. As the Indigenous population declined from epidemic diseases, unscrupulous Spanish magistrates sometimes refused to lower tax and forced labor assessments, leading the communities to use the courts to demand new assessments (*retasas*) commensurate with the population decline.[67] From the 1590s, Indigenous litigants in New Spain pleaded cases before a special court, the *Juzgado General de Indios* in Mexico City.[68] This court was headed by the viceroy and run by a well-trained legal assistant. Indigenous litigants quickly came to prefer this court in the capital to other venues, and they routinely made the trip to Mexico City to present their petitions for royal protective orders (*amparos*).[69] When a Spaniard, Pedro Díaz del Campo, tried to usurp the land of Tlaxcalan colonists on the northern frontier of New Spain in 1640, for example, the Tlaxcalan authorities petitioned the juzgado in Mexico City, which forwarded the petition to the *audiencia*'s attorney. The *audiencia* pronounced in favor of the Tlaxcalans, citing the Tlaxcalans' many services in subduing the nomadic tribes of the north.[70] Of course, not all cases were resolved in favor of Native litigants, but the Spanish court system became a major vehicle for their rights, demonstrating the ways that Amerindians were drawn into the institutional framework of the Spanish.

When they could not gain redress for grievances in local courts and in the capital cities of the Indies, some Indigenous litigants took their case directly to the Spanish court in Madrid, sometimes even demanding an audience with the

---

[66] Galo Román Valarezo, *La resistencia andina: Cayambe, 1500–1800* (Quito, Ecuador: Abya Yala, 1987), 224–30.

[67] For a pioneering study of how the Andean peoples of Huamanga utilized the courts to protect their interests, see Steve J. Stern, *Peru's Indian Peoples and the Challenge of Spanish Conquest: Huamanga to 1640* (Madison: University of Wisconsin Press, 1982), 114–37.

[68] *Recopilación de leyes de los reynos de las Indias* (1680; repr., Madrid: Ediciones Cultura Hispánica, 1973), Tomo II, Libro VI, Título I, ley 47, folio 194.

[69] Brian P. Owensby, *Empire of Law and Indian Justice in Colonial Mexico* (Stanford, CA: Stanford University Press, 2008), 44.

[70] Ibid., 50.

king. In the sixteenth century, Indigenous elites primarily made the expensive trip to Madrid, representing either themselves or their communities. These early travelers often used their connections at the viceregal court or with the religious orders to learn how to present their case before crossing the Atlantic. If they could not travel themselves, sometimes Indigenous litigants hired legal representatives, called *procuradores* (either Spanish or Indigenous), to present their case in Spain.[71] By the seventeenth century, Andean Indigenous representatives took up long residence in Madrid, where they learned Castilian, became Hispanicized, and even assumed leadership positions when they returned to the Indies. While in Spain, many Indigenous travelers asked for rewards (*mercedes*) for various services to the Crown. Some were charlatans, who created a fictionalized identity as important leaders, called *caciques principales*. Jerónimo Lorenzo Limaylla (alias Lorenzo Ayun Chifo) used his connections with Franciscan writer Fray Buenaventura de Salinas y Córdoba to travel to Spain, where he assumed the identity of a *cacique principal* from Jauja, even though he was a commoner from the *llanos* in Reque. When he returned to Peru, he assumed the duties of a cacique, impressing witnesses with his cosmopolitan ways.[72] By the seventeenth century, Indigenous cosmopolitans such as Limaylla often claimed to represent not only their own or their communities' interests, but also the whole Indigenous nation (*nación índica*).[73]

Another way that Amerindian groups became forcibly integrated into the Atlantic world was through Indigenous slavery, particularly in frontier zones. Although the Crown outlawed Indigenous slavery in 1542, the demand for enslaved individuals continued. In the northern frontier of New Spain, where Crown authority remained weak, such servitude continued unabated as Spaniards enslaved Amerindians illegally throughout the seventeenth century, with the excuse that they were captured in "just wars."[74] Indigenous groups also enslaved their enemies and either adopted them to replace a relative lost in war or sold them to eager Spanish merchants in northern New Spain to work as laborers on local estates. Many were shipped to work on Caribbean island plantations.

In 1680, the Pueblo Indians of New Mexico decided to rebel against Spanish rule to end such enslavement, the oppression of Spanish settlers, and the frequent punishments meted out by the local Franciscan friars trying to stamp out all forms of pre-Christian religious rites. The apparent leader of the rebellion, named Po'pay, called on seventy diverse Pueblo communities to rise up together against the Spanish colonizers and the friars. The rebels destroyed houses,

---

[71] José Carlos de la Puente Luna, *Andean Cosmopolitans: Seeking Justice and Reward at the Spanish Royal Court* (Austin: University of Texas Press, 2018), 51–88.
[72] Ibid., 177–78.   [73] Ibid., 89–122, for the evolution of this process.
[74] Alan Gallay, "Slaving, European, of Native Americans," in Miller et al., *Princeton Companion to Atlantic History*, 434.

ranches, missions, and churches in New Mexico, killing some four hundred men, women, and children, and they forced the remaining Spaniards to abandon the capital of Santa Fé and flee to the relative safety of El Paso. The Spaniards did not return to the province for twelve years. Indigenous enslavement, however, returned to New Mexico with the Spaniards, and it lasted along the whole northern frontier of New Spain until the nineteenth century.[75] Just as in the Iberian Reconquista, frontier zones were violent places where law and order did not always prevail.

Cultural Change and Colonial Rule

Although slavery and violence endured along the frontier, in the populous areas of the Indies more peaceful contacts between Amerindian and Spanish peoples led to the emergence of a heterogeneous Hispanicized, bicultural Indigenous group, whom contemporaries called *indios ladinos*.[76] Unlike Jews and Muslims in Iberia, who practiced their religions until the late fifteenth century, the *indios ladinos* were converts to Christianity and taught to reject all past Indigenous religious beliefs. They also spoke and were literate in Castilian and sometimes even Latin, and many served initially as translators (*lenguas*), especially in the early conquest years. Some translators even participated in the conquest of other Indigenous groups and became known as "Indian conquistadors."[77] Apparently, all too many of these *indios ladinos* acquired reputations as tricksters or con men, who used their knowledge of Castilian and colonial law to manipulate the Spanish court system to their advantage, often at the expense of other Amerindians. Others served as intermediaries and clan leaders or Indigenous governors, negotiating between the needs of the Spanish overlords and their Indigenous communities. Some enterprising *indios ladinos* sought opportunities to enrich themselves, becoming landowners or provincial merchants. They also worked as assistants to Spanish clerical *visitadores*, attempting to stamp out enduring pre-Columbian religious practices, or as even translators at Church synods. For example, one *indio ladino*, Juan Tocas, participated as an Andean assistant to the idolatry trials in Cajatambo during the 1650s.[78] *Indios ladinos*

---

[75] Two important books dealing with the Pueblo Revolt are Ramón Gutiérrez, *When Jesus Came, the Corn Mothers Went Away: Marriage, Sexuality, and Power in New Mexico, 1500–1846* (Stanford, CA: Stanford University Press, 1991), 95–140; and Reséndez, *Other Slavery*, 149–71. Reséndez is particularly strong in his view that the enslavement of the Indigenous people was the major cause of the revolt.

[76] A pioneering study of the *indio ladino* is Rolena Adorno, "Images of the *Indios Ladinos* in Early Colonial Peru," in Andrien and Adorno, *Transatlantic Encounters*, 232–70.

[77] Mathew Restall, *Maya Conquistador* (Boston: Beacon Press, 1998).

[78] Adorno, *Polemics of Possession*, 25–29; and John Charles, *Allies at Odds: The Andean Church and Its Indigenous Agents, 1583–1671* (Albuquerque: University of New Mexico Press, 2010), 144–45.

also served as legal agents, petitioning the Crown to recognize the needs of Indigenous communities, to reward their personal service to the monarchy, or to make the king aware of abuses perpetrated by Spanish colonial officials. In short, *indios ladinos* lived in a contact zone between early colonial Spanish and Indigenous societies.[79]

Educated *indios ladinos* worked with friars such as Bernardino de Sahagún, the Franciscan who attempted to preserve knowledge of the Nahua past in New Spain.[80] Still others were genuine public intellectuals, who wrote histories or long petitions about the past and present state of the empire. Often educated in mendicant or Jesuit schools, such as the Colegio de Santa Cruz de Santiago Tlatelolco in Mexico City or the Colegio de San Francisco de Borja in Cusco, they were taught to speak and write in Castilian. They also read European books and became schooled in European styles of pictorial art. Nahua scholars such as Domingo Francisco de San Antón Chimalpahin Quauhtlehuanitzin and the brothers Bartolomé de Alva and Fernando de Alva Ixtlilxochitl wrote histories and contemporary accounts in their own language using the Latin alphabet.[81] The emergence of these bicultural Indigenous intellectuals appeared earlier in New Spain than in the Andes, since Nahua was adapted to the Latin alphabet, and within a generation, they had produced texts in Castilian and their native languages.

By contrast, the first full dictionaries and grammars in the Indigenous languages of the Andes did not appear until the early seventeenth century. The first dictionary and grammar of Quechua, by Diego González Holguin, *Vocabulario de la lengua general de todo el Perú llamada lengua Quechua o del Inca*, appeared in 1608, while the counterpart in Aymara, by Ludovico Bertonio, appeared between 1603 and 1612. Written works produced by Andean *indios ladinos* appeared coincidentally about the same time. The principal languages of the Andes had no known alphabetic writing before the arrival of the Spaniards, so Indigenous scribes and authors produced very few texts in Quechua and Aymara using the Latin alphabet. In the early seventeenth century, a mestizo, El Inca Garcilaso de la Vega, and two Indigenous writers, Juan de Santa Cruz Pachacuti Yamqui Salcamayhua and Felipe Guaman Poma de Ayala, each produced major literary-historical texts that attempted to put the disruptions of the colonial era within the context of the Andean past. They sought to understand,

---

[79] Adorno, *Polemics of Possession*, 23–25.

[80] Elizabeth Hill Boone, "Foreword," in Ramos and Yannakakis, *Indigenous Intellectuals*, x; Camilla Townsend, *Annals of Native America: How the Nahuas of Colonial Mexico Kept Their History Alive* (Oxford: Oxford University Press, 2016).

[81] John Frederick Schwaller, "The Brothers Fernando de Alva Ixtlilxochitl and Bartolomé de Alva: Two Native Intellectuals of Seventeenth-Century Mexico," in Ramos and Yannakakis, eds., *Indigenous Intellectuals*, 39–59. On Chimalpahin, see Susan Schroeder, *Chimalpahin and the Kingdom of Chalco* (Tucson: University of Arizona Press, 1991).

explain, and ameliorate the plight of their people. For these Andean intellectuals, writing became a political act.

The use of writing to rework history and to oppose the corruption and abuses of Spanish colonialism emerged most eloquently in the rich, complex study of Guaman Poma, *El primer nueva corónica y buen gobierno* (ca. 1615). A self-proclaimed Andean nobleman, he apparently learned to write from his half-brother, a priest, and from his service as an interpreter in the campaigns of Cristóbal de Albornoz to root out the Taqui Onqoy movement in the 1560s. Guaman Poma declared his account an objective history of events in the Andean region from creation to his own day, but it was actually a polemical contribution to contemporary political debates. He argued that a Christian prophet, St. Bartholomew, had come to the Andes and converted the Native peoples to Roman Catholicism until the Inca conquered the region, usurped power from preexisting polities, and introduced paganism and idolatry. He denounced the abuses visited on the Indigenous people by Spanish clerics and colonial officials alike, arguing that the king should return power to the Indigenous peoples, who would establish a sovereign Andean empire loyal to King Philip III of Spain.[82] Guaman Poma fashioned his argument from Andean oral traditions, earlier European chronicles, European biographies of kings and saints, and Catholic sermons. He used Castilian, Quechua, and a host of pictorial images to create his complex but cohesive text—repudiating the Inca past, scornful of some clerics and colonialism, but pro-Andean and orthodox in his Christianity.[83]

After giving his account of the pre-Columbian past and the Spanish conquest, Guaman Poma devoted the final two-thirds of the *Nueva corónica* to a scathing, repetitive account of the abuses perpetrated by Spanish officials and clergyman against the hapless Andeans. He listed a host of Spanish crimes— greed, envy, corruption, and unwarranted sexual license—directing some of his harshest criticisms against the sexual immorality of Spaniards and people of mixed blood in the Andes.[84] Guaman Poma was particularly harsh on racial mixing, arguing against the abuses of mulattos and particularly mestizos, whom he believed diluted the racial and cultural purity of the Andean peoples. To illustrate this wanton licentiousness, Guaman Poma skillfully integrated both

---

[82] Rolena Adorno, *Guaman Poma: Writing and Resistance in Colonial Peru* (1986; repr., Austin: University of Texas Press, 2000), 5.

[83] Ibid., 3–56.

[84] According to Guaman Poma, he had a personal reason for disliking the appropriation of Indigenous women for sexual purposes because the Mercederian friar Martín de Murúa tried to force Guaman Poma's wife into a sexual encounter in the town of Yanaca. Felipe Guaman Poma de Ayala, *The First New Chronicle and Good Government*, abridged ed., selected, trans., and ann. David Frye (Indianapolis, IN: Hackett, 2006), 284; Felipe Guaman Poma de Ayala, *El primer nueva corónica corónica y buen gobierno*, ed. John V. Murra and Rolena Adorno, trans. and textual analysis of the Quechua Jorge Urioste, vol.3 (Mexico City: Siglo Veintiuno, 1980), (906) 920.

textual arguments and pictorial pen-and-ink images to reinforce his point. For example, he depicts a drunken banquet offered by a Spanish priest for a mestizo, an Andean, and a mulatto, all being served by a diminutive Indigenous waiter (see Fig. 3.2). The small figure on the tray resembles the body of a headless woman, while the fruit on the priest's left resembles a phallus, with an arrow pointing to his groin. Guaman Poma suggests that the surly priest and his companions intend to seek sexual favor from unspecified women, probably Indigenous. He continued this theme even more graphically in another image that shows a *corregidor* and his lieutenant peering into the window of a naked, sleeping Andean woman, with both men pointing to her exposed genitalia (see Fig. 3.3). Finally, in another image, Guaman Poma denounced the lust and licentiousness among Spanish men and women (see Fig. 3.4). With one hand, the Spanish man makes the sign of the *figa* (a crude symbol for sexual intercourse), while the other grasps his sword, positioned like an erect penis. For her part, the woman offers a rose, a symbol of the female sex, while her other hand rests over her genitals.[85] In each of these cases, the text and drawings communicate the author's outrage, reinforcing his argument that the Indigenous people of the Andes were abused by a mixture of immoral Spaniards; traitorous, Native Andean collaborators; and ignoble individuals of mixed blood.

Despite his carefully constructed arguments, by the end of his book Guaman Poma presented himself as an aged, broken, and unsuccessful petitioner. He lamented a world turned upside down (*mundo al revés*), with the king residing in Castile and the pope in Rome, leaving the Indigenous people to be despoiled by corrupt Europeans. His monumental opus had failed to unite the histories of Europe and the Andes. Guaman Poma tried using writing to resist Spanish domination, but in the end, this did not empower the Andean peoples. The old, disenchanted man could only carry his manuscript to Lima, perhaps knowing that it would probably never be read by his intended audience.[86]

Painting proved another medium for Indigenous artists in the Andes to take up naturalistic, figurative designs. According to numerous Spanish chroniclers, painting had existed in the Inca Empire, but these works probably employed abstract and geometrical motifs, rather than figurative images. After the conquest, the Catholic Church needed skilled Indigenous artists and artisans to decorate their churches, so they trained Andean artists in the European figurative tradition. The apogee of Indigenous painting came during the seventeenth century with the Cusco school, which flourished until approximately 1800. The

---

[85] This analysis is drawn from Mercedes López-Baralt, "From Looking to Seeing: The Image as Text and the Author as Artist," in *Guaman Poma de Ayala: The Colonial Art of an Andean Author*, ed. Rolena Adorno (New York: The Americas Society, 1992), 28–31; and López-Baralt, *Icono y conquista: Guaman Poma de Ayala* (Madrid: Hiperón, 1988), 189–267.

[86] Adorno, *Guaman Poma: Writing and Resistance*, 139–43.

Fig. 3.2 A dinner involving a priest, a mestizo, a mulatto, and an Andean.
Source: El primer nueva corónica y buen gobierno, p. 603, 617, GkS 2232 4. Courtesy of the Royal Library of Denmark, Copenhagen.

Fig. 3.3 A *corregidor* and his lieutenant uncovering a naked, sleeping Andean woman.

Source: El primer nueva corónica y Buen gobierno, p. 503, 507, GkS 2232 4. Courtesy of the Royal Library of Denmark, Copenhagen.

Fig. 3.4 Lust and licentiousness among Spanish men and women.
Source: El primer nueva corónica y Buen gobierno, p. 534, 538, GkS 2232 4. Courtesy of the Royal Library of Denmark, Copenhagen.

former Inca capital had always been a center of Indigenous painting, but a devastating earthquake in 1650 led to a tremendous architectural and artistic rebirth as its citizens tried to reconstruct the city. Members of the city's Indigenous and mestizo artistic community formed their own guild, whose artists developed their distinctive hybrid style.

Among the most famous paintings to emerge from the Cusco school dealt with the Virgin Mary, the patroness of the city, who had allegedly appeared in a miracle to save it during the siege by Manco Inca in 1537. Many of the city's Indigenous citizens embraced the veneration of the Virgin, apparently because they identified her with the Andean earth mother, Pachamama, or some other female deity. Regardless of the cult origins, Indigenous artists painting in Cusco ignored European notions of perspective and space, creating images of the Virgin in a flat, two-dimensional style called statue painting. Among the images of the Virgin created by Indigenous artists, the Virgin of Bethlehem was much favored among Cusco's devotional images (see Fig. 3.5). Artists in the Cusco school typically depicted both the Virgin and her child dressed in elaborate triangular vestments, which also resembled the shape of a mountain. Visually, this technique merged the image of the Virgin with the Andean landscape. Moreover, the intricate brocade pattern on both gowns is composed of the kind of repetitive geometric designs reminiscent of those found on Inca-era textiles. What appears an overly stylized, stiff rendition of the Virgin of Bethlehem merely conveyed Andean artistic preferences in representing a Christian religious icon.

During the mature colonial era, the artistic worlds of Europe and the Indies merged, creating dynamic new artistic practices spanning a number of mediums—painting, drawings, and even ceramics. Indigenous artists in New Spain and Peru began producing works in the European style for churches, public buildings, and private homes. When Indigenous painters, for example, produced religious images, they did so by blending European and Indigenous artistic forms. Likewise, writers such as Guaman Poma and a variety of Indigenous artists produced their written (and in some cases illustrated) works using a blend of European and Indigenous literary and artistic conventions.[87] They did not deny (and in some cases strongly affirmed) Indigenous history and culture, but at the same time they allowed for an openness to European culture, language, and customs. Their work interwove the diverse cultural landscapes that emerged in the New World, as Native American, European, mestizo, African, and mulatto cultures merged to form extended, complex, and diverse cultural identity formations.[88]

---

[87] Adorno, *Guaman Poma: Writing and Resistance*, 131.

[88] The pioneering work on transculturation is Fernando Ortiz, *Cuban Counterpoint: Tobacco and Sugar*, trans. Harriet de Onís (New York: Knopf, 1947). For more recent studies of the concept for contemporary literature, see Mikhail N. Epstein, "Transculture: A Broad Way between Globalism and Multiculturalism," *American Journal of Economics & Sociology* 68, no. 1 (2009): 327–51.

Fig. 3.5 Virgin of Bethlehem, eighteenth century.
Source: Museo Pedro de Osma, Lima.

In short, over the long colonial era artistic expressions throughout the Spanish Atlantic world linked and mixed blooded cultures of the past with the ever-changing colonial present.

Silver, Gold, and the Colonial Economy

Silver and gold formed the basis of the early modern monetary system and fueled market exchanges throughout the Atlantic world in the sixteenth and early seventeenth centuries. After 1640, however, official figures for bullion output, tabulated in accounts by the royal treasury in Spanish America, began a serious decline (see Fig. 3.6). Silver production dropped in value from 102,830,000 pesos in the 1640s to 85,730,000 pesos in the 1660s. It then recovered to over 100 million pesos from 1671 to 1690, but fell again to 78,250,000 pesos, a new low for the seventeenth century. New Spain became the new leader in silver production, as discoveries of new deposits and more abundant supplies of mercury contributed to the northern viceroyalty's passing the Viceroyalty in Peru in registered silver output, a position it maintained throughout the rest of the colonial era. Production in Peru declined, particularly at the formerly dominant mines at Potosí, from 69,330,000 pesos in the 1640s to a low of 27,410,000 pesos in the period from 1711 to 1720.[89] Meanwhile, gold production fluctuated from a high of 12,750,000 pesos in the opening decade of the seventeenth century to a low of 4,540,000 pesos in the decade from 1671 to 1680. It always remained the less abundant metal in the Spanish Atlantic world.

Despite the declining productivity of official output from silver and gold mines in the Indies, figures drawn from French and British consular reports in Seville and Cádiz published in Dutch economic gazettes of the period present a strikingly different view about New World bullion imports.[90] These sources indicate that, after a fall in American treasury receipts around 1650, bullion imports from 1660 to 1680 reached 297,800,000 pesos, which was substantially higher than in the boom years of official sources between 1580 and 1620, when Potosí's production was at its apogee (see Fig. 3.7). These high import figures continued throughout the second half of the seventeenth century, rising to 171,500,000 pesos from 1670 to 1679 and falling to 129,500,000 pesos from 1680 to 1689, but recovering to 146,300,000 pesos in the final decade of the century. Such production figures are even more incredible given

---

An important study of the concept that summarizes the literature on globalization and its role in shaping the modern transcultural novel is Arianna Dagnino, *Transcultural Writers in an Age of Global Mobility* (West Lafayette, IN: Purdue University Press, 2015), 4, 140–41, 201–3; for a discussion of race and *mestizaje*, see Ben Vinson III, *Before Mestizaje: The Frontiers of Race and Caste in Colonial Mexico* (Cambridge: Cambridge University Press, 2017), passim.

[89] Kenneth J. Andrien, "Economies, American: Spanish Territories," in Miller et al., *Princeton Companion to Atlantic History*, 171.

[90] Michel Morineau, *Incroyables gazettes et fabuleux metaux* (Cambridge: Cambridge University Press, 1985). Henry Kamen has also used consular reports to present figures for bullion imports well above the official records. See Kamen, *Spain in the Later Seventeenth Century*, 132–40.

THE MATURE COLONIAL ORDER

Years	Silver	Gold	Total
1492–1500	0	0.7	0.7
1501–1510	0	8.2	8.2
1511–1520	0	7.21	7.21
1521–1530	0.34	3.92	4.26
1531–1540	7.55	11.12	18.67
1541–1550	28.12	8.73	36.85
1551–1560	42.71	10.64	53.35
1561–1570	56.05	8.85	64.9
1571–1580	71.47	13	84.47
1581–1590	100.19	10.18	110.37
1591–1600	113.4	11.91	125.31
1601–1610	121.81	12.75	134.56
1611–1620	124.28	10.43	134.71
1621–1630	123.63	9.91	133.54
1631–1640	128.6	5.24	133.84
1641–1650	102.83	6.72	109.55
1651–1660	92.16	6.73	98.89
1661–1670	85.73	4.74	90.47
1671–1680	100.02	4.54	104.56
1681–1690	109.85	5.85	115.7
1691–1700	92.8	8.24	101.04
1701–1710	78.25	33.24	111.49
1711–1720	92.61	37.05	129.66

Fig. 3.6 New World Gold and Silver Output in millions of Pesos of 272 Maravedis, 1492–1810.

Source: John J. TePaske and edited by Kendall W. Brown, *A New World of Gold and Silver* (Leiden and Boston, Brill, 2010), Table 1-2, p. 20.

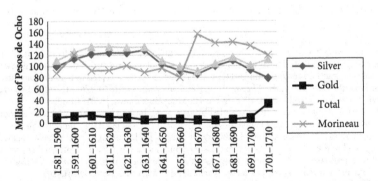

Fig. 3.7 New World gold and silver output in millions of pesos of 272 maravedís, 1581–1710.

Source: John J. TePaske and edited by Kendall W. Brown, *A New World of Gold and Silver* (Leiden and Boston, Brill, 2010), Table 1-2, p. 20; Table 7.2, p. 314, Table 7.3, p. 315.

that sizeable shipments of Mexican bullion were left on the Manila galleons bound for Asia. If these figures are correct, only rampant contraband—at levels well above the 15 to 20 percent estimated by contemporaries—can explain the rise in bullion imports to Europe. Moreover, given that the number of sailings of the *flotas* and *galeones* declined during the century, more silver would have had to travel on each fleet sailing from the Indies to Spain, if the gazettes are accurate.[91] These unconfirmed reports written by foreign consuls and printed in Dutch gazettes, however, do not explain how the New World gold and silver mines continued to produce at such high levels after 150 years of operation.[92] No new advances in mining technology can explain the surge in productivity. Indeed, given the declining production of mercury at the Almadén (in Spain) and Huancavelica (in Peru) mercury mines, the upsurge could only have relied on using unprecedented levels of less efficient smelting methods.[93] The fall in production at Potosí, smelting and new deposits in New Spain must have reached historically high levels in New Spain from 1650 to 1700. Silver imports declined rapidly by the early eighteenth century, when the gazette's figures more closely parallel the official figures. After 1710, official silver production was greater than the amounts recorded in the gazettes, sometimes substantially more.[94] It is not clear, however, who provided the figures published in the gazettes, nor is it certain that these figures were accurate. Did the authors of the gazettes get their information on bullion arrivals from the Indies from personal inspections, insider knowledge, or merely rumors?[95] As a result, the controversy over mining production in the Spanish Atlantic world remains unresolved.

Regardless of whether production at the silver mines in the Americas rose or fell during the seventeenth century, American silver found its way all around the world. Although the bulk of the silver made its way to Seville, much of the specie passed on to Dutch, French, and British merchants, who apparently provided much of the finished goods sold in America through the legal trading system. Dutch ships carried precious metals from the Indies to Asia, where it

---

[91] There were twenty-five *flotas* sent to New Spain and sixteen *galeones* sent from Spain to Tierra Firme from 1650 to 1700. The tonnage of the vessels did not increase during this period, fluctuating between one hundred and four hundred tons, and 77 percent of these vessels were under four hundred tons. Litgardo García Fuentes, *El comercio español con América (1650–1700)* (Seville: Diputación Provincial de Sevilla and Escuela de Estudios Hispano-Americanos, 1980), 411–13.

[92] Morineau's figures have been accepted by several established historians, without questioning the veracity of the sources. See Lynch, *Bourbon Spain, 1700–1808*, 18–21. In a more recent edition of his classic study of Habsburg Spain, Lynch argues that the fall in output in Peru and New Spain was exaggerated in the official figures or that treasury remittances may have been drawn from accumulated reserves preserved from more prosperous times. See John Lynch, *Spain under the Habsburgs: The Hispanic World in Crisis and Change* (Oxford: Basil Blackwell, 1992), 282n136.

[93] This point is made in a very intriguing article draft by Mark A. Burkholder, "Spanish American Bullion and European Importation of Treasure in the Late Seventeenth Century: A Comment" (unpublished essay provided by the author), 17–19. I would like to thank Professor Burkholder for making this work available to me.

[94] TePaske, *New World of Gold and Silver*, 310.   [95] Ibid., 311.

was traded for Asian luxury goods, such as tea, silks, damasks, and spices. Other European merchants carried silver to the North Sea and the Baltic, exchanging it for furs and lumber. Italian traders also took American bullion to the eastern Mediterranean and the Ottoman Empire, purchasing luxury goods from the East. In addition, silver made its way from Acapulco to the Philippines and then to China, where it bought Asian luxury goods and met the Chinese economy's need for circulating currency. Finally, enterprising Peruvian merchants, known as *peruleros*, bypassed the official convoy system and carried silver, most often illegally, from the mines of the southern viceroyalty to Asia and Europe.[96]

During the century, the Spanish Atlantic economy also underwent a period of consolidation and diversification. The Indigenous populations slowly recovered from epidemic diseases of the previous century, immigration from Europe continued, and large numbers of enslaved Indigenous and African people were imported to work in the cities, placer gold mines, and burgeoning plantation economies. The market economy expanded apace, and although silver mining remained important in the central regions of New Spain and Peru, colonial economies became more diverse and integrated. Investment capital flowed to other productive sectors, such as agriculture, grazing, textile manufacturing, and artisan production, particularly in areas where mining declined. Population centers shifted and commercial exchanges became more widespread as formerly peripheral provinces (such as Chile, Buenos Aires, Colombia, and Venezuela in South America and Guanajuato and Guadalajara in New Spain) rose to prominence. Intercolonial trade in legal and contraband goods expanded throughout the Indies, particularly as the legal system of *flotas* and *galeones* declined. Overall, regional economies in the Indies experienced cycles of growth and contraction as they became more politically and economically independent of the metropolis.[97]

Merchant houses in Mexico City and Lima, centered on the powerful merchant guilds (*consulados*) in those cities, dominated commercial transactions in the Americas, relying on a sophisticated network of family, patronage, clerical, and private and state connections. These transactions were linked by sophisticated credit mechanisms—bills of exchange, certificates of deposit, and letters of credit—which funded wide-ranging commercial exchanges. Mercantile interests advanced loans and bought annuities (*juros*) to keep the colonial state solvent, and by 1660 they had even gained control over the collection of commercial taxes in the capital cities. One *limeño* banker, Juan de la Cueva, maintained branch offices in Potosí, Cusco, and Arica, and each office advanced credit to colonial treasury offices, local governors, *corregidores*, miners, smaller-scale merchants, and clerical organizations. As the legal system of *flotas* and *galeones* slowly declined in the second half of the century, large commercial

---

[96] Ibid., 305.   [97] This argument is advanced in Andrien, *Crisis and Decline*, 11–41.

houses opened direct trade with Acapulco and Seville, plied intercolonial trade networks, and supplied regional markets. These merchants often relied on the forced distribution of goods or by advancing credit (*repartimiento de comercio*) as the interior markets expanded with the recovery of Amerindian populations in Peru and New Spain.[98] A number of these merchants were Portuguese *conversos*, who operated openly in the Spanish Atlantic, particularly during the union of the Spanish and Portuguese Crowns from 1580 to 1640. With the rebellion of Portugal in 1640, however, the Inquisition prosecuted these *conversos* for being crypto-Jews and broke their commercial power in the Indies.[99] Nonetheless, merchants in Lima and Mexico City (and their counterparts in the merchant guild of Seville) found ways to use their political ties to promote legal and contraband commerce throughout the Spanish Atlantic world.

The wealth of the Spanish Indies also attracted the attention of its European competitors, particularly the Dutch, who were the first power to challenge the Iberian commercial monopoly. The spread of Calvinism in the Netherlands beginning in the 1560s, conflicts over threats of the Habsburg monarch to allow the Inquisition to operate in the Netherlands, and fiscal pressure from Madrid all encouraged the Dutch to revolt. By the early seventeenth century, the Dutch states of Holland and Zeeland dominated overseas expansion by gaining a controlling interest in two state-licensed joint-stock companies, the Dutch East India Company (founded in 1602) and the Dutch West India Company (WIC, founded in 1621). These companies opened trading posts, engaged in contraband trade, and raided Iberian shipping.[100] In 1628, WIC warships commanded by Piet Heyn captured the entire Spanish silver fleet at Matanzas, off the coast of Cuba, after the fleet was scattered during a hurricane. Company warships took Salvador de Bahia in Brazil in 1624, and after they were expelled, the WIC established a foothold in the province of Pernambuco in 1630, which they held until 1654. Company warships commanded by Joris von Spilbergen raided in the Pacific between 1614 and 1617. Later expeditions between 1623 and 1626, commanded by Jacques l'Hermite, and Hendrick Brouwer's incursions from 1642 and 1644 also preyed on Spanish shipping and tried unsuccessfully to establish a foothold in South America.[101] Despite early successes, these WIC operations ultimately proved disappointing, and the company went bankrupt in 1674. The English and the French followed in the footsteps of the Dutch,

---

[98] The two major books on the merchants and *consulados* of Mexico City and Lima in this period are Louisa Schell Hoberman, *Mexico's Merchant Elite, 1590–1660: Silver, State, and Society* (Durham, NC: Duke University Press, 1991); and Suárez, *Desafíos transatlántico*.

[99] Studnicki-Gizbert, *Nation upon the Ocean Sea*, 151–81.

[100] The best new work on the Dutch Atlantic World is Wim Klooster, *The Dutch Moment: War, Trade, and Settlement in the Seventeenth-Century Atlantic World* (Ithaca, NY: Cornell University Press, 2016).

[101] See Peter T. Bradley, *The Lure of Peru: Maritime Intrusion into the South Sea, 1598–1701* (New York: St. Martin's Press, 1989).

beginning with modest privateering ventures to raid Spanish and Portuguese shipping. By 1634, the Dutch had established a foothold on Curacao off the Venezuelan coast, however, and in 1654, the English captured Jamaica. Both islands became major centers of contraband trade in the Caribbean to the Spanish Indies. These overseas operations by the Dutch, English, and French disrupted Spanish commerce and introduced competing contraband goods in markets throughout the Spanish Indies.

Ursula de Jesús and the Souls in Purgatory

During the lifetime of the Afro-Peruvian mystic Ursula de Jesús, Lima was a vibrant, prosperous, and cosmopolitan capital of the Viceroyalty of Peru. It was the seat of the viceregal court, the most important *audiencia* in the realm, and the center of a prosperous colonial economy. As the commercial entrepôt for South America, silver from the highland mines was exchanged for merchandise from Europe and elsewhere in the Americas. Although social mobility remained more common in the Indies than in metropolitan Spain, as a viceregal capital Lima had a highly stratified urban society, particularly compared to provincial capitals or frontiers zones. In Lima, people of European ancestry (both peninsular-born Spaniards and Creoles) occupied the highest position, followed by those of mixed racial ancestry, Amerindian residents, and large numbers of Afro-Peruvian freedman and enslaved individuals. Between 1581 and 1640, some six hundred thousand African slaves had arrived in Spanish America, many destined for urban areas and the growing number of plantations in the Caribbean, Peru, and New Spain. After 1640, the Spanish territories in the New World received less than seventy-five thousand, but the numbers in prosperous, growing urban centers, such as Lima, remained a substantial and highly visible part of the urban landscape.[102] Whether enslaved or free, Africans typically were considered the lowest social class in the viceregal capital.

As the religious hub of the viceroyalty, Lima was home to a plethora of stately churches and religious houses, including the large convent of Santa Clara, founded in 1605 in what is today the poor neighborhood of Barrios Altos. As at the other female religious houses, life at Santa Clara served as an expression of Catholic religiosity, but it also reflected colonial social stratification. Convent life was rigidly hierarchical, with nuns of the black veil occupying the highest rank, followed by nuns of the white veil, novices preparing to take final vows, *donadas* (religious servants, sometimes recognized for their spiritual gifts), regular servants, and enslaved persons, mostly of African origin. One of the

---

[102] Antonio Feros, *Speaking of Spain: The Evolution of Race and Nation in the Hispanic World* (Boston: Harvard University Press, 2017), 139–40.

enslaved Black individuals serving at the Convent of Santa Clara was Ursula de Jesús. Much is known about this Afro-Peruvian woman because, at the request of her confessor, she left a diary of her visions and mystical life from 1647 to her death in 1666. This journal details her daily routine and much about spiritual life in the convent.[103]

Ursula de Jesús began as a simple enslaved woman serving the needs of her mistress, Inés del Pulgar, a nun of the black veil. As a young woman, Ursula chafed at her humble status, displaying signs of vanity and a rebellious spirit. After narrowly escaping death by falling into a deep well, Ursula changed her ways and led an exemplary holy life. In fact, she became a famous mystic who had divinely inspired visions. She claimed to communicate with souls in purgatory, a liminal space between heaven and hell, often praying on their behalf to release them from their suffering and allow the worthy to ascend to heaven. She had many conversations with these tormented souls, particularly with deceased religious figures, some even former nuns at Santa Clara. She even had a vision of Jesus, who expressed his disappointment with the moral laxity of some female religious at the convent. Her fame eventually led one of the convent's nuns of the black veil, Rafaela de Esquivel, to purchase Ursula's freedom so she could devote more time to God's service. As a result, Ursula became a respected religious servant, or *donada*, in the convent, who enjoyed fame for her efforts to save the souls in purgatory. Despite her notoriety, reputation for self-abnegation, and good works, Ursula did not escape the racial prejudices held against Afro-Peruvians, even in the convent of Santa Clara. Although renowned for her piety and holiness, Ursula could never hope to attain the status of a nun or even gain a measure of the recognition afforded other holy women of European descent in Lima. In many ways, her life reflected the strictures society placed on all Afro-Peruvians in the viceregal capital. Ursula believed that her long hours spent serving the nuns, doing laundry and kitchen work, were simply a reflection of the suffering that Jesus endured during his passion and death on the cross. When she died on February 23, 1666, the nuns of Santa Clara mourned the passing of this pious former enslaved woman and buried her beneath the chapel in the convent. They even commissioned a painting of her, which remains hanging in the convent to this day.

Conclusion

During the seventeenth century, a more stable colonial political and institutional culture emerged as the Indies drifted into an era of greater autonomy from

---

[103] The story of Ursula de Jesús is drawn from Nancy E. van Deusen, "Ursula de Jesús: A Seventeenth-Century Afro-Peruvian Mystic," in Andrien, *Human Tradition*, 101–16; and Van Deusen, *Ursula de Jesús*.

Spain. This stemmed both from Spain's preoccupation with its European wars and from the resilience of the Habsburg composite monarchy. Composite monarchy was inherently a decentralized, but flexible political system that involved ongoing negotiations about political power between the monarch, his ministers, and powerful elites in each province or kingdom. Given the geographical and ethnic diversity of the Indies, this allowed political institutions to evolve as Spain's New World possessions matured. Although the law initially prohibited Creoles from holding most high-ranking bureaucratic posts, local citizens in the Indies often forged economic and social alliances with government officials to influence policy decisions. Bribery, corruption, and influence peddling, which the Crown considered illegal, became tools used by colonial officials and Creole allies to make the viceregal regimes increasingly responsive to local rather than metropolitan needs. Later, the sale of key public appointments accelerated this process of local empowerment, allowing colonial elites to gain possession of many strategic bureaucratic positions, previously dominated by peninsulars. This may have strengthened the government by garnering greater support from Creole elites, but it came at a cost to the beleaguered Crown. During the century, the Crown, desperate for revenues to fight its European wars, attempted to heighten fiscal pressure and exert greater control over the Spanish Indies. This contributed to nearly three decades of political disorder in New Spain and serious rebellions in Catalonia, Portugal, Sicily, and Naples. Colonial officials in Peru resisted the pressure to raise taxes by selling *juros* and contracting loans and forced donations, which allowed viceregal treasury officials to maintain income levels until the 1660s. When such expedients were exhausted, revenue levels and remittances to Spain began to decline. In the hands of these venal officeholders, the colonial regimes in the Indies had evolved from an accessary union with Castile into a looser confederation, an *aeque principaliter*.

Socioeconomic changes in the Spanish Atlantic world followed trends in political developments. The peninsula and the Indies, however, followed different trajectories. While metropolitan Spain suffered military defeat and lost its hegemony in Europe, the Indies experienced an era of greater economic diversification, expanding beyond markets fueled by silver mining and the transatlantic trade. Population shifts led to the growth of formerly peripheral regions of the Indies, such as Chile, the Río de la Plata, and northern South America and the frontiers of northern New Spain. Legal and contraband commerce expanded throughout the region, extending even to Spanish holdings in the Philippines and from there to China. This wealth of the Spanish Atlantic world also attracted the attention of Spain's enemies in Europe, who began preying on Spanish shipping and founding their own colonies in the Americas. Steady socioeconomic change continued in New Spain throughout the century, but Peru suffered a severe setback in 1687 when an earthquake devastated Lima, precipitating an economic decline for the rest of the century.[104]

Despite the efforts of the Crown and the Church to establish rigid Roman Catholic orthodoxy and social hierarchies, society became multiracial, with unplanned levels of social mobility. Popular religious traditions such as local shrines, festivals, chapels, and confraternities flourished. Signs even persisted that the Indigenous peoples had not fully abandoned their old religious beliefs. Some officials saw this blending of Catholic and "pagan" beliefs as merely religious error, while other churchmen favored harsh punishments to stamp out persistent evidence of idolatry. Moreover, local empowerment at the expense of metropolitan Spain did not ameliorate the abuses of the colonial government visited on the Indigenous population, people of mixed racial ancestry, and those descended from Africans. At the same time, a new generation of Hispanicized educated Indigenous groups emerged and served as intermediaries between the colonial order and the Indigenous society. Men such as Guaman Poma protested eloquently against the exploitation of the colonial order, and Amerindians of all backgrounds routinely used the colonial court system to ameliorate such oppression and push for their rights. Although the Afro-Peruvian Ursula de Jesús gained her freedom and became a respected paragon of popular piety in seventeenth-century Lima, she could never overcome her low social position. Clearly, such social hierarchies endured and shaped urban life, and the Spanish Atlantic world of the seventeenth century remained a hybrid but unequal colonial social, religious, and cultural order.

On the whole, the seventeenth century stands out as a formative period. As Creoles slowly gained political clout, Indigenous people, denied a direct voice in governmental affairs, relied on access to the courts and extralegal resistance to defend their rights. They expanded their socioeconomic opportunities by migrating to evade excessive taxes and forced labor and by taking advantage of whatever limited opportunities existed in the colonial system. Pervasive movement to urban areas and Spanish rural estates enabled Spaniards, Creoles, and Indigenous workers to forge a new social order in the countryside. Likewise, alphabetic writing, creating histories in Castilian and Native languages, new forms of artistic expression, and notions of private property became commonplace. Repeated attempts by Roman Catholic clergymen and friars to end Indigenous religious practices continued, but by the end of the century, the merging of Christian and Indigenous beliefs prevailed. As the dramatic events of the conquest had receded, the basic outlines of the Spanish Atlantic world were well established by 1700.

---

[104] Andrien, *Crisis and Decline*, 26.

Timeline: The Mature Colonial Order, 1610–1700

1607	On November 28, Crown officials in Mexico City begin the Real Disagüe de Huehuetoca to drain the lakes around the city to prevent flooding
1608	Publication of Diego González Holguin's dictionary and grammar of the Quechua language
1609–27	Francisco de Avila denounces idolatry in San Damián de Checa, beginning the campaign to extirpate idolatry in the archbishopric of Lima
1612	Publication of Ludovico Bertonio's dictionary and grammar of the Aymara language
1614	The Crown decrees that only legislation formulated specifically for the Indies would have the force of law
1614–17	Dutch West India Company warships raided in the Pacific under the command of Joris von Spilbergen
1615	Completion of Felipe Guaman Poma de Ayala's *El primer nueva corónica y buen gobierno*
1623–26	Dutch West India Company warships raid in the Pacific under Jacques l'Hermite
1624	Riots in Mexico City overthrow the viceroy, the Marqués de Gelves
1628	A Dutch West India Company fleet commanded by Piet Heyn captures the silver fleet returning to Spain at Matanzas, off the coast of Cuba
1633	The Crown begins auctioning appointments to treasury office in the Indies to the highest bidder
1634	Dutch establish a colony at Curacao, off the coast of Venezuela
1640–49	*Visita* of Juan de Palafox y Mendoza in New Spain
1641–71	Second campaign to extirpate idolatry under Archbishop Pedro de Villagómez
1642–44	Dutch West India Company warships commanded by Hendrick Brouwer raid in the Pacific
1648	The debasement of coinage at the Potosí mint leads to the investigation of Francisco Nestares Marín
1654	The English capture Jamaica from Spain and establish a colony
1659	Alleged abuses of the mita lead the viceroy of Peru to appoint special prosecutor Francisco de la Cruz, who dies mysteriously in his sleep on April 23, 1660
1678	The Crown begins selling appointments to *corregimientos* in the Indies
1680	*Recopilación de leyes de los reynos de las Indias* completed
1680	On August 10, Pueblo Revolt in New Mexico
1687	The Crown begins selling appointments to *audiencia* judgeships in the Indies

4

War and Reform in the Spanish Atlantic World, 1700–1796

On May 18, 1781, in the main plaza of Cusco, Spanish authorities conducted a grisly public execution of a notorious rebel, José Gabriel Condorcanqui, who took the name Tupac Amaru II. The last Inca emperor, Tupac Amaru I, had been executed in the same square over two hundred years earlier. Tupac Amaru II, who claimed descent from the Inca royal family, had led a bloody rebellion, which threatened to expel the Spaniards from the Andean highlands and establish a new Inca realm, with himself as Sapa Inca. On the day of his execution, Spanish authorities bound Tupac Amaru and the other rebel leaders in handcuffs and leg irons and tied them to the tails of horses, dragging them along the ground to the city's Plaza de Armas. Tupac Amaru watched the execution of his key followers and family members, including his wife, Michaela Bastidas, and their young son, Hipólito. After their gruesome deaths, Tupac Amaru was led to the center of the plaza. Then the executioner cut out his tongue, threw him face down on the cobblestones, and tied the rebel's hands and feet to four horses, each driven in separate directions, to pull him apart. The horses apparently lacked the strength for the task, and instead, Tupac Amaru remained suspended in the air, with his limbs dislocated but still in place. At this point, the visitor general and presiding judge, José Antonio de Areche, ordered the rebel untied from the horses and beheaded, with his body quartered. Areche ordered Tupac Amaru's body parts, along with those of his son and wife, sent to principal centers of the revolt as a grim reminder of the price of rebellion against the Spanish monarchy. Spanish authorities forced the rebel's nine-year-old son, Fernando, to watch the execution and dismemberment of his parents and brother before he was sent to serve a sentence of permanent exile in Africa.[1]

The execution of Tupac Amaru II was only one brutal incident in the Spanish Atlantic world in an era characterized by reform, political conflict, internal rebellions, and international wars. Violence and expanding the coercive power

---

[1] On the death of Tupac Amaru, see Charles F. Walker, *The Tupac Amaru Rebellion* (Cambridge, MA: Harvard University Press, 2014), 152–67; Kenneth J. Andrien, *Andean Worlds: Indigenous History, Culture, and Consciousness under Spanish Rule, 1532–1825* (Albuquerque: University of New Mexico Press, 2001), 194–95.

of the state became important features in centralizing the monarch's political control throughout his domains. This turbulent period began in 1700, when the last member of the Habsburg dynasty, Charles II, died childless. The king had been ill for most of his reign, and Spain's rivals conspired to divide the kingdom and its rich overseas empire.[2] In a final gesture before dying, King Charles II chose a French claimant to succeed him, Philip of Anjou, the grandson of King Louis XIV. This choice set off the bitter War of the Spanish Succession, involving the principal European powers, which lasted from 1700 to 1713. The British, Dutch, and Austrians supported the candidacy of Archduke Charles, brother of the Habsburg Holy Roman emperor, while the French fought for Philip. The loyalties of the nobility and various provinces of Spain were divided between the French and the Austrian claimants. Although Philip of Anjou finally emerged victorious and the Treaties of Utrecht ensured that the Spanish Atlantic world remained largely intact, the young king (crowned Philip V) inherited a war-torn patrimony badly in need of reform and renovation.[3]

Political reform in Spain began during the war and its aftermath, aimed at creating a unitary state in Spain responsive to the monarch. The Kingdom of Aragon had sided with Archduke Charles during the succession war, and as King Philip V and his armies conquered Valencia and Aragon, they imposed the Nueva Planta (New Plan) that stripped these provinces of their traditional laws, liberties, and privileges (*fueros*); replaced the viceroys with captains general; established new administrative districts ruled by *corregidores* on the Castilian model; abolished their parliaments (*cortes*); and subjected them to the laws of Castile. When Barcelona fell to the armies of Philip, it too was subjected to the New Plan, transforming Spain from a collection of semiautonomous provinces of Castile, Aragon, Valencia, and Cataluña to a single, centralized state.[4] Finally, on November 30, 1714, the Crown created four ministries of state, war, justice and government, and marine and the Indies, headed by secretaries appointed by the king and more directly accountable to him, instead of relying on councils alone for the administration of government affairs.[5]

---

[2] As early as 1668, France and the Holy Roman emperor signed a treaty to divide Spanish territories between them if Charles II died childless. Over the ensuing decades, England and the Dutch also entered the discussion about the partition of the Spanish territories, and in 1698 they decided that the throne of Spain would pass to the Bavarian prince, Joseph Ferdinand, with France and Austria receiving Spanish territories in Italy. In March 1700, after the unexpected death of the Bavarian prince, the European powers agreed to pass the throne of Spain to Archduke Charles of Austria, with other Spanish territories going to the signees. See Henry Kamen, *Philip V of Spain: The King Who Reigned Twice* (New Haven, CT: Yale University Press, 2001), 1–3.

[3] Under the terms of the treaties of Utrecht, Spain lost Milan, Sicily, Naples, Sardinia, Belgium, Gibraltar, and Minorca. Ibid., 79–82.

[4] Elliott, *Imperial Spain, 1469–*, 376–78; Lynch, *Bourbon Spain, 1700–1808*, 62–66.

[5] The ministerial system was borrowed from France, the birthplace of King Philip V, and it emphasized individual accountability to the monarch over the collective responsibility of the

Philip and his sons and successors, Ferdinand VI (1746–59) and Charles III (1759–88), pushed a reformist agenda for the Indies designed to curb the rampant contraband commerce and regain control over the transatlantic trade, raise taxes and fill the depleted royal coffers, modernize state finances and the military, and end the sale of bureaucratic appointments in order to recover authority over the governance of Spain's overseas empire.[6] During the entire eighteenth century, Spain also had to fight in Europe and the Americas to keep its rival colonial powers, Britain, France, and the Netherlands, from attaining direct commercial access to Spanish possessions in the Indies. War and reform thus enjoyed a symbiotic relationship, with conflicts sometimes interfering with Crown attempts at renovation and at other times impelling change, as Spain's ministers attempted to prepare for impending wars with rivals.

The so-called Bourbon reforms during the century initiated fundamental changes in the political and institutional culture in the Spanish Atlantic world, replacing the composite monarchy of the Habsburg dynasty with a more centralized absolutist state. These changes were influenced by intellectual currents in Europe associated with the Enlightenment, which began in northern Europe and spread throughout the Atlantic world. Crown ministers in Spain and its overseas possessions pulled together Enlightenment ideas and merged them with more traditional beliefs to fashion concrete proposals aimed at putting the Spanish Indies more firmly under metropolitan control. The fundamental ideas of the Enlightenment stressed reason and observation, promoting a greater sense of justice and material well-being, as well as the need to compile empirical information to address specific political, scientific, economic, and social issues, instead of relying on tradition and articles of religious faith. Enlightened reformers sought to advance "public happiness" (*felicidad pública*), which involved expanding the power of the monarchy to promote economic growth, public well-being, and national strength.[7] This process involved much more than tightening political control over the composite monarchy and ending the seventeenth-century era of Creole empowerment. Instead, reformist ministers, known as regalists, sought to turn the traditional composite monarchy into a more centralized state by curtailing the power of vested-interest groups and the Church to limit their control over national resources, which they believed impeded economic growth and national prosperity. These policies sought to

---

councils, which remained in place, but more direct administrative power tended to reside with the ministries. Allan J. Kuethe and Kenneth J. Andrien, *The Spanish Atlantic World in the Eighteenth Century: War and the Bourbon Reforms, 1713–1796* (Cambridge: Cambridge University Press, 2014), 42–43.

[6] Ibid., 3–12.

[7] Gabriel B. Paquette, *Enlightenment, Governance, and Reform in Spain and Its Empire, 1759–1808* (Basingstoke, UK: Palgrave Macmillan, 2008), 57–67.

exploit the resources of the Indies for the benefit of metropolitan Spain, making the American provinces more responsive to the needs of the monarchy. Bourbon regalists also attempted to stimulate commerce and tax revenues from the Indies to enrich Spain and ensure that the monarchy had the military resources to defend against the ambitions of its European rivals.

The reforms gathered momentum during the century and reached their apex during the reign of King Charles III (1759-88) as the Crown sponsored a wide array of fiscal, military, administrative, clerical, and commercial changes within the Spanish Atlantic world. The cumulative effect of these reforms was to turn the "kingdoms" of the Indies, established by the Habsburg monarchs, into "colonies" subordinated to the metropole, Spain. The reforms and the dynastic ambitions of the Bourbon monarchs and power politics also led to diplomatic and military conflicts with Spain's rivals. Although this ongoing century of reform produced real successes, it also provoked bitter opposition from Spanish and colonial interest groups who found the innovations a challenge to their prerogatives. Bureaucrats, churchmen, middling and subaltern groups in the Indies, and conservative interests in Spain, such as the merchant's guild in Cádiz, attempted to oppose or at least shape the reform process for their own ends. The configurations of these conflicting interest groups varied throughout the different regions, engendering political clashes that, at times, erupted into violence, such as the Andean rebellion of Tupac Amaru II. As Spanish reformers attempted to create a more centralized absolutist state, such serious political conflicts often influenced the outcome of the reform process throughout the eighteenth-century Spanish Atlantic world.[8]

The Impact of the War of the Spanish Succession in the Indies

The War of the Spanish Succession severely disrupted legal commerce in the Spanish Atlantic world and encouraged British, French, and Dutch contrabandists to supply markets in the Indies with needed merchandise. There was no operating Spanish navy to protect merchant vessels from Seville to the Indies, and wartime disruptions to Iberian commerce made it virtually impossible to secure provisions for the *flotas* and *galeones*. Such foreign smuggling efforts could only continue, however, with the connivance of colonial officials, at one point even involving the viceroy of Peru, Don Manuel de Oms y Santa Pau Olom de Sentmenat y de Lanuza, the first Count of Castelldosríus (1707-10). As a Catalan aristocrat loyal

---

[8] Kuethe and Andrien, *Spanish Atlantic World*, 3-12.

to the Bourbon Philip of Anjou, Castelldosríus had his family assets confiscated when most of Cataluña supported the Habsburg claimant, Charles of Austria. For his loyalty, King Philip V named Castelldosríus viceroy of Peru, but the nobleman arrived in Lima in 1707 deeply in debt.[9] The viceroy quickly moved to gain control over the contraband trade in the Pacific by placing friends, family, and cronies in key strategic positions, such as the ports of Pisco and Ica. He also forged alliances with those already serving in other key ports (Arica, Callao, Concepción, Guayaquil, and Trujillo). The viceroy then allowed French merchants, who plied the Pacific with near impunity, to unload goods while he and his allies allegedly extracted a 25 percent tax on all merchandise sold.[10]

Despite reaping large profits from illicit trade, Castelldorfus shamelessly bullied the Lima merchant community to participate in the legal trade fair of 1707. The *limeño* merchants balked, given that contraband goods already saturated Peruvian markets, making it fruitless to try to sell higher-priced European wares obtained at Portobelo. The viceroy convinced them to attend the fair by promising to curtail his own contraband activities in their absence, but when they returned to Lima in 1709, they found that Castelldosríus had betrayed them. French contraband goods had continued to flood viceregal markets, making it virtually impossible to profit from the sale of goods obtained legally at Portobelo. The viceroy's enemies denounced him, leading to his suspension from office in 1710; only his untimely death that same year spared him the disgrace of prosecution. An inventory of his estate, however, revealed that he had amassed a personal fortune of nearly 1,300,000 pesos during his three-year reign.[11]

Corruption and the contraband trade did not end with the downfall of the Count of Castelldosríus, since his successor, Diego Ladrón de Guevara, the bishop of Quito, engaged in similar shenanigans. As a prelate of the Church, Ladrón de Guevara was named to curtail illegal activities, but he quickly angered the Lima merchant community by his unabashed support for French trade and his own alleged participation in contraband trading. In 1712, for example, he had allowed French traders to unload large cargos in Callao, ostensibly so the government could collect tax revenues from the sale of this merchandise. By 1716, the Council of the Indies had relieved Ladrón de Guevara dishonorably, and after his judicial review, the Crown fined the bishop 40,000 pesos for his

---

[9] Núria Sala i Vila, "Una corona bien vale un virreinato: El Marqués de Castelldosríus, Primer Virrey Borbónico del Perú," in *El "premio" de ser virrey: Los intereses públicos y privados del gobierno virreinal en el Perú de Felipe V*, ed. Alfredo Moreno Cebrián y Núria Sala i Vela (Madrid: Consejo Superior de Investigaciones Científicas, 2004), 19–34, 47–50.

[10] Geoffrey J. Walker, *Spanish Politics and Imperial Trade, 1700–1789* (Bloomington: Indiana University Press, 1979), 38–42; Sala i Vela, "Una corona bien vale un virreinato," 54.

[11] Walker, *Spanish Politics and Imperial Trade*, 47–49; Sala i Vela, "Una corona bien vale un virreinato," 50–78, 111.

transgressions.[12] During this same period, the viceroy of New Spain, the Duke of Albuquerque, was accused of similar contraband trafficking; he only escaped prosecution by paying 700,000 pesos in indemnity to the Royal Treasury.[13]

Apart from problems with corruption at the highest levels, royal authority suffered from the practice of selling key government appointments in the Indies, which reached an apex during the War of the Spanish Succession.[14] The practice had numerous critics in Spain and the Indies, particularly the sale of *audiencia* judgeships, which had begun in 1687.[15] The difficulties involved in selling appointments, which diminished Crown authority over these venal bureaucrats, became all too obvious in the Audiencia of Quito. The judges of Quito's high court were an eccentric and fractious group in the first half of the century, but matters became particularly vexed during the War of the Spanish Succession. One justice, who purchased his appointment, Cristóbal de Ceballos, was infamous for his unorthodox religious beliefs. At a birthday party, Ceballos claimed to have seen the Virgin Mary arise from a meat pie and urged the bishop to hold a special mass for our Lady of the Meat Pie (Nuestra Señora de la Empanada). Instead, the prelate took immediate steps to quell the incipient cult.[16] Another judge who bought his appointment, Juan de Ricuarte, was notorious for beating his wife and even trying to poison her. In 1705, Ricauarte got into a dispute with a fellow justice, Tomás Fernández Pérez, that apparently led both men to draw their swords, until a colleague, Fernando de Sierra Osorio, intervened. Both justices wrote a series of angry letters to Madrid denouncing the other, which prompted the Council of the Indies to transfer Fernández Pérez to Santo Domingo and Ricuarte to Panama.[17]

Despite the transfer order, the two judges were still serving in Quito when a prominent Lima merchant, Juan de Sosaya, assumed the presidency of the *audiencia* after buying the appointment for 20,000 pesos. The presidency must have seemed a valuable prize for the scion of an enterprising merchant clan, giving Sosaya control of overland roads to Quito and the sea lanes to the Pacific port of Guayaquil to market either legal or contraband merchandise. Rumors

---

[12] Walker, *Spanish Politics and Imperial Trade*, 61–62.

[13] Rosenmüller, *Patrons, Partisans and Palace Intrigues*, chap. 8; Sala i Vela, "Una corona bien vale un virreinato," 56–57.

[14] Mark A. Burkholder and D. S. Chandler, *Biographical Dictionary of Audiencia Ministers in the Americas, 1687–1821* (Westport, CT: Greenwood Press, 1982), xiii; Burkholder and Chandler, *From Impotence to Authority*, appendix III.

[15] According to two authorities on the sale of *audiencia* appointments, "Although accounting for less than half of the appointments during the period (1687–1750) the presence of purchasers set the tone for many of the courts well beyond the conclusion of the sales." Burkholder and Chandler, *Biographical Dictionary of Audiencia Ministers*, xiii.

[16] Ibid., 85.

[17] Kenneth J. Andrien, *The Kingdom of Quito, 1690–1830: The State and Regional Development* (Cambridge: Cambridge University Press, 1995), 167–68.

quickly spread that Juan de Sosaya used his powers to trade in contraband cacao, cloth, and oriental goods. When a cargo of allegedly illegal merchandise was uncovered, two of the president's allies in the *audiencia*, Cristóbal de Ceballos and Lorenzo Lastero de Salazar (both venal officeholders), refused to unpack the merchandise to inspect it before sending it to Quito. When the city's *corregidor*, Juan Gutiérrez Pelayo, insisted on opening the crates to verify whether they were contraband, the two justices suspended and later exiled him. The crates went unopened to Sosaya's partner, who sold the contents openly in Quito.[18]

Gutiérrez Pelayo and other prominent *quiteños* sent numerous letters to Madrid denouncing Sosaya for widespread contraband, nepotism, and corruption. In response, the Council of the Indies named a judge on the Lima tribunal, serving as the interim governor of Panama, Juan Bautista de Orueta, to investigate the president's activities in office. Soon after arriving, Orueta suspended the irascible Juan de Ricuarte and Sierra Osorio from investigating the case and removed Sosaya from office. Meanwhile, Sosaya had a formidable array of allies on the court, including justices Juan de Ricauarte, Fernando de Sierra Osorio, Cristóbal de Ceballos, and José de Laysequilla, who was allegedly engaged to the sister-in-law of Sosaya. Orueta also suspended Ceballos and Laysequilla, making a total of four judges excluded from office. In the end, the Council of the Indies ruled that Juan Bautista de Orueta's case against Sosaya was not convincing enough, and it reversed the suspensions of the four judges, reinstating Sosaya as president. Such sordid episodes reflected the deep-seated political culture of corruption that had permeated Spain's colonial bureaucracy by the early eighteenth century. These imbroglios also demonstrated the challenges ahead for the new Bourbon monarch in the reform and renovation of the Spanish Atlantic world.[19]

Alberoni, Patiño, and the First Phase of Reform, 1715–36

Although the Treaties of Utrecht affirmed Philip V as the king of Spain and its overseas empire, the monarch ruled a divided and exhausted nation and an empire in disarray. To complicate matters further, the new king suffered from chronic emotional instability, and he relied heavily on the support and advice of his Savoyard wife, Marie Louise and, after her death in 1714, on that of his

---

[18] Ibid., 166–69.
[19] Ibid. In the end, vengeance also came for the enemies of Sosaya. One of the elderly president's enemies in Quito, an irascible young justice named Simon de Ribera y Aguado, lived openly with Sosaya's young wife. When the former president tried to seek redress in Spain, Ribera blocked the trip and allegedly conspired to assassinate Sosaya in Cartagena. Ibid., 166–73.

second Italian wife, Elizabeth Farnese.[20] Although the king initially trusted French advisors from his grandfather's court, in time, he and his wives came to depend on an unlikely Italian favorite, Abad (later Cardinal) Julio Alberoni, the son of a humble gardener from a village near Piacenza in the Duchy of Parma. Alberoni had achieved fame as the quartermaster of the French commander in the succession war, the rough-hewn Duke de Vendôme. Once at court, Alberoni dazzled both Marie Louise and later Elizabeth with his mastery of Italian cooking, a welcome alternative to the uninspiring fare served at court before his arrival. Although his portrait strikes a dignified pose, Alberoni was a diminutive, rotund man who one contemporary derisively described as a mere "pygmy whom fortune made a colossus" (see Fig. 4.1).[21] The Italian held no public office and relied solely on the good will of the king and queen to maintain power, but he recognized

Fig. 4.1 Julio Alberoni by Rafael Tegeo.
Source: Museo Naval, Madrid: 00816.

---

[20] According to Henry Kamen, the symptoms of Philip V indicate that he suffered throughout his life from bipolar disorder, which explains his periods of lucidity and activism, followed by long periods of debilitating depression. See Kamen, *Philip V of Spain*, 105.

[21] Quoted in Lynch, *Bourbon Spain, 1700–1808*, 76; and taken from William Coxe, *Memoirs of the Kings of Spain of the House of Bourbon, from the Accession of Philip V to the Death of Charles III, 1700–1789* (London: Longman, Hurst, Rees, Orme, and Brown, 1813), 2:108.

that the key to Spain's recovery rested on improving royal finances, rebuilding the navy, and, most important, reviving trade with the Indies.[22] Despite his lack of political connections in Spain, Alberoni oversaw bold policy innovations, although his accomplishments often came at the price of alienating many in the Madrid political establishment.

The key to the renovation of Spain was commerce with the Indies, but commercial reforms faced powerful opponents throughout Spanish Atlantic world, along with foreign rivals. During the succession war, French traders had captured markets in the Pacific, while British, French, and Dutch contrabandists made inroads into the Spanish possessions in the Caribbean and South Atlantic. Many corrupt officials served the colonial bureaucracy in the Indies, and these poorly paid, often venal officeholders had little incentive to curtail the contraband trade, with its lucrative bribes and kickbacks. Moreover, the Treaties of Utrecht allowed Britain's South Sea Company the right to introduce four thousand enslaved people annually into the Indies for thirty years and to have a five hundred-ton ship of permission trade at the fairs at Portobelo and Veracruz for the same period. The slave contract allowed the company to introduce contraband goods along with their slave cargoes, while the ships of permission often attempted to bring merchandise well above the five hundred-ton limit. In addition, these concessions effectively committed the monarchy to the now-failing system of *flotas* and *galeones*, restricting Spain's ability to modernize the transatlantic commercial system.[23] While the powerful Consulado of Seville deplored the intrusion of foreign smugglers into the Indies, the guild worked tirelessly to preserve its monopoly over trade with the Americas and the *flotas* and *galeones* established in the sixteenth century. Although corrupt officials and contraband traders undermined the fleet system, it also had powerful domestic and foreign interests committed to preserving it, even though the fleets never produced the profits gained in previous centuries.

The most pressing issue facing Alberoni was to gain control over Spain's major ports, which had direct implications for commerce with the Indies. Not only did foreign traders ply the contraband trade with the Indies, but French, English, and Dutch traders often supplied much of the merchandise through the legal fleet system, as a result of trade concessions granted to them in the seventeenth century. These foreign merchants residing in Spain enjoyed extraterritoriality, they received favorable tax rates, and the king's customs agents were forbidden to inspect their goods warehoused in Spanish ports. In contravention of custom and the treaties, Alberoni instructed Spanish customs agents to harass and inspect foreign cargos, and in March 1716 a series of incidents along the Mediterranean coast elicited protests from French consulates in Barcelona,

---

[22] Kuethe and Andrien, *Spanish Atlantic World*, 32.   [23] Ibid., 37–40.

Valencia, and Alicante. Customs agents boarded foreign vessels to inspect their cargos and even entered a French warehouse in Valencia. Dutch and later English merchant houses received similar treatment. Protests from these rival powers grew strident as Alberoni's intentions to ignore their treaty privileges and restrict foreign influence at Spanish ports became clear. Discussions among these foreign powers concerned framing a joint response to these bold Spanish actions, which ultimately resulted in the triple alliance of France, Britain, and the Dutch to resist Spanish harassment at its port cities.[24]

At the same time that Alberoni attempted to control Spanish ports, he initiated a number of policies that promised sweeping reforms. On May 18, 1717, he began the process of transferring the Consulado of Seville to Cádiz, where he hoped to lessen the influence of foreign merchants. This caused an uproar among the guild members, who enjoyed a comfortable lifestyle in Seville and had no wish to transfer their operations to the Atlantic port.[25] Alberoni also began the process of elevating the captaincy general of New Granada in northern South America into a viceroyalty to curtail the rampant contraband trade in the area. By appointing new officials and expanding the bureaucracy, he hoped to slow or stop the passage of New Granada's gold to buy contraband manufactures and enslaved individuals, particularly from British Jamaica.[26] Finally, he established a tobacco monopoly in Cuba to ensure a steady flow of leaf to the tobacco factory in Seville, and he initiated a reform of the military on the island to improve the defense of the Caribbean. The imposition of the tobacco monopoly provoked strong opposition among Cuban tobacco growers, who rose up in a rebellion against the Crown, but Spanish troops on the island rapidly quelled the revolt.[27] Taken together, Alberoni's audacious reforms led to conflicts with elites in Spain and the Indies, as well as the growing hostility of Spain's European rivals.

Just as diplomatic tensions over his commercial policies threatened war, Alberoni pursued an ill-advised policy in Italy to advance the dynastic ambitions of the king and queen. After the birth of her first son in 1716, Elizabeth Farnese hoped to find territories in Italy for her son Charles (who had three healthy half-brothers ahead of him to inherit the Spanish throne) and any future children. The queen had dynastic ties in northern Italy, but Alberoni first turned his attention to the southern territories (Sardinia, Sicily, and Naples) that Spain had ceded at Utrecht. When Spanish forces occupied first Sardinia and then Sicily, Austria joined the anti-Spanish front of France, Great Britain, and Savoy, making it a powerful quadruple alliance.[28] Armed conflict began even before a

---

[24] Ibid., 49–54.   [25] Ibid., 73–84.   [26] Ibid., 84–88.   [27] Ibid., 89–95.
[28] The Dutch withdrew from the alliance before the outbreak of hostilities, preferring to settle their differences with Spain diplomatically, but they were replaced by Savoy, whose leaders were outraged over the Spanish capture of Sardinia, where it had dynastic claims. Ibid., 60.

declaration of war, when the British admiral George Byng attacked and destroyed a large Spanish naval force at Cape Passaro, off the coast of Sicily, on August 18, 1717. The allies rapidly declared war on Spain in late 1718 and 1719 and inflicted a series of decisive defeats on land and sea. The Spanish sued for peace, and on December 5, 1719, Philip V delivered a handwritten note to Alberoni notifying him of his dismissal and exile.[29] The era of reform had ended temporarily, as conservatives hostile to the Italian (whom they had always viewed as an interloper) gained power. Over the next few years, conservatives opposed to reform overturned most of Alberoni's innovations, such as the tobacco monopoly and military reform in Cuba and the establishment of the Viceroyalty of New Granada.

Despite reverses suffered in the War of the Quadruple Alliance and the downfall of Alberoni, the central problems facing the Spanish Atlantic world continued—contraband, corruption, treaty concessions to the South Sea Company, and foreign incursions into the Spanish Main. The man who confronted these challenges in the period from 1726 to 1736 was a protégé of Cardinal Alberoni, José Patiño. Patiño's portrait depicts a stern, serious, but burdened minister (see Fig. 4.2). Given the king's periodic mental incapacity, Queen Elizabeth Farnese effectively ruled, and Patiño, who had grown up in Italy and spoke fluent Italian, enjoyed the confidence of the royal family.[30] Indeed, Patiño controlled the key ministerial portfolios for most of his decade in power, and this experienced, well-connected, and skillful politician revived and extended Alberoni's reforms with more lasting success.

One of Patiño's first major changes was to re-establish the tobacco monopoly in Cuba in 1727, and he did so by reaching an accommodation with local growers in Cuba. The goal remained directing Cuban tobacco to the royal tobacco factory in Seville, which provided much-needed funds for the Royal Treasury and insured a steady supply of leaf for the factory. The new monopoly operated in a more flexible way than Alberoni's scheme; this time the Crown allowed Cuban producers to sell their surplus tobacco on the open market after they met the monopoly's official quotas. The new tobacco monopoly gave Cuban growers a steady market for their tobacco at reasonable prices, and this time it continued until 1817.

A major goal of Patiño was to curtail contraband trading in the Indies, particularly in the Caribbean. In 1728, the historic monopoly of the Cádiz

---

[29] Ibid., 61. After leaving Spain, Alberoni went to Italy, where he participated in the conclave to choose a new pope, after the death of Clement XIII. His arrival in Rome was greeted by large crowds anxious to see the gardener's son who had risen to such political heights in Spain and become a cardinal of the Catholic Church. Coxe, *Memoirs of the Kings of Spain*, 2:245.

[30] The king's mental difficulties led him to abdicate in favor of his eldest son, Louis, who died of smallpox shortly after assuming the throne, having reigned only seven months. Philip then resumed the throne, but the queen had him watched constantly, fearful on several occasions that Philip might try to escape and abdicate again. Kuethe and Andrien, *Spanish Atlantic World*, 80.

Fig. 4.2 José Patiño by Rafael Tegeo.
Source: Museo Naval, Madrid: 00818.

merchant guild in the transatlantic trade ended with the founding of the joint-stock Real Compañía Guipuzcoana de Caracas to gain firm control over the commerce in Venezuelan cacao to Spain and New Spain. The company undercut much of the illicit commerce with the Dutch in their colony at Curacao (off the coast of Venezuela), which had taken a large share of the cacao trade. To secure its monopoly, the company agreed to patrol the coast with armed vessels to suppress foreign interlopers, and it promoted an increase in royal tax revenues, particularly on the sale of cacao. Foreign contrabandists still operated in other parts of the Spanish Caribbean, however, and Patiño urged the Consulado of Cádiz to assume financial responsibility for financing a much-expanded Royal Coast Guard in the region. On March 28, 1732, the guild agreed to pay a 4 percent tax on silver and gold to support the Coast Guard. This levy produced over 16.6 million pesos between 1739 and 1761.[31] Private enterprise also played a role

---

[31] AGI, Consulados, 62, Report of Contador Mayor of the Casa de la Contratación, Cádiz, 29 May 1762. An excellent new book on contraband in Venezuela is Jesse Cromwell, *The Smugglers' World: Illicit Trade and Atlantic Communities in Eighteenth-Century Venezuela* (Chapel Hill: Omohondro Institute and the University of North Carolina Press, 2018).

in suppressing foreign contrabandists because the Crown licensed privateers to aid the official Coast Guard ships in patrolling the Caribbean. These Caracas Company and Crown ships, along with licensed privateers, harassed British vessels, particularly those of the South Sea Company operating in the Caribbean.

Although the Spanish never had the resources to supplant Great Britain as the preeminent naval power, Patiño wanted to rebuild the navy after its disastrous defeat at Cape Passaro. Spain needed a strong navy to protect the *flotas* and *galeones* traveling between Cádiz and the Indies, transport troops defending colonial fortresses, and provide tactical support during sieges. The bulk of the naval vessels ultimately came from the new shipyards at Havana, and over the course of the eighteenth century, these facilities produced 198 warships, including 74 ships of the line.[32] Havana had access to essential materials, especially the hardwood timber needed to construct vessels. Funding these tasks was beyond the resources of Cuba, however, and the Crown directed annual subsidies (*situados*) from the treasuries of New Spain to support both the activities of the Havana shipyards and the defenses of the Caribbean. During the crucial years of constructing the shipyard in the 1730s, the Mexican treasuries sent between 700,000 and 1,100,000 pesos annually for the *situado*.[33] The resurgence of both the Indigenous population of New Spain and its mining industry from the early eighteenth century made this support feasible.

In 1734, Patiño began the process of restoring another of Alberoni's projects, the establishment of a Viceroyalty of New Granada. The aim of the policy was to appoint more loyal, honest officials to staff the new bureaucracy in northern South America, police against the contraband trade, supervise the potentially rich gold mines in Chocó and Antioquia, and provide a more effective defense establishment for the region. Re-establishing the viceroyalty took until 1739, three years after Patiño's death, but contraband trading continued, and the ongoing seizure of British vessels eventually poisoned relations between the two nations. According to a British captain, Robert Jenkins, when the Spanish Coast Guard had seized his ship in 1732, they boarded the vessel and a Spanish officer cut off his ear. Parliament used the resulting jingoist hysteria as a pretext to declare war on Spain. In the ensuing conflict, the War of Jenkins' Ear, the British captured Portobelo in Panama and laid siege to Cartagena de Indias in 1741. The viceroy of New Granada, Sebastián de Eslava, provided important military leadership, which stalled the British invaders outside the city until disease took its toll on the foreigners, who withdrew in defeat.[34]

---

[32] Kuethe and Andrien, *Spanish Atlantic World*, 116.
[33] Carlos Marichal and Matilde Souto Mantecón, "Silver and Situados: New Spain and the Financing of the Spanish Empire in America," *Hispanic American Historical Review* 74, no. 4 (November 1994): 594, 612–13.
[34] Kuethe and Andrien, *Spanish Atlantic World*, 125.

The overworked José Patiño died on November 3, 1736, at the age of seventy, after a brief illness. Taken together, he and Alberoni had initiated changes that advanced four key goals of the reform agenda: commercial, fiscal, administrative, and military matters. While the contributions of this first phase of the Bourbon reforms have generally been downplayed or ignored, Alberoni and Patiño's policies yielded impressive and enduring results, which laid the foundation for later, more substantial changes. One important measure of these early Bourbon reforms was the rising levels of income remitted from the Indies to the Depositaría de Indias, the treasury of the House of Trade. The income remitted to the Depositaría from the American treasuries remained sluggish in the aftermath of the War of the Spanish Succession, yielding only 224,346 copper reales de vellón in 1727, but thereafter it rose steadily throughout the Patiño years, reaching peaks between 40,000,000 and 60,000,000 copper reales de vellón, an annual average increase of 4.8 percent.[35] In short, the reforms of Alberoni and Patiño may not have produced revolutionary changes, but their efforts did reverse the long decline of public revenues collected in the Indies for Spain, which served as the means to rebuild a stronger, more fiscally stable state to govern the Spanish Atlantic world.

Carvajal, Ensenada, and the Second Phase of Reform, 1741–54

The pace of reform slowed under the leadership of Patiño's more conservative protégé, Sebastián de la Quadra.[36] During this period, Spain became embroiled in the War of Jenkins' Ear, which merged with dynastic conflicts in Europe into the War of the Austrian Succession that ended in 1748. Although Spain was able to turn back the British invasion and siege of Cartagena de Indias in the conflict, it was a dangerous struggle fought with an increasingly aggressive British foe. The pressures imposed on the transatlantic trade by the conflict led the Madrid government to abandon temporarily the traditional system of *flotas* and *galeones* in favor of individually licensed register ships. It proved so successful that the Crown continued it after the war and later abolished the *galeones* for South America. The merchant guilds of Mexico City and Cádiz lobbied successfully, however, to restore the *flotas* supplying New Spain in 1754, arguing that contraband through the single port of Veracruz was negligible. Powerful interest groups, such as the merchant guilds, could still defend their interests against

---

[35] Jacques A. Barbier, "Towards a New Chronology for Bourbon Colonialism: The 'Depositaría de Indias' of Cádiz, 1722–1789," *Ibero-Amerikanisches Archiv* 6, no. 4 (1980): 335–39, 352–53.

[36] Kuethe and Andrien, *Spanish Atlantic World*, 136–37. For comparative purposes, one colonial peso de ocho real equaled 20 reales de vellón during this period. Lynch, *Bourbon Spain, 1700–1808*, xi.

Bourbon regalists. Nonetheless, the war ended the Utrecht treaties' concessions to the British South Sea Company, which allowed new efforts at reforming the transatlantic commercial system.[37]

During the war years, strong ministers emerged to lead Spain, particularly José de Campillo y Cossío, who championed a wide range of reforms. Campillo was born in Asturias to an hidalgo family, and his thinking about reform was clearly influenced by the Enlightenment, particularly in his most well-known tract, *Nuevo sistema de gobierno económico para la América*. The treatise, which appeared in 1743, was not published until long after Campillo's death, but it apparently circulated widely among reformers. The *Nuevo sistema* presented a mercantilist vision of how the colonies might reach greater levels of economic prosperity and how Spain might benefit from this progress to enrich itself. The principal reform that Campillo advocated was the end of Cádiz monopoly and the promotion of free trade within the empire. Campillo also proposed lower tax levies on commerce to stimulate trade with America. Moreover, he encouraged the production of export crops in the Indies; efforts to revive mining; the establishment of regional trade fairs, both to enhance trade and to curtail contraband; and a modernized mail system that could furnish and circulate more updated market information on supply and demand throughout the Spanish Atlantic world. Campillo also proposed a series of inspection tours (*visitas*) to enact administrative reforms, such as establishing a new intendency system to eliminate corruption, and royal monopolies over tobacco, *aguardiente* (cane liquor), and other products. Most surprisingly, Campillo advocated education for America's Indigenous population, teaching them Castilian and encouraging them to wear Spanish dress, in an effort to turn the Amerindians into consumers and producers in the New World, ending their poverty, inertia, and oppression.[38] In the end, Campillo's reformist agenda influenced succeeding generations of regalist reformers during the reigns of Ferdinand VI (1746–58) and his half-brother and successor, Charles III (1758–88).

Campillo's death in 1743 at the age of forty-three allowed his protégé, a man of modest hidalgo origins from La Rioja, Zenón de Somodevilla, the Marqués de la Ensenada, to rise to political prominence. Ensenada was a military man who rose to power by securing the safe passage of then-Prince Charles to Naples to assume his throne as king of the Two Sicilies. Unlike the stern-visaged portraits of Alberoni and Patiño, he was portrayed with a wry "smirk," common among Enlightenment-inspired Crown servants of the period (see Fig. 4.3). Along with his aristocratic political ally and sometimes rival, José de Carvajal y

---

[37] Ibid., 162.
[38] José del Campillo y Cossío, *Nuevo sistema económico para América*, ed. Manuel Ballesteros Gaibrois (Oviedo, Spain: Editorial Asturiano, 1993).

Fig. 4.3 Zenón de Somodevilla, Marqués de la Ensenada, by Jacopo Amigoni.
Source: Museo del Prado, Madrid: P02939.

Lancaster (the personal secretary of Campillo, who took over as minister of state in 1746), Ensenada took charge of the reform effort by centralizing his control over the Ministries of War, Finance, and Marine and the Indies.[39] As one of his first acts, he turned on the Seville merchants who still controlled the merchant guild at Cádiz, charging them with fraud and then imposing a new system for the apportionment of electors, which effectively placed guild members under greater Crown control.[40] He then established the Royal Havana Company in 1740 and gave it a legal monopoly over Cuba's trade in agricultural exports, lowering tariffs on the island's goods entering Cádiz. This was part of a larger policy of stimulating vulnerable imperial peripheries in the Caribbean and elsewhere. As part of the bargain, the company had to finance the Havana shipyard and transport military supplies to Havana at its own cost.[41]

---

[39] Somodevilla was a military man and Patiño entrusted him with organizing the expedition that escorted Prince Charles to Naples, where he would assume the throne. This achievement won him the title of the Marqués de la Ensenada. Kuethe and Andrien, *Spanish Atlantic World*, 143.

[40] This reform came in AGI, Indiferente General 2302, Royal order, 17 December 1743. The details are presented in Kuethe and Andrien, *Spanish Atlantic World*, 145.

[41] Ibid., 145–46.

Under Ensenada's leadership, reform reached new heights, making the period between 1748 and 1754 the first golden age of enlightened absolutism. The so-called secretary of everything promoted an expansion of the armada, and he extended Patiño's reformed model of military organization pioneered in Cuba to Cartagena, Veracruz, and the Yucatan. During the same period, the Madrid government focused on frontier defenses. Fearing the incursions of the French, Ensenada sent two expeditions to the Texas frontier to consolidate Spanish positions north of the silver mines of New Spain. Private sponsors also promoted an extensive colonization program, transferring hundreds of families protected by a system of missions and armed presidios. Local frontier militias supplemented the regular troops at the presidios in defending vulnerable settlements on the northern frontier of New Spain. Moreover, the rights of citizenship and political participation in these Spanish border provinces were linked to military service, just as they were during the Reconquista in the violent frontier zones of medieval Spain.[42] Whereas previously Franciscan missions extended the northern reach of frontier outposts in New Spain, in this more secular age, missionaries came only after soldiers and local militias secured the imperial peripheries. Similar initiatives developed in northern South America to close off expansion of the Dutch in Surinam and the French in Guyana.

One of the initiatives sponsored by Ensenada was a French scientific expedition—accompanied by two young Spanish naval officers, Jorge Juan and Antonio de Ulloa—to traverse the Andes to measure a degree on the equator. Such information was needed to make accurate measurements of meridians of longitude, critical for navigation and the drawing of precise, accurate maps. While involved in this expedition, Juan and Ulloa also made scientific observations about the geography, resources, flora, and fauna of the king's Andean possessions, which had the potential to serve concrete economic and political ends. The prospects for making profitable economic ventures to exploit the resources of the Andes was another important goal of the expedition, along with using the data to determine reasonable taxation rates for the region's provinces.[43] At the behest of Ensenada, however, Juan and Ulloa compiled a secret report of the political problems of the region, notoriously known as the *Noticias secretas de América*, which uncovered widespread evidence of clerical and political corruption and bad government in the southern Viceroyalty of Peru.

---

[42] Luis A. García, *Frontera armada: Prácticas militares en el noreste histórico, siglos XVII a XIX* (Mexico City: Fondo de Cultura Económica, 2021), David J. Weber, *Bárbaros: Spaniards and Their Savages in the Age of Enlightenment* (New Haven, CT: Yale University Press, 2005), passim.

[43] Neil Safier, *Measuring the New World: Enlightenment Science and South America* (Chicago: University of Chicago Press, 2008), 1–23.

Juan and Ulloa's report was only one of many memorials written by literate subjects of the Crown decrying the problems, ills, and needs of local subjects. Echoing seventeenth-century authors such as Guaman Poma, Indigenous elites also sent memorials to the Crown, written in Castilian, most often complaining about the oppression of the king's servants in the Andes. An Indigenous ethnic leader from Chimo y Chica, near Lambayeque, in Peru, Vicente Morachimo, penned one of the most famous and influential of these memorials in 1732. Morachimo's report provided a blunt recitation of rampant corruption by local officials and parish clergy. In an even more detailed report from 1749, a mestizo lay brother in the Franciscan order, Fray Calixto de San José Túpac Inka, wrote to the Crown, proposing that it end the mita and the forced distribution of European wares by the *corregidores*. He argued that Andeans should be appointed to public offices, receive schooling, and serve in a tribunal composed of Spanish, mestizo, and Andean leaders (independent of the viceroy and the *audiencias*) to set policy for the viceroyalty. Although Fray Calixto never challenged the legality of Spanish rule, he did propose changes that would have allowed the Indigenous peoples unprecedented access to self-rule and economic power. These reports and memorials served as important, but more traditional, sources of information about the various provinces of the Indies, which Ensenada and other ministers used to prepare specific proposals to reform the Spanish Empire.[44]

While earlier Bourbon efforts to reform the imperial system focused largely on administrative and commercial matters, under Ensenada new initiatives involved a fundamental re-examination of the close relationship between the monarchy and the Roman Catholic Church. The power of the more independent-minded regular clergy—the Franciscans, Dominicans, Augustinians, and Mercedarians, except the Jesuits—came under particular scrutiny. A number of royal officials and travelers, such as Jorge Juan and Antonio de Ulloa, had condemned the abuses and corruption of the regular clergy, particularly those administering rural Amerindian parishes.[45] In addition, a series of letters

---

[44] AGI, Lima, 442, Madrid, Vicente Morachimo to Crown, September 2, 1732, Manifiesto de los agravios, vexaciones, y molestias que padacen los indios del reyno del Peru. Fray Calixto de San José Tupac Inca a Mui Ilustre Cabildo de la Ciudad de Lima, Madrid, 14 noviembre de 1750, AGI, Lima, legajo 988. Francisco A. Loayza, ed., *Fray Calixto Túpak Inka: Documentos originales y, en su mayoría, totalmente desconocidos, auténticos, de este apóstol indio, valiente defensor de su raza, desde el año 1746 a 1760* (Lima: Bibliografía Particular Indígena, 1948), 85–94; Alcira Dueñas, *Indians in the "Lettered City:" Reshaping Justice, Social Hierarchy, and Political Culture in Colonial Peru* (Boulder: University of Colorado Press, 2010), 59–92; Andrien, *Andean Worlds*, 98–99.

[45] Jorge Juan and Antonio de Ulloa, *Discourse and Political Reflections on the Kingdoms of Peru. Their Government, Special Regimen of Their Inhabitants and Abuses Which Have Been Introduced into One and Another, with Special Information on Why They Grew Up and Some Means to Avoid Them*, ed. and intro. John J. TePaske, trans. John J. TePaske and Besse A. Clement (Norman: University of Oklahoma Press, 1978), 102, 300, 154–88.

written by the viceroy of Peru, José Manso de Velasco (a close friend and protégé of Ensenada), complained about the overabundance of clergy in Lima and called for the removal of the regular orders from parish work. The problem was particularly obvious after a major earthquake in 1746 damaged many of the religious houses of the city, causing the friars to take refuge in private homes and makeshift dwellings in the capital. As a result, on October 4, 1749, the Crown issued royal edicts (*cédulas*) ordering that all the Indigenous *doctrinas* (parishes) administered by the religious orders in the archdioceses of Lima, Mexico City, and Santa Fe de Bogotá be transferred to the secular clergy when vacancies occurred.[46] These edicts removed the religious orders from lucrative parishes they had controlled since the spiritual conquest of the sixteenth century.[47] All of the orders suffered financial losses, except the Jesuits, who had few such Indigenous parishes. The only parishes exempt from secularization were the few that supported active missions proselytizing along the frontiers of the empire, which the Jesuits largely controlled.[48] These *cédulas* secularizing the parishes naturally elicited strong protests from the regular orders, particularly the Franciscans, but the Crown remained firm in its decision. Nonetheless, no popular upheavals emerged, so the Crown issued a further *cédula* of February 1, 1753, extending the process of secularization to parishes in all the dioceses of the Indies.[49]

The secularization of the largely rural parishes ministering to the Indigenous population limited both the wealth and the prestige of the orders. In the Viceroyalty of Peru, Crown officials estimated that before the edicts of 1749 and 1753, the orders had controlled 190 parishes that paid salaries worth nearly 450,000 pesos annually.[50] Separating the orders from their lucrative parishes led them to curtail the number of regular clergymen admitted to the orders throughout the Indies.[51] This attack on the power of the regular clergy

---

[46] AGI, Lima, 1596, Royal Cédula, Buen Retiro, 4 October 1749.

[47] Ensenada and Manso de Velasco were very close friends, who addressed each other in private correspondence in intimate terms as "paisano del alma" (countryman of my soul) and "amigo de mi vida" (friend of my life). See Adrian J. Pearce, "Minister and Viceroy, Paisano and Amigo: The Private Correspondence of the Marqués de la Ensenada and the Conde de Superunda, 1745–1749," *The Americas* 73, no. 4 (October 2016): 477–90; and Adrian J. Pearce, *The Origins of Bourbon Reform in Spanish South America, 1700–1763* (New York: Palgrave Macmillan, 2014), 145. AGI, Lima 415, Manso de Velasco to Crown, 12 October 1746.

[48] On the protests of the orders and the response of the Crown, see Kuethe and Andrien, *Spanish Atlantic World*, 167–93.

[49] AGI, Lima, 1596, Royal Cédula, Madrid, 1 February 1753.

[50] AGI, Lima, 1596, Resumen general de las Pensiones consignados en las reales cajas y provincias del distrito del tribunal y audiencia rl de quentas de este reyno, con Separacion de sus repectivas aplicaciónes, Lima, 30 June 1748.

[51] According to Juan and Ulloa, shrinking the size of the regular orders would allow more men to live productive lives as laymen, marrying and adding wealth to the kingdom instead of becoming lascivious, nonproductive friars. This was a view held by a number of Enlightenment-influenced commentators of the day. Juan and Ulloa, *Discourse and Political Reflections*, 154–88.

fundamentally altered the traditional partnership between church and state in the Spanish Indies and signaled an important step in the advance of a regalist and increasingly absolutist Bourbon state.

The thorniest issue facing the reformers was trade liberalization with the Indies following the War of Jenkins' Ear. The merchant guilds of Cádiz, Mexico City, and Lima wanted to end the system of register ships and reintroduce the historic system of *flotas* and *galeones*, which wartime necessities had forced the Crown to abandon.[52] Ensenada and Carvajal inclined toward abandoning the fleets and commercial monopolies in favor of free trade within the empire, a position proposed publicly by their former patron, Campillo. Nonetheless, both reformers proceeded very carefully. After all, ending the fleet system represented a direct attack on the long-held monopoly of the powerful merchant guild of Cádiz. In May 1750, Ensenada summoned six leaders from the Consulado of Cádiz to propose methods of enhancing transatlantic commerce, but guild members tried to avoid serving on the special council (junta). Ensenada's instructions made his intentions clear: "His majesty's will be that the freedom to conduct commerce not be limited or inhibited under the label of monopoly."[53] Nonetheless, powerful enemies in the *consulados* did everything within their power to block or at least delay the reformer's commercial innovations, and in 1754, the *flota* to New Spain resumed, while the use of register ships to South America continued.

At the same time that discussion over commercial reform took place, a subtle but profound transformation occurred in appointments to the colonial bureaucracy. The Crown phased out the sale of appointments to judicial offices in the Indies between 1750 and 1751, a practice dating back to the seventeenth century. Beginning in 1745, the viceroys of New Spain and Peru could bar purchasers from taking office if they found the candidates unsuitable.[54] By 1750, with the advent of peace, the Crown could afford to end the policy, which had concerned reformers since the accession of the Bourbon dynasty. This was part of a well-thought-out policy of excluding Creoles from holding high office, particularly in their home districts, replacing them instead with better trained, educated, and loyal peninsular-born Crown officials. This remained a sore point between Madrid and colonial elites throughout the second half of the eighteenth century.

Despite significant accomplishments, Ensenada's political fortunes experienced a rapid decline with the unexpected death of José de Carvajal y Lancaster on April 8, 1754. Afflicted with frail health, the overworked minister of state died at

---

[52] The lynchpin of the galleon trade with South America, the Panamanian port of Portobelo, had fallen to the British before they laid siege to Cartagena, effectively forcing the Crown to use register ships to supply the Viceroyalty of Peru. See Kuethe and Andrien, *Spanish Atlantic World*, 148.
[53] AGI, Indiferente General, 2304, Royal Order, Buen Retiro, 14 September 1750.
[54] Rosenmüller, "Corrupted by Ambition," 25–27.

the age of fifty-six, removing Ensenada's political bridge to the traditional aristocrats at court. Ensenada replaced Carvajal with a former political ally, Ricardo Wall, recently returned from a mission to London. The pro-British Wall had negotiated a treaty with London that Ensenada had criticized, since the terms violated the minister's traditional pro-French sympathies. The angry and now alienated Wall allied himself with the British ambassador and conservatives at court to secure the downfall of Ensenada. The issue that enabled the coup concerned allegations that Ensenada, on his own authority, had ordered military action to dislodge British loggers operating on the Mosquito Coast in Honduras, which King Ferdinand and Queen Barbara feared would lead to war. As a result, on July 20, 1754, Ensenada received the shocking news of his dismissal and exile to Granada in the middle of the night, and he was summarily taken away in a waiting coach. The second phase of the Bourbon reforms had ended. When Queen Barbara died in 1758, King Ferdinand lapsed into a deep, debilitating depression before his own death in 1759. He was succeeded by his younger half-brother, Charles, the eldest son of Elizabeth Farnese, who had reigned as king of Naples from 1735 to 1759. In the end, Elizabeth Farnese did live to see one of her sons take the throne of Spain.

The Pinnacle of Reform, 1759–96

As the king of Naples, Charles had worked with his chief minister, Bernardo Tenucci, to enact a series of reforms to centralize the state, and he was inclined to purse a similar regalist agenda in Spain. The old concept of composite monarchy that had emerged from the Reconquista did not suit the needs or inclinations of the new monarch, who wanted sweeping changes in the institutional culture of the Spanish Atlantic world. The eighteenth century was a time of nearly perpetual conflict with European rivals, and the new king needed a strong state apparatus to meet the fiscal exigencies of modern warfare. King Charles III had to postpone his reformist ambitions, however, when Spain intervened in the Seven Years' War, which led to defeat and humiliation at the hands of the British and the loss of Havana in 1762. The loss of that Caribbean fortress was a huge blow because the city served as the key to defending the sea lanes to New Spain. Although Spain recovered the city in the Treaty of Paris that ended the war, the king and his ministers used the defeat as an excuse to pursue a wide range of fiscal, administrative, commercial, military, and religious reforms, which built on the achievements of Ensenada, Patiño, and Alberoni.

To implement his reformist agenda, the king relied on a new generation of enlightened, regalist ministers; several came from the lower nobility or even the middle class. All were loyal to the king and committed to reform. From the advent of the Bourbon dynasty after the War of the Spanish Succession in 1713, King Philip V and his advisors had attempted to create a power elite, based on "men of letters" (men of talent and skill, educated in a modern, enlightened curriculum). The king and his successors also attempted to create a more professional military (loyal men of honor and merit, trained in modern military tactics and strategy). Both the military men and the men of letters were drawn from provincial elites and middle classes, rather than the traditional aristocracy, and they formed the core of a new, more centralized Bourbon state, first in Spain and then in the Indies. They played an important role in advancing the Bourbon reforms to new heights during the reign of Charles III.[55]

In one of their first reforms, Charles III and his ministers established a Crown-operated modern mail system on August 24, 1764.[56] Government officials and merchants required up-to-date information about market trends and prices to levy effective taxes and conduct commercial exchanges. In the new system, small ships would leave La Coruña for Havana each month and fan out to deliver and collect mail. To help offset expenses of the voyages, mail ships carried European goods to exchange for colonial products. From 1718, the Consulado of Cádiz had been responsible for operating the mail system by sending eight small *navios de aviso* (mail ships) each year to transport the mail, so the shift to direct royal control came as a shock to guild members, whom the Crown failed to consult about the change. Moreover, allowing the mail ships to carry merchandise on voyages opened yet another breach in the guild's monopoly over trade with the Indies.

The king and his ministers used "military imperatives" as a justification for an ambitious reforming agenda following the loss of Havana.[57] In these early years, Charles relied heavily on an Italian minister he had brought from Naples, the Marqués de Esquilache, who held the Ministries of War and Finance. The army and navy required modernization and expansion and fortifications needed updating, and the treasury had to find the means to pay for these innovations. The king and his French allies viewed the Treaty of Paris, ending the Seven Years' War, merely as a truce, with a renewed outbreak of hostilities as inevitable. As a result, military reform would become a major priority, and Charles and Esquilache began with the lynchpin of their Caribbean defenses, Cuba. The king supported a radical plan by the Count of Ricla to reorganize

---

[55] For a full discussion of the role of men of letters and men of arms, see Mónica Ricketts, *Who Should Rule: Men of Arms, the Republic of Letters, and the Fall of the Spanish Empire* (New York: Oxford University Press, 2017).

[56] Reglamento provisional que manda S. M. observar para el establecimiento del Nuevo Correo mensual que ha salir de España a las Indias Occidentales, San Ildefonso, 24 August 1764, AGI, Correos, legajo 484.

[57] Kuethe and Andrien, *Spanish Atlantic World*, 236–37.

the armed forces in Cuba and systematically arm the American colonists for the first time by creating disciplined militia units to counter the British threat in the Caribbean. The reforms also rewarded militia members with the *fuero militar*, the right to be tried in military, not civilian, courts. To implement the changes, the Crown named Ricla the governor and captain general of Cuba, delegating military reform to his close friend and a descendant of Irish nobility, Field Marshall Alejandro O'Reilly, in 1763.[58]

While O'Reilly concentrated on creating disciplined militia units, Ricla sought to raise revenue, establishing an intendancy to streamline the collection of revenues in 1764. He also increased the sales tax from 2 to 4 percent and levied new taxes on locally produced liquor.[59] Learning from the mistakes of Alberoni, both Ricla and O'Reilly consulted widely with the habanero elite to gain their trust and support, which involved liberalizing trade in the Caribbean to stimulate the island's sugar economy. As a result of their recommendations, in 1765 the Madrid government opened free trade between Havana, Santo Domingo, Puerto Rico, Margarita, and Trinidad with nine ports in Spain, chipping away further at the trade monopoly of the Consulado of Cádiz.[60]

As Ricla and O'Reilly continued their reforms in Cuba, Esquilache turned to New Spain, where he dispatched Lieutenant General Juan de Villalba to reform the military and Francisco Anselmo Armona as visitor general to reform revenue collection, establish a tobacco monopoly, and impose an intendancy system to improve administration. Armona died on the passage to New Spain, however, and the Crown selected José de Gálvez to replace him. After his arrival, Gálvez introduced monopolies on tobacco and aguardiente, imposed a 4 percent sales tax (*alcabala*) on all goods sold in Veracruz, and replaced tax farmers and customs officials with salaried royal officials, mostly cronies who had accompanied him from Spain.[61] He also installed a system for registering all goods destined for the trade fair at Jalapa. All of these innovations brought strong protests from the merchant guilds of Mexico City and Cádiz and the *audiencia* in the capital, but Gálvez doggedly imposed his changes.[62]

Like previous generations of reformers, the ministers of Charles III faced powerful enemies, and one of these opponents was the independent-minded Society of Jesus. The Jesuits were a wealthy and powerful order, with international

---

[58] Allan J. Kuethe, *Cuba, 1753–1815: Crown, Military, and Society* (Knoxville: University of Tennessee Press, 1986), 37–45.

[59] The military reform also involved establishing two battalions of free *pardos* and one of free Black people. Herbert S. Klein, "The Colored Militia of Cuba, 1568–1868," *Caribbean Studies* 4 (July 1966), 17–27.

[60] Kuethe and Andrien, *Spanish Atlantic World*, 246.

[61] Linda K. Salvucci, "Costumbres Viejas, 'hombres nuevos': José de Gálvez y la burocracia fiscal novohispana (1754–1800)," *Historia Mexicana* 33 (Octubre–Diciembre 1983): 224–60.

[62] Kuethe and Andrien, *Spanish Atlantic World*, 247–52.

connections and a well-deserved reputation as a bastion of antiregalist sentiment. They maintained a firm allegiance to the papacy, resisting the Crown's efforts to subordinate the Spanish Church to royal authority. The Jesuits also opposed many Roman Catholic reformers, influenced by French Jansenism, who favored greater episcopal, not papal, power and a return to the simplicity of early Christianity. These Church reformers frequently found common cause with the king's enlightened ministers. King Charles himself mistrusted the society, and when he took the throne, he broke with custom and named a Franciscan, not a Jesuit, as his confessor. The king also entered into a long-standing dispute with the society over whether the order was exempt from paying the tithe (*diezmo*) on its extensive landholdings in the New World. In New Spain, the dispute over the Jesuits' payment of the tithe went back at least to the *visita* of Juan de Palafox y Mendoza in the 1640s. The tithe was a tax of 10 percent on all rural produce and two-ninths (*dos novenos*) of every tithe collection went to the Crown, while the rest supported the various activities of the secular clergy. The Jesuits claimed that Pope Pius IV in 1561 had exempted them from paying the tax in recognition of their missionary activities in the Indies. The king's brother, Ferdinand VI, had reached a compromise with the order, allowing them to pay only 3 1/3 percent for the tithe. King Charles III, however, issued a final judgment on the matter on December 4, 1766, demanding that the order pay the full 10 percent of the tithe.[63]

After this acrimonious controversy, relations between the Crown and the Jesuits continued to deteriorate, particularly after popular riots broke out in Madrid in 1766. The riots took place against a backdrop of high food prices, rising taxes, and the Marqués de Esquilache's municipal reforms—including the installation of streetlights in Madrid and an incendiary edict forbidding Madrileños from wearing their traditional long capes and large-brimmed hats, ostensibly to prevent criminals from hiding both weapons and their identity. The rioters broke the newly installed streetlights, looted the house of Esquilache (who went into exile), and killed several of the king's guardsmen. The king escaped his palace under the cover of darkness for Aranjuez. The violence then spread to other Spanish cities. When the king felt safe enough to return to Madrid, he set up a commission to investigate the so-called *motín* (riot) of Esquilache, a task that fell to the regalist *fiscal* of the Council of Castile, Pedro Rodríguez Campomanes. Campomanes used the opportunity to blame the Jesuits for organizing the uprising, reiterating many of the claims about the sinister actions of the order found in contemporary anti-Jesuit literature.[64]

---

[63] Ibid., 262–66; Kenneth J. Andrien, "La reforma clerical durante el Reinado de Carlos III: La expulsión de los Jesuitas, 1762–1773," *Tempus: Revista en Historia General* 4 (Septiembre–Octubre, 2016): 242–46; Dale K. Van Kley, *Reform Catholicism and the International Suppression of the Jesuits in Enlightenment Europe* (New Haven, CT: Yale University Press, 2018).

[64] Andrien, "La reforma clerical," 246–49.

The explosive report of Campomanes gave the regalists at court an unpopular scapegoat for the urban unrest, and on February 27, 1767, the king ordered the expulsion of the Jesuits from the Spanish Empire. He sent the order secretly to the Conde de Aranda, the head of the Council of Castile, who forwarded it on March 1 to viceroys, captains general, and governors in the Indies and the Philippines and in Spain, giving instructions on how to execute the task. Aranda told the pertinent officials to open the secret order on the day the expulsion was to be carried out, ordering that each Jesuit house be surrounded with troops. Members of the society could then take only their personal possessions and go to the nearest port, where they would be loaded on a ship bound ultimately for exile in Italy. Any Jesuit caught returning to lands under the control of the Spanish monarchy would face criminal charges. Crown authorities also confiscated all Jesuit religious houses, both urban and rural properties, and turned any other possessions of the order over to Crown authorities.[65] Not content with his expulsion of the Jesuits, King Charles allied with monarchs in Portugal and France to lobby for the complete extinction of the order, which the papacy finally agreed to do on September 12, 1773.[66]

Although the expulsion proceeded without provoking serious unrest in much of the Spanish Atlantic world, anger over the reforms of the Gálvez *visita* and the Jesuits' expulsion led to violent riots in the mining zones in north-central New Spain. The violence began near San Luis Potosí and Guanajuato and spread westward to Michoacan. Resentment about higher taxes, the recruitment of militiamen, land disputes, the imposition of the tobacco monopoly, and anger over the expulsion of the Jesuits created a volatile situation. When local governments proved unable to restore order, the viceroy sent a military force under the command of *visitador* José de Gálvez to quell the violence, restore order, and punish the guilty parties.[67] Gálvez and his force left Mexico City on July 9, 1767, with full authority to deal with the rioters. They proceeded north to the mining zones, and at each stop Gálvez oversaw the expulsion of the Jesuits and proceeded with trials of anyone arrested for promoting public disorder and violence. In all, Gálvez brought 3,000 people to trial; he condemned 85 to death, ordered 73 to be severely whipped, imprisoned 674, and sent 117 into permanent banishment.[68]

---

[65] Ibid., 249-50.

[66] AGI, Indiferente General, 3087, Breve de Nuestro Muy Santo Padre Clemente XIV. Por el qual su santidad suprieme, deroga, y extingue el instituto y orden de los Clérigos Regulares, denominados de la Compañia de Jesus, que ha sido presentado en el Consejo para su publicación. Año 1773 en Madrid. En la Imprenta de Pedro Marion. The original brief was issued in Rome on July 21, 1773, and published in Madrid on September 12, 1773, 22.

[67] Felipe Castro Gutiérrez, *Nueva ley, nuevo rey: Reformas borbónicas y rebelión popular en Nueva España* (Michoacan, México: El Colegio de Michoacán, Universidad Autónoma de México, Instituto de Investigaciones Históricas, 1996).

[68] Herbert Ingram Priestley, *José de Gálvez: Visitor General of New Spain (1765-1771)* (Berkeley: University of California Press, 1916), 228.

After his return to Spain, King Charles named José de Gálvez minister of the Indies in 1776. Gálvez immediately turned his attention to strengthening the imperial peripheries, to guard against any enemy incursions as Spain prepared to enter the American colonists' revolution against Britain. To shore up the northern frontier of New Spain, Gálvez had established the Comandancia General of the Interior Provinces, which united the whole region from Texas to California in a single administrative district. He also introduced an intendancy in Caracas and made the whole region a captaincy general. To secure the Southern Cone of South America, Gálvez dispatched ten thousand troops to the Portuguese city of Colônia do Sacramento, a major source of contraband goods into the Río de la Plata, and the expedition captured the city in 1777. Gálvez also approved the establishment of the Viceroyalty of the Río de la Plata with its capital at Buenos Aires in 1776, which placed the Southern Cone of South America under one unified government. In 1782, the Madrid government approved an intendancy system for the viceroyalty. The Ordinance of Intendants established eight districts for the Río de la Plata, and each intendant received a generous salary and exercised control over administration, finance, the military, certain judicial matters, and some authority over clerical patronage. The office of *corregidor de indios* was abolished and replaced with subdelegates, paid with 3 percent of tribute receipts from the districts. The intendants represented a new administrative layer, linking the viceroy and the *audiencias* with provincial administrators (see Fig. 4.4).

After the fall of Colônia do Sacramento, many Portuguese families moved to the Spanish port of Montevideo, where they served as a commercial conduit for merchandise and slaves from Rio de Janeiro in Brazil to the Río de la Plata. By the 1790s, this transimperial trade between Montevideo and Portugal and Brazil grew in scale and became more regularized. The city's elites also profited from the creation of new political offices, such as the customs house in Montevideo, after the establishment of the viceroyalty. Montevideo became the region's mandatory port of call for all transatlantic ships entering or leaving the estuary. As a result, social networks of Portuguese merchant families mediated transatlantic commercial relations along the Southern Cone. Other foreign merchants, especially from Britain, entered the estuary, often under the guise of getting their vessels repaired, to trade in the region.[69] In short, along the southern frontier, transimperial commercial and social networks underlay much of the prosperity of Montevideo and the entire Southern Cone.[70]

---

[69] Frabrício Prado, *Edge of Empire: Atlantic Networks and Revolution in Bourbon Río de la Plata* (Berkeley: University of California Press, 2015), 34–107.

[70] To protect its far southern frontier, the Spanish Crown established a program to settle more than nineteen hundred Spanish peasants from Galicia, Asturias, and northern Castile to the remote frontier zone of Patagonia in the Río de la Plata between 1778 and 1784. Allyson M. Poska, *Gendered Crossings: Women and Migration in the Spanish Frontier* (Albuquerque: University of New Mexico Press, 2016).

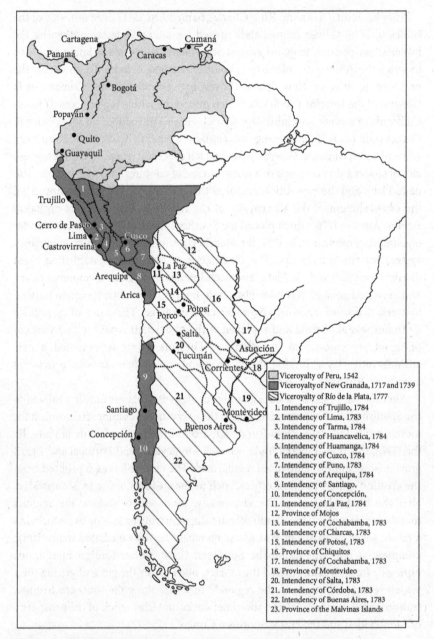

Fig. 4.4 Map of eighteenth-century viceroyalties and intendencies in South America.

Source: Adapted from Cathryn L. Lombardi, John V. Lombardi, with K. Lynn Stoner, *Latin American History: A Teaching Atlas* (Madison: University of Wisconsin Press, 1983), p. 32.

The Bourbon monarch's attempts to control the frontiers of the Spanish Indies even extended to missionary outposts. The Franciscans had maintained an extensive missionary complex on the eastern slopes of the Andes in Peru (called the *montaña* or *oriente*), but an Indigenous rebellion led by a highlander, Juan Santos Atahualpa, had expelled them from their mission outposts in the region in 1742.[71] The order maintained its headquarters in the region at Santa Rosa de Ocopa, but its missions remained confined to smaller centers in the region of Huánuco, Manoa, and Cajamarquilla. The Franciscans did not return to their outposts in the Cerro de la Sal and the Gran Pajonal until the 1780s, when the viceregal government gave them the monetary and military support needed to reopen their lost mission outposts. Nevertheless, the price of this government support was a loss of autonomy. As the Franciscans continued their evangelization efforts, they also followed Crown frontier policies that emphasized encouraging commerce, scientific exploration—particularly finding marketable plants from the region—and protecting the borders with Portuguese Brazil. The viceroy had to approve the placement of new missionaries in the region, and secular authorities even intervened in the election of a new head of the missionary complex in 1787 to secure the victory of a candidate more aligned with royal frontier policies.[72]

In the same year as the creation of the Viceroyalty of Río de la Plata, Gálvez turned his attention to promoting free trade within the Spanish Atlantic world, a goal set by Campillo over thirty years earlier. A royal decree of October 3, 1776, brought Santa Marta and Ríohacha into the Caribbean free trade zone. On February 2, 1778, Spain opened all of South America south of New Granada to imperial free trade, and Gálvez expanded the number of Spanish ports allowed to trade directly with the Indies. These breaches in its traditional monopoly outraged the merchant guild of Cádiz, but further resistance was impossible. Gálvez now had political momentum and a strong ally from 1777 in José Moñino, the Conde de Floridablanca, who had emerged as a dominant political figure and a strong proponent of reforms such as imperial free trade. Finally, on October 12, 1778, the Crown issued the Regulation of Free Trade, which included Cartagena, Panama, and Guayaquil in the new free trade system. The new system of imperial free trade excluded only New Spain, where the powerful Consulado of Mexico City successfully defended its privileges, and Caracas, where the Caracas Company still held monopoly trade rights. The king and his ministers

---

[71] Cameron D. Jones, "The Evolution of Spanish Governance during the Early Bourbon Period in Peru: The Juan Santos Atahualpa Rebellion and the Missionaries of Ocopa," *The Americas* 73, no. 3 (July 2016): 325–29.
[72] Cameron D. Jones, *In Service of Two Masters: The Missionaries of Ocopa, Indigenous Resistance, and Spanish Governance in Bourbon Peru* (Stanford, CA: Stanford University Press, 2017), especially chap. 5.

feared that New Spain's large, prosperous economy would dominate the commercial system, crowding out the participation of the imperial peripheries, which they wanted to stimulate. These last two zones would not be included in imperial free trade until 1789. In the end, imperial free trade undercut contraband, broadened markets, and drew the colonial economies into greater dependency on the metropolis. After the commercial disruptions caused by the American Revolution, exports from the Indies increased from 111,983 copper reales de vellón in 1782 to over 1,201,263, 356 reales de vellón by 1784.[73]

Another important step in trade liberalization came on February 28, 1789, when the Crown allowed Cuba, Santo Domingo, Puerto Rico, and Caracas to obtain enslaved persons directly from African suppliers. African enslavement had been an integral part of the societies of the Spanish Atlantic world from the sixteenth century, but foreign suppliers—first the Portuguese, then the French and British—had provided the bulk of the enslaved individuals in the Spanish Indies. Moreover, the eighteenth century saw the massive influx of 5.7 million enslaved people to the Americas, mostly to Brazil and the English and French Caribbean islands.[74] Over the course of the eighteenth century, Spanish America imported an average of 6,000 slaves annually.[75] This new policy came about only after consistent lobbying from Cuban planters who wanted to participate in this slave trade, and it was part of Spain's strategy of using freer trade—in this case with Africa in enslaved persons—to develop the economies of strategic frontier zones, particularly the sugar plantations of Cuba. In 1791, the policy included New Granada and the Río de la Plata, leading to a large influx of African bondsmen in both regions. The older and more populous region of New Spain and Peru, with their large Indigenous populations, did not participate actively in this new stage of Spanish American slavery.[76]

Despite his successes, the minister of the Indies was an imperious and impatient man, who seldom utilized the customary practice of consultation and compromise with American elites in favor of a more authoritarian approach. Gálvez sent a series of his political protégés on *visitas* to Peru, New Granada, Quito, and Chile, where their high-handed, arbitrary behavior resembled that of their mentor in his earlier inspection tour of New Spain. The missions of *regentes visitadores* José Antonio de Areche to Peru, Juan Francisco Gutiérrez Piñares to New Granada, Tomás Álvarez de Acevedo to Chile, and José García

---

[73] Antonio García Baquero, "Los resultados del libre comercio y el punto de vista: Una revisión desde la estadística," *Manuscrits* 115 (1997): 303–22.

[74] Spanish America received 1.2 million of the over 10 million enslaved individuals imported into the Americas from the sixteenth through the eighteenth century. Herbert S. Klein, *The Atlantic Slave Trade* (Cambridge: Cambridge University Press, 2010), 216–17.

[75] Paquette, *European Seaborne Empires*, 135.

[76] Herbert S. Klein and Ben Vinson III, *African Slavery in Latin America and the Caribbean* (New York: Oxford University Press, 2007), 76–77.

de Leon y Pizarro to Quito all attempted to reorganize colonial finances and administration. These *visitadores* enforced existing taxes more effectively and raised monopoly prices and the sales tax. They also took more accurate censuses of the Indigenous populations, which led to a considerable upsurge in tribute revenues. To accomplish these innovations, the *visitadores* purged colonial bureaucracies of local Creoles and put their own men in positions of power. They also imposed the intendancy system in Peru, Chile, Guatemala, and New Spain by 1786. These actions succeeded in raising revenues, but they alienated American elites accustomed to exercising power through local bureaucratic offices. The innovations also angered colonial middle-class and subaltern groups who had to pay higher taxes and face stricter government regulations. Gálvez and his *visitadores* achieved much, but the price in colonial anger and disaffection was very high, including outbreaks of rebellion much more serious than those that Gálvez had suppressed in New Spain in 1767.

The first outbreak of this violence began as a series of local protests in 1777 by the Aymara people of Macha (in Chayanta, north of Potosí), led by an illiterate Andean peasant, Tomás Katari. The people of Macha wanted redress over abuses in tribute collection and the forced allocation of European wars (*repartimiento de comercio*; also called the *reparto*) by the local *corregidor de indios*, Joaquin Alós. This practice of forcing Indigenous communities to buy often low-quality European and colonial goods, usually at inflated prices, began in the first half of the eighteenth century to take advantage of the rising Indigenous population. Merchants in Lima usually supplied the merchandise to *corregidores* throughout the viceroyalty, and both groups could make handsome profits from the practice. The viceregal government began regulating the prices and the quantity of the goods and levied the sales tax in 1750, but by the 1780s, the practice had become notoriously corrupt and abusive as the magistrates and their merchant allies conspired to distribute poor-quality goods at inflated prices. A man of humble origins, Katari led the ten ethnic communities of Macha in a series of legal confrontations with the *corregidor* and the Audiencia of Charcas, who were implicated in the abusive *reparto* practices. Katari then made the long, three-month, two thousand–mile trek from Chayanta to Buenos Aires, where he took his case directly to the new viceroy. Although authorities in Buenos Aires supported Katari's claims against the corrupt elites in Charcas, these local authorities remained opposed to this popular movement, triggering violent confrontations. The protests led to the expulsion of Spanish authorities from the region, the assumption of power by Katari, and a widespread insurrection of the Aymara peoples against the colonial regime. Even after local officials arrested and later murdered Katari in December 1780, rebellion engulfed the region. Within a year, however, Spanish troops had defeated the rebels and restored order.

At the same time as the unrest in Chayanta, an even more violent insurrection threatened Spanish power southeast of Cusco in Tinta. This rebellion was led by José Gabriel Condorcanqui, who called himself Tupac Amaru II after the name of the last Sapa Inca executed by the Spanish in 1572. The Bourbon reforms had led to economic woes and high taxes, while local political corruption in tribute rates and the *reparto* allocations produced much unrest among the Indigenous peoples. After Tupac Amaru and his troops arrested and executed the apparently corrupt local *corregidor*, Antonio de Arriaga, a rebellion inflamed the whole Cusco region. Although the bulk of the troops were Andean peasants, the leadership consisted of Spaniards, Creoles, mestizos, and a few Indigenous and mulatto officers. Tupac Amaru used a diverse set of Christian and Inca symbols in forging a program to attract a broad coalition of different ethnic groups to protest Spanish abuses. Tupac Amaru took the title of Sapa Inca, dressed in traditional Inca tunics, and drew on messianic beliefs that foretold the return of the last Inca, Tupac Amaru I, who would expel the Spaniards and bring justice and social order. After some initial victories, the Indigenous rank and file took out years of pent-up anger by killing Creoles, peninsulars, and noncombatants indiscriminately. After failing to take Cusco with an army of thirty thousand rebel troops, Tupac Amaru retreated to Tinta, where a Spanish force from Cusco defeated, captured, and later executed the rebel.

Despite the defeat and execution of Tupac Amaru II, segments of the rebel army under the command of his cousin, Diego Cristóbal Tupac Amaru, retreated to Upper Peru (Bolivia), where they established connections with Aymara rebels led by the Katari brothers and a third force commanded by an illiterate petty trader, Julián Apasa. Apasa pretended to be the incarnation of the deceased Tomás Katari, which helped him to raise an army and later take the name Tupac Katari. When the Spanish forces captured one of the original Katari brothers and another died in battle, command of the Aymara forces fell to Tupac Katari, who attempted to coordinate with the Quechua army commanded by Diego Cristóbal. The Aymara and Quechua commanders often experienced strained relations, and they had to speak to each other through interpreters. After failing to capture La Paz, bitter divisions emerged between the two camps, and the Tupac Amaru clan abandoned their Aymara allies to negotiate a surrender and a pardon from Spanish authorities. A few days after learning of this betrayal, Spanish authorities lured Tupac Katari into a trap, captured him, and later executed him, ending the Andean rebellions. Despite the victory, the revolts had badly shaken Spanish authority in the Andes.

The last major upheaval directed against the reforms in South America began in New Granada in March 1781 in the town of Socorro in Tunja Province (in upland central Colombia), and this Comunero Rebellion soon spread through much of the interior of the viceroyalty. The rebellion was in response to vigorous enforcement of tax and monopoly laws and efforts to reduce inefficiency and eliminate bureaucratic corruption by the *regente visitador*, Juan Francisco Gutiérrez Piñares, a protégé of Gálvez. The center of the revolt, Socorro, suffered from reforms that raised taxes on local cotton production and restricted local tobacco cultivation, causing economic hardship. Over four thousand protestors gathered in April 1781 to protest the new revenue measures, under the command of a local Creole, Juan Francisco Berbeo. The viceroy deployed the bulk of the royal army in Cartagena to defend the city during the American Revolution, so the authorities in Bogotá sent only a small force to crush the insurgents, but these royal troops were routed at the Battle of Puente Real. After the victory, the rebel army swelled to fifteen thousand and encamped outside the defenseless capital of Bogotá. The rebels issued their demands in the thirty-four Capitulations of Zipaquirá, which dealt with Comunero's complaints against the Bourbon innovations. Without an army to defend the city, local authorities accepted the capitulations, which they later repudiated when the rebels returned home. With this repudiation, the rebellion flared again, but this time viceregal authorities defeated the rebels and restored order in the region. Although Spanish authorities put down this bloody rebellion, colonial discontent continued to fester.

Despite the deaths of José de Gálvez in 1787 and King Charles III in 1789, under the leadership of the Conde de Floridablanca the Crown continued to consolidate and refine gains made in its reformist agenda by advancing additional administrative, fiscal, military, and commercial innovations aimed at thoroughgoing changes in the political and institutional culture of the Spanish Atlantic world. Floridablanca's government incorporated New Spain and Caracas, for example, into the system of imperial free trade in 1789 and created six new *consulados* in the Indies between 1793 and 1810—Buenos Aires, Santiago de Chile, Havana, Caracas, Cartagena de Indias, and Veracruz.[77] Bolstered by increased trade and fiscal remittances from America, Spain emerged as an important military power, particularly after its successes in the American Revolution added strategically important Florida (which had been under British control from 1763 to 1783) to the Spanish Indies. Although the Crown used its resources from the Indies to develop its military, it invested little to develop the economic infrastructures of the metropolis or the Indies. As a result, when Spain was drawn into international conflicts, first into the wars of the French Revolution and ultimately into two disastrous conflicts with the British beginning in 1796, the reforming impulse in the Spanish Atlantic world came to an end.

---

[77] See Gabriel Paquette, "State–Civil Society Cooperation and Conflict in the Spanish Empire: The Intellectual and Political Activities of the Ultramarine *Consulados* and Economic Societies, c1710–1810," *Journal of Latin American Studies* 39 (May 2007): 263–98.

Bourbon Social and Scientific Policies

By the late eighteenth century, the Bourbon monarchs advanced an Enlightenment-inspired social agenda that expanded the power of the state over the individual lives of ordinary citizens. The Crown issued a landmark piece of legislation in 1778, for example, with the Royal Pragmatic on Marriages, which gave parents and royal officials more control over children's marriage choices. Previously, the Church had taken a strong stand in favor of spousal choice, even in cases of marriages between persons of unequal social standing, but the pragmatic effectively allowed parents to petition royal officials to prevent a marriage, if either the bride or the groom had a "defect" of birth or race. Moreover, efforts to advance secular education, public hygiene, and even the custody of minors made the courts the "patriarch" of last resort for all parents and children.[78] The Bourbon state also attempted to police local morals in cities and prosecute a wide range of property, criminal, and civil disputes within families.[79]

In 1789, the Crown issued a very controversial edict to regulate the treatment of enslaved individuals. After reiterating prohibitions about working enslaved persons on Sundays and the master's obligation to feed and clothe bondsman, as well as fostering marriages among enslaved persons, the Crown limited the types of punishments that masters could inflict on them. The legislation also authorized the courts to enforce Crown legislation, guaranteeing the rights of enslaved individuals to evangelization, education, and manumission at a fair price.[80] Finally, the Crown gave town councils and members of the clergy the right to inspect and report on any crimes masters and overseers committed against enslaved individuals. The new legislation provoked outrage among elites in Havana, Caracas, and other areas with large enslaved populations, who argued that they had the legal right to suspend the enforcement of the new law. In the end, opposition from owners of enslaved people forced the monarchy to repeal the law, asking only that owners respect the spirit of the protective legislation.[81]

---

[78] Bianca Premo, *Children of the Father King: Youth, Authority, and Legal Minority in Colonial Lima* (Chapel Hill: University of North Carolina Press, 2005), 137–78.

[79] Despite Bourbon centralizing efforts to reinforce patriarchy, women in late-colonial Quito asserted their personal rights by invoking customary law and representing themselves in court cases, despite the legal requirement that a male figure (a husband, father, or judge) speak for them. Chad Thomas Black, *The Limits of Gender Domination: Women, the Law, and Political Crisis in Quito, 1765–1830* (Albuquerque: University of New Mexico Press, 2010), 121–62.

[80] For a discussion of how enslaved Africans, often born in America, utilized the Spanish court system to seek some redress, see Sherwin K. Bryant, *Rivers of Gold, Lives of Bondage: Governing through Slavery in Colonial Quito* (Chapel Hill: University of North Carolina Press, 2014). Enslaved individuals in Mexico even used blasphemy to appear before the courts and attempt to leave an abusive master. See Javier Villa-Flores, *Dangerous Speech: A Social History of Blasphemy in Colonial Mexico* (Tucson: University of Arizona Press, 2006), 127–47.

[81] Ada Ferrer, *Freedom's Mirror: Cuba and Haiti in the Age of Revolution* (Cambridge: Cambridge University Press, 2014), 28–30.

Bourbon policies toward poverty in multiracial societies of the Indies shifted in the late eighteenth century, from an emphasis on Christian charity to Enlightenment-inspired, state-sponsored welfare programs. This change led government officials to round up vagabonds, beggars, prostitutes, and other "social undesirables" and place them in state-supported poorhouses, where they would be taught to work and live a productive, socially responsible life. In Mexico City, for example, Crown officials sent many destitute people to work in the royal tobacco factory, while in Quito, the *audiencia* president, Juan José de Villalengua y Marfil, rounded up poor children between the ages of twelve and sixteen who appeared to be vagrants and sent them to a state poorhouse.[82] Although most of these government social engineering programs failed to meet the Crown's ambitious goals, they represent a serious attempt to expand the state's power to intervene in the lives of private citizens.

The monarchy also involved itself in social engineering when it decided in 1795 to publish a price list, which allowed people to erase "defects" of birth or race. Those who were illegitimate could purchase an official edict of legitimation, while people of mixed racial ancestry could purchase "whiteness" or even buy the honorific title *don* or *doña*. The edicts (called *cédulas de gracias al sacar*) expanded on the traditional Spanish idea that the king could alter rank, status, or heritage, even changing an individual's birth or race.[83] Negotiations were delicate matters, however, that had to be scrutinized, adjudicated, and debated carefully by the Cámara of the Indies, a subcommittee of the Council of the Indies, on a case-by-case basis. A crucial principle guiding members of the Cámara was whether a person could "pass" as white or legitimate in the wider society despite any defects in birth or racial status. By granting an edict of legitimation or whiteness, the Cámara was validating honor and status already acknowledged in wider society, allowing the monarchy and its ministers to mediate and promote social order.[84]

The Cámara often struggled with cases where race, honor, and status were questionable. Between 1795 and 1807, a dark-skinned (*pardo*) Panamanian merchant with connections throughout the region, Pedro de Ayarza, petitioned for official whiteness and the honorific title *don* for himself and his three sons. Ayarza was clearly a well-respected man, a captain in the local *pardo* militia, and prominent officials felt comfortable staying at his house, but he was of

[82] Susan Deans-Smith, *Bureaucrats, Planters, and Workers: The Making of the Tobacco Monopoly in Bourbon Mexico* (Austin: University of Texas Press, 1992). Cynthia E. Milton, *The Many Meanings of Poverty: Colonialism, Social Compacts, and Assistance in Eighteenth-Century Ecuador* (Stanford, CA: Stanford University Press, 2007), 137–41.

[83] Ann Twinam, *Public Lives, Private Secrets: Gender, Honor, Sexuality, and Illegitimacy in Colonial Spanish America* (Stanford, CA: Stanford University Press, 1999).

[84] Ann Twinam, "Pedro de Ayarza and the Purchase of Whiteness," in Andrien, *Human Tradition*, 221–22.

dubious ancestry. Ayarza argued that his wealth, his social standing in Panama, and the virtues of his children (who were all well educated and respected by their teachers) outweighed the defect of his birth, and many prominent local citizens and public officials supported his request. Because he was the son of a *pardo*, Ayarza's eldest son, Josef Ponciano, could not graduate from the university in Bogotá nor could he hope to practice law, which led Ayarza, an apparently loving, dutiful father, to begin his original petition for whiteness. After several years, the Cámara declared Josef Ponciano "white" and a *don*, but they failed to approve a change in status for Pedro de Ayarza and his younger sons, Antonio Nicanor and Pedro Crisólogo. This odd compromise left the family divided, with one member white and the others *pardos*, and it demonstrated the Crown's difficulties in negotiating ethnicity, race, and honor in the closing decades of Spanish rule.[85]

The Enlightenment and the assertion of Crown authority also inspired efforts to promote useful science. During the reign of Charles III (1759-88) and that of his son and successor Charles IV (1788-1808), the Crown sponsored almost sixty scientific expeditions throughout the Spanish Empire.[86] These expeditions explored and cataloged the flora and fauna of the New World, mapped imperial frontiers and coastlines, conducted astronomical observations and measurements, and investigated the political and administrative problems of the empire.[87] In 1735, a Swedish botanist, Carl Linnaeus, developed a new nomenclature and taxonomy of plants that was widely used in Europe. Botanists sought to observe the plant species of the Americas to compare them to known varieties of plant life. Since it was impractical to preserve and send the plants themselves to Madrid, scientific expeditions to the New World attempted to observe, classify, and draw pictures of plant life, which men of science could publish and analyze in Europe. Apart from their value in advancing scientific knowledge, a major goal of these expeditions was to find plants and herbs that the Crown could sell to make dyes, medicines, and other useful products that would produce wealth for the empire.[88] In this way, useful science had the potential to advance the reform and economic renovation in the Spanish Atlantic world.

The twin goals of economic utility and observation and proper cataloging of the natural plant and animal resources of the Indies motivated the expedition

---

[85] The case is summarized in ibid., 221-37. For a full discussion of the case and its place within the controversies about edicts of whiteness, see Ann Twinam, *Purchasing Whiteness: Pardos, Mulattos, and the Quest for Social Mobility in the Spanish Indies* (Stanford, CA: Stanford University Press, 2015), 138-39, 240-46, 302-3, 334-47.

[86] Daniela Bleichmar, *Visible Empire: Botanical Expeditions and Visual Culture in the Hispanic Enlightenment* (Chicago: University of Chicago Press, 2012), 18. See also Cañizares-Esguerra, *Nature, Empire, and Nation*, 96-111.

[87] Bleichmar, *Visible Empire*, 18.   [88] Ibid., 19, 22-41.

of José Celestino Mutis in New Granada. Mutis was born in 1732 in Cádiz and studied surgery and medicine in Spain. In 1760, he moved to New Granada, where he developed an interest in the natural resources of the Indies. It was not until 1783 that the Crown authorized him to lead a botanical expedition in the region with the goal of finding useful natural commodities, which Spain could use to break the trade monopolies of rival nations. To this end, he assembled a team of plant collectors and spent two years trying to locate American varieties of cinnamon, tea, pepper, nutmeg, and cinchona, which yielded quinine used in the treatment of malaria. At the same time, Mutis hired sixty artists from Bogotá, Madrid, Quito, and Popayán to draw illustrations of the wide variety of plants that they encountered in New Granada to send back to Spain, where they could be studied, compared to known varieties of plants, and classified according to Linnaean principles. Enlightenment science rested on a visual epistemology coupled with a desire to exploit and profit from the bounty of the natural world.[89]

Scientific expeditions could also originate in the Spanish Indies. Between 1782 and 1784, the Enlightenment-educated bishop of Trujillo, Baltasar Jaime Martínez Campañón, conducted a *visita* of his diocese, 93,205 square miles of territory that included rainforests, agricultural valleys, mountains, and coastal desert.[90] While conducting this inspection, the bishop collected twenty-four large crates of preserved zoological, botanical, and mineral specimens to be shipped to Spain. Martínez Campañón also hired artists to draw 1,372 watercolor images of the people, plants, animals, and minerals found in the Trujillo region.[91] This enterprise was part of the bishop's ambitious plan to transform Trujillo into a modern, economically prosperous region of the empire. In this modernization project, Martínez Campañón oversaw the rebuilding of the cathedral and the construction of thirty-nine churches, founded twenty new towns, and ordered the construction of fifty-four primary schools, largely to educate the region's Indigenous population in Castilian, modern ways of living. King Charles III promoted this project in the wake of the Tupac Amaru rebellion to integrate the Indigenous peoples into the colonial society as consumers and producers, a project promoted by Campillo in his *Nuevo sistema* in 1743.[92] The tenure of Martínez Campañón as bishop of Trujillo marked an experiment by this enlightened prelate to put into practice the types of policies favored by Spain's regalist ministers in Madrid.

---

[89] Ibid., 39–41.
[90] Emily Berquist Soule, *The Bishop's Utopia: Envisioning Improvement in Colonial Peru* (Philadelphia: University of Pennsylvania Press, 2014), 50.
[91] Ibid., 176, 186–87. Because the bishop did not follow the nomenclature and taxonomy of Linnaeus, scientists in Spain showed little interest in his work.
[92] Ibid., 92–113.

Silver, Gold, and the Bourbon Reforms

A major objective of the Bourbon reforms was to stimulate mining, particularly the output of precious metals, to boost tax revenues. The Madrid government did this by cutting the mining tax of 20 percent (*quinto*) to 10 percent (*diezmo*); introducing new technology, such as blasting with dynamite; and augmenting supplies of mercury for silver miners by increasing output at the Almaden mine in Spain and purchasing additional amounts from the Idria mines in Slovenia. In New Spain, the discovery of rich mines, such as at Guanajuato, also increased the output of silver. All contributed to an impressive growth in the output of silver and gold (see Fig. 4.5). Legal silver production more than doubled, from 130,650,000 pesos of eight reales in the 1730s to over 279,460,000 pesos between 1800 and 1810. The Viceroyalty of New Spain expanded its domination of silver production in the Indies, producing between 62 and 72 percent of the New World total.[93] Output also rallied in Peru, which accounted for most of the remaining production of silver. Increased bullion extraction, more efficient tax collection, new levies and royal monopolies, and greater trade liberalization all paid for the expanded military establishment and the royal bureaucracy, which oversaw the shipment of remittances to Spain.[94]

The increased output of precious metals clearly led to rising levels of tax remittances from the Indies into the General Treasury in Madrid, which attests to the overall financial success of the Crown's various reforms by the 1790s (see Fig. 4.6). Income from the Indies rose from over 58,000,000 copper reales de vellón in 1763 to 312,290,000 reales in 1796.[95] A three-year moving average of Indies income flowing into the General Treasury in Madrid demonstrates the high levels of revenue shipments. During three major periods, remittances increased noticeably, from 1733 to 1740, from 1749 to 1762, and after 1783. The first period corresponds to the implementation of initiatives under Patiño, which had begun under Alberoni, while the second corresponds to the end of the War of Jenkins' Ear and the revival of reform under Ensenada. Although the Seven Years' War interrupted commerce in the Spanish Atlantic, leading

---

[93] Kenneth J. Andrien, "Economies, Spanish Territories," in Miller et al., *Princeton Companion to Atlantic History*, 174.
[94] A technological expedition of European mining and metallurgical experts headed by Baron Nordenflicht also arrived in Potosí in 1789 to improve refining techniques by heating rotating barrels that mixed ore, mercury, salt, and magistral, but this barrel method produced disappointing results and refiners abandoned the new process. See Kendall W. Brown, *A History of Mining in Latin America: From the Colonial Era to the Present* (Albuquerque: University of New Mexico Press, 2012), 27–28. On the failure of the Nordenflicht expedition, see also J. R. Fisher, *Silver Mines and Silver Miners in Colonial Peru, 1776–1824*, Monograph Series, No. 7 (Liverpool, UK: Center for Latin-American Studies, University of Liverpool, 1977), 54–73.
[95] Kuethe and Andrien, *Spanish Atlantic World*, 340.

Years	Silver	Gold	Total
1492–1500	0	0.7	0.7
1501–1510	0	8.2	8.2
1511–1520	0	7.21	7.21
1521–1530	0.34	3.92	4.26
1531–1540	7.55	11.12	18.67
1541–1550	28.12	8.73	36.85
1551–1560	42.71	10.64	53.35
1561–1570	56.05	8.85	64.9
1571–1580	71.47	13	84.47
1581–1590	100.19	10.18	110.37
1591–1600	113.4	11.91	125.31
1601–1610	121.81	12.75	134.56
1611–1620	124.28	10.43	134.71
1621–1630	123.63	9.91	133.54
1631–1640	128.6	5.24	133.84
1641–1650	102.83	6.72	109.55
1651–1660	92.16	6.73	98.89
1661–1670	85.73	4.74	90.47
1671–1680	100.02	4.54	104.56
1681–1690	109.85	5.85	115.7
1691–1700	92.8	8.24	101.04
1701–1710	78.25	33.24	111.49
1711–1720	92.61	37.05	129.66
1721–1730	112.45	74.25	186.7
1731–1740	130.65	99.12	229.77
1741–1750	147.94	108.73	256.67
1751–1760	174.58	90.41	264.99
1761–1770	166.72	95.41	262.13
1771–1780	216.55	104.65	321.2
1781–1790	241.88	102.27	344.15
1791–1800	289.94	102.59	392.53
1801–1810	279.46	82.06	361.52

Fig. 4.5 New World Gold and Silver Output in millions of Pesos of 272 Maravedis, 1492–1810.

Source: John J. TePaske and edited by Kendall W. Brown, *A New World of Gold and Silver* (Leiden and Boston, Brill, 2010), Table 1–2, p. 20.

to a downturn in remittances, shipments of public revenues began to rise again during the 1770s until the disruptions of trade during the American Revolution. Then they rose steadily until the war with Great Britain in 1796. Remittances from the Indies also formed an increasingly large share of the Crown's total income, rising from over 12 percent of total income in the 1760s to over 33 percent in 1796.[96] From the Crown's perspective, the century-long process of reform and renovation in the Spanish Atlantic world paid huge financial dividends.

[96] Ibid.

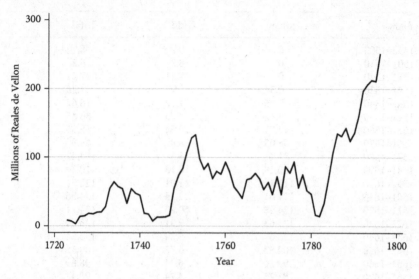

Fig. 4.6 Remittances of public revenue to Spain, three-year moving average.

Sources: Jacques A. Barbier, "Towards a New Chronology for Bourbon Colonialism: The 'Depositaría de Indias' of Cádiz, 1722–1789," *Ibero-Amerikanisches Archiv* 6, no. 4 (1980): 335–53; Jacques A. Barbier and Herbert S. Klein, "Revolutionary Wars and Public Finances: The Madrid Treasury, 1784–1807," *Journal of Economic History* 41, no. 2 (June 1981): 315–37; Carlos Marichal, "Beneficios y costes fiscales del colonialismo: Las remesas Americanas a España, 1760–1814," *Revista de Historia Económica* XV, no. 3 (Otoño–Invierno, 1997): 475–505.

Revolutionary Hysteria: Juan Barbarín and the French Conspiracy in Buenos Aires

In the late eighteenth century, three great revolutions erupted in the Atlantic basin (in English North America in 1776, in France in 1789, and in Haiti in 1791), producing reactions ranging from enthusiasm to abhorrence in the Spanish Indies. Many Creole and peninsular elites, members of the middle classes, mixed-race plebeian groups, and Amerindians had chafed under the negative consequences of the Bourbon reforms, yet the prospect of revolutionary change produced even greater unease, particularly in ruling circles on both sides of the Atlantic. In Buenos Aires, the large influx of enslaved Africans after trade liberalization in 1791 made the city's elites particularly sensitive to the possible political chaos and social upheaval that independence might bring. As a result, by 1795, rumors of a revolt by enslaved individuals, perhaps led by radical elements of the city's French citizenry, swept through the viceregal capital in 1795, creating a tense, fearful atmosphere. After all, the number of enslaved people in the city had surpassed ten thousand and accounted for perhaps 20 percent of the total urban population.⁹⁷ Rumors of insolent behavior by enslaved persons, secret nighttime meetings by Frenchmen, and stockpiled weapons and ammunition were difficult to substantiate, but they caused fearfulness among the Buenos Aires (*porteño*) elites.

When subversive posters with only the word "liberty" mysteriously appeared around the city, Viceroy Nicolás de Arredondo appointed Martín de Alzaga to investigate the matter. Alzaga was a dour, self-important member of the city council who harbored no sympathies for foreigners or revolutionaries. Alzaga's investigation soon focused on the city's French community, particularly a prosperous thirty-eight-year-old merchant named Juan Barbarín (also called Jean Capdepón). Witnesses testified that Barbarín served as a sponsor for a Black religious sodality, had Afro-Argentines visit his house, and maintained a close and apparently affectionate relationship with his own enslaved person, Manuel. Barbarín and Manuel took public walks in the city, chatting amiably like two friends. Witnesses said that Barbarín allegedly defended Maximilien Robespierre and the bloody revolution in his native France. To a staunch defender of the traditional social hierarchies in the colony such as Alzaga, Barbarín's behavior was odious, subversive, and probably revolutionary. He had the merchant jailed, along with Manuel. Although evidence that Alzaga compiled apparently cleared Barbarín of complicity in any enslavement conspiracy, the merchant remained in jail and suffered financial ruin. After being exiled to Spain, Barbarín disappeared from known historical records. Juan Barbarín was merely a pawn or scapegoat for a society fearful of revolution; his belief in liberty, equality, and fraternity—the mottos of the French Revolution—was his undoing.⁹⁸ Manuel, who took the name Manuel Macedonio Barbarín, secured his freedom by fighting heroically in Argentina's independence wars and later for the dictator Juan Manuel de Rosas. He died in 1836, leaving a wife and seven children.⁹⁹

Conclusion

The cycles of war and reform over the course of the eighteenth century indicate that the renovation of the political and institutional culture of the Spanish Atlantic world emerged from a long, complicated political process in which the Crown,

---

[97] Lyman L. Johnson, "Juan Barbarín: The 1795 French Conspiracy in Buenos Aires," in Andrien, *Human Tradition*, 270–72. For a fuller discussion of the French conspiracy and Barbarín, see Johnson, *Workshop of Revolution*, 149–78.
[98] Johnson, "Juan Barbarín," 269–87; Johnson, *Workshop of Revolution*, 149–78.
[99] Johnson, *Workshop of Revolution*, 249–50.

conservatives in Spain and the Indies, and Spain's European rivals engaged in prolonged struggles for power. The century-long process of political reform involved a major expansion of royal power at the expense of vested-interest groups on both sides of the Atlantic. The Habsburg composite monarchy recognized a broad array of local privileges granted to towns, provinces, different kingdoms, influential corporate groups such as the nobility merchant guilds, and the Church. The Bourbon effort to change this composite monarchy into a more centralized, absolutist state prompted dissention, opposition, and even periodic political unrest or rebellion. The many changes in policy over time made the whole process of imperial reorganization appear a halting piecemeal effort, often fraught with inconsistencies and contradictions. Bourbon regalists took Enlightenment ideas from Europe with a variety of discourses on reform from the Indies to fashion practical policies of reform. The political reforms proceeded in stages, moving from the policies of Alberoni and Patiño to the more extensive changes initiated by Ensenada, finally reaching their pinnacle during the reign of Charles III. Politics was always a disorderly process, with numerous interest groups fighting to shape, impede, or even destroy efforts to reshape the ties binding the Indies and the metropolis. Political disputes between reformers and opponents also led to different outcomes in the diverse provinces of the Spanish Atlantic world. The chronology of the reforms differed across regions as well. Some changes, such as the expulsion of the Jesuits in 1767, contributed to unrest in New Spain, although they proceeded without such violence in Peru and New Granada. The most serious opposition to reform came later in both of these regions, with the Comunero Revolt and the Andean rebellions of the 1780s, which severely disrupted the reform process and threatened the foundations of Spanish rule in both regions. On other occasions, reforms led to social and political tensions, particularly after the revolutions in North America, France, and Haiti, as elites feared the consequences of any move against the established order. Such fears gave rise to the so-called French conspiracy in 1795, leading to the arrest and exile of Juan Barbarín in Buenos Aires.

Political and commercial reform also led to conflicts with European rivals seeking to gain access to markets in the Indies. These recurrent outbreaks of war, complicated by conflicting dynastic ambitions in Europe, sometimes derailed reform and interrupted policy changes in the Spanish Atlantic world, leading to the downfall of powerful royal ministers such as Alberoni and Ensenada. On other occasions, war could impel reform as Bourbon ministers enacted policies to prepare Spain for looming conflicts with her rivals. The loss of Havana, for example, allowed Charles III and his ministers to justify some of the most important political and commercial changes of the century, such as the formation of colonial militias, the proclamation of imperial free trade, and administrative reforms such as the imposition of the intendency system and the establishment of the Viceroyalty of the Río de la Plata. In short, war and the threat of war was an ongoing theme in the eighteenth century, and it was intimately linked with efforts to reform and renovate the Spanish Atlantic world. War and the constant political struggles over reform and renovation explain why no single coherent plan of reform emerged during the century, which gave the Bourbon reforms their apparently muddled, inconsistent appearance.

While political and commercial reforms emerged in fits and starts over the course of the century, Bourbon attempts to undermine the power of the Church took place from mid-century. The effort to remove the regular orders from their lucrative Indigenous parishes clearly diminished the wealth, power, and size of the mendicant orders. The expulsion of the powerful Society of Jesus in 1767 was probably the most significant religious reform of the century, and the extinction of the order in 1773 removed one of the most threatening rivals to the efforts of Bourbon regalists to establish a strong, centralized state apparatus. By the end of the century, the institutions of the Roman Catholic Church were largely subordinated to the power of the Bourbon monarchy.

Bourbon social innovations came later. In the late eighteenth century, regalists attempted to insert the Bourbon state into individuals' personal lives and to use the patronage of the monarchy to advance science. Bourbon ministers issued the Royal Pragmatic on Marriage in 1786 and efforts to regulate the treatment of enslaved individuals in 1789 attempted to make the state, not the Church, the final arbitrator in marriage choice and in protecting the rights of bondsmen. Bourbon social reformers even granted edicts of legitimation or whiteness, allowing the monarch to change the social status of citizens. The Bourbon state also tried to police public morality in cities and prosecute a wide array of property, criminal, and civil disputes within families. Enlightened ideas not only influenced political and social policies, but also led to the promotion of useful science by the late eighteenth century. The reigns of Charles III and his son and heir, Charles IV, were a time of promoting scientific expeditions to explore and benefit from the flora and fauna of the Indies. Some scientific initiatives even originated in the Indies, such as the efforts of Bishop Baltasar Jaime Martínez Campañon in northern Peru.

Despite the Crown's successes in centralizing power in the monarchy and creating a more absolutist state, the reforms had negative consequences that reverberated throughout the Indies. The decision to end the sale of appointments, the policy of replacing Creoles in high office with peninsulars, and increased fiscal pressure from Madrid alienated elites throughout the Indies. When José de Gálvez was minister of the Indies, he essentially ignored the long-held practice of consulting and compromising with American elites, taking a more authoritarian approach and unleashing an ambitious regalist agenda designed to centralize power. Gálvez demonstrated initiative and ambition, but he lacked the tact and good sense to promote change without provoking further colonial resistance. Under the Habsburgs, good government rested on a compact between the monarch and local notables, which respected local laws, privileges, and customs, and on the support of the universal Church. Bourbon regalism undermined this social contract, even weakening the Crown's formerly close partnership with the Roman Catholic Church. These policies toward the Church weakened an institution that had provided religious unity and cohesion in the Spanish Atlantic world since the Reconquista. In the end, the reforms also made considerable headway toward moving the Indies from being separate kingdoms of the monarch to being subordinated colonies. The eighteenth-century reforms achieved much, but at a high price in the alienation of many social groups in the Indies.[100]

Timeline: War and Reform in the Spanish Atlantic World, 1700–1796

1700 Death of the last Habsburg king, Charles II, beginning the War of the Spanish Succession

1713 Peace Treaties of Utrecht end the War of the Spanish Succession with victory of the Bourbon claimant, Philip V, giving Britain the monopoly on enslaved individuals in the Indies and the right to bring a five hundred-ton ship of permission to the trade fairs in the Indies

Alberoni, Patiño, and the First Phase of Reform, 1715–36

1715 Rise of Italian commoner, Abad (later Cardinal) Julio Alberoni

1717 On May 18, Alberoni orders the transfer of the *consulado* from Seville to Cádiz

1717 On August 11, British admiral George Bing defeats the Spanish fleet off Cape Passaro

1718–20 Spain defeated in War of the Quadruple Alliance

1719 Alberoni falls from power and goes into exile

1726 José Patiño, a protégé of Alberoni, rises to power

1727 Patiño establishes tobacco monopoly in Cuba

---

[100] According to an article by Mark A. Burkholder, some writers in the eighteenth century referred to the Indies as colonies of Spain, but the term was not commonly employed in Spain until early in the nineteenth century. Mark A. Burkholder, "Spain's America from Kingdoms to Colonies," *Colonial Latin American Review* 25, no. 2 (June 2016): 125–53.

1728	Consulado of Cádiz agrees to fund a Coast Guard in the Caribbean and gives Caracas Company control over commerce in Venezuelan cacao
1736	On November 3, Patiño dies
1739	The Crown establishes a new viceroyalty in northern South America, the Viceroyalty of New Granada

Carvajal, Ensenada, and the Second Phase of Reform, 1741–54

1739–48	War of Jenkins' Ear merges dynastic conflicts in Europe, producing the War of the Austrian Succession
1740	The Crown abandons the *galeones* to South America, licensing individual register ships during the war
1742	Rebellion of Juan Santos Atahualpa on the eastern slope of the Andes in Peru
1743	José de Campillo circulates *Nuevo sistema de gobierno económico para la América* in ruling circles and dies later in the year
1743	Marqués de la Ensenada appointed minister of war, finance, marine and the Indies, beginning his domination of court politics
1746	Aristocrat José de Carvajal y Lancaster named minister of state, beginning a partnership and rivalry with Ensenada
1746	Massive earthquake and tsunami devastates Lima and destroys Callao
1749–53	The Crown orders regular orders serving in Indigenous parishes be replaced by secular clergy
1750–51	The Crown ends the systematic sale of bureaucratic appointments as part of a policy to replace venal officeholders with well-trained, educated, and loyal peninsular-born officials
1754	On July 20, Ensenada dismissed and sent into exile, ending the second phase of the reform process

The Pinnacle of Reform, 1759–96

1759	King Ferdinand VI dies and is replaced by his half-brother, Charles III, who had been king of Naples (1735–59)
1764	Charles III and his ministers establish a modern mail system
1765	The Crown opens free trade between Havana, Santo Domingo, Puerto Rico, Margarita, and Trinidad with nine ports in Spain
1765–71	Gálvez *visita* to New Spain
1767	On April 27, King Charles orders the expulsion of the Jesuits from the Spanish Atlantic world
1767	Riots erupt in New Spain that were suppressed by *visitador* José de Gálvez
1773	The papacy extinguishes the Jesuit order
1776	José de Gálvez is named minister of the Indies
1776	Creation of the Viceroyalty of Río de la Plata

1777	*Visitas* dispatched to Peru, New Granada, Chile, and Quito
1778	On October 12, the Crown announces free trade within the empire, excluding only New Spain and Caracas
1778	Royal Pragmatic on Marriage
1779	Spain enters the War of the American Revolution
1777–81	Rebellions in New Granada and the Andes
1782	Intendency system imposed in Río de la Plata
1786	Intendency system imposed in Peru, Chile, Guatemala, and New Spain
1789	On February 28, New Spain and Caracas are included in imperial free trade
1789	On February 28, Cuba, Santo Domingo, Puerto Rico, and Caracas are allowed to obtain enslaved individuals directly from Africa
1789	On May 31, Crown issues edict on the fair treatment of enslaved persons
1789	On December 14, death of King Charles III and accession of his son, Charles IV
1791	New Granada and the Río de la Plata are allowed to purchase enslaved persons directly from Africa
1793–95	War with Revolutionary France
1795	The Crown publishes a price list for *cédulas de gracias al sacar*
1796	War breaks out with Great Britain

5

The Collapse of the Spanish Atlantic World, 1796–1825

> That having found our beloved Ferdinand a prisoner of the tyrant Napoleon, all the nation occupied by the French, the Junta Central dissolved and Quito governed by suspect, inept, creatures of Godoy, who scheme to deliver us to the usurper, with whom they are in accord: this noble and loyal city with the authority of the people has seen fit to form a *Suprema Junta Governativa* for the defense of this kingdom, and its preservation, to restore it to its legitimate owner whenever providence wishes to restore him to the throne.
>
> Juan Pío de Montúfar, Quito, October 25, 1809

At his death on December 14, 1788, King Charles III left his son and heir heightened commercial ties with the Indies, a more centralized political system, and a stable treasury, which had financed Spanish victories in the war against Britain during the American Revolution. Within a decade, however, Spain was embroiled in the wars surrounding the French Revolution of 1789 and later with two disastrous wars with Great Britain. To pay for nearly three decades of war, the Crown borrowed heavily, issued annuities (*vales reales*), and ultimately seized assets of the Church, first in Spain in 1798 and then in the Indies in 1804. After Napoleon Bonaparte rose to power in France, his army invaded the Iberian Peninsula in 1807 to attack Portugal, a traditional ally and trading partner of Great Britain, the French emperor's bitter foe. Napoleon then decided to make Spain a vassal state and forced the Spanish monarch, Charles IV, to abdicate the throne in 1808; he also compelled the Prince of Asturias, Ferdinand, to renounce his right to the Spanish throne. Napoleon then made his elder brother, Joseph, the Spanish king, his power bolstered by a large French army of occupation. The French invasion and the abdications of the royal family, however, led to popular uprisings against the foreign occupying army, which spread throughout the peninsula. Regional committees (juntas) formed in Spain to rule until the return of the monarch and to coordinate resistance against the French. Even after the French withdrew, struggles ensued between supporters of Ferdinand VII, who had returned from his exile in France by 1813 and demanded a return to absolutism, and Liberal groups favoring a constitutional monarchy. This continued for much of the nineteenth century.

This tumult in Spain also promoted a serious constitutional crisis in the Indies, where many Creoles believed that without a legitimate monarch, power reverted to the people. As a result, Creole elites established their own juntas in many major cities of the Indies, usually intending to rule until the restoration of a legitimate monarch or stable government in Spain. The quote at the outset of this chapter by Juan Pío de Montúfar of October 25, 1809, presents the sentiments of such provincial juntas in the Indies, boldly expressing the desire to claim sovereignty until the return of the monarch.[1] Meanwhile, Royalists, particularly in the colonial bureaucracy in the Indies, argued that in the absence of the sovereign, his appointed representatives in the Indies still ruled in his name. As a result, these Royalists used military force to quell any uprisings or political movements in their provinces of the Indies, provoking civil wars in the Indies between Royalists and Creole nationalist armies. Even the return of Ferdinand VII from his exile did not end the conflicts in the Indies. Ferdinand even prolonged the rebellions by demanding that the rebels lay down their arms, recognize his absolute authority, and return to their pre-1808 status as colonies. The result was bloodshed, political chaos, and economic devastation that enveloped the Spanish Atlantic world from 1808 to 1825.

Under these pressures, the Spanish Atlantic world slowly collapsed between 1808 and 1825. In the Viceroyalty of New Spain, the Loyalists fell to the rebel forces of Agustín de Iturbide by 1821. The downfall of Spanish authority in South America came by 1825, after the rebel victory at Ayacucho. New Spain soon broke into the independent state of Mexico and the Central American nations of El Salvador, Guatemala, Honduras, Costa Rica, and Nicaragua. The South American Viceroyalties of Peru, New Granada, and the Río de la Plata ultimately splintered into the nations of Peru, Chile, Ecuador, Colombia, Venezuela, Bolivia, Argentina, Uruguay, and Paraguay by 1830. Over sixteen million people in the Spanish Indies, about half of the total population of the Spanish Atlantic world, wrested political control from Spain and began on the path of creating independent nation states. By this time, the Spanish Empire had shrunk to encompass Spain, Cuba, and Puerto Rico, and the Philippines.

The French Invasion and the Constitutional Crisis, 1807–9

After members of the revolutionary regime in France executed King Louis XVI in 1793, Spain became entangled in European conflicts to stop the spread of

---

[1] Archivo General de Indias, Estado, 72 (hereinafter AGI), Memoria de la Revolución de Quito en 5 cartas escritas a un amigo (hereinafter Memoria de la Revolución), Quito, 25 Octubre de 1809, carta 1, folio 4 v, 5.

social revolution from France. In these conflicts with revolutionary France between 1793 and 1795, a series of disastrous defeats forced King Charles IV and his ministers to sue for peace and revive the traditional alliance with France. This, in turn, led to wars with France's principal enemy, Great Britain, in 1796 and 1804. The first war led to the loss of much of the Spain's navy at the Battle of Cape St. Vincent in 1797, effectively ending the reforms of the Bourbon dynasty and seriously curtailing commercial ties between Spain and the Indies. This prompted the Crown to take the unprecedented step of allowing the vessels of neutral powers to trade with the Indies and to convey American bullion and produce to Spain between 1797 and 1799. A second conflict with Britain from 1804 to 1808 resulted in the British fleet's destruction of the Franco-Spanish naval force off Cape Trafalgar in 1805. The renewal of war with Britain once again forced the Spanish government to allow direct neutral trade with the Indies from 1805 to 1808.[2]

To fund these conflicts, Charles IV and his ministers relied on loans from European bankers and both loans and forced donations from clerical institutions in Spain and the Indies. Loans had to be repaid, however, and war frequently disrupted deliveries of Indies revenues, especially during the conflicts with Britain. With such extraordinary revenues exhausted, the Crown turned to selling government annuities, *vales reales*, which normally paid 3 percent interest. Initially, the annuities attracted clerical buyers and private citizens looking for secure investments, but after the French war, the government had sold nearly 1 million reales de vellón, and their actual market value of fell to 40 percent of the face value. The first war with Britain forced the Crown to sell additional annuities, and by the end of that conflict in 1798, the Royal Treasury faced bankruptcy. As a result, the Crown took the controversial, extraordinary measure in 1798 of seizing and selling most Church assets in Spain. In 1803, Napoleon forced Charles IV to sign a secret treaty to pay France a subsidy of 24,000,000 reales de vellón for nine years as the price of remaining neutral in his war with Great Britain. When the second conflict with Great Britain broke out anyway, the Crown extended the policy of seizing Church assets in the Indies in 1804. The urgent fiscal needs of the Madrid government led an

---

[2] Barbara H. Stein and Stanley J. Stein, *Edge of Crisis: War and Trade in the Spanish Atlantic, 1789–1808* (Baltimore: Johns Hopkins University Press, 2009), 207–20; Jacques A. Barbier, "Commercial Reform and *Comercio Neutral* in Cartagena de Indias, 1788–1808," in *Reform and Insurrection in Bourbon New Granada and Peru*, ed. John Fisher, Allan J. Kuethe, and Anthony McFarlane (Baton Rouge: Louisiana State University Press, 1990), 60–61; Jacques A. Barbier, "Comercio neutral in Bolivarean America," in *América Latina en la época de Simón Bolívar: La formanción de las economías y los intereses económicos europeos, 1800–1850*, ed. Reinhard Liehr (Berlin: Colloquium Verlag, 1989), 369; Patricia H. Marks, *Deconstructing Legitimacy: Viceroys, Markets, and the Military in Late Colonial Peru* (University Park: Pennsylvania State University Press, 2007), 108–11.

architect of the confiscation policy, Jorge Escobedo, to call the Indies merely "those provinces from which we want to suck out the juice."[3] Such predatory Crown fiscal attitudes and policies proved deeply unpopular in Spain and particularly in the Indies, alienating members of the regular and secular clergy and pious laity from the monarchy.[4]

The French invasion of the Iberian Peninsula in 1807 emerged from the imperial competition between Britain and Napoleonic France, and it embroiled the peninsula in a bloody conflict against the French that lasted until 1813. In response to a British naval blockade of the French coasts, Napoleon had issued the Berlin decree of November 21, 1806, which placed an embargo on continental European trade with Great Britain. The flaw in this policy was that Britain's close traditional ally, Portugal, served as a conduit for European commerce flowing between Lisbon and British ports. To deal with this defect in the continental system, Napoleon signed the Treaty of Fontainebleau with Spain, which permitted French troops to cross Spain and mount a joint Franco-Spanish invasion of Portugal. The provisions of the treaty divided Portugal into three parts. The royal favorite, the Spanish chief minister Manuel Godoy, was granted control over the southern territories of the Algarve, the central region was placed under French rule, and the northern provinces went to Spain (to be ruled by the former queen of Etruria, María Louisa, a member of the Spanish royal family). Vain and ambitious, Manuel Godoy came from a modest hidalgo family, and he lacked high-level connections among the wealthy and politically powerful nobles in Madrid. Moreover, he was a reputed lover of Queen María Luisa and despised by the heir to the throne, Prince Ferdinand, and his Conservative allies. As French forces poured into Spain, popular resentment against Godoy and the king and queen erupted into a riot at Aranjuez, where the royals and Godoy were temporarily in residence. An alliance between Prince Ferdinand and Conservatives at the court led to the imprisonment of Godoy and forced the abdication of Charles IV in favor of Ferdinand.

---

[3] Escobedo was at the time a minister of the Council of the Indies, but he had served as a reforming *visitador general* in Peru and was the man who presided over the execution of Tupac Amaru. AGI, Indiferente General, 1702, Jorge Escobedo to Francisco Viaña, no location given, 25 November 1804; cited in Jacques A. Barbier, "Peninsular Finance and Colonial Trade: The Dilemma of Charles IV's Spain," *Journal of Latin America Studies* 2, no. 1 (May 1980): 33.

[4] The seizure of Church assets in 1798 and 1804 is called the Consolidación de Vales Reales. In Spain, most Church assets consisted of property, but in the Indies the Church was a major lender, so these assets were largely liens and loans on rural and urban properties, so the confiscations threatened to disrupt credit markets and thus the colonial economies in the Americas. The best summary of the confiscations may be found in Gisela von Wobeser, "El orígen y la finalidad que se perseguía con el real decreto sobre la enajenación de bienes eclesiásticos (Consolidación) en América. 1804," in *El proceso disvinculador y desamortizador de bienes eclesiásticos y comunales en la América Española siglos XVIII y XIX*, coord. Hans-Jürgen Prien y Rosa María Martínez de Codes (Ridderkerk, The Netherlands: Asociación de Historiadores Latinoamericanistas Europeos, 1999), 188–214.

Charles quickly regretted his abdication and tried to reclaim the throne, while Ferdinand, recognizing the insecurity of his position, attempted to flatter the French commander in Spain, Joachim Mura, to secure official recognition from Napoleon. Meanwhile, Napoleon, who apparently never intended to honor the terms of the Treaty of Fontainebleau, summoned Charles and Ferdinand to Bayonne, where he forced both men to abdicate the throne. Napoleon declared his elder brother, Joseph (then king of Naples), king of Spain.[5] Next, Napoleon then placed Charles, his wife, and Godoy in confinement at Compiègne in France, while Ferdinand remained a prisoner for six years in a country estate at Château de Valençay. This stunning sequence of events provoked an unexpected constitutional crisis in the Spanish Atlantic world over who should rule in the absence of a legitimate Bourbon monarch.

Before the French invasion of Iberia, the British aggressively attempted to make inroads into the Spanish Indies. Six months after defeating the Franco-Spanish fleet at Trafalgar, Britain sponsored an unsuccessful expedition in 1806, led by a Venezuelan revolutionary, Francisco de Miranda, to attack Caracas.[6] Later that year, the British launched the first of two unsuccessful expeditions to the Río de la Plata, aimed at capturing Buenos Aires and Montevideo and gaining control over the silver trade from Upper Peru. Local militias, who had expelled the British invaders, effectively controlled the Río de la Plata, which became virtually independent of Spain. A second British invasion in 1807 also failed to take Buenos Aires. British forces might have returned for a third attempt at taking control of the Río de la Plata, but the French invasion of Portugal and Spain transformed the diplomatic landscape. Later that year, Britain sponsored an expedition under the command of Arthur Wellesley (later named Duke of Wellington) to organize the military effort in Iberia against the French, in cooperation with the Portuguese, loyal members of the Spanish army, and local Spanish partisans known as *guerrillas*.[7] Britain and Spain signed a formal alliance to defeat Napoleon in Europe on January 9, 1809.[8] In exchange for this military assistance, British vessels gained direct access to trade with the Indies, which brought an influx of foreign goods into American markets.[9]

Many senior government officials, the nobility, the Church hierarchy, and key senior officers in the army initially accepted Joseph Bonaparte as king, but the Spanish people spontaneously rebelled against the French invaders in the name of Ferdinand VII, utterly rejecting Joseph as a usurper. On May 2, 1808, the citizens of Madrid rose up against the invaders, but the French suppressed

---

[5] Stein and Stein, *Edge of Crisis*, 391–474. [6] Ricketts, *Who Should Rule?*, 118.
[7] In fact, the word *guerrilla* (Spanish for "little war") came into common usage during the war against the French invaders.
[8] Ricketts, *Who Should Rule?*, 119. [9] Ibid.

the uprising and retaliated with widespread executions. The abdication of the Bourbon monarch and his heir also provoked a profound political and constitutional crisis throughout the Spanish Atlantic world. In the absence of the monarchy, where did sovereignty lie? Employing medieval legal practices that, in the absence of the monarch, sovereignty rested with the people, regional governing committees (juntas) emerged throughout Spain to rule until the return of Prince Ferdinand as the rightful king, who was revered among the populace as the beloved one (*el deseado*). By the end of May, when news of the abdications reached the provinces, local authorities began to organize themselves into governing juntas to direct political and military affairs. The first provincial junta formed in Oviedo, followed by such committees in Santander, La Coruña, Segovia, Logroño, León and Zamora, Ciudad Rodrigo, Zaragoza, Valencia, Murcia, and Seville.[10] Popular insurrections against the French spread throughout the countryside, harassing the invaders at every opportunity. The junta in Seville soon styled itself the Supreme Junta of Spain and the Indies, declared war on the French, and proclaimed its loyalty to Ferdinand VII, who quickly became a national symbol of resistance against the invaders. In July, an army organized by the junta in Seville decisively defeated the French at Bailén, leaving twenty-five hundred dead and forcing the French general, Pierre Dupont, to surrender with ten thousand men to the Spanish general, Francisco Javier Castaños.[11] After the defeat, Joseph Bonaparte and his government temporarily evacuated Madrid.

The juntas of several cities called for the formation of a single Junta Central, which met in 1808 to direct the resistance against the French invaders. In January 1809, members of the Junta Central decreed that the imperial possessions were integral parts of the Spanish nation and not colonies, and its members decided to call elections in America for membership on the governing body. There were to be thirty-six representatives in total in the newly reformed Junta Central, but only nine seats went to elected members from the Indies, even though the population of the Spanish American territories probably exceeded the number of people in Spain.[12] The elections were a complicated and lengthy process, and procedures were not standardized throughout the Spanish Indies, which meant that some representatives from Guatemala, Chile, and the Río de la Plata did not complete the electoral process before the Junta Central disbanded in January 1810.[13] Moreover, other provinces, such as Charcas and Quito, were not granted

---

[10] Timothy E. Anna, *Spain and the Loss of America* (Lincoln: University of Nebraska Press, 1983), 27.
[11] Ibid., 29–30.
[12] Brian R. Hamnett, *The End of Iberian Rule on the American Continent, 1770–1830* (Cambridge: Cambridge University Press, 2017), 112.
[13] Jaime Rodríguez O., *The Independence of Spanish America* (Cambridge: Cambridge University Press, 1998), 62.

the right to elect representatives.[14] An important reason for the elections was to legitimize the Junta Central and to prevent the Indies (now often labeled as colonies rather than kingdoms) from creating their own regional juntas.[15]

Civil War in the Indies, 1809–12

Despite gaining modest representation in the Junta Central, regional juntas sprang up in cities such as Quito, La Paz, and Chuquisaca (the capital of Charcas) in 1809 to rule until Ferdinand returned to Spain.[16] All of the juntas proclaimed their loyalty to the Bourbon dynasty, and they supported the active struggle against the Bonapartist usurpation and the French invaders. Members of the royal bureaucracy in the Indies opposed these regional governments, arguing that in the absence of the sovereign, his appointed representatives in the New World legally ruled in his name. In many cases, juntas in capital cities failed to secure the loyalty of provincial cities, unwilling to submit to Creole-led governments in their colonial capitals. In consequence, civil wars broke out between Royalists, mostly led by the Bourbon-appointed colonial governments, and those who supported the regional juntas, often led by Creole urban elites.

In Quito, for example, news of the French invasion, the abdications of the monarchs, and the excitement surrounding impending elections to the Junta Central led many Creoles in the city to discuss forming their own junta to rule until Ferdinand returned to the throne. Rumors also spread that the president of the Audiencia of Quito, the Conde de Ruíz de Castilla, and other peninsular authorities wanted to recognize Joseph Bonaparte as king and planned to jail key members of the Creole nobility.[17] There was even gossip about an impending British invasion of the region. A group of conspirators met clandestinely on the evening of August 9, 1809, and hatched a plan to overthrow the royal government and establish a junta, headed by a prominent member of the *quiteño* nobility, the Marqués de Selva Alegre, and supported by leading members of the Creole aristocracy.[18] When the meeting broke up at 4:00 a.m., the commander of the local garrison, Juan de Salinas, mustered his soldiers to occupy government buildings, placing Ruíz de Castilla under house arrest later that morning. When the city awoke, there was a new government, all without even calling an open meeting of the city council (*cabildo abierto*). The junta mirrored colonial

---

[14] Ibid., 61.   [15] Hamnett, *End of Iberian Rule*, 113.   [16] Ibid.
[17] Demetrio Ramos Pérez, *Entre el plata y Bogotá, cuatro claves de la emancipación Ecuatoriana*, (Madrid: Ediciones Cultura Hispánica, 1978), 180; Rodríguez O. *Independence of Spanish America*, 67.
[18] According to a Loyalist observer, Cañizares was from "familia honrada e interesante, que vende placers a buen precio, y donde tienta hecha su contrata el exmo. Quiroga." AGI, Estado, 72, Memoria de la Revolución, carta 1, f. 1.

quiteño society—closed, aristocratic, hierarchical, and insular. The conspirators had seized power in a simple coup d'état.[19]

Leaders of the junta lacked a long-range governing plan, and they did not attempt to gain any popular support in Quito or in other cities of the kingdom.[20] They naively assumed that, as the aristocratic elite of the capital city, they were the natural leaders of the entire kingdom after the downfall of the monarchy. The governors of Popayán, Guayaquil, and Cuenca wanted no part of the Junta Suprema, and they organized military forces to resist the Creole-led government in the capital. When the Junta Suprema mounted a northern expedition against Pasto, Loyalist troops defeated the *quiteño* army. As a Royalist critic of the junta commented, Cuenca, Popayán, and Guayaquil did not depend on trade or political support from Quito. In fact, the declining economy of the north-central highlands produced largely wheat, barley, potatoes, corn, and some sugar, and high transportation costs made it difficult to export these items any distance. Moreover, returns from trading textiles had diminished substantially by 1809. Cut off and isolated by its political defiance of royal authority, Quito was much more dependent on goods from Popayán, Cuenca, and Guayaquil than those provinces were on Quito.[21]

The imminent arrival of forces from Cuenca and Guayaquil, reinforced by major punitive expeditions to besiege the capital from Peru and New Granada, prompted changes in the junta. The Marqués de Selva Alegre resigned, and the remaining members of the junta negotiated a deal with the Conde Ruíz de Castilla on October 24, 1809. For his part, Ruíz de Castilla agreed to head the junta, rule in the name of King Ferdinand VII, and prohibit the former justices of the *audiencia* from returning to power. Salinas remained head of the army, and Ruíz de Castilla gave all the rebels immunity from any punishment for their role in overthrowing the royal government.[22] Within a few weeks, however, Ruíz de Castilla had reinstated the taxes and royal monopolies abolished by Selva Alegre, and he dissolved the army that had supported the coup. The Junta Suprema collapsed after the arrival of Loyalist troops from Lima. The failure of the junta in Quito mirrored what was happening in Chuquisaca and La Paz,

---

[19] AGI, Estado, 72 Memoria de la Revolución, carta 1, f. 5; Rodríguez O., *Independence of Spanish America*, 68.

[20] The elite's reluctance to gain popular support in Quito for the junta was likely a legacy of the popular insurrection in Quito in 1765, which overthrew the colonial regime for nearly one year. See Kenneth J. Andrien, "Economic Crisis, Taxes, and the Quito Insurrection of 1765," *Past and Present* 129 (November 1990), 104–31; Anthony McFarlane, "The Rebellion of the Barrios: Urban Insurrection in Bourbon Quito," *Hispanic American Historical Review*, 49 (May 1989): 283–330.

[21] AGI, Estado, 72, Memoria de la Revolución, Carta 2, ff. 8v., 9. These events are summarized in Kenneth J. Andrien, "Soberanía y revolución en el reyno de Quito," in *En el umbral de las revoluciones hispanicas: el bienio 1808–1810*, ed. Roberto Breña (Mexico City: Colegio de México y Centro de Estudios Políticos y Constitucionales, 2010), 313–34.

[22] Rodríguez O., *Independence of Spanish America*, 69.

where royal authorities in Peru sent a Loyalist army under General José Manuel de Goyeneche, who swiftly took control and suppressed the Creole-led governments in those cities.[23]

While the early juntas established in 1809 were quickly crushed, Creole-led governments that emerged in Caracas, Bogotá, and Buenos Aires by 1810 precipitated violent conflicts with forces loyal to the colonial bureaucracy and metropolitan Spain. Most of these juntas favored ruling until the return of the legitimate sovereign, Ferdinand VII, but over time, Creole leaders began to advocate independence and even republican forms of government. Loyalist forces, opposed to any breakup of the old colonial system, vigorously resisted these movements, often relying on Spanish troops stationed in the Indies to suppress any efforts at home rule. The center of loyalism in South America was the Viceroyalty of Peru, where Viceroy José Fernando de Abascal y Sousa controlled the largest and most well-equipped army in South America.[24] Likewise, in New Spain viceregal troops attempted to maintain peace and order. Provincial cities often aided these Loyalist forces, unwilling to accept the leadership of Creole juntas in capital cities such as Bogotá, Buenos Aires, and Caracas. In Iberia, the conflict against the French invaders also weakened the authority and power of government in metropolitan Spain.

On April 19, 1810, the leading citizens of Caracas established a new governing body, "The Supreme *Junta* and Defender of the Rights of Ferdinand VII."[25] The province of Caracas represented more than half of the captaincy's eight hundred thousand inhabitants and dominated the production and commerce in regional cacao, indigo, and coffee. The new government expected quickly to gain the allegiance of local provincial capitals, but few accepted its leadership. Within these provinces, smaller cities and towns rejected the leadership of both Caracas and the provincial capitals. While centralized political authority began to dissolve in those places, Coro, Maracaibo, and Guyana remained firmly under the control of Royalist authorities.[26] The Caracas government mobilized an army consisting of regular soldiers from the colonial defense forces along with urban militias of "patriotic volunteers" to launch an attack on Coro.[27] Before the onset of hostilities, however, the new government fell under the influence of Francisco de Miranda and his more radical supporters, who pushed a newly formed constituent congress to declare independence and establish a republic in the former captaincy general on July 5, 1811.

---

[23] Hamnett, *End of Iberian Rule*, 129–30.   [24] Ricketts, *Who Should Rule?*, 142–52.
[25] Anthony McFarlane, *War and Independence in Spanish America* (New York: Routledge, 2014), 85.
[26] Ibid., 86–87.   [27] Ibid., 88.

The Spanish Loyalists were too weak to attack the new republic in Caracas, but bases in the Caribbean sent reinforcements to centers of Loyalist control. When a Royalist rebellion erupted closer to Caracas in Valencia, the congress sent Francisco de Miranda, who had military experience in France and Spain, to put down the Loyalist rebels.[28] Although successful, the republican cause suffered a huge setback after a devastating earthquake struck Caracas.[29] The republican government faced bankruptcy, unable to meet the expenses of both fighting a war and rebuilding the city. Miranda also had to confront a new Loyalist threat when forces from Coro, under the command of Juan Domingo de Monteverde, forced a retreat of republican forces to Caracas. Monteverde bolstered his forces by recruiting enslaved Africans in Venezuela, offering them freedom if they fought for the Royalist cause. Miranda also tried to recruit enslaved people, but his efforts alienated plantation owners, who valued keeping their slaves above aiding the Creole-led government.[30] With his unpaid army decimated by desertion, Miranda faced a hopeless military situation and negotiated the surrender of Caracas, which was occupied by Monteverde and his Loyalist army on June 30, 1812, ending the first Republic of Venezuela.[31]

During 1810, Creole-led juntas replaced royal authorities in New Granada, beginning with Cartagena in June, followed by Cali, Pamplona, Socorro, and finally Santa Fé de Bogotá in July. Royalist strongholds continued in Santa Marta in the north and Pasto and Popayán in the south. Cartagena had already denied the authority of Bogotá in August 1809, and the city acted largely as an independent political entity.[32] New Granada lacked a preeminent city, so several regional juntas claimed to rule in the name of King Ferdinand as centralized political authority broke down. Nevertheless, the self-styled Supreme Junta in Bogotá claimed authority over the whole viceroyalty and called a congress of all the regions to act as a provisional government, but only six provinces sent representatives. In 1811, the Supreme Junta created a new political entity for the capital and the surrounding province of Santa Fé, which they called the state of Cudinamarca, as New Granada divided into advocates of a strong central government and those favoring a federal system. The political squabbles even broke out into armed conflict, which also failed to resolve the divide between Centralists and Federalists, even though both sides opposed Loyalist authorities.[33]

While Cudinamarca and the Federalist congress vied for power, one Loyalist center in Popayán remained strong. The governor, Miguel Tacón, resisted any

---

[28] Ibid., 91.   [29] Ibid., 93.
[30] Peter Blanchard, *Under the Flags of Freedom: Slave Soldiers and the Wars of Independence in Spanish South America* (Pittsburgh: University of Pittsburgh Press, 2008), 26.
[31] Ibid.   [32] Hamnett, *End of Iberian Rule*, 133.
[33] McFarlane, *War and Independence in Spanish America*, 98–100.

efforts to establish a junta in the south of New Granada. When forces from Quito attempted to annex the region in 1809, Tacón had mustered support from the Indigenous population of Popayán and Pasto by offering a one-third reduction in tribute rates. He also secured the loyalty of many of the region's enslaved population of fifteen thousand to twenty thousand (who worked in the gold mines and on regional haciendas that supplied the mining zones) by offering freedom to those willing to fight for the Crown.[34] After defeating the *quiteño* army, Tacón strengthened Loyalist forces and resisted efforts by juntas in the Cauca valley to subdue Popayán by force. Tacón demonstrated that Indigenous towns and enslaved communities were viable military recruiting centers. In 1810, rebel towns of the Cauca valley and a military force under the command of Antonio Baraya attacked Tacón's smaller Loyalist army, forcing the Loyalists to retreat southward. Nonetheless, using funds and gold taken from the Popayán treasury, Tacón kept Loyalist resistance alive until he was defeated at Iscuandé in 1812. Despite this defeat, Loyalist troops, bolstered by their Indigenous and enslaved soldiers, kept their cause alive in the region for several more years, carving out territory in Pasto, Popayán, and the Magdalena River valley.[35]

In Buenos Aires, the militias that expelled the British invasions in 1806 and 1807 effectively controlled the Río de la Plata, and the interim viceroy, Santiago Liniers (1808–09) and his successor, Baltasar Hidalgo de Cisneros, sent from Spain (1809–10), governed at the pleasure of the local militias. As a result, a revolutionary junta, supported by the urban Creole elite and the city militia, took power on May 25, 1810, and deposed Cisneros. The junta vowed to rule as an emergency government until the return of Ferdinand VII.[36] Although the rebel government exhorted the interior provinces of the Río de la Plata to support them, Royalist strongholds held out in Paraguay, Montevideo in the Banda Oriental, and Córdoba, where the ex-viceroy and hero of the resistance to the British invasions, Santiago Liniers, joined with the intendent to resist the Buenos Aires junta. At the same time, the viceroy of Peru, José Fernando de Abascal y Sousa, sent General José Manuel de Goyeneche to take control over the silver-rich provinces of Upper Peru. Both sides coveted Upper Peru and the important port of Montevideo for their resources and strategic value.[37]

---

[34] The most detailed treatment of loyalism in the Pasto region is Marcela Echeverri, *Indian and Slave Royalists in the Age of Revolution: Reform, Revolution, and Royalism in the Northern Andes, 1780–1825* (Cambridge: Cambridge University Press, 2016). See also Blanchard, *Under the Flags of Freedom*, 20; Hamnett, *End of Iberian Rule*, 284; McFarlane, *War and Independence in Spanish America*, 101–2.

[35] Ibid.

[36] For an excellent discussion of the British invasions and the efforts of the Creole elite to recruit members of the working class in Buenos Aires, first to repel the invaders and later to fight for independence, see Johnson, *Workshop of Revolution*, 249–82.

[37] McFarlane, *War and Independence in Spanish America*, 145–47.

The Loyalist forces under Goyeneche's command hoped to use their base in Upper Peru to attack the army of Buenos Aires and join up with Royalist forces in Montevideo and Paraguay to extinguish the junta in the capital city.[38] They suffered two major setbacks when the *porteño* army invaded Upper Peru, capturing Córdoba, and when the city of Cochabamba declared its loyalty to the government in Buenos Aires. After suffering defeat at the hands of the *porteño* invaders at Suipacha and a reverse at Aroma a week later by an army from Cochabamba, the Loyalist forces retreated to the Desaguadero River, leaving the five major cities of Upper Peru, Potosí, La Paz, Cochabamba, Oruro, and Chuquisaca, in rebel hands late in 1810.[39] Viceroy Abascal now faced a serious dilemma: Peru appeared surrounded by hostile juntas in Chile, a revived junta in Quito, and the forces of Buenos Aires in Upper Peru (see Fig. 5.1). To the chagrin of Abascal, Goyeneche used his time at the Desaguadero to train and prepare his army for the invasion of Upper Peru, which finally began in June 1811. In a series of military victories, Goyeneche's forces swept across the Desaguadero River, pushing back the *porteño* forces and retaking all the major cities of Upper Peru.[40] Meanwhile, invasions from Buenos Aires to reclaim control of Paraguay and Montevideo had failed, leaving the overall military and political balance of power in favor of the Loyalists by early 1812.[41]

While Creole aristocrats established juntas in relatively peaceful seizures of power in South America, the rebellion in New Spain involved a widespread popular uprising headed by provincial Creoles. This was largely the result of the coup perpetrated by peninsular members of the merchant guild (*consulado*) of Mexico City, who overthrew the viceroy, José de Iturrigaray, in 1808. These peninsular groups (disparagingly called *gachupines* by Creoles) suspected that Iturrigaray would allow Creoles a role in government following the royal abdications. Because of the coup in Mexico City, Creole political opposition shifted from the capital to provincial cities, where they gambled on calling for a violent, popular insurrection to seize power. When the Crown began jailing Creoles suspected of conspiring against the government in Mexico City, a popular but eccentric priest from Dolores in the Bajío, Miguel de Hidalgo, incited local people to rise up in rebellion on September 16, 1810.[42] Those who responded to Hidalgo's call to arms were chiefly Indians and *castas* displaced by recent drought, famine, and other economic dislocations in the Bajío. Moreover, Hidalgo rallied the populace to defend the deposed King Ferdinand and used the imagery of the Virgin of Guadalupe (representing the Church against what

---

[38] Ibid., 149–51.   [39] Ibid., 153–56.
[40] Ibid., 157–64. On the character and life of Hidalgo, see Hugh M. Hamill, *The Hidalgo Revolt: Prelude to Independence* (Gainesville: University of Florida Press, 1966), 78–80.
[41] Ibid., 165–75.   [42] Hamnett, *End of Iberian Rule*, 154.

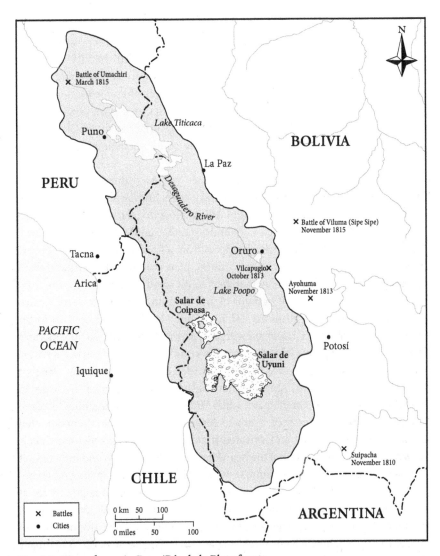

Fig. 5.1 Map of wars in Peru/Río de la Plata front.
Source: Based on a map from John Fletcher, *The Wars of Spanish American Independence, 1809–29* (Oxford: Osprey, 2013), 50, 54.

they termed godless peninsulars).[43] The insurrection spread rapidly as Hidalgo's followers moved southward, first to Celaya and then to the rich mining city of Guanajuato, gaining the support of displaced workers and peasants and even provincial militias along the way. The rebel entry into Guanajuato became a

---

[43] McFarlane, *War and Independence in Spanish America*, 222.

bloody affair as the peninsulars, commanded by the intendent, Juan Antonio Riaño, took refuge in the city granary (*alhóndiga*). Hidalgo's troops stormed the granary, killed all the Spaniards inside, and later sacked the city. Hidalgo's followers (sometimes accompanied by wives and children) resembled a large popular migration more than a disciplined army, but they moved inexorably through Zacatecas to San Luis Potosí, where they set up a provisional government. Hidalgo took the rebellion to Jalisco and captured the city of Guadalajara on November 11, 1810 (see Fig. 5.2), moving south to their ultimate target, Mexico City.[44]

The newly arrived viceroy sent to replace the ousted Iturrigaray, Francisco Javier Venegas, was an experienced military man, and he immediately began preparing for the defense of the capital. He called on regular troops and civilian volunteers drawn from Mexico City and its hinterland; he even armed local Indian militias. This army received support from a force in the north of Mexico, commanded by Félix María Calleja, and the plan was to have Venegas defend the capital while Calleja's forces marched south to attack Hidalgo's army from the rear.[45] Hidalgo's force of perhaps eighty thousand pressed toward Mexico City, but before arriving at the capital, he fought a battle against Loyalist forces at Las Cruces. Although Hidalgo emerged victorious, he suffered considerable losses. Worried that his bloodied troops could not take Mexico City by a direct assault after Las Cruces, Hidalgo retreated on November 3, 1810. He sent his second in command, Ignacio Allende, to take a portion of the army to Valladolid and then to Guanajuato, while Hidalgo took the remaining forces to Guadalajara.[46] Calleja pushed south to Mexico City, but he first encountered Hidalgo's retreating army and defeated it at Aculco. After this victory, Calleja took his army across the Bajío, the heartland of the insurgency, and inflicted yet another defeat on the rebels commanded by Allende at Guanajuato and recaptured the city.[47] He then turned his attention to attacking Hidalgo's forces at Guadalajara. Hidalgo positioned his army at the Bridge of Calderón, on a main road outside the city, where he hoped to use his artillery and massive numbers of troops to overwhelm Calleja's much smaller force. The battle began on January 17, 1811, when Calleja split his force, with one group sent to capture Hidalgo's artillery battery and the other force to attack the main body of Hidalgo's troops. Calleja's army was successful on both fronts, and Hidalgo's soldiers fled in a rout. Hidalgo escaped to Aguascalientes, where Loyalist forces captured him, had him defrocked as a priest, and then executed him.[48] The victory at the Bridge of Calderón effectively ended the rebel insurrection. Thereafter, Hidalgo's troops scattered into smaller guerrilla groups throughout the surrounding countryside.

[44] Ibid., 225–29.   [45] Ibid., 226.   [46] Ibid., 226–29, 242–43.
[47] Ibid., 231–33.   [48] Ibid., 233–36.

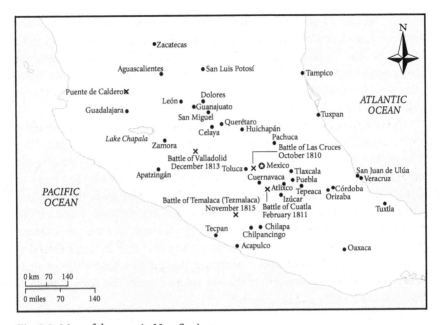

Fig. 5.2 Map of the wars in New Spain.
Source: Based on maps from Anthony McFarlane, *War and Independence in Spanish America* (New York: Routledge, 2014), 250; and John Fletcher, *The Wars of Spanish American Independence, 1809–29* (Oxford: Osprey, 2013), 36.

By 1812, the military balance of power favored Spain in both South America and New Spain, but violence and casualties forced both Loyalists and rebels to recruit from the lower ranks of colonial society, which had profound potential consequences for the future of the Indies. In Venezuela, Loyalist General Monteverde had recruited enslaved persons, promising freedom if they fought for the king, while Miguel Tacón recruited both enslaved individuals and Indigenous soldiers in Popayán and Pasto. Given the peninsular coup that had overthrown Viceroy Iturrigaray, Hidalgo and his fellow Creole conspirators in New Spain relied on plebeian recruits (discontented with the economic downturn in the Bajío) in the insurrection of 1810. Even after Hidalgo's defeat at the Bridge of Calderón, peasant guerrilla bands roamed the countryside, disturbing the peace in rural New Spain.[49] In the military operations in Upper Peru too, Loyalists and the rebel armies recruited local (largely Indigenous recruits) to fill the rank and file of their armies. As General Goyeneche complained to Viceroy Abascal, high levels of desertion required him to rely on local Indigenous and

---

[49] For an important book on the popular insurgency in New Spain from 1810 to 1821, see Erick Van Young, *The Other Rebellion: Popular Violence, Ideology, and the Mexican Struggle for Independence, 1810–1821* (Stanford, CA: Stanford University Press, 2001).

mestizo recruits of doubtful loyalty, whom he claimed were "without honor, self-confidence...so downtrodden and apathetic that they wanted nothing more than to be idle."[50] In short, the mobilization of the lower classes and their active participation in the civil wars between Loyalists and rebels had the potential to redraw social hierarchies. Once mobilized, the lower classes demanded greater political power and social equality after the violence ended.

The civil wars in the Indies led to a serious breakdown in the political order of the Spanish Atlantic world. In Spain, the conflict had turned against the French, but there was little consensus about what form of government would emerge after the invaders withdrew. In the Indies, matters were even more dangerous. The conflicts between Loyalist and the rebels made the chance of restoring a stable political order remote. Intrigue and political infighting like that of medieval Spain took place in both the Loyalist and the rebel camps, mostly over political ideology. Did the future rest with establishing a federal or a more centralized governmental structure? Was political Liberalism or some more conservative restoration of the old colonial order the correct political path toward stability and progress?

The Constitutional Era and Ongoing Struggles in the Indies, 1812–14

In Spain, the Junta Central decided on January 1, 1810, to summon the old Spanish assembly, or *cortes*, to serve as a platform for restoring a stable political order in Spain and the Indies. After a series of defeats in 1809 discredited the Junta Central, its members decided on June 29, 1810, to dissolve that body in favor of a small regency council to direct resistance against the French invaders. Despite the reluctance of some members, the regency called for new elections to a *cortes* that would convene on September 1. It asked all provinces of the Spanish Atlantic world to organize elections and send delegates to this unprecedented assembly.[51] When the new *cortes* opened, it was dominated by middle-class Liberals, who favored an end to Bourbon absolutism. The *cortes* declared that it represented the people and that it was the repository of national sovereignty. By extension, the regency (representing the absent monarch) and the judiciary were subordinate to the legislative branch, which established clear limits on the king's power when he returned. The *cortes* also abolished the office of viceroy, but those holding the office retained military power as *capitanes generals* and *jefes políticos superiores*. Authorities in Spain also turned the *audiencias*

---

[50] Ibid., 158. [51] Rodríguez O., *Independence of Spanish America*, 78–79.

into high courts, with no administrative or legislative powers; provincial deputations, elected by the people, and elected town councils (*ayuntamientos*) in the cities would perform those functions.[52]

The Constitution of 1812 that emerged from the constituent *cortes* defined the Spanish nation as consisting of all the territories of the monarchy, "composing one sole Monarchy, and one sole nation, and one sole family."[53] The political center of the nation remained metropolitan Spain, with elections held for a single one-house legislature, or *cortes*. The constitution also curtailed the powers of the monarch and Church. Even though the constitution did not refer specifically to the Inquisition, it ended censorship and provided for freedom of the press and the right of publication, without the need to obtain a royal or inquisitorial license.[54] The constitution extended the franchise in future elections to all males, except some *castas* and those of African ancestry, without regard to owning property or even literacy.[55] People of Indigenous ancestry (including most mestizos), however, were granted full citizenship and voting rights in all future elections.[56] Although citizenship and the franchise were denied to some *castas* and people of African ancestry, members of these excluded groups might become citizens if they met stringent requirements of virtue and merit. The constitution also abolished Indigenous tribute in the Indies. Nonetheless, the Indies, now seen as colonies, received slightly fewer than half of the elected delegates to the new legislature.[57] Despite these restrictions, all of the constitutional provisions regarding citizenship and the franchise expanded dramatically the scope of political participation. The document clearly provided a liberal blueprint for restoring political order, leaving little room for compromise with those who favored a restoration of Bourbon absolutism.

Although the resulting Constitution of 1812 gave broad liberties and citizenship to most in the empire, its definition of the nation excluded sharing power with any regions and former kingdoms and principalities of Iberia and the Indies. There would be no recognition of any special privileges or *fueros* enjoyed by various regions before the Bourbon dynasty acceded to the throne. At the same time, the constitution still saw the civil wars raging in America as a threat to the indivisible Spanish "nation," which included the colonial possessions in the Indies. As a result, the delegates refused to support concessions to the American "rebels" that might recognize any form of "home rule."[58] It was a last-ditch attempt by Liberal constitutionalists to bring the Indies, fractured by a decade of war and rebellion, back into a reformed Spanish monarchy. The Spanish Liberal regime even rebuffed an offer by its British ally to mediate the conflicts

---

[52] Ibid., 87–89.   [53] Hamnett, *End of Iberian Rule*, 182.
[54] Ibid., 187.   [55] Rodríguez O., *Independence of Spanish America*, 83–85.
[56] Ibid., 83.   [57] Ibid., 85.   [58] Hamnett, *End of Iberian Rule*, 181–85.

in the Indies. Efforts by American delegates to obtain freer access to trade outside the imperial system also met with opposition. After all, the *cortes* met in Cádiz, and the powerful business and political interests of that city's merchant community lobbied effectively to prevent any liberalization of trade. The Cádiz merchants provided needed financial support to the government during these years, including aid to fight against insurgents in the Indies.[59] In short, the constitution provided that the unity of the nation trumped other concerns, even efforts to deal with the rebellions in the Indies. In this sense, the Liberals who framed the Constitution of 1812 shared similar views about maintaining the integrity of the Spanish Atlantic world with absolutists (called *serviles*) in Spain.

In areas of Loyalist control, the implementation of this constitution posed some daunting challenges. In New Spain, for example, Viceroy Venegas saw his powers curtailed to largely military matters in the wake of the Hidalgo insurrection. He feared that elections might send Creole groups favoring home rule to the *cortes* in Spain and to control local *ayuntamientos*, so he postponed elections. A few days later, he suspended Article 371 of the constitution, which called for freedom of the press.[60] When Félix Calleja succeeded Venegas in March 1813, he, too, banned press freedom. Moreover, Calleja did not approve of some delegates elected to the *cortes*, so he denied them funds for travel to Spain.[61] Likewise, Viceroy Abascal in Peru feared the consequences of imposing a new system of government amid an ongoing struggle with rebels in Buenos Aires. He continued to exercise his viceregal powers and attempted, like Venegas, to impede freedom of the press by imposing a Junta de Censura. Abascal also sponsored pro-Loyalist publications to counter those of his critics in Lima.[62] In other areas, such as Quito, despite some confusion about how to proceed, the elections took place without incident. Ongoing military conflicts complicated the calling of elections in many other parts of the Indies. When the *cortes* met in October 1813, of the 149 delegates assigned to the Indies, only 23 elected delegates took part.[63]

In the meantime, wars between Loyalists and rebel forces continued, as leaders from the failed first Republic of Venezuela urged a rebel attack on the Royalist outpost in Santa Marta. When this struggle settled into a stalemate, Simón Bolívar succeeded in convincing authorities in New Granada to support a renewal of the conflict in Venezuela. Bolívar began his campaign in 1813 with approximately one thousand men, while the Loyalist commander, Monteverde, mustered ten thousand to twelve thousand soldiers. Given the unequal strength of the two armies, Bolívar's strategy in the so-called Admirable Campaign was

---

[59] Ibid., 192–94.   [60] Ibid., 195–96.   [61] Ibid., 199.
[62] Ricketts, *Who Should Rule?*, 155.
[63] Rodríguez O., *Independence of Spanish America*, 101–3.

to avoid battle with large enemy forces, outflank the Loyalists, and rely on quick victories that demoralized and confused his opponents.[64] Within six months, Bolívar had won a series of such victories, taking La Grita, Mérida, Valencia, and, most important, Caracas on August 7, 1813. He was aided in this campaign by an independent rebellion on the coast led by Manuel Piar. Piar commanded a force supplemented by *llanero* horsemen (mostly racially mixed-blooded cowboys and small freeholders) who defeated the Loyalists at Maturín in March 1813.[65] The *llaneros* notoriously gave no quarter to Royalist prisoners, and to encourage loyalty to the Second Venezuela Republic, on June 15, 1813, Bolívar famously announced a "war to the death," declaring that all captured Spaniards would be executed. Despite his successes, Bolívar's rapid advance allowed him to control the capital and its hinterland, but the bulk of the Loyalist army remained intact, and the Second Venezuelan Republic held power only tenuously.[66]

In many respects, Simón Bolívar was an unlikely revolutionary leader. He was born into a wealthy family in Caracas, and he had inherited property in the city and estates producing cacao, large herds of cattle, and worked by enslaved people. Bolívar traveled twice to Europe, visiting Spain, France, and Italy, and read voraciously, particularly the works of Enlightenment thinkers such as Hobbes, Locke, Montesquieu, Raynal, and Voltaire. While living in Europe, Bolívar made the acquaintance of famed savant Alexander von Humboldt. During this first trip abroad, he married a Caracas aristocrat, María Teresa Rodríguez del Toro, who tragically died soon after. He never remarried, although his affairs with women in Europe and South America were notorious. Bolívar had little formal military training, but he had charisma, self-confidence (bordering on egomania), and legendary physical endurance, which marked him as a natural leader.[67] What Bolívar lacked in military experience, he quickly learned on the battlefield. Moreover, his political ideas and dedication to the independence movement evolved, making him the leader who would soon be called the "Liberator" of Spanish South America.[68]

The Royalists held three strategic regions of Venezuela: the port of Puerto Cabello, the coastal towns of Coro and Maracaibo, and much of southern Venezuela, including the llanos. Here, the Spaniard José Tomás Boves now commanded the irregular forces, composed largely of *llanero* cavalry. The military and strategic situation turned into a stalemate, despite Bolívar's major

---

[64] McFarlane, *War and Independence in Spanish America*, 115–20.
[65] Ibid., 118.   [66] Ibid., 120.
[67] The *llanero* cavalry in Bolívar's army referred to him as *culo de hierro* (iron butt). See Jay Kinsbruner, *Independence in Spanish America* (Albuquerque: University of New Mexico Press, 1994), 81.
[68] For biographies that discuss Bolívar's background and life before the independence era, see John Lynch, *Simón Bolívar: A Life* (New Haven, CT: Yale University Press, 2006), 22–40; and David Bushnell, *Simón Bolívar: Liberation and Disappointment* (New York: Pearson Longman, 2004), 1–16.

victory at Araure on December 5, 1813.[69] Early in 1814, after Loyalist reinforcements arrived, the royal troops began an offensive from all three of their bases to destroy the rebel army defending Caracas. The most serious threat came from Boves and his *llaneros*, who moved northward from the Calabozo plains to the hinterland of Caracas. Boves behaved like an independent warlord, and his promises of plunder allowed him to mobilize the *llaneros* into a fearsome cavalry force that offered no quarter to civilians and rebel prisoners. Although Bolívar won a major battle at Carabobo, Boves defeated the rebel forces at La Puerta on June 14, 1814, forcing Bolívar to abandon Caracas a month later. Boves continued his rampage from Caracas to Cumaná, winning a victory at Urica that defeated the last sizeable rebel army, but he was killed in the fighting.[70] Despite the loss of Boves, the Loyalists had regained control over Venezuela, but the war had left much of the region devastated. Bolívar took refuge in Cartagena.

While Royalist fortunes won in Venezuela by 1814, the situation in Peru and Upper Peru had settled into a stalemate. Viceroy Abascal wanted General Goyeneche to launch an invasion of the Río de la Plata that would coordinate with Royalist armies in Paraguay and Montevideo. It was the *porteño* army under the command of Manuel Belgrano that first took the offensive, capturing Salta from the Loyalists in 1813, opening the way for the army of Buenos Aires to re-enter Upper Peru. The Loyalist army under Goyeneche retreated from Potosí to Oruro, leaving the wealthy mining town and its treasury to Belgrano and his troops.[71] This military reversal led Abascal to replace Goyeneche with Joaquín de la Pezuela, an army general with experience fighting against the British and the French. He took command of the Loyalist army on August 7, 1813. Pezuela found the condition of the Loyalist army of Peru appalling. The bulk of troops were unpaid, without uniforms or supplies, and on the verge of desertion. Moreover, most of the troops were Indigenous or mestizos; few even spoke Spanish, and they survived largely by foraging, since the army lacked a commissariat to obtain food and supplies.[72] Pezuela also faced a *porteño* army that was well entrenched in Potosí and reinforced by a regiment of former enslaved people, who had been recruited with the promise of freedom if they fought for Buenos Aires. In part, to encourage recruitment of enslaved people, the government in Buenos Aires also passed a free womb law in 1813, declaring that all children of enslaved individuals born in the United Provinces of the Río de la Plata were free.[73] Moreover, Pezuela found that the rebels had established stable, insurgent governments in Potosí, Cochabamba, and Santa Cruz loyal to Buenos Aires. Guerrilla forces (composed largely of Indigenous and mestizo fighters in Upper Peru) also supported Belgrano's army and harassed the Loyalist forces.[74]

---

[69] Ibid., 122–25.   [70] Ibid., 128–30.   [71] Ibid., 191–94.   [72] Ibid., 194–97.
[73] Blanchard, *Under the Flags of Freedom*, 47.
[74] McFarlane, *War and Independence in Spanish America*, 197–98.

After preparing his army for combat, Pezuela attacked Belgrano's position on October 1, 1813, at Vilcapugio, where the Loyalists won a hard-fought victory. Belgrano tried to fall back to Potosí and defend the rich mining city, but Pezuela's forces cornered him and inflicted a major defeat at Ayohuma on November 14, 1813. The army of Buenos Aires left six hundred men dead on the battlefield, and the Loyalist cavalry cut down even more of the retreating *porteño* soldiers as they attempted to flee. Belgrano, and what remained of his army, retreated to Jujuy and then Salta.[75] The second invasion of Upper Peru by the army of Buenos Aires had ended in failure. When José de San Martín, a general with combat experience in the Peninsular War against France, relieved Belgrano in January 1814, he found a tattered, defeated army, with few supplies and resources to pay the soldiers. Despite his victories, Pezuela had to contend with a rebel army of irregular soldiers, mostly gauchos (cowboys) commanded by Martín Guëmes, which forced the Loyalist army to halt any planned invasion of the Río de la Plata. The Loyalist troops also had to deal with pockets of hostile (largely Indigenous) guerrilla forces in Upper Peru.[76]

Despite setbacks in Upper Peru, the *porteño* rebels had cause for celebration when Montevideo fell on June 23, 1814, and a dangerous rebellion of disgruntled Creoles broke out in Cusco, a bastion of the Royalist political and military operations. The discontent in the old Inca capital began with a struggle between the *audiencia* and the city's cabildo, which only worsened with the onset of elections and the publication of the Constitution of 1812. A group of disaffected Creoles believed that they were not receiving the rights conferred by the constitution, and they blamed the largely peninsular-controlled *audiencia* and Viceroy Abascal. The Angulo brothers, José, Vicente, and Mariano, were early leaders of the conspiracy, and they formed a junta with other Creole malcontents to rule the city and its hinterland. When the Angulos began to raise an army, they recruited a prominent Andean leader, Mateo García Pumacahua, who had fought for the Royalists against Tupac Amaru. Pumacahua was angry with Abascal for not choosing him to succeed Goyeneche as leader of the army in Upper Peru. A powerful, wealthy, Indigenous nobleman, he possessed considerable military experience and the connections to recruit Indigenous soldiers for the uprising. Pumacahua commanded the rebel army, which proceeded to capture Puno, La Paz, and Arequipa. Viceroy Abascal sent General Juan Ramírez from the army of Upper Peru to quell the rebellion, and by 1815, he had retaken the major cities, except Cusco. When Ramírez defeated Pumacahua and his army at Umachiri, northwest of Puno, on March 11, 1815, he had the Indigenous commander executed before his troops.[77] Ramírez then entered Cusco and hanged the Angulo brothers and the remaining rebel leaders.

---

[75] Ibid., 198–200.   [76] Ibid., 198–202.
[77] Ibid., 207–10; Ricketts, *Who Should Rule?*, 167–69; Charles F. Walker, *Smoldering Ashes: Cuzco and the Creation of Republican Peru, 1780–1840* (Durham, NC: Duke University Press, 1999), 97–105.

After the defeat of Hidalgo, the rebellion in New Spain had fragmented into a series of regional guerrilla bands. While the Royalists held the major cities, the insurgents dominated throughout the countryside. In the south, the insurgency flourished under the leadership of a mixed-blooded priest, José María Morelos. Despite his lack of military experience, Morelos won the support of leading Creole families, and he used their networks of kin and retainers to build a disciplined army of over three thousand men, which invaded the heartland of the viceroyalty.[78] Morelos threatened to lay siege to Puebla, but instead moved west to capture the town of Cuautla on December 26, 1811. The Loyalist army, under the command of Félix María Calleja, laid siege to the city. As the Loyalist blockade of Cuautla tightened and food supplies dwindled in the city, Morelos attempted to withdraw under the cover of darkness. The Royalists discovered the evacuation, however, and inflicted great losses on the rebel troops, who nonetheless managed to retreat to Izúcar and regroup.[79] After his defeat at Cuautla, Morelos returned to the offensive to the south and captured the regional capital of Oaxaca in December 1812, which became a base for an insurgent government. He then moved east and captured the city of Acapulco after a lengthy siege on August 20, 1813. With these victories, Morelos convoked a national congress at Chilpancingo in September 1813, which declared the independence of Mexico on November 6.[80] Morelos was clearly the head of a dangerous insurgency by 1813.

When Morelos left the government in Chilpancingo, he marched his army to Valladolid to establish an insurgent base in the Mexican heartland. When his army assaulted the city, however, Royalist generals Agustín de Iturbide and Ciriaco de Llano arrived with an army of three thousand Loyalist troops and defeated Morelos and his army.[81] Iturbide and Llano pursued the retreating insurgents, inflicting a second major defeat at Temalaca on November 5, which led to the dispersal of the insurgent forces. After these losses, the congress removed Morelos from the high command of the rebel army. Loyalist forces captured Morelos in November 1815, took him away for trial, defrocked him as a priest, and then executed him on December 22, 1815.[82] The insurgents then reverted to small guerrilla bands in the countryside, which the viceregal government attempted to suppress with a brutal counterinsurgency strategy.

The Return of *el deseado* and the Repression, 1814–15

By the summer of 1813, the combined Spanish and British forces under Wellesley's command drove the French out of Spain, after routing the French army at Vitoria

---

[78] McFarlane, *War and Independence in Spanish America*, 254–55.   [79] Ibid., 257–62.
[80] Ibid., 262–65.   [81] Ibid., 267–69.   [82] Ibid., 269.

on June 21. In December, Napoleon signed the Treaty of Valençay, which established peace between France and Spain, recognized Ferdinand as the rightful king of Spain, and allowed him to leave his exile and assume his throne.[83] According to the Constitution of 1812, however, the king had to take an oath of allegiance to the constitution before the *cortes* would accept his right to rule. When Ferdinand returned to Spain early in 1814, it remained an open question as to whether he would accept constitutional limits on his powers or attempt to re-establish Bourbon absolutism. It was the last possible moment to restore political order and reconstruct a Spanish Atlantic world fractured by a decade of war and civil conflict. When the king saw the Spanish people's enthusiastic response to his return and the support that he received from the army and from Conservatives at court, he decided to order the suppression of the constitution, turning his back on both the Liberals in Spain and the rebels in the Indies. As he announced on May 4, "I declare than my royal will is, not only not to swear or accede to the said Constitution of 1812, nor to any decree of the general and extraordinary Cortes…but to declare that Constitution and those decrees null and of no value nor effect, now and for all time, as if those acts had never been passed."[84] The king then ordered the arrest of thirty-eight deputies, termed the ringleaders of Liberalism, which he saw as a "reprehensible ideology."[85] The repression of the Liberals who had governed Spain in Ferdinand's captivity had begun. Although the king did not realize it, the time had passed to restore lasting peace and order within his domains.

Despite the euphoria surrounding Ferdinand's return to Spain, the monarch faced daunting fiscal problems. The war against the French left much of Spain devastated—as many as a million people (10 percent of the total population) may have died of famine, epidemics, and wartime deaths and atrocities. The legacy of guerrilla war was widespread banditry, and rural areas had repeatedly suffered the depredations of competing armies that had lived off the land.[86] The Crown had financed the disastrous wars of the 1790s by borrowing, and by the time of the French invasion, state coffers were empty. Moreover, foreign creditors were unwilling to advance more funds, particularly since the wars in the Indies meant that no help was forthcoming from colonial treasuries, such as the large sums that had bolstered the Liberal government in Cádiz. The conflicts in America disrupted the critical mining industry, and taxes on trade diminished during periods of wartime, leaving colonial treasuries little to remit to the metropolis.[87] Moreover, the king had little talent or experience in government.

---

[83] Anna, *Spain and the Loss of America*, 118.
[84] Ibid., 125.   [85] Hamnett, *End of Iberian Rule*, 211.
[86] McFarlane, *War and Independence in Spanish America*, 291.
[87] Carlos Marichal, *Bankruptcy of Empire: Mexican Silver and the Wars between Spain, Britain, and France, 1760–1810* (Cambridge: Cambridge University Press, 2007), 255–56, 262–65; John J. TePaske,

He appointed and dismissed ministers frequently—on average they served only six months, leading to vacillating, inconsistent policies. In a two and a half year period, for example, there were seven ministers of finance.[88] Instead, Ferdinand relied on an informal group of very conservative advisors who held no official positions, but they exerted a great deal of influence on him and encouraged his hatred of Liberal constitutionalism. As a result, political conflict, instability, and fiscal bankruptcy plagued Spain in the years following the restoration of absolutism.

Despite initially offering the hope of reconciliation with insurgent and constitutional groups in the Indies, King Ferdinand opted for a military solution. After the French withdrew, Spain had a large army (estimated at 148,643 men) in need of employment, and by 1815, the prospects for a military victory over the American insurgents seemed bright. Mexico was largely pacified after the defeat and execution of Morelos, and Abascal had defeated the rebel regime in Chile, was in possession of Upper Peru, and had quelled the dangerous revolt in Cusco. Only the rebel regime in the Río de la Plata remained, and Crown officials seriously considered sending a large expeditionary force from Spain to crush this last insurgent stronghold. The king ultimately decided to send an expeditionary force of 12,254 men in twenty-nine warships and forty-nine smaller vessels in 1815 to New Granada, since the fall of Montevideo to the rebel regime had deprived the Royalist army of a base to launch an attack on Buenos Aires. This army, under the command of General Pablo de Morillo (a veteran of Spain's Peninsular War), was the largest military force ever sent from Spain to the Indies. Its task was to crush the insurgency in New Granada.[89]

The Breakup of the Spanish Atlantic World, 1815–25

When Morillo arrived in Venezuela in May 1815, the Second Republic had already fallen to Loyalist forces. His main task was to restore public order after the plunder and rapine of the *llaneros* and prepare his army to destroy the rebel regime in New Granada. His forces retook Cartagena and quickly subdued the rebel governments of the interior, entering Bogotá on May 6, 1816.[90] Morillo assumed dictatorial powers, setting up military governments in Venezuela and New Granada, which gained a well-deserved reputation for the arbitrary use of authority, confiscating local resources to support his army, and jailing anyone

---

"The Fiscal Disintegration of the Royal Government in Mexico during the Epoch of Independence," in *The Independence of Mexico and the Creation of the New Nation*, ed. Jaime Rodríguez O. (Los Angeles: University of California Press, 1989), 63–84.

[88] Hamnett, *End of Iberian Rule*, 210–11; McFarlane, *War and Independence in Spanish America*, 288.
[89] McFarlane, *War and Independence in Spanish America*, 290.   [90] Ibid., 301.

accused of "infidelity" to the Royalist cause.[91] The problem of establishing royal control became difficult because insurgent pockets persisted along the frontiers. This disorder was a daunting problem in the llanos, where José Antonio Páez, loyal now to the insurgency, commanded the insurgent *pardos*, who formed the bulk of the soldiers in the *llanero* cavalry. As a result, Morillo took the main body of his forces to Venezuela to quell the insurgency.[92]

When Bolívar returned from exile in Haiti on December 31, 1816, he attempted to unite the various insurgent forces under his command to gain control over the Orinoco basin in the south. From this base, he planned to launch an offensive against Morillo's army in Venezuela. Bolívar installed a system of military justice to transform the clusters of insurgent guerrillas into a more disciplined army capable of fighting an open battle with Morillo's veterans.[93] After his return from Haiti, Bolívar also began to recruit enslaved individuals systematically. Nonetheless, he continued to own enslaved persons, and his commitment to the eventual abolition of slavery remained secondary to his desire for independence. Like Bolívar, Morillo relied on local men to fill his ranks, including freed enslaved, Amerindian, and *pardo* recruits.[94] When the two forces met at Semen (La Puerta) on March 16, 1818, Morillo emerged victorious, halting Bolívar's advance from southern Venezuela.[95] This left the key cities under Royalist control and a military deadlock. Bolívar then returned to Angostura, where he called a national congress to establish a constitutional assembly, which met in early 1819 and elected him president.[96] Bolívar used his new political authority to undertake a bold new strategy, attacking the Loyalist forces in New Granada, where he could gain new resources to liberate Venezuela (see Fig. 5.3).[97]

Bolívar decided to gamble on starting his offensive from the llanos in the winter season, when the Loyalists would least expect it. Moving men and war materiel across the flooding grasslands and then to the highland basins of New Granada was difficult, but his army made the trip in about five weeks, without suffering irreparable losses. After reaching the highlands, Bolívar replenished his army with new local recruits and supplies for an advance in early July on the Loyalist army commanded by Colonel José María Barreiro.[98] Bolívar intercepted the Royalist army at Boyacá on the road to the viceregal capital of Bogotá on August 7, 1819. In a bitter struggle, the insurgent troops and cavalry broke through and encircled the Loyalist's left and center, inflicting heavy losses.

---

[91] Ibid., 302.   [92] Ibid., 313.   [93] Ibid., 319–20.
[94] Blanchard, *Under the Flags of Freedom*, 65, 70.
[95] McFarlane, *War and Independence in Spanish America*, 321.
[96] The Congress at Angostura ended the trade of enslaved people to Venezuela, but the delegates failed to support abolition, except in those cases where enslaved persons had provided military service. Blanchard, *Under the Flags of Freedom*, 73.
[97] McFarlane, *War and Independence in Spanish America*, 325.   [98] Ibid., 327.

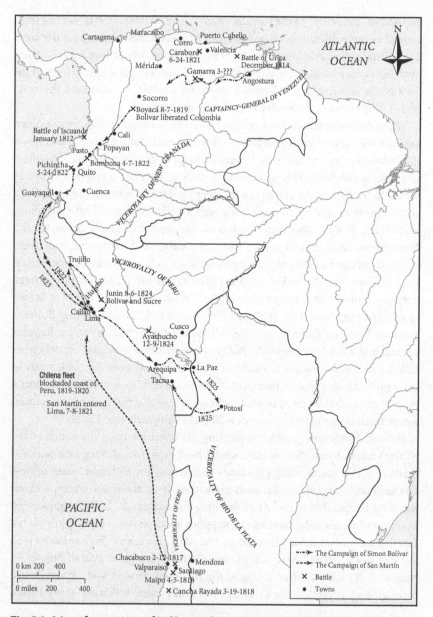

Fig. 5.3 Map of campaigns of Bolívar and San Martín in South America.
Source: Based on maps from Cathryn L. Lombardi and John V. Lombardi, with K. Lynn Stoner, *Latin America: A Teaching Atlas* (Madison: Conference on Latin American History and the University of Wisconsin Press, 1983), 48; and John Fletcher, *The Wars of Spanish American Independence, 1809–29* (Oxford: Osprey, 2013), 40, 54.

Barreiro decided to end the potential slaughter, surrendering his army of sixteen hundred soldiers.[99] Although the Loyalist commander probably expected clemency after the defeat, Bolívar ordered his execution, along with that of thirty-eight Spanish officers. The "Liberator" then entered Bogotá and proclaimed the Republic of Colombia.

While Bolívar's victory at Boyacá provided a strategic advantage in the north, an attempt to invade Upper Peru by the forces of Buenos Aires, led by José Rondeau, failed after Pezuela's Loyalist army defeated him decisively at Wiluma (also called Viluma or Sipe Sipe) on November 29, 1815.[100] Viceroy Abascal strongly urged Pezuela to follow his victory with an invasion of the Río de la Plata, but the army of Peru stalled fighting a counterinsurgency against largely Indigenous guerrilla groups in Upper Peru and the gauchos of Martín Güemes operating in Salta. Frustrated with Pezuela's inability to invade the Río de la Plata, Abascal replaced him with José de la Serna, a battle-hardened veteran of the Peninsular War, but his forces also bogged down fighting the insurgent guerrillas and the gauchos under Güemes.

Buenos Aires could not launch a new invasion of Upper Peru because of warfare in the Banda Oriental (now Uruguay), where the irregular forces of José Artigas (composed largely of gauchos and former enslaved individuals) threatened the capital city. Artigas, a prominent landowner in the Banda Oriental, had originally fought with Buenos Aires against the Spanish, but later he and his army wanted to be free of domination from both Spain and Buenos Aires. Artigas envisaged a federal government (modeled on the United States) where the individual states would have the right to elect representatives to their own state assembly, with a governor to serve as executive and an elected judiciary.[101] When the Portuguese sent an army of ten thousand men in June 1816 to control the region, Artigas turned against the foreign invaders and forces from Buenos Aires. In the end, the army of Artigas was not able to resist the Portuguese regular army, and he took refuge in Paraguay in 1820.[102]

While La Serna's army exerted control over Upper Peru, José de San Martín proposed a new strategy for Buenos Aires: an attack over the Andes into Chile, followed by an invasion by sea to the viceregal capital of Lima. While politicians in Buenos Aires squabbled over the conduct of the war in Upper Peru and the Banda Oriental, San Martín began building an army in the mountainous central western region of Cuyo, with its capital at Mendoza. He started recruiting men, including large numbers of enslaved Africans (freed to serve in the military), who formed over half of his invasion force of five thousand men.[103] To supply the force, San Martín requisitioned cattle, food, and local supplies.[104]

[99] Ibid., 327–28. [100] Ibid., 345. [101] Ibid., 338–39. [102] Ibid., 342.
[103] Blanchard, *Under the Flags of Freedom*, 62.
[104] McFarlane, *War and Independence in Spanish America*, 351.

After elaborate preparations—approximately twenty-two thousand horses, draught animals, mules, and oxen accompanied the army—San Martín's troops crossed the Andes into central Chile, arriving well supplied and ready to attack the Loyalist army.[105] San Martín benefited from the participation of influential Chilean allies, particularly Bernardo O'Higgins, who provided military service and intelligence about the best invasion route in Chile and served as the basis for a Chilean insurgent government once inside the country. After crossing the Andes successfully, San Martín's army and the Loyalists met at Chacabuco on February 12, 1817, and the rebels won a decisive victory. O'Higgins established a government (to replace the Loyalist governor who had fled Santiago), which declared the independence of Chile. Viceroy Pezuela sent an army from Lima under the command of Manuel Osorio that combined with the remaining Loyalist forces in Chile to defeat San Martín and O'Higgins at Cancha Rayada on February 19, 1818.[106] As Osorio moved toward the capital at Santiago, San Martín concentrated his forces on the plain at Maipú, south of the capital. Here, San Martín won a decisive victory on April 5, and despite pockets of Royalist resistance, Chile had secured its independence. San Martín was free to develop an invasion plan for Lima, Peru.[107]

Despite some Loyalist successes, the insurgent forces began to win the war in South America, while conflict in New Spain settled into a stalemate. The insurgents controlled much of the countryside while the Loyalists held the major cities. In Spain, King Ferdinand and his ministers vacillated in both their domestic policies and their support for the war effort in America. At the root of the government's inept and ineffective policies was the failure to solve the fiscal and economic problems that had plagued Spain since before the French invasion. The metropolitan state was bankrupt, and discontent spread to the military because officers resented the financial cutbacks and career insecurity that accompanied the shrinking of the army after the French withdrawal. Conscripts went unpaid and supplies needed for war were in short supply. Few officers or men wanted to go fight in America against insurgent forces that were more like cousins, not natural enemies. Officers and men in the Loyalist army in America faced similar challenges, as defeat and poor support from the Crown made it difficult to win the war. In addition, many junior officers in the Spanish army had Liberal sympathies and blamed the Crown for its failure to provide the financial support for the military. This volatile state of affairs led soldiers, who were suffering an outbreak of yellow fever, to rally behind the Liberal colonel

---

[105] Ibid., 353.
[106] Abascal was skeptical of Ferdinand's policy of restoring the Inquisition in the Spanish Atlantic world, and the king removed him from office in 1816, making Pezuela the viceroy of Peru. Hamnett, *End of Iberian Rule*, 213.
[107] McFarlane, *War and Independence in Spanish America*, 353–57.

Rafael Riego, who launched a coup on January 1, 1820, forcing Ferdinand to accept the Constitution of 1812. Over the next two months, the revolt spread to other regiments and towns throughout Spain as military and civil protests increased to end absolutism. Ultimately, these Liberal protests forced the reluctant king to accept constitutional limitations.

Despite the second triumph of Liberal constitutionalism, moderate and radical Liberals disagreed over the future direction of the country, with Ferdinand and the *serviles* attempting to disrupt the squabbling Liberals at every turn. Moreover, peasant guerrilla bands rampaged in much of the countryside, particularly in Navarre and Catalonia.[108] The new Liberal governments that came to office in 1820 could not solve Spain's economic and financial problems, and they were still unwilling to make serious concessions to the American insurgents. As a result, the war in America continued to go badly for the Loyalists. In the end, fearful of the spread of Liberal revolution, Bourbon France mounted an invasion of Iberia to re-establish absolutism in Spain in 1823, which crushed the hopes of Liberal constitutionalists. Spain lapsed into political disorder, which further complicated efforts to defeat the insurgency in America.

This political chaos in Spain promoted political and military disorder in New Spain. The Liberal regime in Spain refused to sanction free trade or give equal electoral representation to the Americans. Their reforms also alienated the corporate privileges of the Church and the army in New Spain. The bitter insurgency had increased the army's role, which grew to ten thousand soldiers as reinforcements from Spain arrived over the period 1811–16.[109] The head of the Loyalist army in southern New Spain, Agustín de Iturbide, had been prominent in the rural counterinsurgency campaigns, so he knew and had negotiated with insurgent leaders, particularly Vicente Guerrero. Guerrero was a former gunsmith from Tixtla (a town inland from Acapulco) who gained fame as an insurgent leader under Morelos and later commanded his own guerrilla force. On February 24, 1821, Iturbide proclaimed the Plan of Iguala (with Guerrero's support), which called for New Spain to become an independent monarchy, ruled by a member of the Spanish royal family. Until the framing of its own constitution, the Spanish Constitution of 1812 would obtain in New Spain. Iturbide attempted to build a coalition around three guarantees—the Church, independence, and union—a vague platform that he used to attract widespread support. Viceroy Juan Ruíz de Apodaca faced an increasingly bankrupt treasury, since total revenues had dropped from 28 million pesos in 1809 to under 9 million in 1817, so he lacked the fiscal and military resources to oppose Iturbide.[110] To add to the political disorder in New Spain, two leading army

---

[108] Hamnett, *End of Iberian Rule*, 251.
[109] McFarlane, *War and Independence in Spanish America*, 371.   [110] Ibid., 297.

officers, Pascual Liñan and Francisco Novella, staged a coup that overthrew Apodaca. Novella took the title of viceroy, but he too failed to muster sufficient troops to oppose Iturbide.[111] By June and July, most Loyalist army garrisons had joined Iturbide, and when the incoming captain general, Juan O'Donojú, arrived in Mexico City, he recognized New Spain's independence. On September 28, 1821, Iturbide entered Mexico City and took over the government, effectively ending Spanish rule in New Spain.

The return to the Spanish Constitution of 1812 had caused political unrest in New Spain, and news of the Riego Revolt and its aftermath arrived in Lima just after the departure of San Martín's army by sea to assault the capital. The insurgent naval force, commanded by the British mercenary Lord Cochrane, had gained control of the seas, and the Army for the Liberation of Peru departed Valparaíso on August 19, 1820, in the largest amphibious assault of the insurgents in Spanish America. Consisting of forty-three hundred men, eight hundred horses, and thirty-five artillery pieces, the army landed at Pisco, south of Lima.[112] Viceroy Pezuela commanded a Loyalist force of twenty-three thousand men to oppose San Martín, who divided his army, sending General Alvarez de Arenales to the Peruvian highlands with one thousand men to isolate the capital from the highlands. Meanwhile, San Martín moved his army slowly and cautiously to encircle Lima. Pezuela believed the insurgent army was too small to capture Lima, and he expected that it would suffer attrition through disease and desertion in the arid coastal desert region. The professional military men remained strong Royalists, and they wanted to confront San Martín's invading army. The Loyalist high command, particularly General José de la Serna, criticized the viceroy's apparent timidity, and on January 29, 1821, they staged a coup and placed Pezuela under house arrest. La Serna then took over as viceroy and as commander of the Loyalist army opposing San Martín.[113]

Once La Serna had consolidated power in Lima and gained the loyalty of the Royalist army, he decided on a strategy of abandoning the capital city and defending Peru from the highlands. La Serna sent half of the Loyalist army to the interior under General José de Canterac in June, and on July 6, 1821, he abandoned Lima to San Martín. Six days later, the insurgent general took possession of the capital city, and on July 28, San Martín declared the independence of Peru. He then assumed the title of "Protector of the State of Peru" and established a military government in the city, which declared all enslaved individuals owned by Spaniards and those willing to serve in the military free.[114]

---

[111] Ibid., 372.   [112] Ibid., 359–61.
[113] The role of Lima's merchants in the downfall of Pezuela is discussed in Marks, *Deconstructing Legitimacy*, 304–305, 311, 318.
[114] McFarlane, *War and Independence in Spanish America*, 378; Blanchard, *Under the Flags of Freedom*, 100.

Once in Lima, San Martín faced daunting challenges. The capital city lacked the resources on the desert coast to sustain its population and the insurgent army, so the government confiscated supplies and imposed heavy fiscal burdens on the city elite, which did little to win them over to the independence cause. Over half of the government's income came from voluntary and forced contributions to the treasury, and the government recognized a national debt of 6,500,000 pesos.[115] San Martín's government could not gain access to specie from the highland mines (now controlled by the Loyalists) and the contraction of commerce by sea led to a decline in port taxes, which left San Martín's government on the verge of bankruptcy. Under these circumstances, it was difficult to finance an attack on the Loyalist positions in the highlands, and he recalled Arenales and his troops to Lima.[116] When a Loyalist army, commanded by Canterac, moved to the coast in September 1821, San Martín abandoned the city temporarily until the enemy withdrew, without attempting to engage the Loyalists in a pitched battle. Meanwhile, La Serna established his capital in Cusco, where he commanded the wealth and resources of the highlands, which he used to sustain and enlarge his army. San Martín remained trapped in Lima, with little hope of launching an assault on the Loyalist strongholds in Cusco, Jauja, Arequipa, and Pisco. The weakness of San Martín's position was exposed when he dispatched Domingo Tristán to recruit soldiers in Ica, and Canterac and his Loyalist troops in Jauja marched to the coast and defeated Tristán's army at Mamacona on April 7.[117]

While San Martín languished in Lima, Simón Bolívar gained control over New Granada, but Loyalist forces in the south (Pasto and Popayán) and Cartagena remained entrenched. The reinstatement of the Spanish constitution in 1820 had divided the Loyalists; some in the Royalist camp were reluctant to support the war with money and recruits and instead favored reconciliation with the insurgents. After Morillo arranged a six-month truce with Bolívar, he handed over command of his army to Miguel de la Torre and returned to Spain.[118] When the truce expired, the insurgents took Popayán and besieged Cartagena, forcing the Royalists in New Granada to go on the defensive. This allowed Bolívar to turn his attention to the main Royalist army in Venezuela.

Bolívar's army controlled much of the south of Venezuela, while the Loyalist troops deployed in defensive positions, blocking the roads into Caracas. Bolívar hoped to go on the offensive, but he had to rebuild his army, depleted by combat losses, desertions, and disease. He solved this problem by conscripting

---

[115] The government also refused to assume responsibility for 11,700,000 pesos in debt. Timothy E. Anna, "Economic Causes of San Martín's Failure in Lima," *Hispanic American Historical Review* 54, no. 4 (November 1974): 678.

[116] McFarlane, *War and Independence in Spanish America*, 379.

[117] Ibid., 381.   [118] Ibid., 388–89.

troops in New Granada and recruiting large numbers of enslaved individuals from Venezuela. Bolívar had come to favor an end to enslavement, since he also knew that offering enslaved persons freedom to fight for independence provided loyal, dedicated soldiers.[119] Once he had built up the strength of his army to about ten thousand men, Bolívar went on the offensive, while the Loyalists defended Caracas. La Torre fell back to Carabobo, which put his army in a strong defensive position to fight against Bolívar's forces advancing from the llanos and the coastal cordillera. The decisive battle at Carabobo took place on June 24, 1821, when Bolívar sent his *llanero* cavalry under José Antonio Páez to attack La Torre's right flank. The *llaneros* dislodged the Royalist cavalry from their defensive position and attacked their infantry. After great carnage, the Loyalist troops who survived withdrew to the fortified town of Puerto Cabello.[120] Most of Venezuela now belonged to Bolívar and the insurgents.

After defeating the Royalists in Venezuela, Bolívar decided to take his army overland to Quito, but in Pasto, the Loyalists held back his forces after a bloody engagement at Bomboná in April 1822, temporarily halting his advance.[121] Nonetheless, the insurgent general, Antonio José de Sucre, was able to advance from Guayaquil into the highlands, aided by fifteen hundred men from San Martín's army. Sucre met the Loyalist troops commanded by the president of the Kingdom of Quito, Melchor Aymerich, and defeated them decisively at the Battle of Pichincha on May 24, 1821; Sucre then accepted the surrender of the city of Quito. Bolívar later incorporated the region into the Republic of Gran Colombia (including modern-day Ecuador, Colombia, and Venezuela). Control of Quito placed Bolívar's army on the old Inca road, the gateway to the highlands of Peru.

The collaboration of San Martín and Bolívar, which bore fruit with Sucre's victory at Pichincha, promised to end the stalemate in Peru if the two generals could agree on a military and political plan of action in the south. San Martín wanted a constitutional monarchy for Peru and military assistance to attack the Loyalists in the highlands, but when the two men met at Guayaquil in July 1822, they could not reach an accord. Bolívar rejected the idea of a monarchy for Peru, and his promise of military aid fell far short of what San Martín needed. Moreover, San Martín was unable to attack the Royalists from his base in Lima, while Bolívar controlled the principal road with access to the Peruvian highlands from his base in Quito. Under those circumstances, San Martín decided to place his army under Bolívar's command, resign his commission, and go into exile in Europe. Bolívar had the prestige of victory in the north, and his strategy was to take the fight to the Peruvian highlands and defeat the armies of La Serna.[122]

---

[119] Ibid., 390.   [120] Ibid., 392.
[121] Echeverri, *Indian and Slave Royalists*, 251.
[122] McFarlane, *War and Independence in Spanish America*, 393–95.

Despite two unsuccessful campaigns and Canterac's second occupation of Lima for one month in June 1823, Bolívar was able to take possession of the capital city and assume dictatorial powers in 1824. Nonetheless, the Royalist army was a formidable fighting force. Canterac had eight thousand men in Huancayo, Gerónimo Valdés had three thousand in Arequipa, Pedro Antonio de Olañeta commanded four thousand soldiers in Upper Peru, and Viceroy La Serna had a reserve force of one thousand in Cusco.[123] In April 1823, however, a French army invaded Spain, the Liberal regime collapsed, and Ferdinand VII once again imposed an absolutist regime that persecuted the Liberal opposition. With Spain again in disarray, divisions appeared in the Loyalist army. Olañeta proclaimed an independent government in Upper Peru in the name of Ferdinand VII, disrupting any cohesive military plans by Viceroy La Serna. Before La Serna could discipline Olañeta, Bolívar and his army advanced to the highlands in search of Canterac's army. The two armies met on the plains of Junín on August 6, 1824, in a battle fought with lances and swords, with no shots fired.[124] The *llanero* cavalry Bolívar had brought from Colombia won the day, forcing Canterac to retreat to Cusco. Bolívar returned to Lima to attend to political matters, leaving Antonio José de Sucre in command of an army of six thousand.[125]

Sucre took his army to the plains of Ayacucho, near the city of Huamanga, while La Serna and the Loyalist army of nine thousand men took up positions on the hills overlooking the rebel force. The battle began on December 9, 1824, when the viceroy sent Gerónimo Valdés to engage Sucre's left with artillery and musket fire. Meanwhile, La Serna himself led an attack along Sucre's front. The Royalist infantry attack failed as the troops broke ranks and ran, while Sucre's cavalry decisively defeated the Royalist horsemen. In the ensuing carnage, Sucre's forces took La Serna prisoner, winning a decisive victory. The victory at Ayacucho effectively secured the independence of Peru. The Loyalist army of General Pío Tristan in Arequipa soon surrendered. Sucre then moved his army from Cusco to Upper Peru, where Olañeta's forces began to disintegrate before the rebel advance. Olañeta himself was mortally wounded trying to escape on April 1, 1825, at Tumsula, near the border with the Río de la Plata, and the independence of Bolivia was won. As in New Spain, Spanish rule in South America was effectively over.[126] At this point, the fragmentation of the Spanish Atlantic world was complete and permanent.

Loyalism and Agustín Agualongo

Despite the ultimate victory of the independence forces, loyalty to the Crown remained a potent force during the years between the French invasion and the

[123] Ibid., 400. [124] Ibid., 402. [125] Ibid. [126] Ibid., 403–4.

Battle of Ayacucho, particularly in Pasto and Popayán in southern New Granada. Pasto was a strategic food-producing region, supplying the gold mines of the Pacific littoral and located on a commercial crossroads between the highlands surrounding the viceregal capital of Bogotá and the Audiencia of Quito to the south. After the French invasion of Iberia in 1807, a regional junta arose in Quito to govern in the name of the deposed Bourbon monarch, Ferdinand VII. When word of this insurgent government reached Popayán, Governor Miguel Tacón enlarged Royalist forces in the region by recruiting the local Indigenous population with promises of lower tribute rates. He even recruited large numbers of enslaved individuals by offering freedom to any who fought against the insurgent forces sent from Quito. Tacón's policies upset local miners and landowners, who feared the loss of Indigenous and African laborers. His efforts to recruit Amerindians also angered local Indigenous clan leaders who were resentful of their declining power over ethnic groups once they left their traditional villages to fight in the Royalist army. Tacón's policy of arming Amerindians and enslaved people made southern Colombia a strong Loyalist outpost, which resisted efforts by insurgent armies to pacify the region.[127] From the Reconquista onward, the image of the king served as a powerful symbol of unity in the Spanish monarchy, which Governor Tacón could use, along with strategic concessions to Indigenous and enslaved peoples, to secure their unwavering loyalty to the Royalist cause.

One of those who joined the Loyalist cause was a young mestizo, Agustín Agualongo, a painter by trade, who distinguished himself in a number of early battles against insurgent forces.[128] Agualongo joined the Royalist army in 1811 as a volunteer in the militia organized by Governor Tacón in Popayán to stop any planned invasions from Creole-led juntas in Quito, Cali, and Santa Fé. He participated in Royalist victories over invaders from Quito and Cali in 1811, earning him a reputation as a savvy and brave soldier. Agualongo quickly moved up the ranks, particularly after he fought against an insurgent army commanded by Antonio Nariño, an educated member of the "enlightened" elite from the government of Cudinamarca. Later, Agualongo fought in victorious battles in the Audiencia of Quito. Young Agualongo not only proved his valor and military skills, but also gained confidence in the ultimate victory of loyalism over the insurgent cause, particularly after Ferdinand VII's decision to crush the rebels in America.

---

[127] The efforts of Miguel Tacón to build a Loyalist army relying on Indigenous and enslaved recruits are developed in the work of Marcela Echeverri. Please see Echeverri, *Indian and Slave Royalists*, 53–54, 123–32, 157–69, 177–78; and Marcela Echeverri, "Agustín Agualongo and the Royalist Cause in the Wars of Independence," in *The Human Tradition in Colonial Latin America*, 2nd ed., ed. Kenneth J. Andrien (New York: Rowman & Littlefield, 2013), 289–304.

[128] The role of Agustín Agualongo as a Loyalist leader is developed in Echeverri, *Indian and Slave Royalists*, 194–203; and in Echeverri, "Agustín Agualongo and the Royalist Cause," 289–304.

When the forces favoring independence won the key victory at Carabobo in 1821, Bolívar turned his attention to reducing the Loyalist army in Pasto, on the road to Quito. Despite long odds, a majority of the local population continued to support the Loyalist cause. The Liberator's response to antirepublican revolts in 1822 and 1823 was to burn and sack Pasto. Bolívar deemed the *pastusos* rude, backward, and uneducated Indians and enslaved people because of their unyielding support for the Loyalist cause. For Agualongo and his Loyalist force, Bolívar was a brutal tyrant, and they denounced the efforts of the Liberal government of Colombia to privatize Indigenous lands and allow slavery. Agualongo attempted to continue the fight and expand his control over the Pacific littoral while maintaining ties with Loyalists in Peru. In the end, Bolívar's troops caught Agualongo and took him to Popayán, where they tried and shot him on July 13, 1824. Agualongo had commanded the loyalty of his troops against Bolívar, an outsider who had little knowledge about the needs and desires of the *pastusos*.

Throughout Agualongo's long struggle in southern Colombia, he remained dedicated to the king and the monarchist cause. He was aided in this by the belief of common people—Amerindians, enslaved individuals, free Black people, and mestizos—that loyalism offered the hope of greater autonomy and a better life than the elite-controlled republican governments headed by leaders such as Simón Bolívar. Given the tenacity of Agualongo and his popular army, they managed to hold the insurgent forces at bay for several years. Agualongo and his followers truly believed that loyalism would produce a more egalitarian nation than the independent republic of Gran Colombia. Given what transpired after Agualongo's defeat and death and the brutal pacification of the *pastusos*, it is no small wonder that loyalty to the Crown, which had mobilized the subaltern groups in the region, persisted for so long.

Conclusion

The wars of independence shattered the unity of the Spanish Atlantic world that had formed in the decades following the voyages of Christopher Columbus. The international conflicts of the eighteenth century continued with even greater intensity in the early nineteenth century. The French Revolution and the later rise of Napoleon Bonaparte in France led to conflict throughout Europe that inevitably spilled into the Atlantic world. Two wars with Great Britain led to the virtual destruction of the Spanish navy, so carefully funded and assembled under Charles III, and they seriously curtailed the commercial linkages with the Indies. In fact, to keep trade to the Indies open at all, Spanish authorities took the unprecedented step of allowing trade with neutral vessels in the Spanish commercial system. The greatest blow, however, came with the French invasion of Iberia in 1807 and the abdications of the Bourbon monarchs. This prompted a popular upheaval in Spain and a constitutional crisis over where sovereignty lay in the absence of the monarchs. Both led to a serious disruption of political affairs on both sides of the Atlantic. It also hastened the fiscal collapse of the royal treasuries in Spain and the Indies, already in a precarious state because of the wars of the 1790s.

The war and disorder in Spain and the Indies led to an escalating cycle of violence that produced independence movements throughout the Americas. At first, most Creole-led juntas in the New World wanted to rule until the return of Ferdinand, since the institutions, political practices, and cultural tradition of monarchy were deeply embedded in the Spanish Atlantic world. The civil wars between loyalists and insurgents gradually expanded and became more violent. These conflicts moved from elite-led efforts to forge juntas to govern at least until the return of the monarchy to mass-based efforts of all social groups to attain independence. This mass mobilization occurred first in New Spain with the Hidalgo revolt, but later spread throughout the Indies. These bitter struggles mobilized the masses of people in the Indies to fight on both the Loyalist and the insurgent sides over time.

The Constitution of 1812 offered a vision of a new Hispanic political and institutional order, which involved both Americans and Spaniards jointly participating in ruling the Spanish Atlantic world. Nonetheless, the unwillingness of the Liberal constitutionalists to consider commercial and greater political concessions to Spanish Americans led many in the Indies to continue the struggle first for home rule and later for complete independence. The Liberals fundamentally considered the Spanish Indies colonies, not kingdoms ruled by the Spanish monarch, with their own rights and privileges. The return of King Ferdinand VII offered another possible moment of reconciliation among factions in Spain and the Indies, but the monarch wanted to restore absolutism and conquer, not compromise with, his opponents. Swayed by his enthusiastic reception in Spain in 1814 and the relatively strong position of Loyalist regimes in the Indies, the king overestimated his power to restore Bourbon absolutism in the Spanish Atlantic world. The king lacked the vision and intelligence to see that re-establishing absolute monarchy was neither desirable nor possible. The conflict between *serviles*, who favored the absolutism of Ferdinand VII, and Liberal constitutionalists also led to political instability, vacillating fiscal policies, and social disorder within Spain, which ultimately made defeating the insurgencies in the Americas virtually impossible. The events between 1808 and 1814 profoundly altered the political and military landscape in Spain and the Indies, and violence and political disorder only escalated from 1814 to 1825, which ultimately tore the Spanish Atlantic world apart.

The civil wars among Loyalist and insurgent elites weakened social hierarchies and opened racial, ethnic, and class tensions as plebeians, peasants, castes, Amerindians, and enslaved individuals mobilized to participate in the violent struggles for power. From New Spain to the Río de la Plata, Loyalists and insurgents recruited subaltern groups in the independence struggles in the Indies. Loyalist leaders such as Miguel Tacón and Domingo de Monteverde quickly realized the military potential of arming Indigenous peasants with offers of lower tribute and enslaved persons with promises of freedom. They could also call on long-held faith and loyalty to the monarchy. Military leaders such as Simón Bolívar, himself an owner of enslaved individuals, did not favor abolishing enslavement or arming Indigenous groups, but over time, Bolívar and other rebel leaders recognized that the only way to replenish their armies with new recruits involved arming popular groups and enslaved persons. All armies recruited locally, and many Loyalist and insurgent leaders decried the need to rely on peasants and enslaved individuals, whom they saw as social inferiors. Peasant guerrilla forces in Spain during the Peninsular War and Indigenous and caste guerrilla groups in Mexico, Upper Peru, and the llanos of New Granada all played a major role in the violent struggles within the Spanish Atlantic world. One army or the other conscripted these subaltern groups or the popular groups entered the military conflicts for their own local reasons, such as to acquire plunder, settle old scores, or preserve their communities. These popular sectors did not so easily return to their subservient social position after the fighting stopped. Banditry, violence, and crime continued after the formal hostilities ended. Independence did not make cohesive nation states in the former Spanish Indies. That process would take a great deal more time.

Timeline: The Collapse of the Spanish Atlantic World, 1796–1825

Spain

1797–99   During the war with Great Britain, Spain allows neutral vessels to convey American bullion and produce to Spain

1805–8   During renewed hostilities with Britain (1804–8), Spain again allows neutral vessels to trade directly with the Indies

1806   Napoleon of France signs the Treaty of Fontainebleau with Spain, which permits French troops to cross Spain to invade Portugal; the treaty promises to divide Portugal into three parts, with the royal favorite, Manuel Godoy, granted control over the southern portion, the French ruling the central territories, and the northern portion going to the former queen of Etruria, María Luisa

1807	The French invade Iberia and depose King Charles IV and his son Ferdinand, making Napoleon's older brother, Joseph, king of Spain
1808	British expedition commanded by Arthur Wellesley, loyal members of the Spanish and Portuguese armies, and guerrillas wage war on the French, ratified by a treaty of alliance between Spain and Britain on January 9, 1809
1808	Provincial juntas in Spain form to resist the French until the return of Prince Ferdinand as the legitimate monarch
1809	The Junta Central, which directed Spanish resistance against the French, calls elections, even in the Indies, to take part in the junta proceedings
1810	After a series of military defeats by the French, on January 29 the Junta Central dissolves itself and creates a Council of the Regency, which calls for elections to a constituent *cortes* to create a new constitution for Spain
1810	On September 1, the *cortes* convenes to write a new constitution
1812	On March 19, the *cortes* in Cádiz proclaims a new Liberal constitution that provides for universal manhood suffrage, including extending the vote to the Indies, including the Indigenous peoples
1813	Allied army under the command of Arthur Wellesley pushes the French army out of Iberia after defeating them decisively at Vitoria on June 21
1814	Ferdinand is released by Napoleon in late 1813; he returns to Spain and denounces the Constitution of 1812 on May 4
1820	On January 1, Colonel Rafael Riego launches a coup to force Ferdinand VI to accept the Constitution of 1812
1823	A French invasion of Iberia topples the Liberal government and reinstates royal absolutism in Spain

New Granada

1809	On August 10, Creoles in Quito proclaim a junta to rule until the return of Ferdinand VII and depose the Crown government—similar juntas arose in La Paz and Chuquisaca
1810	On April 19, leading citizens in Caracas establish the Supreme Junta and Defender of the Rights of Ferdinand VII
1810	Creole-led juntas proclaimed in Cartagena, Cali, Pamplona, Socorro, and Bogotá
1811	Francisco de Miranda and his supporters push a constituent congress to declare the independence of Venezuela and the establishment of a republic, which collapses on June 30, 1812
1813	Simón Bolívar begins his "admirable campaign," captures Caracas in August, and on June 15 declares a "war to the death"
1813	On August 7, Bolívar captures Caracas, which he is forced to abandon in July 1814

1815 On March 11, Royalist army defeats the rebel troops of the Cusco Rebellion, commanded by Mateo García Pumacahua at Umachiri

1815 In April, a Spanish army of 10,500 men arrives in Cartagena from Spain under the command of General Pablo Morillo, which captured Bogotá on May 6, 1816

1816 On December 31, Bolívar returns to Venezuela from his exile in Haiti and takes command of the rebel forces in the region, executing his rival, Manuel Piar

1818 On March 16, Morillo defeats Bolívar's army at Semen/La Puerta

1819 Rebel Congress of Angostura meets in February and elects Bolívar president of Gran Colombia

1819 On August 7, Bolívar defeats the Royalist army of José María Barreiro at the Battle of Boyacá

1821 On June 24, Bolívar defeats the Royalist army at Carabobo, securing the independence of Venezuela

1822 On May 24, Antonio José de Sucre defeats the Royalist army under Melchor Aymerich at the Battle of Pichincha near Quito

1822 Bolívar and San Martín meet at Guayaquil in July and fail to agree on a joint plan to end the independence conflicts

Río de la Plata/Peru/Chile

1806–7 Two British invasion forces unsuccessfully attempt to take control of Buenos Aires

1810 On May 25, Creole-led junta takes power in Buenos Aires in the name of Ferdinand VII

1810 On November 7, rebel army of Buenos Aires defeats Royalist forces at Suipacha and a week later at Aroma, but Royalist forces recapture Upper Peru by the end of the year

1813 On October 1, the Royalists defeat the rebel army commanded by Manuel Belgrano at Vicapugio; the Royalists win another viceroy on November 14 at Ayohuma

1814 On June 23, Montevideo falls to rebel troops commanded by Juan José Rondeau and José Artigas

1815 On November 29, the Royalist army defeats rebels from Buenos Aires at Wiluma (Viluma or Sipe Sipe), pushing them from Upper Peru

1817 On February 12, after crossing the Andes into Chile, José de San Martín defeats Royalists at Chacabuco

1818 On April 5, San Martín wins a decisive victory over the Royalists at Maipú, securing the independence of Chile

1821   On July 6, San Martín captures Lima and on July 28 declares the independence of Peru

1824   Bolívar defeats Viceroy José La Serna and his Royalist army at Junín

1824   On December 9, Sucre defeats La Serna and the Royalists at Ayacucho, effectively securing the independence of Peru

New Spain

1810   On September 16, Miguel de Hidalgo proclaims rebellion in Dolores

1810   On November 11, Hidalgo's rebel army captures Guanajuato, sacking the city and killing the Royalist defenders

1811   On January 17, Hidalgo's army is defeated by Royalist forces at Bridge of Calderón, outside Guadalajara, and Hidalgo is captured and executed at Aguascalientes

1813   On August 20, rebel forces of José María Morelos capture Acapulco

1813   On November 6, the rebel Congress of Chilpancingo declares the independence of Mexico

1815   On November 5, Morelos is defeated at Temalaca and captured; he is executed on December 22

1821   On February 24, the former Royalist general, Agustín de Iturbide, proclaims the Plan of Iguala, calling for the independence of Mexico

1821   On September 28, Iturbide enters Mexico City and takes over the government

1822   On July 21, Iturbide is crowned Agustín I, emperor of Mexico

Conclusion

From Kingdoms to Colonies to Independence, 1492–1825

The voyages of Christopher Columbus led to changes in the political and institutional culture, along with social, religious, and economic forces that shaped the Spanish Atlantic world over its three hundred-year history. From a few scattered Caribbean outposts, Spanish conquistadors invaded mainland North America and gradually expanded southward to the Inca Empire, allowing the first Spanish settlers to gain control over vast human and economic resources. Over time, the Spanish Atlantic world formed around a Crown-appointed imperial bureaucracy, the Roman Catholic Church, ongoing commercial exchanges, and the movement and mixture of peoples from all four continents surrounding the Atlantic Ocean. By the seventeenth century, Creole elites and peninsular-born Spaniards gained great power over the bureaucracy in the Indies by establishing ties of clientage, family connections, and political corruption and influence peddling that weakened royal authority. This process of local empowerment only accelerated after the Crown began selling important government appointments in 1633. The Indies operated as separate kingdoms united by a common monarch, especially as the Crown became preoccupied with a series of expensive and ruinous foreign wars in Europe. When the Bourbon dynasty came to power by 1713, the Crown slowly implemented a series of political, fiscal, economic, and social reforms that attempted to establish a strong, centralized state apparatus in Spain and the Indies, which reversed this trend toward greater autonomy. The reforms also undermined the power of the Roman Catholic Church, the Crown's traditional partner in governing the Indies. By the end of the eighteenth century, the Madrid government viewed the Indies not as important kingdoms of the monarchy but as dependent colonies, subordinated to the metropole, Spain. When the enormous fiscal pressures of war and the French invasion of Iberia led to the downfall of the Bourbon monarchy, political ties holding the vast Spanish Atlantic world unraveled, leading to its slow-motion collapse between 1808 and 1825.

The first union of the Christian kingdoms of Castile and Aragon led to the formation of a dynastic or composite monarchy after the marriage of Ferdinand and Isabel when the couple acceded to their thrones in 1479. With the joint resources of both kingdoms, the Catholic kings secured the military conquest of the last Muslim kingdom at Granada in 1492, the year that Columbus sailed on his historic first voyage. This monarchy had the flexibility to annex new lands in the Indies, and by the mid-sixteenth century, the Spanish Crown boasted extensive domains in the Americas. The Indies formed just one more territorial component to those kingdoms already controlled by the monarchs in Europe. The Spanish Crown viewed the Indies as kingdoms, united by a common monarchy, and within a generation it had established new bureaucratic institutions to subordinate the unruly conquistadors and establish peace and stability. The conquests in the Americas provided enhanced prestige and an immense source of wealth in land, labor, and natural resources, particularly in silver and gold, which were in great demand around the globe in the sixteenth century. These extensive resources allowed the Spanish monarchy to become Europe's only truly global power, whose wealth and military power eclipsed that of its rivals.

With the addition of large mainland Indigenous populations after the expedition of Cortés, authorities in Madrid established the Council of the Indies in 1524 to advise the Crown about all major policies regarding the Americas. This council was to ensure that the king received the best advice, and it allowed him an institutional mechanism for negotiating with key elites throughout his diverse holdings in America. The king's subjects expected all Crown councils to respect the rights, privileges, and laws of each of the various domains of the Spanish Atlantic world. The Crown dispatched Crown-appointed bureaucrats and churchmen to govern, populate, and impose Roman Catholic orthodoxy in its rich possessions in the Indies. New waves of Spanish settlers also helped entrench royal control. The Crown set up an extensive bureaucracy to rule the newly conquered lands, patterned on governmental institutions in Castile. This bureaucracy was headed by a viceroy in each of the two principal political units, the Viceroyalties of New Spain and Peru (and later New Granada in 1739 and the Río de la Plata in 1776), which tied the Indies to Spain. These viceroys were prominent men, often nobles, who had powerful allies among the king's ministers in Madrid. They also came to the viceregal capitals with an entourage of loyal attendants (called *criados*), to whom the viceroy routinely gave key positions in the local government hierarchy. The most successful viceroys used this network of well-placed *criados* to form alliances with local elites, who had ties to both prominent clergymen and influential lay families in the capital cities. This network of allies or relatives enacted policies that also enriched themselves and their families. Such alliances often shifted during a viceregal term, but they endured as long as participation in the wider Spanish Atlantic world gave its participants greater opportunities for wealth and power tied to this global entity.

Rich silver deposits and fertile agricultural lands in the Indies promised great wealth for Spain, but silver could easily be smuggled, and so the Crown established a network of courts (*audiencias*), magistracies (*corregimientos*), treasury offices (*cajas reales*), and city councils (cabildos) to tax, regulate, and govern its New World possessions. The *corregidores de indios* replaced the *encomenderos* in collecting taxes and assessing labor services on Indigenous peoples. The councils in Spain and bureaucrats in the Indies allowed the monarch to consult and negotiate with key elites about maintaining peace and stability in the overseas provinces. By 1610, the Spanish Crown incorporated the Indies as an "accessory union" with metropolitan Spain, making the new possessions a subordinate, legal appendage of the Castilian monarchy. Governmental institutions provided a sense of collective identity that held the diverse provinces of the Indies together with the monarch's other kingdoms.[1]

The Crown regulated commerce by funneling trade with America through Castile's Atlantic port of Seville (and, after 1717, Cádiz) and by establishing a series of licensed ports in the Indies (Veracruz, Cartagena, and Portobelo), where trade fairs led to the official exchange of European wares for New World products, particularly silver. To protect this commerce, in 1564 the Crown sent merchant ships sailing to and from the Indies in a convoy accompanied by warships; this system was known as the *flotas* to New Spain and the *galeones* to trade with Peru. A stable series of regional markets developed in the Indies to supply the needs of the Spanish settlers; the Indigenous, enslaved African, and free inhabitants; and the growing population of mixed racial ancestry (*castas*). In short, by the end of the sixteenth century, the plundering conquest economy founded by the conquistadors gave way to a more stable colonial political, social, and economic order. This society had the Europeans at the pinnacle of the social hierarchy, followed by the castes, Indigenous populations, and the people of African ancestry, usually imported as enslaved individuals. The exact nature of this social hierarchy differed, often significantly, in populous central regions and the more unstable societies of the frontier, and society also evolved in different ways in most areas of the Indies over time.

The Church became a vital partner of the monarchy in governing the Indies by maintaining religious purity and providing the moral and ethical principles for colonial society. Since Ferdinand and Isabel ordered the conversion of Jews and later Muslims in Iberia, the Crown favored the conversion of the Indigenous peoples of the Indies to Roman Catholicism. At first, the religious orders took

---

[1] Theoretically, the Indies were a legal appendage of Castile, and only Castilians could move to the New World. After 1516, when Castile and Aragon had one king, these restrictions on people from Aragon coming to the New World eased. The Crown still tried to restrict the movement of Portuguese subjects to Spanish America, but this too proved difficult to enforce.

the lead in evangelization, but later the secular clergy, supervised by the hierarchy of bishops, played a more important role in converting and ministering to the Indigenous population. Although the royal government in the Indies allowed Indigenous clan leaders some latitude in administering their communities, there would be only one religion and one legal order, administered by the Crown's appointed officials in the Indies. Over time, the Indigenous people occupied a subordinate position in the evolving multiracial and hierarchical society, although both the state and the Church considered them neophytes, not full citizens, in need of protection in a separate República de Indios.

Despite the ties of loyalty to one monarchy and one Church, the political and institutional order in the Indies had a fragile quality that could threaten its long-term viability if this loyalty was undermined. The two principal areas of weakness by the seventeenth century were religious divisions and the fiscal pressures of war. The Inquisition took care of maintaining religious uniformity among the settlers, but it had no jurisdiction over the Indigenous population, whom the Crown believed was in need of ongoing instruction in the faith, even after the first formal conversions. The very wealth, power, and success of the Spanish Indies, however, attracted the envy and attention of European rivals, anxious to gain commercial access to the kingdoms of the Indies and their great wealth, particularly in precious metals. As a result, the late sixteenth and seventeenth centuries were times of war in Europe, attempts by European rivals to plunder the Spanish *flotas* and *galeones* and engage in ongoing contraband trade to penetrate American markets.

The Indies underwent a period of consolidation, economic diversification, and greater political autonomy from the metropolis during the seventeenth century. This time of evolutionary change in America contrasted with the era of war, defeat, and decline for Spain in Europe. Imports of American silver encouraged the assertive imperialism of Philip II and his grandson, Philip IV, leading to a series of expensive and ultimately unsuccessful foreign wars. By 1640, Spain faced bankruptcy and near collapse, as both Portugal and Catalonia (and later Sicily and Naples) revolted to secede from the composite monarchy of the Habsburgs. Beginning in 1633, the fiscally strapped Crown began systematically selling bureaucratic appointments to treasury positions in the Indies, which allowed Creoles and Native sons to buy these positions, even in their own locales, giving colonial elites increased political clout at the expense of embattled Spain. The Crown extended the sales to *corregimientos* in 1678 and to *audiencia* judgeships in 1687. Corruption, graft, and inefficiency also became commonplace, as the venal officeholders advanced their own personal agendas, often at the expense of metropolitan needs. In the second half of the century, remittances of tax revenue and the overall transatlantic trade also stagnated and then diminished, exacerbating this overall decline of Spain. Beginning in 1614, the Crown also decreed that only colonial laws be observed in the Indies, and by 1680, the Crown issued a compilation of this colonial legislation, the *Recopilación de leyes de los reynos de las Indias*. As a result of this growing legal separation between Castile and the Indies and the drift toward rising local power and the overall decline of royal authority, the two principal viceroyalties entered into a new, more independent political and institutional relationship (*aeque principaliter*) with the Crown.

Spanish regular and secular clergymen worried that evangelization efforts failed to produce a pure and fully orthodox Roman Catholic order, which could undermine religious unity in the Indies. The Church had successfully converted millions of Amerindians since the conquest, but Catholic authorities found persistent signs of enduring pre-Christian religious practices. Some zealous churchmen initiated systematic efforts to uncover and "extirpate" such idolatry, which appeared to demonstrate the shortcomings of the "spiritual conquest" of the Native peoples. In their view, the Spanish Atlantic world must remain Roman Catholic, and they saw any form of religious toleration as a dangerous sign of social disorder. Campaigns by churchmen to extirpate idolatry began early in the seventeenth century in Peru and somewhat later and with less intensity in New Spain. The history of the Iberian Peninsula, with the long Reconquista tradition of religious conflict, seemed to validate this position of intolerance. As the Indigenous population converted to Christianity, however imperfectly, a new hybrid colonial culture developed, producing a society that was a mixture of European, Indigenous, and African cultural influences.

The economy began to diversify and expand beyond the formerly dominant silver mining sector as investment capital flowed into agriculture, grazing, manufacturing, and artisan production. New market centers developed outside the older Indigenous population centers of the former Aztec and Inca Empires as the range of colonial market connections expanded, but the overall trend was toward greater self-sufficiency. Commerce in legal and contraband goods also spread beyond the transatlantic monopoly trading system of convoys and licensed ports established in the previous century. In fact, the fleets sailed less frequently from the 1660s, as the American economies became more self-sufficient and less dependent on the declining metropolis, Spain. While the Crown stubbornly attempted to maintain the closed commercial system established in the sixteenth century in the Spanish Atlantic world, by the end of the seventeenth century it had become increasingly porous.

The eighteenth century was an era of war but also vigorous reform, as the Crown made a concerted effort to gain greater control over the governance, commerce, and resources of the Indies. Trade between Spain and the Indies had declined alarmingly by the early eighteenth century, as colonial officials failed to curb various forms of illicit commerce. British and French merchants began introducing large quantities of cheaper contraband merchandise, which undermined the legal trading system of *flotas* and *galeones*, exacerbating the declining Spanish commerce with the Indies. To deal with this broad array of problems, the Spanish kings initiated a series of economic, political, religious, and social measures (known collectively as the Bourbon reforms) to expand the centralizing power of the monarchy. This involved creating an absolutist state apparatus capable of mustering the resources necessary to revitalize Spain and consistently tap the wealth of its overseas possessions. The Madrid government needed enhanced trade and tax revenues to fund conflicts with ever more belligerent European rivals, changing in fundamental ways the political and institutional culture of the previous Habsburg era. The Bourbon monarchs attempted to curb contraband commerce, regain control over the transatlantic trade, modernize government and Crown finances, raise taxes, and fill the depleted royal coffers. The reforms aimed to use trade with the Indies as a means of reviving the Spanish economy, damaged by disastrous wars and ruinous taxation of the seventeenth and early eighteenth centuries. Another major objective of the reforms was to end the previous century's drift toward greater colonial autonomy, using the stronger Bourbon state apparatus to increase the flow of resources from the Indies to renovate Spain and fund its foreign conflicts. By 1750, the Crown had ended the sale of offices in the Indies and systematically began replacing Creole officeholders with peninsular Spaniards. This reforming impulse reached its apogee during the reign of Charles III (1759–88), when political, military, social, and economic reforms strengthened royal power and fiscal control, leading to a clear rise in trade and fiscal remittances from the Indies to Spain. The price, however, was steep. In essence, the Bourbon monarchs in stages curtailed what elites in the Americas had come to view as their rights to greater autonomy.

Bourbon regalist ministers also undermined the traditional partnership between church and state in the eighteenth century by attempting to limit the power and wealth of clerical organizations, particularly the more independent religious orders. Officials such as the Spanish naval officers Jorge Juan and Antonio de Ulloa denounced the corruption and the overabundance of clergy in the Indies. Even Catholic reformers within the Church, influenced by French Jansenism (which sought to purify the Church of baroque forms of piety and ritual and return to the simplicity of the early Church), often sided with Bourbon regalist ministers seeking to undermine the power and influence of the religious orders and the papacy. Bourbon regalists removed the religious orders from their lucrative Amerindian parishes between 1749 and 1753. King Charles III took the drastic step of expelling the rich and powerful Society of Jesus from the Spanish Atlantic world in 1767 and lobbied successfully to have the pope extinguish the order in 1773. The Crown also expanded state power over matters previously policed by the Church by advancing reforms over marriage choice, social programs, secular education, public morality, and even child custody cases. Finally, in 1804 the Crown confiscated much of the wealth of the regular and secular clergy with the Consolidación de Vales Reales. By weakening the traditional power of the Church, the Crown further alienated the clergy and many among pious colonial elites. Weakening the Church, however, undermined the institution that provided religious unity, one of the principal forces holding the Spanish Atlantic world together.

The Bourbon efforts to create an absolutist state by the late eighteenth century had undermined the interlocking ties of clientage, family connections, and political alliances that created loyalty to the monarchy. After ending the sale of judicial offices around 1750 and systematically replacing Creole officeholders with peninsular Spaniards who were more loyal to the Crown, elites in the Indies lost a great deal of political power. In addition, efforts to tighten administrative controls with the imposition of the intendency system and the creation of a larger organized militia system to enforce royal decrees only lessened the need for bureaucrats in Spain and the Indies to consult and develop ties with Creole elite families. From the 1760s, some Spanish authors began referring to the Crown's overseas kingdoms in the Indies as mere colonies.[2] The growth of a more centralized absolutist state reached its peak under José de Gálvez, who as *visitador* in Mexico and later as minister of the Indies demonstrated little regard for the views of Creole magnates in the Indies.[3] Even efforts to liberalize trade within the empire and the revival of mining production increased royal revenues and heightened the dependency of the Indies on Spain and the monarchy. By the end of the eighteenth century, the kingdoms of the Indies had evolved into colonies dependent on the Spanish Crown, rather than separate kingdoms that formed an essential part of the Spanish monarchy.[4]

Bourbon innovations produced serious grievances in some regions of the Indies that erupted into violence. The more autocratic Bourbon *visitadores* sent from Spain largely abandoned the traditional policies of consultation to seek the advice and opinion of local elites in the Indies about policy innovations. In 1767, the *visitador* José de Gálvez imposed higher taxes, raised disciplined militias throughout New Spain, and oversaw the expulsion of the Jesuits, triggering violence in the mining regions in the north, which had to be suppressed with military force. Even more serious were uprisings in New Granada and the

---

[2] Mark A. Burkholder, "Spain's America: From Kingdoms to Colonies," *Colonial Latin American Review* 25, no. 2 (June 2016): 143.

[3] The colonial policy of Gálvez and his near contempt for Creole interests are reviewed in Kuethe and Andrien, *Spanish Atlantic World in the Eighteenth Century*, 288–90, 311–16, 321–22.

[4] This process is reviewed carefully by Burkholder, who argues that Spain sought to "emulate British success," in "Spain's America," 142–43.

Andes in the 1780s. In New Granada in 1781, efforts by *visitador* Juan Francisco de Gutiérrez Piñares to enforce tax and monopoly laws and eliminate corruption in local government led to an uprising of regional elites and plebeians in the Socorro region, which forced concessions from the government until it was suppressed by royal troops. Similar policies, along with the high-handed efforts of corrupt *corregidores* to replace local Indigenous clan leaders with more pliable leaders, provoked three separate rebellions centered in Chayanta, the Cusco region, and La Paz, which nearly drove the Spaniards from the Andean highlands before each was defeated. Bourbon reforms aimed at raising revenues, tightening administrative controls, and eliminating local elites from decision-making led to the alienation of elite and popular groups in the Indies, undermining ties of loyalty to the Crown in the Indies by the early nineteenth century.

While periodic rebellions in the Indies protesting the Bourbon reforms and wars with foreign rivals damaged the political order, the French invasion of the Iberian Peninsula in 1807 led to the slow collapse of the Spanish Atlantic world by 1825. Napoleon forced the Spanish monarch, Charles IV, to abdicate on May 6, 1808, and his heir, Ferdinand, to renounce his rights to the throne. The French then took both men off to captivity in France, and Napoleon placed his elder brother, Joseph, on the Spanish throne. In the absence of a legitimate monarch, a series of regional councils (juntas) developed to coordinate resistance against the French. The invasion and abdication of the royal family led to a massive popular uprising against the government of Joseph Bonaparte, widely considered a French usurper, which spread throughout the peninsula. The fiscal pressures of war led to policies that clearly weakened ties of loyalty to the monarchy, and the French invasion led finally to its collapse in Spain.

This tumult in Spain also promoted a serious constitutional crisis in the Indies, where many Creoles believed that without a legitimate monarch, power reverted to the people. As a result, Creole elites felt emboldened to establish provincial juntas in major cities of the Indies, usually to rule until the restoration of a legitimate monarch or stable government in Spain. Other zones of the Indies, such as Peru, with its large royal army, remained loyal and under the firm grip of royal officials. Even the Constitution of 1812 put constraints on Crown power, but it also declared the Spanish Atlantic world an indivisible unity and offered no political concessions regarding autonomy or greater home rule for rebellious groups in the Indies. Nevertheless, local Creoles inexorably moved from favoring local rule until the return of the Ferdinand VII to complete independence, although the strength of such sentiments varied over time and from region to region of the vast Spanish Indies. When King Ferdinand returned to the throne, his weak governments did not even try to achieve a reconciliation with his Liberal opponents in Spain or with the rebel groups in the Indies. The final victories of the insurgent leadership ultimately culminated in the independence of Mexico and Central America by 1821 and of South America by 1825.

Independence destroyed the unity of the Spanish Atlantic world, but it did not lay the foundation for peace and prosperity. Spain, the former metropolis, suffered from conflicts between Liberals and Conservatives, leading to decades of political instability. During their return to power following the Riego revolt in 1820, the Liberals divided over which policies to pursue for Spain into moderates (*moderados*) and more radical Liberals (*exaltados*, later called *progresistas*). After the French restored Ferdinand VII and the absolutist regime in 1823, more extreme Conservatives rallied around the king's brother, Carlos. After the death of Ferdinand in 1833, Prince Carlos, an extreme political Conservative, invoked the Salic Law (which prohibited women from taking the throne) to press his claim to the throne over the king's young daughter and heir, Isabel. Between 1833 and 1840, the Carlist Wars raged in Spain, with the Basque provinces, Catalonia, and parts of Andalusia largely favoring the Carlists, while most cities and the rest of Spain favored Isabel II and moderate Liberalism. While the Liberal forces favoring Isabel ultimately prevailed, the divisions among Liberals and the lingering power of Conservatives plunged Spain into decades of political instability that retarded economic development and promoted regionalism.

Things were even more chaotic in the former Spanish Indies, where independence did not create stable, cohesive national states.[5] As the political apparatus of colonialism slowly collapsed from 1808 to 1825, colonial market economies, ordered into a complicated series of trunk and feeder lines, unraveled. Regions united by market ties and the colonial state apparatus—whether oriented for export or for local and regional consumption—fractured as political, economic, and social disorder in the various regions of the Indies impeded the formation of stable national economies and governments. Moreover, the colonial fiscal system collapsed under the pressures of the destructive independence wars, leaving the new independent states in relative fiscal penury.[6] Conflict among elites further undermined national unity, as they divided between Conservatives and Liberals.[7] Compounding these

---

[5] Brian R. Hamnett made this point in a pioneering article, "Process and Pattern: A Reexamination of the Ibero-American Independence Movements, 1808–1826," *Journal of Latin American Studies* 29, no. 2 (May 1997): 279–328.

[6] This point is made in a controversial article on the colonial financial system: Alejandra Irigoin and Regina Grafe, "Bargaining for Absolutism: A Spanish Path to Nation-State and Empire Building," *Hispanic American Historical Review* 88, no. 2 (May 2008): 173–209.

[7] On the one hand, although the Conservative political agenda varied from region to region, in general they favored a strong central government directed from the former colonial capitals, continued support for the Church, and some government controls over trade to protect traditional

political and economic problems was an overall decline in trade with Europe, suffering an economic downturn following the end of the Napoleonic Wars, which led to diminished demand for imported primary goods from the former Spanish Indies.

In this time of elite factionalism, regional political warlords (called *caudillos*) became political arbiters among competing national, regional, and local interest groups. As in Spain, regionalism, not nationalism, characterized much of the postindependence era in the Latin American nations, leading to endemic strife and instability for much of the nineteenth century. Despite the mobilization of popular groups by both Loyalist and insurgent armies, the states that emerged from the wars of independence remained under elite control, with limitations on citizenship and even the endurance of enslavement. As the disillusioned liberator, Simon Bolívar, remarked shortly before his death to a comrade, Juan José Flores, in 1830, "You know that I have been in command for twenty years; and from them I have derived only few sure conclusions: first, America is ungovernable for us; second, he who serves the revolution ploughs the sea."[8] During this long period of unrest and instability, the independent Spanish American nations became less well integrated into the Atlantic world, at least until the second half of the nineteenth century. By then, commercial ties with Europe and later the United States slowly drew these states directly into a new, stronger Atlantic commercial system. This favored the liberal political agenda of free trade, which promoted a new political consensus around their ideology, leading ultimately to greater political stability. These new, more stable regimes generally did not promote greater political inclusion or social rights for the masses of people of the former Spanish Atlantic world.

---

colonial interest groups. These Conservative elites wanted to preserve or restore key elements of the old colonial order. On the other hand, Liberals also favored policies that varied from region to region, but in general they wanted a clear break from the past. They favored free trade, foreign investment, private property, individual liberty, free enterprise, and a federal political system, with power shared by the central government and the regions. In the United Provinces of Argentina, however, Liberal elites in Buenos Aires favored a strong central government that could control the interior regions. Liberals were also frequently anticlerical, although the strength of this sentiment varied in different parts of the former Spanish Indies.

[8] Quoted in Bushnell, *Simón Bolívar* 202; Lynch, *Simón Bolívar: A Life*, 276.

Glossary of Terms

Accessory union—A union headed by a monarch, whereby the dominant power subjects the acquired province, such as an overseas possession, to its laws and privileges.

Adelantado—Frontier governor during the Reconquista or the leader of an expedition of conquest to the New World.

Aeque principaliter (equally important)—A loose confederation or union headed by a monarch, where each province is treated as a distinct entity, subject to its own laws and privileges.

al-Andalus—Muslim Iberia until 1031 CE with its capital at Córdoba.

Alcabala—Sales tax.

Alcalde—Mayor of a Spanish or Indigenous city or town.

Alcántara—A military order licensed by Pope Alexander III in 1176 CE whose knights observed the same rules as the Cistercian order of Calatrava, but its activities were largely confined to León.

Aljama—Muslim community.

Amparos—A degree of royal protection sought by Indigenous petitioners, usually in the Juzgado General de Indios in Mexico City.

Arbitrio judicial—Spanish officials in the Indies had the legal power to resist or delay the imposition of any Crown directive that they felt violated local justice, custom, or the common good.

Audiencia—High courts in Spain and the Indies that heard civil and criminal cases and, in the Indies, enforced issued laws.

Autos-da-fé—Public punishments for those found guilty of crimes of faith by the Holy Office of the Inquisition.

Cabildo—City council, sometimes called an *ayuntamiento*.

Cabildo abierto—Open meeting of the city council, often called in the Indies following the French invasion of Iberia in 1807.

Cacique—Traditional Indigenous clan or community leader, called a *kuraka* in the Andes.

Calatrava—Military order organized in 1164 CE whose knights had the same status as monks of the Cistercian order and were subject to its rules, including celibacy.

Capellanía—A chantry, a financial bequest to support a certain number of masses for the soul of the donor, family members, or close friends.

Capitulación—Legal agreement usually between the Crown and a private citizen, often used to support commerce and settlement in the Indies. The Capitulaciones of Santa Fé in 1492 gave broad rights to Christopher Columbus by Queen Isabel of Castile in the Americas, naming him an admiral, viceroy, and governor general over any lands he discovered and giving him a tenth of any treasure he found and the right to trade duty free with inhabitants of the Americas.

Casa de la Contratación, or Board of Trade—Founded in 1503 to control colonial commerce, license travelers across the Atlantic, and inspect cargos entering Seville, the only port allowed to trade with the Indies until 1717, when the licensed port was moved to Cádiz.

Castas—People of mixed racial ancestry in the Indies.

Cédula—Royal edict.

Cédulas de gracias al sacar—A royal edict that could alter the social status; any of defect of birth, such as illegitimacy; or even the race of any citizen who paid an established fee and received the approbation of the *Cámara* of the Council of the Indies by the late eighteenth century.

Chicha—Andean fermented maize beer often used for ritual occasions in the Inca Empire and sold commercially in the colonial period.

Circum-Atlantic history—A work of history giving a transnational view of the region, seeing the Atlantic basin as a unified zone of exchange, circulation, and the transmission of people, ideas, goods, and even warfare.

Cis-Atlantic history—A work of history that examines particular places, regions, empires, or even institutions within a wider Atlantic context.

Cofradía—Christian religious sodality.

Composite monarchy—A kingdom composed of different provinces or kingdoms, each subject to its own laws and customs, united by a common monarch.

Consejo de Indias, or Council of the Indies—Founded in 1524 to serve as a court of appeals in civil cases, a legislative body, and an executive authority to frame laws for the Indies for the king's signature. The Council of the Indies also dispatched royal inspectors to the Indies to ensure good governance.

Consolidación de Vales Reales—Effort to consolidate the debt in vales; later, the term used to sequester Church assets in Spain in 1798 and the Indies in 1804.

Consulado—Merchant guild in cities such as Seville (and, after 1717, Cádiz), Mexico City, and Lima participating in transatlantic commerce. In the eighteenth century, the number of *consulados* expanded to include other colonial cities.

Conversos—Jews who converted (often forcibly) to Christianity.

Convivencia—Period when Muslims, Christians, and Jews lived in relative peace and with some level of religious toleration.

Corregidor de españoles—Spanish magistrate who served in municipalities to hear court cases and to regulate local affairs in conjunction with the city council (cabildo).

Corregidor de indios—Spanish rural magistrate who regulated contact between Spaniards and Amerindians, collected the Indigenous head tax or tribute, and assigned forced (corvée) labor service for state projects.

Cortes—Traditional representative assembly in Iberia; during the Peninsular War, an elected assembly that produced the Constitution of 1812 and governed Spain.

Criados—Retainers who accompanied the viceroys from Spain to the Indies and usually received patronage appointments to enrich themselves and establish ties to local elites.

Cumbi—Cloth made from the finest camelid wool in the Andes.

Depositaría de Indias—Treasury of the House of Trade or Casa de la Contratación.

Derecho indiano—Laws designed specifically for the Indies.

Deseado, el—the desired one; name given to Ferdinand VII when he was in exile in France from 1806 to 1813.

Dhimmi, Ahd al—Special pact of protection accorded to "people of the book" allowing Christians and Jews living under Muslim control religious freedom and some level of political and economic autonomy, if they paid a special poll tax (*jizya*).

Diezmo—Tithe, usually set at 10 percent of rural produce.

Doctrina de indios—Indigenous parish.

Donada(o)—Servant in a religious house.

Dos novenos—Two-ninths of tithe, which was the traditional portion paid to the Crown.

Encomendero—The holder of an encomienda grant.

Encomienda—In the New World, a grant of a number of Indigenous towns, almost always to a Spaniard (often a conquistador), allowing the grant holder, called an *encomendero*, to collect taxes and labor from his Indigenous charges in return for military protection and instruction in Roman Catholicism. In Iberia, it also gave the *encomendero* some control over or ownership to land, in addition to taxes and labor service.

Extirpation of idolatry—Religious campaigns to end lingering Indigenous religious practices in New Spain, but especially in Peru from the early seventeenth century to around 1750.

Felicidad pública—A effort to promote public happiness, economic growth, social well-being, and national strength.

Fiscal—Attorney.

Flotas y galeones—Legally sanctioned convoys, dispatched from Seville to designated locations in the Indies where trade fairs (at Veracruz, Cartagena, and Portobelo) were held to exchange European wares for American products, particularly silver from the mines in New Spain and Peru. The *flota* serviced New Spain until 1789, and the *galeones* serviced South America until 1740.

238 GLOSSARY OF TERMS

Forastero—An Andean who left his home community to live elsewhere and paid a lower tribute rate than normal community members (called *originarios*) but had little or no legal right to have access to community lands.

Fueros—Special rights or privileges from the crown to cities, regions, or kingdoms of Iberia.

Gachupines—A disparaging slang term for a peninsular-born Spaniard.

Gauchos—Cowboys (herders and keepers of cattle) in Argentina.

Grandees—Highest echelon of the Castilian nobility.

Guerrilla—Literally meaning little war; a term used to describe small-scale, irregular forces that harassed regular armies, usually harassing them in small skirmishes; it originated in the Peninsular War when Spanish partisans fought the French invaders of Iberia from 1808 to 1813.

Hakhamim—Legal scholars in Jewish law.

Halakha—Jewish law.

Hidalgo—Lowest echelon of the Castilian nobility.

Imam—A leader of Muslim prayers.

Indios de faltriquera—Literally pocket or purse Indians, who paid their way out of serving in the mita at Potosí by paying the wage of one wage laborer (*minga*).

Indios ladinos—A group of Indigenous intellectuals who were literate in both Castilian and their Indigenous language and often served as intermediaries between their native communities and Spaniards.

Ingenuos or engenho—Sugar plantation.

Jefes politicos superiores—Title given to viceroys in the Indies after the Spanish *cortes* abolished the office of viceroy in 1810, since the king was in exile.

Jihad—Muslim holy war.

Jizya—Special poll tax levied by Muslim governments in Iberia on non-Muslims.

Juderías (in Castile) and juerias (in the Kingdom of Aragon)—Jewish neighborhoods often walled off in Iberian Christian cities.

Junta—Special council, often ad hoc; after the French invasion of Iberia in 1807, such councils arose in Spain and the Indies to govern until the return of the deposed king, Ferdinand VII.

Juros—Government-issued annuities usually paying 3 to 5 percent interest annually.

Juzgado de Capellanías y Obras Pias—A clerical agency that managed pious works and endowments according to canon law, often lending this money to local entrepreneurs.

Juzgado General de Indios—Court in Mexico City that heard cases involving Indigenous litigants, most often seeking *amparos*.

Kahal or kehilla—Jewish community.

Khatib—Muslim preachers.

Limpieza de sangre—Purity of bloodlines; any person wishing to enter a university or receive a government position or any number of other jobs had to go before the Inquisition to prove that they were from an Old Christian family, with no Jewish or Muslim blood. In the Indies they had to prove that they had no taint of African or Indigenous blood.

Llanero—Term given to horsemen, mostly racially mixed blooded cowboys and small farmers from the llanos of Colombia and Venezuela, who fought (first for the Spanish army and later for the rebel armies) in the wars of independence in northern South America.

Llanos—Plains of Colombia and Venezuela.

Mercaderes de plata—Silver merchants, most notably powerful at Potosí.

Merced—A reward, often awarded by the Crown for meritorious service.

Mesta—Sheep-growers guild in Castile.

Mestizo—The offspring of a Spaniard and an Amerindian in the New World.

Minga—Wage labor at Andean silver mines.

M'ita—Hispanicized as mita; cyclical state corvée labor in the Andes.

Moderados—Moderate Liberals in nineteenth-century Spain.

Montaña or Oriente region—Eastern slopes of the Andes, a largely jungle frontier region.

Motín—Riot, uprising, or mutiny.

Mudéjars—Muslims in Christian-controlled regions of medieval Iberia.

Mufti—Experts rendering legal and religious opinions, or *fatwas*.

Mundo al revés—In the Andean region, it meant a world turned upside down.

Morería—Muslim district or neighborhood in a Christian-controlled town or city.

Obraje—A textile workshop that most often made rough woolen cloth.

Obras pias—Catholic foundations created to support the spiritual activities of the clergy.

Pardo—A person with dark skin and usually some African blood.

Patria potestad—Paternal right that allowed fathers to take children from the care of their mothers (in the Indies, often by Indigenous mothers) as long as they provided for the material and spiritual well-being of the children.

Peruleros—Peruvian merchants who bypassed the convey system and carried merchandise, mostly silver, directly to Asia and Europe.

Porteño—Resident of the "port" of Buenos Aires.

Presidio—Garrison, usually on the frontiers, staffed by regular army troops and often supported by local militias.

Probanza de Méritos—A legal document sent to the Crown to attain a reward for services to the Crown, normally complete with eyewitness testimony verifying the truthfulness of the assertions and certified by a notary.

Progresistas or exaltados—Radical Liberals in nineteenth-century Spain.

Pulperías—Stores selling groceries, alcoholic beverages, and various sundries.

Quinto—Mining tax of 20 percent.

Real Compañia Guipuzcoana de Caracas—Joint-stock company founded in 1728 to control the commerce in cacao from Venezuela. It ended the historic monopoly of the Cádiz merchant guild over trade with the Indies.

Recogimientos—Homes for pious or wayward women or women whose husbands were away.

Reconquista—The intermittent seven hundred-year struggle between Christians and Muslims to control the Iberian Peninsula.

Recopilación de leyes de los reynos de las Indias—Compilation of colonial law completed in 1680.

Regalists—Crown ministers in the eighteenth century who attempted to strengthen the monarchy at the expense of vested interest groups in Spain and the Indies.

Relaciones Geográficas—Questionnaires sent out by royal cosmographer Juan López de Velásco to learn about local history and natural history and to compile economic data, trade and navigation, and geographical information, including maps of each locale.

Remença—Mandatory payment by Catalan peasants to be relieved of their feudal duties.

Repartimiento de comercio, repartimiento de mercancías, or reparto—Forced distribution of goods to Indigenous communities in the Andes or in parts of Mexico; credit advanced to Indigenous communities to produce a commodity, most often cochineal dye.

República de Españoles—Corporate legal category for Spaniards from Iberia, people of Spanish descent born in the Indies (called Creoles), people of mixed ancestry (*castas*), and free and enslaved Africans. The *República de Españoles* was subject to the laws of Castile and, later, the Indies, with its own privileges and obligations, such as paying taxes and rendering various services to the Crown.

República de Indios—Corporate legal category for Amerindians, giving them access to their traditional landholdings in return for paying a head tax, tribute, accepting conversion to Christianity, and serving periodic labor services.

Requirement—A document read aloud in Castilian before a battle with Amerindian groups requiring the enemy to submit and convert to Christianity or face the loss of their material wealth and their very lives. It was based on Muslim warnings issued before beginning a jihad, or holy war.

Santa Hermandad—Rural police force and judicial tribunal in Castile to maintain order in the Castilian countryside, established by the Cortes of Madrigal in 1476.

Santiago—Military order founded in 1175 CE by Pope Alexander III, who subjected the knights directly to the Holy See and laid down its rules, including the right of its members to marry.

Sapa Inca—Unique Inca or emperor of the Inca Empire, or *Tawantinsuyu*.

Sentencia de Guadalupe—Treaty in 1486 that abolished the six evil customs in Aragon; it freed the kingdom's peasants from serfdom, but allowed the nobility to retain ownership of their lands.

Servicios—Tax contributions voted by the *cortes* of the various Christian realms of Iberia.

Serviles—Absolutists, who supported the return to absolute monarchy under Ferdinand VII.

Shariah—Muslim law derived from the Qur'ān, the direct revelation of God (Allah); it was a moral and ethical guide to all private and public behavior and Muslims had to obey its precepts.

Situado—Government subsidy usually paid from wealthy central treasuries in the Indies, such as Lima or Mexico City, to support the defense of frontier zones.

Sunnah—Statements and deeds of the prophet Muhammad, preserved by legal scholars in written form in the Hadith (reports or accounts of the Prophet Muhammad).

Taifas—Muslim city states that emerged by 1031 CE in al-Andalus after the downfall of the Muslim caliphate centered in Córdoba.

Taqui Onqoy—A sixteenth-century Andean revivalist movement that called for vanquishing the Spanish settlers, abandoning their God, and returning to Andean religion. Its adherents were called *taquiongos*.

Tianques—Indigenous marketplace.

Tocapu—Checkerboard pattern on Inca tunics.

Trajines—Llama caravans in the Andes transporting a range of locally produced goods and foodstuffs and even European wares.

Transatlantic history—A work of history that gives international comparisons across the ocean and the continents that face onto it.

Treaty of Tordesillas—Agreement between the Spanish and Portuguese Crowns to divide the world between them, with Spain getting most of the New World except Brazil and Portugal getting Africa and most of Asia.

242 GLOSSARY OF TERMS

Vales reales—Government-issued annuities paying 3 to 5 percent interest annually for purchasers, issued in the eighteenth and early nineteenth centuries.

Válido—Chief minister of the king of Spain.

Vecino—Urban citizens in Iberia with political rights tied to military service during the Reconquista.

Visita—A government or clerical inspection tour.

War of the Quadruple Alliance—War between Spain and an alliance of Great Britain, Austria, France, Great Britain, and Savoy, which defeated Spain decisively from 1718 to 1719, leading to the downfall of Julio Alberoni, the chief advisor to King Philip V.

Bibliography

Adelman, Jeremy. *Sovereignty and Revolution in the Iberian Atlantic*. Princeton, NJ: Princeton University Press, 2006.
Adorno, Rolena, ed. *Guaman Poma de Ayala: The Colonial Art of an Andean Author*. New York: The Americas Society, 1992.
Adorno, Rolena. *Guaman Poma: Writing and Resistance in Colonial Peru*. 1986. Reprint, Austin: University of Texas Press, 2000.
Adorno, Rolena. *The Polemics of Possession in Spanish American Narrative*. New Haven, CT: Yale University Press, 2007.
Altman, Ida. *Emigrants and Society: Extremadura and America in the Sixteenth Century*. Berkeley: University of California Press, 1989.
Altman, Ida. *Transatlantic Ties in the Spanish Empire: Brihuega, Spain, and Puebla, Mexico, 1560–1620*. Stanford, CA: Stanford University Press, 2000.
Alvarez de Toledo, Cayetana. *Politics and Reform in Spain and Viceregal Mexico: The Life and Thought of Juan de Palafox, 1600–1659*. Oxford: Clarendon Press, 2004.
Amelang, James S. *Parallel Histories: Muslims and Jews in Inquisitorial Spain*. Baton Rouge: Louisiana State University Press, 2013.
Andrien, Kenneth J. *Andean Worlds: Indigenous History, Culture, and Consciousness under Spanish Rule, 1532–1825*. Albuquerque: University of New Mexico Press, 2001.
Andrien, Kenneth J. "Corruption, Inefficiency, and Imperial Decline in the Seventeenth-Century Viceroyalty of Peru." *The Americas* XLLI (July 1984): 1–20.
Andrien, Kenneth J. *Crisis and Decline: The Viceroyalty of Peru in the Seventeenth Century*. Albuquerque: University of New Mexico Press, 1985.
Andrien, Kenneth J. "Economic Crisis, Taxes, and the Quito Insurrection of 1765." *Past and Present* 129 (November 1990): 104–31.
Andrien, Kenneth J., ed. *The Human Tradition in Colonial Latin America*. 2002. Reprint, New York: Rowman & Littlefield, 2013.
Andrien, Kenneth J. *The Kingdom of Quito, 1690–1830: The State and Regional Development*. Cambridge: Cambridge University Press, 1995.
Andrien, Kenneth J. "La reforma clerical durante el reinado de Carlos III: La expulsión de los Jesuitas." *Tempus: Revista en Historia General* 4 (Septiembre–Octubre 2016): 239–55.
Andrien, Kenneth J. "The Sale of Fiscal Offices and the Decline of Royal Authority in the Viceroyalty of Peru." *Hispanic American Historical Review* 62, no. 1 (February 1982): 49–71.
Andrien, Kenneth J. "The Sale of Juros and the Politics of Reform in the Viceroyalty of Peru, 1608–1695." *Journal of Latin American Studies* 13 (May 1981): 1–19.
Andrien, Kenneth J., and Rolena Adorno, eds. *Transatlantic Encounters: Spaniards and Andeans in the Sixteenth Century*. Berkeley: University of California Press, 1991.
Anna, Timothy. "Economic Causes of San Martín's Failure in Lima." *Hispanic American Historical Review* 54, no. 4 (November 1974): 657–80.
Anna, Timothy. *Spain and the Loss of America*. Lincoln: University of Nebraska Press, 1983.
Anthony, Danielle Tina. "Intimate Invasion: Andeans and Europeans in 16th Century Peru." Ph.D. diss., The Ohio State University, 2018.
Armitage, David and Michale J. Braddock. *The British Atlantic World, 1500–1800*, edited by David Armitage and Michael J. Braddick. Basingstoke, UK: Palgrave Macmillan, 2008, 15–27.
Arriaga, Pablo José de. *The Extirpation of Idolatry in Peru*. Translated by L. Clark Keating. 1621. Reprint, Lexington: University of Kentucky Press, 1968.

Assadourian, Carlos Sempat. *El sistema de la economía colonial: El mercado interior, regiones, y espacio económico*. Mexico City: Editorial Nueva Imagen, 1983.

Bailyn, Bernard. *Atlantic History: Concepts and Contours*. Cambridge, MA: Harvard University Press, 2005.

Ballone, Angela. *The 1624 Tumult of Mexico in Perspective (c. 1620-1650): Authority and Conflict Resolution in the Iberian Atlantic*. Leiden: Brill, 2018.

Barbier, Jacques A. "Peninsular Finance and Colonial Trade: The Dilemma of Charles IV's Spain," *Journal of Latin America Studies* 2, no. 1 (May 1980): 21-37.

Barbier, Jacques A. "Towards a New Chronology of Bourbon Colonialism: The 'Depositaría de Indias' of Cádiz." *Ibero-Amerikanisches Archiv* 6, no. 4 (1980): 335-353.

Barr, Juliana. *Peace Came in the Form of a Woman: Indians and Spaniards in the Texas Borderlands*. Chapel Hill: University of North Carolina Press, 2007.

Barrera Osorio, Antonio. *Experiencing Nature: The Spanish American Empire and the Early Scientific Revolution*. Austin: University of Texas Press, 2006.

Barton, Simon. *Conquerors, Brides, and Concubines: Interfaith Relations and Social Power in Medieval Iberia*. Philadelphia: University of Pennsylvania Press, 2015.

Benjamin, Thomas. *The Atlantic World: Europeans, Africans, Indians, and Their Shared History*. Cambridge: Cambridge University Press, 2009.

Bernal, Antonio-Miguel. *La financiación de la Carrera de Indias (1492-1824)*. Seville: Escuela de Estudios Hispano-Americanos, 1992.

Berquist Soule, Emily. *The Bishop's Utopia: Envisioning Improvement in Colonial Peru*. Philadelphia: University of Pennsylvania Press, 2014.

Black, Chad Thomas. *The Limits of Gender Domination: Women, the Law, and Political Crisis in Quito, 1765-1830*. Albuquerque: University of New Mexico Press, 2010.

Blanchard, Peter. *Under the Flags of Freedom: Slave Soldiers and the Wars of Independence in Spanish South America*. Pittsburgh, PA: University of Pittsburgh Press, 2008.

Blaufarb, Rafe. "The Western Question: The Geopolitics of Latin American Independence." *American Historical Review* 112, no. 3 (June 2007): 742-63.

Bleichmar, Daniela. *Visible Empire: Botanical Expeditions and Visual Culture in the Hispanic Enlightenment*. Chicago: University of Chicago Press, 2012.

Bolton, Herbert Eugene. "The Epic of Greater America." *American Historical Review* 38, no. 3 (April 1933): 448-74.

Borah, Woodrow, and Sherburne Cook. *The Aboriginal Population of Mexico on the Eve of the Spanish Conquest*. Berkeley: University of California Press, 1963.

Borucki, Alex. *From Shipmates to Soldiers: Emerging Black Identities in the Río de la Plata*. Albuquerque: University of New Mexico Press, 2015.

Boswell, John. *The Royal Treasure: Muslim Communities under the Crown of Aragon in the Fourteenth Century*. New Haven, CT: Yale University Press, 1977.

Boyd-Bowman, Peter. *Índice geobiográfico de cuarenta mil pobladores Españoles de América en el siglo XVI*. 2 vols. Bogota, Colombia: Instituto Caro y Cuervo, 1964.

Bradley, Peter T. *The Lure of Peru: Maritime Intrusion into the South Sea, 1598-1701*. New York: St. Martin's Press, 1989.

Breña, Roberto. *El primer liberalismo Español y los procesos de emancipación de América, 1808-1824: Una revision historiográfica del liberalismo hispánico*. Mexico City: El Colegio de México, 2006.

Brooks, James. *Captives and Cousins: Slavery, Kinship, and Community in the Southwest Borderlands*. Chapel Hill: Omohondro Institute and the University of North Carolina Press, 2002.

Brown, Kendall W. *A History of Mining in Latin America: From the Colonial Era to the Present*. Albuquerque: University of New Mexico Press, 2012.

Bryant, Sherwin K. *Rivers of Gold, Lives of Bondage: Governing through Slavery in Colonial Quito*. Chapel Hill: University of North Carolina Press, 2014.

Burkholder, Mark A. "Spain's America: From Kingdoms to Colonies," *Colonial Latin American Review* 25, no. 2 (June 2016): 143.
Burkholder, Mark A., and D. S. Chandler, eds. *Biographical Dictionary of Audiencia Ministers in the Americas, 1687–1821*. Westport, CT: Greenwood Press, 1982.
Burkholder, Mark A., and D. S. Chandler, eds. *From Impotence to Authority: The Spanish Crown and the American Audiencias, 1687–1808*. Columbia: University of Missouri Press, 1977.
Burns, Kathryn. *Colonial Habits: Convents and the Spiritual Economy of Cuzco, Peru*. Durham, NC: Duke University Press, 1999.
Bushnell, David. *Simón Bolívar: Liberation and Disappointment*. New York: Pearson Longman, 2004.
Campillo y Cossío, José del. *Nuevo sistema económico para América*. Edited by Manuel Ballesteros Gaibrois. Oviedo, Spain: Editorial Asturiano, 1993.
Candiani, Vera. *Dreaming of Dry Land: Environmental Transformation in Colonial Mexico City*. Stanford, CA: Stanford University Press, 2014.
Cañeque, Alejandro. *The King's Living Image: The Culture and Politics of Viceregal Power in Colonial Mexico*. London: Routledge, 2004.
Cañizares-Esguerra, Jorge. "The Core and the Peripheries of Our National Narratives: A Response from IH-35." *American Historical Review* 112, no. 5 (December 2007): 1423–33.
Cañizares-Esguerra, Jorge. "Entangled Histories: Borderland Historiographies in New Clothes." *American Historical Review* 112, no. 3 (June 2007): 787–99.
Cañizares-Esguerra, Jorge. *How to Write the history of the New World: Histories, Epistemologies, and Identities in the Eighteenth-Century Atlantic World*. Stanford, CA: Stanford University Press, 2001.
Cañizares-Esguerra, Jorge. *Nature, Empire, and Nation: Explorations of the History of Science in the Iberian World*. Stanford, CA: Stanford University Press, 2006.
Cañizares-Esguerra, Jorge. *Puritan Conquistador: Iberianizing the Atlantic, 1550–1700*. Stanford, CA: Stanford University Press, 2006.
Canny, Nicholas, and Philip Morgan, eds. *The Oxford Handbook of the Atlantic World, 1450–1850*. Oxford: Oxford University Press, 2011.
Cardim, Pedro, Tamar Herzog, José Javier Ruiz Ibánez, and Gaetano Sabatini, eds. *Polycentric Monarchies: How Did Early Modern Spain and Portugal Achieve and Maintain Global Hegemony?* Eastbourne, UK: Sussex Academic Press, 2012, 2014.
Castro Gutiérrez, Felipe. *Nueva ley, nuevo rey: Reformas borbónicas y rebelión popular en Nueva España*. Michoacan, Mexico: El Colegio de Michoacán, 1996.
Charles, John. *Allies at Odds: The Andean Church and Its Indigenous Agents, 1583–1671*. Albuquerque: University of New Mexico Press, 2010.
Charney, Paul. *Indian Society in the Valley of Lima, 1532–1824*. Lanham, MD: University Press of America, 2001.
Chaunu, Pierre, and Huguette Chaunu. *Séville et l'Atlantique*. 8 vols. Paris: Colin, 1955–59.
Clayton, Lawrence A. *Bartolomé de las Casas: A Biography*. Cambridge: Cambridge University Press, 2012.
Clendinnen, Inga. *Ambivalent Conquests: Maya and Spaniard in the Yucatán, 1517–1570*. Cambridge: Cambridge University Press, 1987.
Clifford, James, and George E. Marcus, eds. *Writing Culture: The Poetics and Politics of Ethnography*. Berkeley: University of California Press, 1986.
Coclanis, Peter. "*Drag nach Osten*: Bernard Bailyn, This World-Island, and the Idea of Atlantic History." *Journal of World History* 13 (2002): 169–82.
Cohen, Mark R. *Under the Crescent and Cross: The Jews in the Middle Ages*. Princeton, NJ: Princeton University Press, 1994.
Cole, Jeffrey. *The Potosí Mita, 1573–1700: Compulsory Indian Labor in the Andes*. Stanford, CA: Stanford University Press, 1985.

Cook, Alexandra Parma, and Noble David Cook. *Good Faith and Truthful Ignorance: A Case of Transatlantic Bigamy.* Durham, NC: Duke University Press, 1991.

Cook, Noble David. *Born to Die: Disease and the New World Conquest, 1492-1650.* Cambridge: Cambridge University Press, 1998.

Corr, Rachel. *Interwoven: Andean Lives in Colonial Ecuador's Textile Economy.* Tucson: University of Arizona Press, 2018.

Coxe, William. *Memoirs of the Kings of Spain of the House of Bourbon, from the Accession of Philip V to the Death of Charles III.* 3 vols. London: Longman, Hurst, Rees, Orme, and Brown, 1813.

Cromwell, Jesse. *The Smuggler's World: Illicit Trade and Atlantic Communities in Eighteenth-Century Venezuela.* Chapel Hill: Omohondro Institute and the University of North Carolina Press, 2018.

Crosby, Alfred W. *The Columbian Exchange: Biological and Cultural Consequences of 1492.* Westport, CT: Greenwood Press, 1972.

Crosby, Alfred W. *Ecological Imperialism: The Biological Expansion of Europe, 900-1900.* Cambridge: Cambridge University Press, 1986.

Cummins, Thomas B. F. *Toasts with the Inca: Andean Abstraction and Colonial Images on Quero Vessels.* Ann Arbor: University of Michigan Press, 2002.

Curtain, Philip. *The Atlantic Slave Trade: A Census.* Madison: University of Wisconsin Press, 1969.

Cutter, Charles R. *The Legal Culture of New Spain, 1700-1810.* Albuquerque: University of New Mexico Press, 1995.

Dagnino, Arianna. *Transcultural Writers in an Age of Global Mobility.* West Lafayette, IN: Purdue University Press, 2015.

Deans-Smith, Susan. *Bureaucrats, Planters, and Workers: The Making of the Tobacco Monopoly in Bourbon Mexico.* Austin: University of Texas Press, 1992.

Devaney, Thomas. *Enemies in the Plaza: Urban Spectacle and the End of Spanish Frontier Culture, 1460-1492.* Philadelphia: University of Pennsylvania Press, 2015.

Díaz del Castillo, Bernal. *The True History of the Conquest of New Spain.* Translated and with an introduction by Jane Burke and Tod Humphrey. Indianapolis, IN: Hackett, 2012.

Dueñas, Alcira. *Indians in the "Lettered City": Reshaping Justice, Social Hierarchy, and Political Culture in Colonial Peru.* Boulder: University of Colorado Press, 2010.

Duviols, Pierre. *La destrucción de las religiones andinas (conquista y colonia).* Translated by Albor Maruenda. 1971. Reprint, Mexico City: Universidad Autónoma de México, 1977.

Eastman, Scott. *Preaching Spanish Nationalism across the Hispanic Atlantic.* Baton Rouge: Louisiana State University Press, 2012.

Echeverri, Marcela. *Indian and Slave Royalists in the Age of Revolution: Reform, Revolution, and Royalism in the Northern Andes, 1780-1825.* Cambridge: Cambridge University Press, 2016.

Edwards, John. *The Spain of the Catholic Monarchs, 1474-1520.* Oxford: Blackwell, 2000.

Elliott, J. H. *Empires of the Atlantic World: Britain and Spain in the Americas, 1492-1830.* New Haven, CT: Yale University Press, 2006.

Elliott, J. H. "A Europe of Composite Monarchies." *Past and Present* 137 (November 1992): 48–71.

Elliott, J. H. *Imperial Spain, 1469-1716.* 1963. Reprint, London: Penguin, 2002.

Elliott, J. H. *The Revolt of the Catalans: A Study in the Decline of Spain.* Cambridge. Cambridge University Press, 1963.

Elliott, J. H. "The Spanish Conquest and Settlement of America." In Leslie Bethell, ed. *The Cambridge History of Latin America*, edited by Leslie Bethell (Vol. 1, pp. 147–206).

Eltis, David. *The Rise of Atlantic Slavery in the Americas.* Cambridge: Cambridge University Press, 2000.

Epstein, Mikhail N. "Transculture: A Broad Way between Globalism and Multiculturalism." *American Journal of Economics & Sociology* 68, no. 1 (2009): 327-51.

Esdaile, Charles J. *Spain in the Liberal Age: From Constitution to Civil War, 1808-1939.* Oxford: Blackwell, 2000.

Fernández-Armesto, Felipe. *Columbus*. New York: Oxford University Press, 1991.
Fernández-Armesto, Felipe. *Pathfinders: A Global History of Exploration*. New York: W. W. Norton, 2006.
Feros, Antonio. *Speaking of Spain: The Evolution of Race and Nation in the Hispanic World*. Cambridge, MA: Harvard University Press, 2017.
Ferrer, Ada. *Freedom's Mirror: Cuba and Haiti in the Age of Revolution*. Cambridge: Cambridge University Press, 2014.
Fisher, J. R. *Silver Mines and Silver Miners in Colonial Peru, 1776–1824*, Monograph Series, No. 7. Liverpool, UK: Center for Latin-American Studies, University of Liverpool, 1977.
Fisher, John, Allan J. Kuethe, and Anthony McFarlane, eds. *Reform and Insurrection in Bourbon New Granada and Peru*. Baton Rouge: Louisiana State University Press, 1990.
Formisano, Ronald P. "The Concept of Political Culture." *The Journal of Interdisciplinary History* 31, no. 3 (Winter 2001): 393–426.
Francis, J. Michael, comp. *Invading Colombia: Spanish Accounts of the Gonzalo Jiménez de Quesada Expedition of Conquest*. University Park: Pennsylvania State University Press, 2007.
Fuente, Alejandro de la. *Havana and the Atlantic in the Sixteenth Century*. Chapel Hill: University of North Carolina Press, 2008.
Gallay, Allan. *Walter Raleigh: Architect of Empire*. New York: Basic Books, 2019.
García Garcia, Luis Alberto. *Frontera armada: Prácticas militares en el noreste histórico, siglos XVII al XIX*. Ciudad de México: Fondo de Cultura Económica, 2021.
García Baquero González, Antonio. *Cádiz y el Atlántico, 1717–1778. El comercio colonial bajo el monopolio gaditano*. 2 vols. Seville: Escuela de Estudios Hispano-Americanos, 1976.
García Baquero González, Antonio. "Los resultados del libre comercio y 'el punto de vista': Una revisión desde la estadística." *Manuscrits* 115 (1997): 303–22.
García Fuentes, Lutgardo. *El comercio español con América, 1650–1700*. Seville: Escuela de Estudios Hispano-Americanos, 1980.
Gauderman, Kimberly. *Women's Lives in Colonial Quito: Gender, Law, and Economy in Spanish America*. Austin: University of Texas Press, 2003.
Gibson, Charles. *Spain in America*. New York: Harper & Row, 1966.
Glave, Luis Miguel. *Trajinantes: Caminos indígenas en la sociedad colonial, siglos XVI/XVII*. Lima: Instituto de Apoyo Agrario, 1989.
González, Ondina, and Bianca Premo, eds. *Raising an Empire: Children in Early Modern Iberia and Colonial Latin America*. Albuquerque: University of New Mexico Press, 2007.
Gould, Eliga H. "Entangled Atlantic Histories: A Response from the Anglo-American Periphery." *American Historical Review* 112, no. 5 (December 2007): 1415–22.
Gould, Eliga H. "Entangled Histories, Entangled World: The English-Speaking Atlantic as a Spanish Periphery." *American Historical Review* 112, no. 3 (June 2007): 764–86.
Graubart, Karen B. "Learning from the Qadi: The Jurisdiction of Local Rule in the Early Colonial Andes." *Hispanic American Historical Review* 95, no. 2 (May 2015): 195–228.
Graubart, Karen B. *Republics of Difference: Religious and Racial Self-Governance in the Spanish Atlantic World*. New York: Oxford University Press, 2022.
Graubart, Karen B. *With Our Labor and Sweat: Indigenous Women and the Formation of Colonial Society in Peru, 1550–1700*. Stanford, CA: Stanford University Press, 2007.
Greene, Jack P., and Philip D. Morgan, eds. *Atlantic History: A Critical Appraisal*. Oxford: Oxford University Press, 2009.
Griffiths, Nicholas. *The Cross and the Serpent: Religious Resurgence in Colonial Peru*. Norman: University of Oklahoma Press, 1996.
Guaman Poma de Ayala, Felipe. *The First Chronicle and Good Government*. Abridged ed. Selected, translated, and annotated by David Frye. Indianapolis, IN: Hackett, 2006.
Guaman Poma de Ayala, Felipe. *El primer nueva corónica y buen gobierno*. Edited by John V. Murra and Rolena Adorno. Translated and textual analysis of the Quechua by Jorge Urioste. 3 vols. Mexico City: Siglo Veintiuno, 1980.
Gutiérrez, Ramón. *When Jesus Came, the Corn Mothers Went Away: Marriage, Sexuality and Power in New Mexico, 1500–1846*. Stanford, CA: Stanford University Press, 1991.

Hall, Gwendolyn Midlo. *Slavery and African Ethnicities in the Americas: Restoring the Links.* Chapel Hill: University of North Carolina Press, 2005.
Hämäläinen, Pekka. *The Comanche Empire.* New Haven, CT: Yale University Press, 2008.
Hamill, Hugh. *The Hidalgo Revolt: Prelude to Independence.* Gainesville: University of Florida Press, 1966.
Hamilton, Earl J. *American Treasure and the Price Revolution in Spain, 1501–1650.* Cambridge, MA: Harvard University Press, 1934.
Hamnett, Brian R. *The End of Iberian Rule on the American Continent, 1770–1830.* Cambridge: Cambridge University Press, 2017.
Hamnett, Brian R. "Process and Pattern: A Re-examination of the Ibero-American Independence Movements, 1808–1826." *Journal of Latin American Studies* 29 (May 1997): 279–328.
Hanke, Lewis. *The Spanish Struggle for Justice in the Conquest of the Americas.* Philadelphia: University of Pennsylvania Press, 1949.
Haring, Clarence. *The Spanish Empire in America.* New York: Harcourt, Brace & World, 1949.
Hemming, John. *The Conquest of the Incas.* New York: Harcourt Brace Jovanovich, 1970.
Herring, Adam. *Art and Vision in the Inca Empire: Andeans and Europeans at Cajamarca.* Cambridge: Cambridge University Press, 2015.
Herzog, Tamar. *Frontiers of Possession: Spain and Portugal in Europe and the Americas.* Cambridge, MA: Harvard University Press, 2015.
Hoberman, Louisa Schell. *Mexico's Merchant Elite, 1590–1660: Silver, State, and Society.* Durham, NC: Duke University Press, 1991.
Irigoin, Alejandra, and Regina Grafe. "Bargaining for Absolutism: A Spanish Path to Nation-State and Empire Building." *Hispanic American Historical Review* 88, no. 2 (May 2008): 173–209.
Israel, J. I. *Race, Class, and Politics in Colonial Mexico, 1610–1670.* London: Oxford University Press, 1975.
Jacobsen, Nils, and Cristobal Aljovín de Losada, eds. *Political Culture in the Andes, 1750–1950.* Durham, NC: Duke University Press, 2005.
Johnson, Lyman L. *Workshop of Revolution: Plebeian Buenos Aires and the Atlantic World, 1776–1810.* Durham, NC: Duke University Press, 2011.
Jones, Cameron D. "The Evolution of Spanish Governance during the Early Bourbon Period in Peru: The Juan Santos Atahualpa Rebellion and the Missionaries of Ocopa." *The Americas* 73, no. 3 (July 2016): 325–48.
Jones, Cameron D. *In Service of Two Masters: The Missionaries of Ocopa, Indigenous Resistance, and Spanish Governance in Bourbon Peru.* Stanford, CA: Stanford University Press, 2017.
Juan, Jorge, and Antonio de Ulloa. *Discourse and Political Reflections on the Kingdoms of Peru. Their Government, Special Regimen of Their Inhabitants and Abuses Which Have Been Introduced into One and Another, with Special Information on Why They Grew Up and Some Means to Avoid Them.* Edited and with an introduction by John J. TePaske. Translated by John J. TePaske and Besse A. Clement. Norman: University of Oklahoma Press, 1978.
Kamen, Henry. *Philip V of Spain: The King Who Reigned Twice.* New Haven, CT: Yale University Press, 2001.
Kamen, Henry. *Spain, 1469–1714: A Society of Conflict.* New York: Pearson Longman, 2006.
Kamen, Henry. *Spain in the Later Seventeenth Century.* London: Longman, 1980.
Kamen, Henry. *The War of the Succession in Spain, 1700–1715.* Bloomington: Indiana University Press, 1969.
Kinsbrunner, Jay. *Independence in Spanish America.* Albuquerque: University of New Mexico Press, 1994.
Klein, Herbert S. *The Atlantic Slave Trade.* Cambridge: Cambridge University Press, 2010.
Klein, Herbert S. "The Colored Militia of Cuba, 1568–1868." *Caribbean Studies* 4 (July 1966): 17–27.

Klein, Hebert S., and Ben Vinson III. *African Slavery in Latin America and the Caribbean.* Oxford: Oxford University Press, 2007.

Klooster, Wim. *The Dutch Moment: War, Trade, and Settlement in the Seventeenth-Century Atlantic World.* Ithaca, NY: Cornell University Press, 2016.

Kuethe, Allan J. *Cuba, 1753–1815: Crown, Military, and Society.* Knoxville: University of Tennessee Press, 1986.

Kuethe, Allan J., and Kenneth J Andrien. *The Spanish Atlantic World in the Eighteenth Century: War and the Bourbon Reforms, 1713–1796.* Cambridge: Cambridge University Press, 2014.

Lamana, Gonzalo. *Domination without Dominance: Inca–Spanish Encounters in Early Colonial Peru.* Durham, NC: Duke University Press, 2008.

Lane, Kris. *Potosí: The Silver City That Changed the World.* Berkeley: University of California Press, 2019.

Levine, Philippa, and John Marriott, eds. *The Ashgate Research Companion to Modern Imperial Histories.* Surrey, UK: Ashgate, 2012.

Levy, Evonne, and Kenneth Mills. *Lexicon of the Hispanic Baroque: Transnational Exchange and Transformation.* Austin: University of Texas Press, 2013.

Liehr, Reinhard, ed. *La formación de las economías y los intereses económicas europeos, 1800–1850.* Berlin: Colloquium Verlag, 1989.

Liss, Peggy K. *Atlantic Empires: The Network of Trade and Revolution.* Baltimore: Johns Hopkins University Press, 1983.

Liss, Peggy K. *Isabel the Queen: Life and Times.* Oxford: Oxford University Press, 1992.

Loayza, Francisco A., ed. *Fray Calixto Túpac Inka: Documentos originales y, en su mayoría, totalmente desconocidos, auténticos, de este apóstol indio, valiente defensor de su Raza, desde el año 1746 a 1760.* Lima: Bibliografía Particular Indígena, 1948.

Lomax, Derek W. *The Reconquest of Spain.* London: Longman, 1978.

López Baralt, Mercedes. *Icono y conquista: Guaman Poma de Ayala.* Madrid: Hiperión, 1988.

Lynch, John. *Bourbon Spain, 1700–1808.* Oxford: Basil Blackwell, 1989.

Lynch, John. *New Worlds: A Religious History of Latin America.* New Haven, CT: Yale University Press, 2012.

Lynch, John. *Simón Bolívar: A Life.* New Haven, CT: Yale University Press, 2006.

Lynch, John. *Spain under the Habsburgs: The Hispanic World in Crisis and Change.* Vol. 2. Oxford: Basil Blackwell, 1992.

Lynne, Kimberly. *Between Court and Confessional: The Politics of Spanish Inquisitors.* Cambridge: Cambridge University Press, 2013.

MacCormack, Sabine. "Atahualpa and the Book." *Dispositio* 14, no. 36–38 (1989): 141–68.

Maltby, William S. *The Rise and Fall of the Spanish Empire.* Basingstoke, UK: Palgrave Macmillan, 2009.

Mangan, Jane. *Trading Roles: Gender, Ethnicity, and the Urban Economy in Colonial Potosí.* Durham, NC: Duke University Press, 2005.

Mangan, Jane. *Transatlantic Obligations: Creating the Bonds of Family in Conquest-Era Peru and Spain.* Oxford: Oxford University Press, 2016.

Mannarelli, María Emma. *Private Passions and Public Sins: Men and Women in Seventeenth-Century Lima.* Translated by Sidney Evans and Meredith D. Dodge. Albuquerque: University of New Mexico Press, 2007.

Marichal, Carlos. *Bankruptcy of Empire: Mexican Silver and the Wars between Spain, Britain, and France, 1760–1810.* Cambridge: Cambridge University Press, 1989.

Marichal, Carlos, and Matilde Souto Mantecón. "Silver and Situados: New Spain and the Financing of the Spanish Empire in America." *Hispanic American Historical Review* 74, no. 4 (November 1994): 587–613.

Marks, Patricia H. *Deconstructing Legitimacy: Viceroys, Markets, and the Military in Late Colonial Peru.* University Park: Pennsylvania State University Press, 2007.

Martínez, María Elena. *Genealogical Fictions: Limpieza de Sangre, Religion, and Gender in Colonial Mexico.* Stanford, CA: Stanford University Press, 2008.

Matthew, Laura E., and Michael R. Oudijk, eds. *Indian Conquistadors: Indigenous Allies in the Conquest of Mesoamerica*. Norman: University of Oklahoma Press, 2007.

McEnroe, Sean F. *From Colony to Nationhood in Mexico: Laying the Foundations, 1560–1840*. Cambridge: Cambridge University Press, 2012.

McFarlane, Anthony. "The Rebellion of the Barrios: Urban Insurrection in Bourbon Quito." *Hispanic American Historical Review* 49, no. 2 (May 1989): 283–330.

McFarlane, Anthony. *War and Independence in Spanish America*. New York: Routledge, 2014.

McNeil, John Robert. *Atlantic Empires of France and Spain: Louisbourg and Havana, 1780–1763*. Baltimore: Johns Hopkins University Press, 1985.

Meyerson, Mark D. *A Jewish Renaissance in Fifteenth-Century Spain*. Princeton, NJ: Princeton University Press, 2004.

Meyerson, Mark D. *Jews in an Iberian Frontier Kingdom: Society, Economy, and Politics in Morvedre, 1248–1391*. Leiden: Brill, 2004.

Meyerson, Mark D. *The Muslims of Valencia in the Age of Fernando and Isabel: Between Coexistence and Crusade*. Berkeley: University of California Press, 1991.

Miller, Joseph C. *Way of Death: Merchant Capitalism and the Angolan Slave Trade, 1730–1830*. Madison: University of Wisconsin Press, 1988.

Miller, Joseph C., eds. *The Princeton Companion to Atlantic History*. Princeton, NJ: Princeton University Press, 2015.

Miller, Kathryn A. *Guardians of Islam: Religious Authority and Muslim Communities of Late Medieval Spain*. New York: Columbia University Press, 2008.

Mills, Kenneth. *Idolatry and Its Enemies: Colonial Andean Religion and Extirpation, 1640–1750*. Princeton, NJ: Princeton University Press, 1998.

Mills, Kenneth, William B. Taylor, and Sandra Lauderdale Graham, eds. *Colonial Latin America: A Documentary History*. Wilmington, DE: Scholarly Resources, 2002.

Milton, Cynthia E. *The Many Meanings of Poverty: Colonialism, Social Compacts, and Assistance in Eighteenth-Century Ecuador*. Stanford, CA: Stanford University Press, 2007.

Moreno Cebrián, Alfredo, and Núria Sala I Vila, eds. *El "premio" de ser virrey: Los intereses públicos y privados del gobierno virreinal en el Perú de Felipe V*. Madrid: Consejo Superior de Investigaciones Científicas, 2004.

Morineau, Michel. *Incroyables gazettes et fabuleux metaux*. London: Cambridge University Press; Paris: Maison des sciences de l'homme, 1985.

Muldoon, James, and Felipe Fernández Armesto, eds. *The Medieval Frontiers of Latin Christendom: Expansion, Contraction, Continuity*. 2008. Reprint, London: Routledge, 2016.

Mundy, Barbara E. *The Death of Aztec Tenochtitlan and the Life of Mexico City*. Austin: University of Texas Press, 2015.

Mundy, Barbara E. *The Mapping of New Spain: Indigenous Cartography and the Maps of the Relaciones Geográficas*. Chicago: University of Chicago Press, 1996.

Nirenberg, David. *Communities of Violence: Persecution of Minorities in the Middle Ages*. 1996. Reprint, Princeton, NJ: Princeton University Press, 2015.

O'Callahan, Joseph F. *A History of Medieval Spain*. Ithaca, NY: Cornell University Press, 1975.

Ortiz, Fernando. *Cuban Counterpoint: Tobacco and Sugar*. Translated by Harriet de Onís. New York: Knopf, 1947.

Owensby, Brian P. *Empire of Law and Indian Justice in Colonial Mexico*. Stanford, CA: Stanford University Press, 2008.

Pagden, Anthony. *Lords of All the World: Ideologies of Empire in Spain, Britain, and France c. 1500–c. 1800*. New Haven, CT: Yale University Press, 1995.

Paquette, Gabriel. *Enlightenment, Governance, and Reform in Spain and Its Empire, 1759–1808*. Basingstoke, UK: Palgrave Macmillan Press, 2008.

Paquette, Gabriel. *The European Seaborne Empires: From the Thirty Years War to the Age of Revolutions*. New Haven, CT: Yale University Press, 2019.

Paquette, Gabriel. "State–Civil Society Cooperation and Conflict in the Spanish Empire: The Intellectual and Political Activities of the Ultramarine *Consulados* and Economic Societies, c. 1710–1810." *Journal of Latin America Studies* 39 (May 2007): 263–98.

BIBLIOGRAPHY 251

Parker, Geoffrey. *Imprudent King: A New Life of Philip II*. New Haven, CT: Yale University Press, 2014.
Parry, J. H. *The Spanish Seaborne Empire*. Berkeley: University of California Press, 1966.
Pearce, Adrian J. "Minister and Viceroy, Paisano and Amigo: The Private Correspondence of the Marqués de la Ensenada and the Conde de Superunda, 1745–1749." *The Americas* 73, no. 4 (October 2016): 477–90.
Pearce, Adrian J. *The Origins of Bourbon Reform in Spanish South America, 1700–1763*. Basingstoke, UK: Palgrave Macmillan, 2014.
Pease G. Y., Franklin. *Las crónicas y los Andes*. Mexico City: Fondo de Cultura Económica, 1995.
Penry, S. Elizabeth. *The People Are King: The Making of an Indigenous Andean Politics*. New York: Oxford University Press, 2019.
Pérez-Mallaína Bueno, Pablo Emilio. *Los hombres del océano: Vida cotidiana de los tripulantes de las flotas de Indias, siglo XVI*. Seville: Escuela de Estudios Hispano-Americanos, 1992.
Phelan, John Leddy. *The Millennial Kingdom of the Franciscans in the New World*. Berkeley: University of California Press, 1970.
Phillips, William D. Jr. *Enrique IV and the Crisis of Fifteenth-Century Castile*. Cambridge: Medieval Academy of America, 1978.
Phillips, William D. Jr., and Carla Rahn Phillips. *A Concise History of Spain*. Cambridge: Cambridge University Press, 2010.
Phillips, William D. Jr., and Carla Rahn Phillips. *The Worlds of Christopher Columbus*. Cambridge: Cambridge University Press, 1992.
Pietschmann, Horst, ed. *Atlantic History: History of the Atlantic System, 1580–1830*. Gottingen, Germany: Vandenhoeck and Ruprecht, 2002.
Pillsbury, Joanne, Catherine Julien, Kenneth J. Andrien, and Eric Deeds, eds. *Guide to Documentary Sources for Andean Studies*. 3 vols. Norman: University of Oklahoma Press, 2008.
Poole, Stafford. *Juan de Ovando: Governing the Spanish Empire in the Reign of Philip II*. Norman: University of Oklahoma Press, 2004.
Portuondo, María. *Secret Science: Spanish Cosmography and the New World*. Chicago: University of Chicago Press, 2009.
Poska, Allyson M. *Gendered Crossings: Women and Migration in the Spanish Empire*. Albuquerque: University of New Mexico Press, 2016.
Powers, James F. *A Society Organized for War: The Iberian Municipal Militias in the Central Middle Ages, 1000–1284*. Berkeley: University of California Press, 1988.
Powers, Karen Vieira. *Andean Journeys: Migration, Ethnogenesis, and the State in Colonial Quito*. Albuquerque: University of New Mexico Press, 1995.
Prado, Fabricio. *Edge of Empire: Atlantic Networks and Revolution in Bourbon Río de la Plata*. Berkeley: University of California Press, 2015.
Premo, Bianca. *Children of the Father King: Youth, Authority, and Legal Minority in Colonial Lima*. Chapel Hill: University of North Carolina Press, 2005.
Premo, Bianca. *The Enlightenment on Trial: Ordinary Litigants and Colonialism in the Spanish Empire*. Oxford: Oxford University Press, 2017.
Presta, Ana María. *Los encomenderos de La Plata, 1550–1600*. Lima: Instituto de Estudios Peruanos, 2000.
Presta, Ana María. "Undressing the *Coya* and Dressing Indian Women: Market Economy, Clothing, and Identities in the Colonial Andes, La Plata (Charcas), Late Sixteenth and Early Seventeenth Centuries." *Hispanic American Historical Review* 90, no. 1 (February 2010): 41–72.
Priestley, Herbert Ingram. *José de Gálvez: Visitor General of New Spain (1765–1771)*. Berkeley: University of California Press, 1916.
Puente Luna, José Carlos de la. *Andean Cosmopolitans: Seeking Justice and Reward at the Spanish Royal Court*. Austin: University of Texas Press, 2018.
Racine, Karen. *Francisco de Miranda: A Transatlantic Life in the Age of Revolution*. Wilmington, DE: Scholarly Resources, 2003.

Ramos, Gabriela, and Yana Yannakakis, eds. *Indigenous Intellectuals: Knowledge, Power, and Colonial Culture in Mexico and the Andes.* Durham, NC: Duke University Press, 2014.

Ramos Pérez, Demetrio. *Entre el plata y Bogotá: Cuatro claves de la emancipación Ecuatoriana.* Madrid: Ediciones Cultura Hispánica, 1978.

Ray, Jonathan. *The Sephardic Frontier: The Reconquista and the Jewish Community in Medieval Iberia.* Ithaca, NY: Cornell University Press, 2006.

Recopilación de leyes de los reynos de las Indias. 1680. Reprint, Madrid: Ediciones Cultura Hispánica, 1973.

Reséndez, Andrés. *The Other Slavery: The Uncovered Story of Indian Enslavement in America.* Boston: Houghton Mifflin Harcourt, 2016.

Restall, Matthew. *Maya Conquistador.* Boston: Beacon Press, 1998.

Restall, Matthew. *When Cortés Met Montezuma: The True Story of the Meeting That Changed History.* New York: Ecco, Harper Collins, 2018.

Ricketts, Mónica. *Who Should Rule? Men of Arms, the Republic of Letters, and the Fall of the Spanish Empire.* Oxford: Oxford University Press, 2017.

Riley, G. Micheal. *Fernando Cortés and the Marquesado in Morelos: A Case Study in the Socioeconomic Development of Sixteenth-Century Mexico.* Albuquerque: University of New Mexico Press, 1973.

Ringrose, David. *Spain, Europe, and the Spanish Miracle, 1700–1900.* Cambridge: Cambridge University Press, 1996.

Rodríguez O., Jaime, ed. *The Independence of Mexico and the Creation of the New Nation*, Los Angeles: University of California Press, 1989.

Rodríguez O., Jaime. *The Independence of Spanish America.* Cambridge: Cambridge University Press, 1998.

Rodríguez O., Jaime, ed. *Mexico in the Age of Democratic Revolutions, 1750–1850.* Boulder, CO: Lynne Rienner, 1994.

Rodríguez O., Jaime, ed. *Patterns of Contention in Mexican History.* Wilmington, DE: Scholarly Resources, 1992.

Román Valarezo, Galo. *La resistencia andina: Cayambe, 1500–1800.* Quito, Ecuador: Abya Yala, 1987.

Rosenmüller, Christoph. "'Corrupted by Ambition': Justice and Patronage in Imperial New Spain and Spain." *Hispanic American Historical Review* 96, no. 1 (February 2016): 1–37.

Rosenmüller, Christoph. *Corruption and Justice in Colonial Mexico, 1650–1755.* Cambridge: Cambridge University Press, 2019.

Rosenmüller, Christoph. *Patrons, Partisans and Palace Intrigues: The Court Society of Colonial Mexico.* Calgary, AB, Canada: University of Calgary Press, 2008.

Safier, Neil. *Measuring the New World: Enlightenment Science and South America.* Chicago: University of Chicago Press, 2008.

Safran, Janina M. *Defining Boundaries in al-Andalus: Muslims, Christians, and Jews in Islamic Iberia.* Ithaca, NY: Cornell University Press, 2013.

Salvucci, Linda K. "Costumbres Viejas, 'hombres nuevos': José de Gálvez y la burocracia fiscal novohispana (1754–1800)." *Historia Mexicana* 33 (Octubre–Diciembre 1983): 224–60.

Schell, William Jr.. "Silver Symbiosis: ReOrienting Mexican Economic History." *Hispanic American Historical Review* 81, no. 1 (February 2001): 89–133.

Schroeder, Susan. *Chimalpahin and the Kingdom of Chalco.* Tucson: University of Arizona Press, 1991.

Schwaller, John Frederick. *The History of the Catholic Church in Latin America: From Conquest to Revolution and Beyond.* New York: New York University Press, 2011.

Schwaller, John Frederick. "The Ordenanza del Patronazgo in New Spain." *The Americas* 42, no. 3 (January 1986): 253–74.

Schwaller, John Frederick. *Origins of Church Wealth in Mexico: Ecclesiastical Revenues and Church Finances, 1523–1600.* Albuquerque: University of New Mexico Press, 1985.

Schwartz, Stuart. *All Can Be Saved: Religious Tolerance and Salvation in the Iberian Atlantic World.* New Haven, CT: Yale University Press, 2008.
Schwartz, Stuart, ed. *Tropical Babylons: Sugar and the Making of the Atlantic World.* Chapel Hill: University of North Carolina Press, 2004.
Scott, Heidi V. *Contested Territory: Mapping Peru in the Sixteenth and Seventeenth Centuries.* Notre Dame, IN: University of Notre Dame Press, 2009.
Seed, Patricia. *American Pentimento: The Invention of Indians and the Pursuit of Riches.* Minneapolis: University of Minnesota Press, 2001.
Seed, Patricia. *Ceremonies of Possession in Europe's Conquest of the New World, 1492–1640.* Cambridge: Cambridge University Press, 1995.
Seed, Patricia. "Failing to Marvel: Atahualpa's Encounter with the Word." *Latin American Research Review* 26, no. 1 (Winter 1991): 7–32.
Serulnikov, Sergio. *Subverting Colonial Authority: Challenges to Spanish Rule in the Eighteenth-Century Southern Andes.* Durham, NC: Duke University Press, 2003.
Sloan, Dolores. *The Sephardic Jews of Spain and Portugal: Survival of an Imperiled Culture in the Fifteenth and Sixteenth Centuries.* London: McFarland, 2009.
Stein, Barbara H., and Stanley J. Stein. *Crisis in an Atlantic Empire: Spain and New Spain, 1808–1810.* Baltimore: Johns Hopkins University Press, 2014.
Stein, Barbara H., and Stanley J. Stein. *Edge of Crisis: War and Trade in the Spanish Atlantic, 1789–1808.* Baltimore: Johns Hopkins University Press, 2009.
Stein, Stanley J., and Barbara H Stein. *Apogee of Empire: Spain and New Spain in the Age of Charles III, 1759–1789.* Baltimore: Johns Hopkins University Press, 2003.
Stein, Stanley J., and Barbara H Stein. *The Colonial Heritage of Latin America: Essays on Economic Dependence in Perspective.* Oxford: Oxford University Press, 1970.
Stein, Stanley J., and Barbara H Stein. *Silver, Trade, and War: Spain and America in the Making of Early Modern Europe.* Baltimore: Johns Hopkins University Press, 2000.
Stern, Steve J. *Peru's Indian Peoples and the Challenge of Spanish Conquest: Huamanga to 1640.* Madison: University of Wisconsin Press, 1982.
Studnicki-Gizbert, Daviken. *A Nation upon the Ocean Sea: Portugal's Atlantic Diaspora and the Crisis of the Spanish Empire, 1492–1640.* Oxford: Oxford University Press, 2007.
Suárez, Margarita. *Desafíos transatlánticos: Mercaderes, banqueros, y el estado en el Perú virreinal, 1600–1700.* Lima: Pontifía Universidad Católica del Perú/Instituto Riva Agüero, 2001.
Subrahmanyam, Sanjay. "Holding the World in the Balance: The Connected Histories of the Iberian Overseas Empires, 1500–1640." *American Historical Review* 112, no. 5 (December 2007): 1329–58.
Tavárez, David. *The Invisible War: Indigenous Devotions, Discipline, and Dissent in Colonial Mexico.* Stanford, CA: Stanford University Press, 2011.
Taylor, William B. *Theater of a Thousand Wonders: A History of Miraculous Images and Shrines in New Spain.* Cambridge: Cambridge University Press, 2016.
TePaske, John J. *A New World of Gold and Silver.* Edited by Kendall W. Brown. Leiden: Brill, 2010.
TePaske, John, and Herbert S. Klein. *The Royal Treasuries of the Spanish Empire in America.* 4 vols. Durham, NC: Duke University Press, 1982–1990.
TePaske, John, and Herbert S. Klein. "The Seventeenth Century Crisis in New Spain: Myth or Reality." *Past and Present* 90 (February 1981): 116–35.
Titu Cusi Yupanqui. *History of How the Spaniards Arrived in Peru.* Edited with an introduction by Catherine Julien. Translated by Catherine Julien. Indianapolis, IN: Hackett, 2006.
Townsend, Camilla. *Annals of Native America: How the Nahuas of Colonial Mexico Kept Their History Alive.* New York: Oxford University Press, 2016.
Townsend, Camilla. *Malintzin's Choices: An Indian Woman in the Conquest of Mexico.* Albuquerque: University of New Mexico Press, 2006.

Townsend, Camilla. *Tale of Two Cities: Race and Economic Culture in Early Republican North and South America—Guayaquil, Ecuador and Baltimore, Maryland*. Austin: University of Texas Press, 2000.

Tutino, John. *Making a New World: Founding Capitalism in the Bajío and Spanish North America*. Durham, NC: Duke University Press, 2011.

Twinam, Ann. *Public Lives, Private Secrets: Gender, Honor, Sexuality, and Illegitimacy in Colonial Spanish America*. Stanford, CA: Stanford University Press, 1999.

Twinam, Ann. *Purchasing Whiteness: Pardos, Mulatos, and the Quest for Social Mobility in the Spanish Indies*. Stanford, CA: Stanford University Press, 2015.

Urton, Gary, and Adriana Von Hagen. *Encyclopedia of the Incas*. New York: Rowman & Littlefield, 2015.

van Deusen, Nancy E. *Between the Sacred and the Worldly: The Institutional and Cultural Practice of Recogimiento in Colonial Lima*. Stanford, CA: Stanford University Press, 2001.

van Deusen, Nancy E. *Embodying the Sacred: Women Mystics in Seventeenth-Century Lima*. Durham, NC: Duke University Press, 2018

van Deusen, Nancy E. *Global Indios: The Indigenous Struggle for Justice in Sixteenth-Century Spain*. Durham, NC: Duke University Press, 2015.

van Deusen, Nancy E. *Ursula de Jesús, The Souls of Purgatory: The Spiritual Diary of an Afro-Peruvian Mystic*. Albuquerque: University of New Mexico Press, 2004.

Van Kley, Dale K. *Reform Catholicism and the International Suppression of the Jesuits in Enlightenment Europe*. New Haven, CT: Yale University Press, 2018.

Van Young, Eric. *The Other Rebellion: Popular Violence, Ideology, and the Mexican Struggle for Independence, 1810–1821*. Stanford, CA: Stanford University Press, 2001.

Vargas Machuca, Bernardo. *Defending the Conquest: Bernardo de Vargas Machuca's Defense of the Western Conquests*. Edited by Kris Lane. Translated by Timothy Johnson. State College: Pennsylvania State University Press, 2010.

Varón Gabai, Rafael. *Francisco Pizarro and His Brothers: The Illusion of Power in Sixteenth-Century Peru*. Norman: University of Oklahoma Press, 1997.

Velasco Murillo, Dana, Mark Lentz, and Margarita R. Ochoa, eds. *City Indians in Spain's American Empire*. Brighton, UK: Sussex Academic Press, 2019.

Verlinden, Charles. *Précédents médiévaux de la Colonie en Amérique*. Mexico City: I.P.G.H., 1954.

Vila Vilar, Enriqueta. *Los Corzo y los Mañara: Tipos y arquetipos del mercader con América*. Seville: Escuela de Estudios Hispano-Americanos, 1991.

Vila Vilar, Enriqueta. "Las Ferias de Portobelo: Apariencia y realidad del comercio con Indias." *Anuario de Estudios Americanos* XXXIX (1982): 275–340.

Villa-Flores, Javier. *Dangerous Speech: A Social History of Blasphemy in Colonial Mexico*. Tucson: University of Arizona Press, 2006.

Vinson, Ben, III. *Before Mestizaje: The Frontiers of Race and Caste in Colonial Mexico*. Cambridge: Cambridge University Press, 2017.

von Wobesar, Gisela. *Dominación colonial: La consolidación de vales reales, 1808–1812*. Mexico City: Universidad Nacional Autónoma de México, 2003.

von Wobesar, Gisela. *El proceso disvinculador y desamortizador de bienes eclesiasticos y comunales en la América Española, siglos XVIII y XIX*, edited by Hans-Jürgen Prien and Rosa María de Codes (pp. 188–214). Ridderkerk, The Netherlands: Asociación de Historiadores Latinoamericanistas Europeos, 1999.

Walker, Charles. *Smoldering Ashes: Cuzco and the Creation of Republican Peru, 1780–1840*. Durham, NC: Duke University Press, 1999.

Walker, Charles. *The Tupac Amaru Rebellion*. Cambridge, MA: Harvard University Press 2014.

Walker, Geoffrey. *Spanish Politics and Imperial Trade, 1700–1789*. Bloomington: Indiana University Press, 1979.

Warren, Adam. *Medicine and Politics in Colonial Peru: Population Growth and the Bourbon Reforms*. Pittsburgh, PA: University of Pittsburgh Press, 2010.

Weber, David. *Bárbaros: Spaniards and Their Savages in the Age of Enlightenment*. New Haven, CT: Yale University Press, 2006.

Weckman, Luis. *The Medieval Heritage of Mexico*. Translated by Frances M. López-Morillas. New York: Fordham University Press, 1992.

Wheat, David. *Atlantic Africa and the Spanish Caribbean, 1570–1640*. Chapel Hill: Omohondro Institute and the University of North Carolina Press, 2016.

Yalí Román, Alberto. "Sobre alcaldías mayors y corregimientos en Indias." *Jahrbuch für Geschichte von Staat, Wirtschaft, un Gesselschaft Lateinamerikas* 9 (1974): 1–39.

Zavala, Silvio. *Las instituciones jurídicas en la conquista de América*. Madrid: Imprenta Helénica, 1935.

Zeno Conedera, Sam. *Ecclesiastical Knights: The Military Orders in Castile*. New York: Fordham University Press, 2015.

Index

For the benefit of digital users, indexed terms that span two pages (e.g., 52-3) may, on occasion, appear on only one of those pages.

Abascal y Sousa, José Fernando de 193, 195-6, 199-200, 202, 204-5, 208, 211
Absolutism 156, 185, 200-1, 206-8, 212-13, 220
Absolutist state 5-7, 16, 142-3, 158-9, 179-82, 217, 230-1
Accessory union 3, 5-6, 15-17, 48, 55-6, 92-3, 96, 227
Adelantado in Spain 24, 46-7
   In the Indies 46-7, 56-7
Aeque principaliter 4-6, 15-16, 96, 136-7
Agualongo, Agustín 16-17, 217-19
Al Andalus, Muslim Kingdom of 22-6, 29
   Almoravid invasion and dynasty of 23
   Almohad invasion and dynasty of 23, 25-6
   Breakup into taifa kingdoms 22-3
   Muslim invasion to establishment of 22-3
Al Rahmān I, Abd (emir) 22-3
Alberoni, Julio (Abad, later Cardinal) 146-8
   Control of Spanish ports 148-9
   Cuban monopoly and New Granada 149-50, 176-9
   Dynastic interests of Queen in Italy, war, and downfall 149-50
   Reformist platform for future reforms 153
   Reforms and rising revenues 176-7, 179-81
Alcántara, Religious order of knights 20-1, 24-5
Alfonso VIII (King of Castile) 24-6
Alfonso X (King of Castile, *el sabio*) 29-30
Aljama 31-4, 38-9
Almagro, Diego de 1-2, 54-5
Al Nāsir, Muhammed (Almohad King) 25-6
Alzaga, Martín 179
Andean Rebellions 7-8, 143, 179-80
   Tomás Katari Revolt 168-9
   Tupac Amaru Revolt in Tinta 169
   Tupac Katari, (Julián Apasa) 170
Angostura Congress 209
Aquinas, Thomas 29-30
Aragon, Kingdom of 27-8
   Territorial expansion of 39
   Commercial ties in Mediterranean 39
   Jewish population in 34-7

   Muslim population in 26, 31-3, 47-8
   Plague and population loss 39
   Divisions in Barcelona, Biga and Busca 39
   Remença Peasant Revolt 39-40
   Sentencia de Guadalupe 39-40
   Tax returns from 46-7
Arbitrio judicial 104
Areche, José Antonio 140, 168
Ariaga, Pablo José 110-11
Armitage, David 13-14
Artigas, José 211
Asturias, Kingdom of 21, 23
Atahualpa, Sapa Inca 52-5, 58
Atahualpa, Juan Santos 167
Atlantic History 13-14
Audiencias (Spanish high courts in the Indies) 3, 6, 56, 76, 83, 91, 96, 156
   Audiencia of Charcas 102-3
   Audiencia of Cusco 205
   Audiencia of Lima 119, 135
   Audiencia of Mexico City 106-7, 119, 162
   Audiencia of Quito 118-19, 145, 148-9, 173-4, 191-2
   Audiencia of Santo Domingo 90
   Sale of judgeships 96-8, 145
Avila, Francisco de 111
Ayacucho, Battle of 186, 217-18
Ayuntamientos 201-2
Aztec Empire (Mexica) 1-2, 49, 69, 73, 201-2

Barbarín, Juan (Jean Capdepón) 16, 178, 179
Barbarín, Manuel Macedonio 179
Becerra, Baltasar 100-2
Belgrano, Manuel 204-5
Berlin decree 188-9
Bolívar, Simón (the Liberator) 10, 201-3, 208-9, 214, 220
   Background 203
   Battle of Boyacá 209-11
   Battle of Carabobo 204, 215
   Battles in Popayan 217, 219
   Meeting with San Martín 216

Bonaparte, Joseph (King of Spain) 8, 185, 189–92
Bonaparte, Napoleon 7–8, 185, 187–9, 194, 206–7, 219–20
Boves, José Tomás 203–4
Bridge of Calderón, Battle of 197–9
Bubonic Plague 37–40, 46–7
Burgos, Laws of 64

Cabildo (city council) 68, 76–7
Cajamarca, Ambush at 52, 54–7
Cajas Reales (royal treasury offices) 3, 76–8, 227
  In Peru 104–5, 108–9, 133–4
  Sale of 6, 99–100, 136–7, 186, 203–4
Calatrava, Religious order of knights 20, 24–5, 42
Calleja, Feliz María 198, 202, 206
Campillo y Cosío, José de 154–5, 159, 167–8, 175
Campomanes, Pedro Rodríguez de 163–4
Cape St. Vincent, Battle of 186–7
Cape Trafalgar, Battle of 186–7, 189
Carvajal y Lancaster, José de 154–5, 159–60
Casa de la Contratación (Board of Trade in 1503) 73, 76–7
  And Cosmography 82–3
  And Geographical Information 83
  And Ludeña case 90
Castelldosríus, Count of (Manuel de Oms y Santa Pau Olom de Sentmenat y de Lanuza) 143–4
  And contraband trade as viceroy 144–5
  Death 144
Castile, Kingdom of 39–40
  Act of Resumption 42
  Civil wars in 41
  Corregidores in 42
  Cortes at Madrigal 42
  Indies as legal appendage of 5–6
  Jewish population of 36–8
  King Henry IV and succession conflicts 41
  Marriage of Isabel of Castile to Ferdinand of Aragon 40–1
  Muslim population of 31–4
  Pastoral economy 40–1
  Restoration of order by Ferdinand and Isabel 41
Catalan Revolt (1640) 7 n15
Catalina, servant woman 15, 89–90, 92–3
Caudillos 17
Ceballos, Cristóbal (Judge on Quito audiencia) 145–6
Cédulas de gracias al sacar 173

Charles (Archduke of Austria, later Holy Roman Emperor) 140–1, 143–4
Charles I (King of Spain and Holy Roman Emperor 65–6, 87–8
Charles II (King of Spain) 98–9, 140–1
Charles III (King of Spain) 142–3, 154, 176–80, 219
  And Jesuits 6–7, 162–3
  As King of Naples 160
  Ministers of 160–1
  Reforms of 6–7, 142–3, 154, 160–1, 174–6, 179–81, 219–20
  War and strong state 5–7, 159–60
  Death 171, 185
Charles IV (King of Spain) 7, 185–7, 189, 218
  Abdicates throne 8, 188–9
  And vales reales 187–8
Chichimecas (warlike indigenous group in northern New Spain) 72, 91
Colônia do Sacramento 165
Columbian Exchange 84–5
Columbus, Christopher 1–2, 9, 13–15
  Inept management of first settlements 56
  Voyages of 1–6, 20–2, 43–8, 219–20
Composite Monarchy 1–2, 4–5, 16, 133–4, 142–3, 160, 179–80
  Defined 4–5, 179–80
  Examples of 1–2, 4–7, 15, 41, 47–8, 136–7
Comunero Revolt 170–1, 179–80
Constitution of 1812 8–9, 16–17, 212–14, 220
  Provisions of 201
  Implementation obstacles in Indies 201–2
  Suppression by Ferdinand VII 206
Consulado (merchant guild) 76–7, 148–9
  In Cádiz 149–55, 159, 161–2
  In Mexico City 76–7, 133–4, 153–4, 162, 167–8, 196–8
  In Lima 76–7, 108–9, 133–4, 144–6
  In Seville 76–7, 133–4, 148–9, 205
Contraband commerce 4, 11–12, 76–7, 86, 87–8, 100–1, 130–3
  In Caribbean 134–5, 148–52
  In Pacific 137–8, 143–6
  In South Atlantic 148, 165
Conversos 38, 42–3, 45–6
Convivencia 31–2
  Breakdown of 33–5, 37–9
Córdoba 20, 22–3, 26, 43, 46
Corregidores 42
  In Indies 76, 99, 101–3, 123–4, 133–4, 141, 145–6, 157, 165, 169–70, 227
  In Spain 42, 141
  Sale of 99–100

Corruption 18-19
  In eighteenth century 144-6, 150, 154, 156-8, 170-1
  In seventeenth century 100-2, 104-8, 123-4, 136-7
  In sixteenth century 73-6
Cortes 5-6, 33, 42-3, 87-8, 141
  Of Cádiz 200-2, 206-7
Cortés, Fernando 1-2, 57-61, 72
  Encomiendas of 60-1
Cosmography 82
Council of the Indies (1524) 2, 67-8, 73, 76, 78-9, 101-2
  And corruption 144-6
  And Geographical Information 82-3
Covadonga, Battle of 21-2
Criados (retainers of powerful officials) 2, 73-6
Cruz, Francisco de la 103-4
Cudinamarca, State of 194-5, 218
Cusco (Inca capital) 54-5, 58-60, 68, 70-1, 88-9, 113-14, 215
  Cusco school of painting 124-8
  Rebellion in 205, 208

Depositaria de Indias 153
Derecho Indiano 6, 104
Dhimmi, Ahd-al 31-2, 49
Díaz del Castillo, Bernal (conquistador) 66
Dutch West India Company (Geoctroyeerde Westindische Compagnie or W.I.C) 10-11, 134-5

Encomienda 4, 14-15, 27, 30, 42, 49, 55, 60-6, 70
  And struggle for justice 63-6
  Decline in central regions of Indies 69-70
  In the Indies 55-6, 60-1, 68, 227
  In Spain 26-7, 30, 42
Enlightenment 16, 142-3, 154-5, 171, 179
  Scientific advances 174-5
  Social welfare programs 173
Ensenada, Marqués de la (Zenón de Somodevilla) 154-5, 176-9
  And *Noticias secretas* 156-7
  Commercial policies 159
  Fall from power and exile 159-60
  Phases out Sale of appointments 159
  Reformist aims 156
  Secretary of everything 154-5
  Secularization of *doctrinas de indios* 157-8
Enslaved Africans 1-2, 8, 10-12, 15-18
  Buenos Aires fears of 178-9
  Code for treatment of 172

Commerce and labor of 56-7, 67-8, 87, 91, 95-6, 116, 120, 133, 140, 148-52, 168
  Recruitment of in independence struggles 194-5, 199-200, 204, 209, 211-12, 214-18
  Substitute for Indigenous labor 56-7, 118
Escalona, Duke of 107-8
Esquilache, Marqués de (Leopoldo di Gregorio) 161-3
Evangelization of the Indigenous People 7, 79-80, 92, 167, 227
  Indigenous resistance to in Yucatan 80-1, 92
  Indigenous resistance to in Peru (Taqui Onqoy) 81, 92
Expulsion of Jews from Spain 43
Extirpation of indigenous idolatry 5, 110, 135
  Divisions within Church over 110-11
  In New Spain 112
  In Peru 111-12

Farnese, Elizabeth (Queen of Spain) 147-50, 159-60
  Dynastic ambitions for sons in Italy 149-50
Ferdinand III of Castile 25-30, 35, 48
Ferdinand VI (King of Spain) 142, 154, 162-3, 176
Ferdinand VII (King of Spain, el deseado) 8-9, 185
  Forced Acceptance of Constitution of 1812 212-13
  Accession to Throne 188-9
  Forced abdication and captivity 185, 189-91
  Juntas rule in his name 185, 189-95, 217-18
  Military end to rebellions 208, 218
  Restoration of Absolutism 217
  Return to Spain 142, 207-208
Ferdinand, King of Aragon 4-5
  Captures Granada 43
  Marries Isabel 41
  Restores order in Aragon 39-40
  With Isabel, restores order in Castile 41-2
Floridablanca, Conde de (José de Moñino) 167-8, 171, 215-16
Flotas and Galeones 3, 76-7
  Decline of 4-6, 130-4, 145, 148, 152-4, 159
Fontainebleau, Treaty of (1807) 188-9
Franciscan order 156-7, 167
French invasion of Iberia 1, 7, 16-17, 185, 188-9, 207-8, 217-18, 225
French Revolution 7, 16, 171, 185, 219-20
  Fears of Revolt of enslaved population in Buenos Aires 179
Fueros 24, 28, 141, 185, 201-2

Gálvez, José de 7–8, 162, 164, 180–1
　Administrative style 181–2
　Death 171
　Establishes imperial free trade 167–8
　Establishment of Viceroyalty of Río de la Plata 165, 167–8
　Expedition to Capture Colônia do Sacramento 165
　Expulsion of Jesuits in New Spain 164
　Minister of the Indies 165
　Sends *visitas* to Indies 168–9
　Visitador of New Spain 162, 164
Gauchos 205, 211
Gelves, Marqués de 106–8
Godoy, Manuel 185, 188–9
Goyeneche, General José Manuel de 192–3, 195–6, 199–200, 204–5
Granada, Kingdom of 26–8
　Border wars with Christians 27–8, 30
　Downfall 1–4, 21–2, 43, 46–7
Great Britain, Wars with 185–6
Guaman Poma de Ayala, Felipe 96, 128–30, 138, 157
　Background 123
　El primer nueva coronica y buen gobierno 96–8, 120–4
　On abuses of Spanish 123–4
　Road to Lima 96–8, 124
Güemes, Martín 205, 211
Guerrilla warfare 189
　In New Granada 209, 221
　In New Spain 198–200, 206, 213–14, 221
　In Río de la Plata 204–5, 211, 221
　In Spain 189, 207–8, 221
Guerrero, Vicente 213–14
Guilds 6, 115–16, 124–8
　Merchant's guild (*see* Consulado)
　Sheep growers guild (*mesta*) 21–2, 40
Gutierrez Pelayo (Corregidor of Quito) 145–6
Gutierrez Piñares, Juan Francisco 1, 168–71, 232

Havana (Cuba) 89–90
　Company of 154–5
　Consulado of 171
　Free trade in 162
　Loss of in War 160–2, 180–1
　Shipyards of 152
　Unrest over 1789 Slave Code 172
Hidalgo, Miguel 196–200, 202, 206, 220

Indigenous litigation and protest 119–20
Indios ladinos 96–8, 121–3

Inquisition, Holy Office of 2, 11–12, 42–3, 45, 69
　And Conquest of Granada 43
　And Constitution of 1812 201
　Established in the Indies 81–2, 92–3, 109
　Limpieza de sangre (purity of blood) 114–15
　No jurisdiction over Amerindians 110, 228
　Prosecutes Portuguese merchants 109, 133–4
Intendancy reforms 153–4, 165, 181, 231
Isabel I, Queen of Castile 4–5, 15, 18
　Establishes power in Castile 42
　Founds Inquisition in Castile 42–3
　Gains throne of Castile 41
　Heir to Henry IV 40–1
　Marriage to Ferdinand of Aragon 1–2, 21–2, 47–8
　Supports Columbus 43–6
Iturbide, Augustín de 186, 206, 213–14

James I (Jaume) of Aragon 26–7, 31–2, 35–6, 39
Jansenism 6–7, 162–3, 230
Jenkin's Ear, War of (War of the Austrian Succession) 152–4, 159, 176–7
Jesuit order (Society of Jesus) 162
　Education of Amerindian elites 122
　Evangelization efforts of 78–9
　Expulsion of 164, 179–80
　Extinction of order 164
　And extirpation of Idolatry 111–12
　Founded by Ignatius Loyola 58–60
　Quarrels with Crown 157–8, 162–3
　And struggle over tithe 107–8, 163–4
　Wealth of 113–14
Jewish merchants 20–35, 37, 85–7, 124
Juan, Jorge and Antonio de Ulloa 157–8, 230
　Noticias secretas de América 156
Juderías (juerias) 33–6
Juntas 16–17
　In Spain 185, 188–9
　In Indies 185, 189–94
　Junta Central 185, 190–2, 200–1
Juros 108–9, 133–4, 136–7

Kahal (kehilla) 35–9

Ladrón de Guevara, Diego (Bishop of Quito and interim Viceroy of Peru) 144–5
Land tenure 116
Landa, Fray Diego de, *See* evangelization
Las Casas, Fray Bartolomé (Domnican protector of indigenous people) 64–6
　Briefest Relation of the Destruction of and Indies 65–6

Las Navas de Tolosa, Battle of 25–6, 46
La Serna, José 211–12, 216–17
  Abandons Lima 214–15
  Defeat at Ayacucho 217
Lima (capital of Viceroyalty of Peru)
  11–12, 69
  Archbishopric of 106
  Cosmopolitan city 135
  Earthquakes 137–8, 157–8
  Home to indigenous population 116–17
  Site of Inquisition 12, 81–2
  Manco Inca revolt 54–5
  Portuguese merchants in 87
  Site of viceregal court 73–6, 99
Llaneros 201–4, 208–9, 216
López de Velasco, Juan 82–4
Louis XVI (King of France) 186
Ludeña, Francisco de 89–90, 92–3

Mail system 154, 161
Manco Inca 54–5, 58–60
Manso de Velasco, José (Conde de Superunda) 158
María Luisa (Queen of Spain) 188–9
Martínez Campañón, Baltasar Jaime (Bishop of Trujillo) 175
Mestizos 60, 116, 157, 170, 200–1, 204
Mexico City (capital of New Spain) 68, 72–7
  Archbishopric in 78–9
  In independence of Mexico 196–8, 214
  Periodic flooding 105–6
  Riots in 106–7
  Site of Inquisition 12, 81–2
  Site of viceregal court 76, 99
Migration 12–13, 118
  In Spain 28–9, 31, 46
  In the Indies 81, 91–2
Minga (wage laborer in Peru) 11–12, 70–1, 103–4
Miranda, Francisco 189, 193–4
Mita (m'ita, Andean forced labor system) 70–1, 92
  Abuses of 103–4, 116–18
Monteverde, Juan Domingo de 194, 199–200, 202–3, 221
Morachimo, Vicente 157
Morelos, José María 206, 208, 213
Morería 27, 31–4
Morillo, General Pablo 208–9, 215
Moriscos 42–3, 90
  Forced conversions of 47–8
Morvedre 35, 37–8
Motín of Esquilache 163
Mudejars 27, 31, 33–9

Nestares Marín, Francisco 102–3
Neutral Trade 186–7
New Granada, Viceroyalty of 2, 149–50, 152, 168–71, 186
New Laws of 1542 65, 67–8
New Spain, Viceroyalty of 2, 73–6, 85–7, 186
Noguerol de Ulloa, Francisco 62–3
Ñuesta, Beatriz 58–60
Nueva planta (New Plan) 141

Obraje (textile mill) 71–2, 118
Olivares, Count Duke of (Gaspar de Guzmán) 98–9, 106–8
O'Donojú, Juan 214
O'Reilly, Alejandro 161–2
Ortiz de Zárate, Juan 62–3
Orueta, Juan Bautista (Judge of Lima audiencia) 146
Osorio, Manuel 211–12
Ovando, Juan de 82–3

Palafox y Mendoza, Juan de (Bishop of Puebla, visitador) 107–9
Palos de la Frontera 20–1, 43–4
Paris, Treaty of (1763) 160
Patiño, José 150
  Coast guard and privateers in Caribbean 150–2
  Death 153
  Rebuilds navy 152
  Works to restore Viceroyalty of New Granada 152
  Tobacco Monopoly in Cuba 150
Patronato real 106
Pelayo, King of Asturias 20–3, 29
Peninsular War 16–17, 205, 208, 211, 221
Pérez de la Serna, Juan (Archbishop of Mexico City) 106–7
Peru, Viceroyalty of 2, 18, 85–7, 96–8, 186, 192
Pezuela, Joaquín de la 204–5, 211–12
  Overthrown by coup 214
Philip II (King of Spain) 84, 87
  Bankruptcy declared 87–8
  Commissions Relaciones Geográficas 84
  Inherits Portuguese throne 87
  Imperialism of 87–8, 98–9
Philip III (King of Spain) 82–3, 96–9, 123
Philip IV (King of Spain) 4–5, 98–9, 102–3, 106–7, 109
Philip V (King of Spain) 6–7, 140–1, 149–50
Pizarro, Francisco de 1–2, 54–5, 57, 69

Political and Institutional Culture 3, 8, 15–17
  Five Distinct Stages of 3–9
  Influence of Reconquista on 20–2, 48–9
  Conquest era culture 55–6, 58–61, 67–8, 76, 96, 112–15
  Implanting an accessory union of Castile 3, 55–6, 68–71, 73, 76–7, 87–8, 91–3, 96
  Evolving into an aeque principaliter 4–6, 15–16, 96
  An absolutist political culture 5–7, 17, 142–3, 156, 158–9, 171, 179–82, 199–200
Polo de Ondegardo y Zárate, Juan 63
  Disputes over name 63 n22
Portugal, Kingdom of 5–6, 23
  Commerce with Indies 165
  Franco-Spanish attack in 1807 185, 188–9
  Gains Brazil 11–12
  Merchants of 6–7, 86, 133–4
  Revolt (1640) 95–6, 105–6
  Treaty of Tordesillas and 83
  Union with Spain 87
  Union ends 4–5, 98–9, 107–8, 136–7
Potosí (richest silver mine in the Indies) 69–71, 91–2
  Corruption at 102–3
  Declining production and mita 103–4, 130–2
  Faulty accounting at treasury 101
  Harsh working conditions 71
  Location on trunk line 88–9
Pueblo Revolt 120–1
Pumacahua, Mateo García 205

Quadruple Alliance, War of 149–50
Quesada y Sotomayor, Juan 100–2

Raleigh, Walter 10–11
Ramírez, General Juan 205
Real Desagüe de Huehuetoca 105–6
Reconquista 3–5, 9–10, 12–13, 18
  Chronology 46–8
  Crusading zeal 42–3, 48
  Defined 20–1
  Final victory 20–1, 43
  Legacies for Indies 49
  Southward migration 30
Recopilación de Leyes de los Reynos de las Indias 104, 229
Regalist ministers 6–7, 142–3, 154, 160–1, 163, 175, 180–82, 230
Regency Council 200–1
Regulation of free trade (*reglamento de comercio libre*) 162, 167–8, 171
Relaciones Geográficas 83–4

República de Españoles 66–7, 81–2, 92–3
Replica de Indios 3–4, 66–7, 92–3, 228
Requirement 64
Revolutionary France, War with 185–6
Ricla, Conde de (Fuentes Villalpando, Ambrosio de) 161–2
Ricauarte, Juan de (Judge on Quito audiencia) 145–6
Riego, Rafael 213–14, 233
Río de la Plata, Viceroyalty of 2, 16, 165, 167–8, 181, 186–9
Roman Catholic Church 1–4, 8, 18
  Dioceses of the Secular Clergy 78–9, 112–13
  Discord with viceroys 106–8
  Economic role in credit 112–14
  Evangelization of Amerindians 3–4, 8, 15–16, 72, 78–9, 92, *See* evangelization
  Loyalty to 2–3, 18, 47–8, 55–6
  Ordenanza del Patronazgo 78–9
  Religious shrines and images 114
  Religious confraternities 115
  Secularization of indigenous parishes 142–3, 157–9
  Crown Seizure of Economic Assets in Spain and the Indies 144 n4, 191
  Social welfare responsibilities 112–13
Royal Havana Company 154–5
Royal Pragmatic on Marriages 172, 181
Ruiz de Castilla, Conde de 191–2

Sahagún, Bernardo de 122
Sale of Appointments 1, 4–6, 96, 99–101, 136–7
  And bureaucratic corruption 104–5
  In Peru 102–3, 145
  End sales in 1750 5–6, 159, 186
San José Túpac Inka, Fray Calixto de 157
San Martín, José de 205
  Battle of Chacabuco 211–12
  Battle of Cancha Rayada 211–12
  Battle of Maipú 211–12
  Captures Lima 215
  Declares Independence of Peru 214
  Challenges of occupying Lima 214
  Meeting with Bolívar at Guayaquil and Resignation 216
Santangel, Luis 15, 45–6
Santa Hermandad 42
  Funding for Columbus 43–6
Santiago, Religous order of Knights 20–5
Santo Tomás, Fray Domingo (Dominican) 60–1, 65
Science, advances in 82–5, 105–6, 174–5, 181
Secularization of parishes 158–9

INDEX 263

Selva Alegre, Marqués de (Juan Pío de Montúfar) 185, 191–2
Sepúlveda, Juan Ginés 65–6
Shariah 32
Shrines and images, religious See Roman Catholic Church
Siete Partidas 29
Silver and Gold Production 85–6
  Declines 130
  Morineau Figures 130–2
  Global trade 132–3
Situados (subsidies) 152
Social hierarchy 115–16
  Breakdown of 116–17
Solorzano y Pereira, Juan de 5–6
Sosaya, Juan de (President of Audiencia of Quito) 145–6
Spanish conquistadors 3, 10, 17, 24, 226
  See encomienda; Political and institutional culture
  Aleged abuses and defense of 65–6
  Civil disorder and 54–6, 61–2, 69–70, 95–6
  Forge alliances with indigenous groups 30, 57–8
  Forge kinship ties with indigenous leadership 58–60
  Loss of wealth 62–3
  Reconquista values 48–9
Spanish Succession, War of the 140–1, 143–5, 153, 160–1, 185
Sucre, Antonio José (General) 216
  Battle of Ayacucho 217
Superunda, Conde de (Viceroy of Peru) See Manso de Velasco, José

Tacón, Miguel (Governor of Popayán) 194–5, 199, 217–18, 221
Taqui Onqoy, See evangelization in Peru
Tax remittances to General Treasury in Madrid 176
Tenochtitlan (Aztec capital) 57–8, 68, 79–80
Tithe (*diezmo*) 78–9, 107–8, 112–13, 162–3
Tlaxcalans, allies of Spanish 57–8, 119
  Settlers in Northern New Spain 72, 91
Toral, Fray Francisco de, See evangelization in New Spain
Tordesillas, Treaty of (1497) 11–12, 83
Tribunal of Accounts 99, 101–2
Trunk lines and Feeder lines (colonial markets) 88–9, 91–2, 95–6
Tupac Amaru II (José Gabriel Condorcanqui) 140, 143, 170, 175

Union of Arms 98–9, 107–8
Ursula de Jesús 15–16, 135–6, 138
Utrecht, Treaties of (1713) 140–1, 146–50

Valencay, Treaty of (1813) 206–7
Vales reales 6–7, 185, 187–8, 231
Vega, Garcilaso de la (el Inca) 60, 122–3
Viceroy 2, 73, 99–100, 113–15, 156, 200–1
  Discord with Bishops, See Roman Catholic Church
Visitas 101–2, 107–8, 168–9
Vilcabamba 54–5, 58–60, 91

Wall, Ricardo 159–60
Wellesley, General Arthur (Duke of Wellington) 189, 206–7